Mayakovsky

A POET IN THE REVOLUTION

Studies of the Russian Institute **RI** *Columbia University*

MAYAKOVSKY

A Poet in the Revolution

by Edward J. Brown

PRINCETON UNIVERSITY PRESS

PRINCETON, NEW JERSEY

L. C. Card: 72-14022
ISBN: 0-691-06255-2

Publication of this book has been aided by
a grant from the Andrew W. Mellon Foundation

"*About That* and About Some Other Things" is
reprinted here by permission of *Survey*, in which
journal it originally appeared in 1972

The material on the poem *Man* which appears in
Chapter Six is reprinted with permission from
*American Contributions to the VI Congress of
Slavicists*, published by Mouton and Company in 1969

Pictures from the first edition of the poem *Pro eto*
(1923) were provided by Ardis publishers, which produced
a facsimile of the original edition in 1973

This book has been composed in Linotype Caledonia
Printed in the United States of America
by Princeton University Press,
Princeton, New Jersey

Foreword

There are many institutions to whom the author is indebted for assistance in the production of this book. The American Council of Learned Societies appointed me in the fall of 1963 as an Exchange Professor under their agreement with the Soviet Academy of Sciences, and I spent several months in Moscow and Leningrad gathering material and interviewing various authorities on the life and work of Mayakovsky. Indiana University and Stanford University both provided assistance, and the Russian Institute of Columbia University appointed me as a Senior Research Fellow during the academic year 1969-1970. The Humanities Fund supported a final summer of work in 1971 during which the book was virtually completed. For this indispensable assistance I wish to express profound gratitude.

I also owe much to particular persons who provided inspiration, advice, and criticism: Roman Jakobson; Vladimir Zemskov, formerly of the Mayakovsky Museum in Moscow; the group of scholars known as *mayakovedy* and connected with the Institute of World Literature in Moscow, including Pertsov, Papernyi, Ushakov, and others; Robert and Olga Hughes of the University of California at Berkeley, and Nikolai Pashin of Stanford University, who read and criticized certain chapters; Donald Fanger of Harvard and Richard Sheldon of Dartmouth, both of whom made valuable suggestions; Tatiana Liberman of New York City, who read a part of the manuscript with a critical eye; Lily Brik; Ella Wolfe, who supplied some extraordinary photographs; and my wife Catherine, an ever-resourceful reader and critic. To all of you this book is offered, in the hope that it is a worthy gift.

A Note on Transliteration

When we try to represent the Russian Cyrillic alphabet in English letters certain problems arise. A book written in English to be read by nonspecialists as well as by specialists must, it seems, use a transliteration system that will make it possible for someone who knows no Russian to approximate closely the sound of personal and place names. The same principle ought to apply to the transliteration of titles and of words and phrases from poetry; the point of such transliteration is always to approximate the *sound* of the Russian in terms of English letters.

A number of recent books accept this principle in the text but abandon it in favor of the so-called scholarly transliteration system in the footnotes and bibliography, where, as one writer put it "the utmost precision is required." But the distinction seems to the present writer to be quite pointless. Only those who know Russian will consult footnoted titles and bibliographical listings, and anyone who knows Russian (or a librarian aware of the various systems of transliteration) will identify without difficulty the original Cyrillic form of any transliterated matter.

I have therefore opted for the "popular" transliteration system throughout, the system used in D. S. Mirsky's *History of Russian Literature* and in many other recent books. Some of the problems have been treated here in special ways, however. Variations in transliteration arise in only fifteen letters of the Russian Cyrillic alphabet. The following table indicates how each of these letters is transliterated here:

е → e (ye initially in certain names, e. g. *Yesenin*)
ё → yo (o after *ch, shch,* and *sh*)
ж → zh
й → i
х → kh
ц → ts
ч → ch
ш → sh
щ → shch
ъ → omitted
ы → y
ь → omitted

э → e
ю → yu
я → ya

The frequent combination *-ский* at the end of Russian names is always transliterated -sky, and the generally accepted transliterations of the names of well known Russian writers is used, e. g., Tolstoy, Gorky, Burliuk.

Table of Contents

Mayakovsky

A POET IN THE REVOLUTION

Introductory Remarks

In the first entry of his autobiography, *I Myself*, where he announces his major "theme," Mayakovsky makes the point that he is a poet, and worth studying chiefly in that capacity: "I'm a poet. That's why I'm interesting. And that's what I'm writing about. I'll write about all the rest only as it settles down in verbal form." He seems to be advising the future critic to direct his attention to the poems rather than to other things and to suggest that those other matters are worthy of attention only to the extent that they exist in his poetry. Mayakovsky was a fascinating human being and in the course of his life did many interesting things, but his most important deeds were his poems. Those poems could be—indeed, have been—studied in total abstraction from the poet's life. Some of the most important recent work on Mayakovsky deals with the rhythmic patterns of his poetry and of course neglects to mention his father, mother, and sisters, his place of birth and manner of death. His imagery, syntax, and vocabulary exist independently of his life and can be studied without reference to it. A student of his early painting might concentrate on his use of the materials of that craft and need show no interest in the identity of his models or the psychological problems possibly reflected in certain cubist canvases—the one entitled "Roulette," for instance; similarly, the literary critic might analyze his extended and developed metaphors without suggesting that some of them may be interesting studies in psychopathology.

Conversely, his life could be studied quite apart from the poems and without reference to them, and so studied it would offer important political, historical, artistic, erotic, and general psychological evidence. Mayakovsky was a bolshevik agitator as a boy, and had been arrested three times before he turned fifteen. He spent seven months in prison, much of it in solitary confinement. "Kicked out of various schools," as he himself put it, he nonetheless became a leading figure in the cubist movement in Russian painting in 1911 and 1912, and took part in the animated debates among the various avant-garde painters' groups of those days: The Jack of Diamonds, The Donkey's Tail, and the Union of Youth. He was one of the founders of Russian cubo-futurism and co-author, along with David Burliuk, Velimir Khlebnikov, and

Aleksei Kruchonykh (with all of whom we will deal in the course of the narrative), of its famous manifesto, "A Slap at Public Taste" (1912). He helped to create sensational episodes not only in the major cities of the empire but also in the provinces, where the futurists "toured" in 1913 offering noisy and sometimes scandalous recitals of their poetry and exhibitions of their painting in various Russian towns. After the October revolution he was a leading producer of pro-bolshevik propaganda in the form of cartoons and agitational verse. And in addition to all this, his emotional makeup and his erratic and self-consuming love life should invite the attention of any biographer with a bent for psychological analysis. He was a kind of hypochondriac, preternaturally afraid of infection from knives, forks, spoons, drinking glasses, and even other people's hands offered in friendship. He was a compulsive washer of his own hands. He was also a compulsive gambler—ready to bet on anything: the odd or the even, the turn of a card, the last number on the next automobile license plate, the number of peanuts that would drop from a vending machine at the insertion of a coin. And the last act of his life was, according to some evidence, a losing bet in a game of Russian roulette. What a subject that life would be! It's enough to make a psychiatrist's fingers itch, or a novelist squirm with anticipatory pleasure. But what is the literary critic to do?

The long dominance of formalist, "new," and other critics of an intrinsic bent has conditioned us to regard the biography of a poet as a matter of secondary importance if we are concerned with analysis of the poems. But no such doctrine holds for Mayakovsky. On the contrary, the poems cannot be fully understood if they are studied in abstraction from the family, the personality, the life, and from history. Mayakovsky's poetry is intensely intimate, particular, personal, local, directly involved with whatever was happening to him and whomever he knew at any given moment. The one-eyed Burliuk materializes in *A Cloud in Pants*, as does the poet Igor Severyanin in the shape of a long-stemmed wineglass; Lily Brik's address and telephone number are correctly recorded in *About That*; the real Vladimir Mayakovsky was the author, producer, and principal actor in the "tragedy" which has his name as its title; we could go on indefinitely with such examples. The critic Vissarion Belinsky in the nineteenth century spoke of Pushkin's poem *Eugene Onegin* as an "encyclopedia of Russian life," and the modern critic suspects such a statement as gross oversimplification. Yet the body of Mayakovsky's work might be usefully investigated as an "encyclopedia" of Russian life in the early twentieth century and as an auxiliary guide to the history of the Soviet period. Obviously we must be alert to the special character of that "encyclopedia" as a *literary* statement, and consider the *use* made of historical facts in the structure of each poem; but the poetry does offer important evidence of a purely historical character.

The intricate involvement of Mayakovsky's poetry with "life" and "history" can be considered from still another point of view. Burliuk once said about him: "Mayakovsky's memory is like a road in Poltava—everyone leaves a galosh there."[1] It is true that we find innumerable lost galoshes strewn about in the retentive mass of Mayakovsky's verse, and sometimes it's essential to the analysis of a particular poem to find out *whose* galoshes they are; unless we know this it will be difficult to say how a particular galosh functions in a given poem. Sometimes the elucidation of ownership may require careful research and clear exposition of an episode in Mayakovsky's life: the reference to "pearls and furs" in the "Letter to Tatiana Yakovleva" is a case in point. In other poems particular items, historical or personal, undergo in the poetic process a kind of imaginative diffusion, the nature of which will remain obscure unless these items can be identified and named. The interpretation of "difficult" hermetic poets such as Rimbaud, or Kuzmin or Akhmatova (in her *Poem without a Hero*, for instance) at times calls for long and careful erudition in music, art, and literature, since those poets were intensely aware of all existing art as a source of imagery and allusion. Mayakovsky is less demanding in this respect, though we do find in some of his poems, for instance in *About That*, a pattern of literary references. But Mayakovsky demands of the critic that he be aware as much as possible of everything that existed in the bright foreground of the poet's own life: artists, poets, critics, revolutionaries, Roman Jakobson and David Burliuk, Lily Brik and other intriguing women, the "quiet Jew" Pavel Ilych Lavut and the People's Commissar Lunacharsky, as well as the iconic political figures Lenin and Stalin. A quarter-century marked by catastrophic war and revolution provides Mayakovsky with his content; the events

[1] Burliuk's remark is quoted by Mayakovsky in his autobiography, *Ya sam*, in *Polnoe sobranie sochinenii* (Moscow, 1955-1959), I, 9. This edition will hereafter be referred to as *PSS*.

and people of his time enter into an intimate personal relationship with the poet, just as the daylight "luminary" chats with him over a cup of tea in his poem about the sun. It is of course possible for a critic to speak of Mayakovsky without reference to the real world with which his poems are in frequent and fruitful intercourse; but such a critic would emasculate the poetry and, however subtle his own pattern of insights and nuances, obscure rather than elucidate the poetic artifact.

Some poets produce poems that may indeed be read without reference to their biographies. The love poems of Catullus lose very little through the reader's ignorance of particulars, since those poems are lyric verbalizations of widely experienced and immediately recognized emotional states. The best of Fyodor Tyutchev is accessible to us even though we may be ignorant of his long career as a diplomat (though of course it would be well if we knew something about the German philosopher Schelling). But can we understand Byron or Lermontov if we read them in a state of detachment from the individual life reflected in their poems? Similarly the work of Alexander Blok teasingly suggests that a concealed autobiographic commentary is somewhere in the near background of each poem. Sergei Yesenin produced a body of poetry that is openly autobiographical. And in Mayakovsky's case, the poet's ego is flagrantly explicit: it is the major subject of his poetry. We can hardly speak of a biographical commentary to the poems: the biography is in them; many of them deal with particular experiences localized as to date and street address.

The formalist critic Boris Tomashevsky suggests in a very acute article that ". . . the biography that is useful to the literary historian is not the author's curriculum vitae or the investigator's account of his life. What the literary historian really needs is the biographical legend created by the author himself. Only such a legend is a *literary fact*."[2] This may very well be true, and yet the raw facts upon which the legend is based, if they can be discovered, must be of interest to any literary historian concerned with the imaginative process and its end result in the poem. Without them, how are we to trace the shaping and import of the legend? The discovery of each poem as a fact of the poet's real

[2] B. Tomashevsky, "Literature and Biography," in L. Matejka and K. Pomorska, eds., *Readings in Russian Poetics: Formalist and Structuralist Views* (Cambridge, 1971), p. 55.

biography, then, is essential to a full understanding of Mayakovsky.

Modern criticism as a whole tends to regard as its proper business the definition and investigation of something called "literariness," the quality or condition that converts a verbal product into art, and biographical facts are of interest only insofar as they illuminate that particular quality. But I would suggest that the sharp line so often drawn between literature and all manifestations of "life" in and around the poet breaks down, certainly in the case of Mayakovsky, and possibly of many other poets. Even the well-established dogma that the facts of a poet's biography must never be deduced from his poems is subject in his case to radical modification. Indeed, the structure of his poetry as a whole—and by structure I mean the systematic organization of theme and image—was shaped by the events of his life as a piece of bronze statuary is shaped by its mold; the critic may therefore deal with his life and his work as directly and systematically related, and move without embarrassment from one to the other. In fact we might even say that in his case the relation between private life and work is "a simple relation of cause and effect,"[3] as the entries in a diary are "caused" by the events of the day. Mayakovsky was rather unsophisticated in his view of literary creation, and when his "lyrical I" speaks of a razor and a throat we may be certain that the razor and the throat are his, and that if blood flows in the poem it will be real, and his own. Even in the last lines he wrote, where he speaks of his "love-boat smashed against convention," the love-boat is a double image: it is an ironic sentimental cliché, but it is also his own office on Lyubyansky Street, which he really referred to as his "boat." What follows in our account of Mayakovsky's poetry will, I believe, bear out the validity of this approach to his life and work.

Mayakovsky's relationship to the Soviet state and the Communist Party presents a special problem. Quantitatively, the major part of his poetic product after 1917 was political verse. In his career as a Soviet poet he made a consistent and conscious effort to lend his poetic gift to political uses. The pressures on him to do this were complex and varied, but they came largely from

[3] In *Theory of Literature* (New York, 1956), p. 65, René Wellek and Austin Warren make the statement that "the relation between the private life and the work is *not* a simple relation of cause and effect." (Italics mine.)

inside himself. The image we sometimes have of a genuine poet required by a state bureaucracy to give up his real self in favor of agitation and propaganda is totally false; in fact there were powerful pressures upon him to abandon the practice of agitational poetry in favor of his own lyrical gift. The major poets of his day—Pasternak, Mandelshtam, Akhmatova, Yesenin—were distressed by his reduction of poetry to utilitarian artifacts. He might have said of this phase in his career what Stavrogin in Dostoevsky's *The Possessed* said of his own suicide: "Don't blame anyone. I did it myself." He wrote his propaganda poems on demand, his pliable muse producing whatever the client desired at any given moment. The theories that justified this practice were not imposed on him but rather invented, as we shall see, by the members of his own literary group, who were not even averse to imposing them on others. Osip Brik, his principal mentor during the twenties, a brilliant critic and neglected writer, was also an opportunist and a gentle cynic with good connections in the *Cheka*, the secret political police of that day. The subtle ideas he worked out as theoretician of the Left Front of Art had little or nothing to do with Marxist literary criticism: their purpose was simply to rationalize the selling of poetic talent to the state. The positive side of those theories was that a poet—Mayakovsky, for instance—could write anything required of him without compromising, without even enlisting in the enterprise his own inner self. In Mayakovsky's case the inner man remained relatively free, and even during the twenties asserted himself from time to time in lyric poetry of extraordinary power. And when I say that he "sold poetic talent" to the state I intend equal emphasis on "sold" and "talent." What he sold was a set of verbal products that display his rich resources as a poet, and that often repay careful study.

The complex involvement of Mayakovsky's poetry with reality is a fact of which the critic must be aware if he is to throw light on anything except the bare elements of poetic technique. Yet the process by which some "reality" becomes embodied in a work of art is far from simple. A painter of the realistic school, even a "photographic" realist, produces only an illusion of reality when he conveys his retinal impressions to canvas,[4] and the criticism of a given painting can hardly be limited to discussion of the scenes

[4] On this subject E. H. Gombrich in *Art and Illusion*, 2nd ed. (Princeton, 1961), pp. 33-63, is very illuminating.

or figures represented. Writers of the realistic school are actually adept masters in the art of creating the illusion of a direct experience of reality. Mayakovsky rejected and abused the "realistic" school, but he was no less intent than they on explaining a certain kind of reality: in his case the reality of his own psychic makeup. His method in the major lyric poems is interior monologue in which psychic movements are given in terms of abnormal syntax and images—metonymy, metaphor, synecdoche, hyperbole, and simile—presented literally, or, in the usual terminology, "realized." For instance, the emotional pressure inside him when he makes a phone call raises the voltage in an underground telephone cable to a dangerous level and produces an earthquake: we learn of this in the story of that earthquake told many years later by an old fellow who happened to be out shopping that night. The illusion has been created of immediate contact with an emotional upset, the reason for which is then traced in the character of a particular person (whose name we know) and the habits and prejudices of a particular social milieu. The person, the society, history, the fate of the revolution, all are wrapped up implicitly in the lyric hero's psychic problems. To ignore all that would empty the poems of their *raison d'être*. Only by a judicious combination of formal and historical criticism can we elucidate the work of Mayakovsky.

Elucidation is the aim of this study, but elucidation of the work as a whole rather than of its separate parts in serial order. Mayakovsky's work lends itself readily to what we might call a holistic analysis, since each part of it suggests relationships to all the other parts, and the whole product may be referred to literally as well as figuratively as a "corpus"—that is to say, a body made up of numerous and subtly interrelated parts. To a surprising degree Mayakovsky's poems anticipate and allude to one another, and it is possible to reduce the corpus of his work to certain essentials, in fact to treat the multiform array of poems as a single poem. The study of his poetry is in a sense an investigation of the poet's mind itself, of the ways it experiences the world and how it gives form and expression to that experience.

Ezra Pound once defined the function of criticism as "excernment. The general ordering and weeding out of what has actually been performed. The elimination of repetitions. The work analogous to that which a good hanging committee or a curator would perform in a National Gallery or in a biological museum. The ordering of knowledge so that the next man (or generation) can most readily find the live part of it, and waste the least possible time among obsolete issues."[5]

The purpose of this study, in other words, is to clearly identify, sort out, describe, and display what is essential in the work of Mayakovsky.

Presenting the Poetry

The fact that Mayakovsky was a poet gives rise to special problems, since his art depends to a high degree on verbal effects, and many of those effects are inseparable from the Russian language. How can the products of that art be presented so as to be intelligible to readers who don't understand the language in which they were written? Translation can never fully reveal Mayakovsky; even though his imagery and emotional sense can often be successfully reproduced in another language, translators will probably remain helpless before his rhyming puns, his deftly playful broken rhymes, his rich alliterations and assonances, his humorous and happy neologisms, and the declamatory effect of his heavily accented phrase lines.

In the pages that follow I have translated or interpreted crucial passages whose meaning in terms of image or idea could be stated in English, without attempting to reproduce prosodic effects or verbal play. The latter qualities I have from time to time tried to describe in terms of their effect on an ear attuned to the speech instrument Mayakovsky used. Puns may be explained; rhyme schemes can be charted and at times exemplified in phonetic transcription, as can onomatopoeic effects. In other words the presence of sound patterns that translation cannot convey is, whenever necessary, indicated in a commentary.

A final word of explanation is in order as to the system used in citing Mayakovsky's verse lines. Sometimes—but rarely—he printed his poems in complete lines; more often the lines are broken on the page into phrase patterns which usually indicate the emphasis given in an oral presentation of the poetry. These phrase lines sometimes appeared in "ladder" form, one directly under another, and sometimes in "staircase" form, moving in steplike progression down the page. In the case of "laddered" poems I present the phrase lines one directly under another, to the

[5] Ezra Pound, *Literary Essays* (New York, 1918), p. 75.

extent that this is consistent with idiomatic English word order. The steps of a "staircase" I have divided by the use of slash marks. In numbering the lines of longer poems I have followed the *Complete Works of Mayakovsky* (*Polnoe sobranie sochinenii Mayakovskogo*, 1955-1961), where each phrase unit is counted as a line.

Chapter One

PRELUDE: APRIL 9, 1930

There are certain moments in the life of a poet, or perhaps of any human being, that catch that life's significance in a sharp focus. One such moment in the life of Mayakovsky occurred shortly before his suicide in April 1930. In a brief encounter with a hostile audience in Moscow he recapitulated his career as a revolutionary poet, and fully revealed the insolvent state his life had reached. The poetry he performed at that last "recital," and the occasion itself, throw a bright light on Mayakovsky both as a poet and as an agitator.

During the period just before his suicide he was frequently in trouble with proletarian audiences for whom much of the poetry he wrote during the 1920's was ostensibly meant. Of course the experience of contention with a live audience was not a new one for him; provocation of his hearers had been a poetic method in the early days of his literary career when, done up in grease paint and yellow blouse and with a radish in his buttonhole, he recited poems that were an offense to the established literary taste. But the bourgeois café audience of 1913 was a preselected target and the proper object of an avant-garde poet's scorn; its obtuse ridicule could hardly pierce the armor of his grease paint and blouse. Two very revealing lines in the poem *A Cloud in Pants* (*Oblako v shtanakh,* 1915) help us to understand the psychological function of the clown costume he wore in 1913:

It's fine when the soul
is shielded from inspection
in a yellow blouse.[1]

He might have expected that the working-class audience of 1930 would understand him as the "poet of the revolution"; but they didn't. They exhibited, in fact, an obdurate dullness more deadly than the amused disapproval of the pseudo-sophisticates and philistines who once crowded the futurist seances. And Maya-

[1] *PSS*, I, 186.

kovsky in the early months of 1930, no longer wrapped in his clown's mantle, no longer shielded from inspection, seemed defenseless against them. Once he had been an absolute master of repartee, a platform practitioner of the instantaneous verbal thrust, but he seemed to have lost that verbal control. The desolation of his final weeks and his suicide itself are probably best explained by his growing isolation not only from the "workers," but from everyone else—his friends and enemies alike. Loneliness was an established motif of his poetry beginning with the earliest things: "I'm alone," he said in 1913, "like the last eye left/ to a man going to join the blind."[2] The forlornness expressed in his first poems became a fact of the last years of his life.

The poet's last public appearance took place in April 1930, just five days before his suicide. We are in great debt to a close friend and associate, V. I. Slavinsky, who in the face of noisy invective and constant disorder, kept the "minutes" of the meeting at which Mayakovsky appeared.[3] The scene of that meeting was the Plekhanov Auditorium of the Institute of the National Economy in Moscow, and the audience was composed for the most part of students in the Institute. Mayakovsky when he appeared was sullen and sick; he complained of his throat and mentioned grippe. In addition to Slavinsky he was accompanied by Pavel Ilych Lavut, whom he had immortalized in verse as a "quiet Jew," and who was involved as a kind of manager in the poet's many and far-flung recitals. The students wandered into the hall slowly and it was only partly filled when his friends advised Mayakovsky that the time had come to start. According to Slavinsky, who had a sense of drama and an eye to history, the hall was dimly lighted and the poet as he climbed the stairs onto the speaker's platform was in a state of painful irritation, both physical and mental. He started with a half-humorous challenge, explaining that he was actually quite bored with the occasion and had come against his will. He reminded the students that although much stupid gossip circulated about him now, "Yet when I die you will all be reading my poems and shedding tears of tender emotion over them." Slavinsky recorded that there was "laughter in the hall." Mayakovsky continued in this vein of rather old-fashioned *épatage*:

[2] *PSS*, I, 49.

[3] The report of the meeting was published in *V. Mayakovsky v vospominaniyakh sovremennikov*, Z. Papernyi, ed. (Moscow, 1963), pp. 602-615 and 684-685.

"All my life I've been engaged in writing things that nobody would like, so nobody likes them." He offered to recite his recent poem *At the Top of My Voice* (*Vo ves golos*, 1930), which he called the "first introduction to a poem about the Five-Year Plan."[4]

The choice should have been a perfect one, for that poem is a rough paean to communism, a vernacular song about men as workers and builders, and a confident call over the heads of his contemporaries to the future. The poem possesses great power of language and imagery, and its ideological purpose should not conceal from us the quality of the work. The beauty of Dante's verse is not lost even on unbelievers, and Mayakovsky's old-fashioned unlettered Marxism need not obscure the poetic wonder of his hells and heavens.

The poem begins with an invocation to far-off descendants of the future—the only true friends of Mayakovsky—who will some day no doubt "dig in the petrified shit" of the poet's world in an effort to rediscover and understand that world. For the busy scholar of the future whose "erudition will cover a swarm of questions" he offers answers to possible questions about himself, Mayakovsky. He explains that he is a "latrine-cleaner and water-carrier," drawn to such healthful jobs by the revolution, and rescued, almost against his will, from the trivial floriculture of lyric poetry. It is of course no accident that Mayakovsky, who harbored a chronic neurotic fear of infection, should have emphasized the disinfectant function of his poetic work. The poem *At the Top of My Voice* expresses his rejection, not only of the traditional poet's fame—"that capricious old lady"—but of his own first and original poetic self, the poet totally concerned with his own ego, and his espousal of another and quite different poetic personality, the citizen who builds something as useful as an aqueduct or performs a task as healthful as cleaning a street. He had always been a kind of "anti-poet" and a paradoxical motif of his early poetry was the rejection of poetry itself. The bolshevik "anti-poet" of the late twenties rationalized the old motif by claiming precedence in verse for socially useful tasks. That's why he "stepped on the throat of his own song."

It is a long poem, but on this occasion in the Plekhanov Auditorium he was able to get only as far as the lines: "It would hardly be an honor / should roses like these / get my graven im-

[4] *PSS*, x, 279. Book-length poems ("*poemy*") are given in italics.

age set up / on squares where consumption coughs out its lungs/ where hooligans and whores and syphilis . . ." (47-53).[5] Suddenly there were shouts of protest at such coarse language[6] and Mayakovsky abruptly broke off and announced that he could not finish. Notes were forwarded from the floor to the platform—a custom at Russian meetings of this sort—and some of them suggested that "indecent words should not be employed in poetry."

Sensing the hostility of his audience, Mayakovsky tried to initiate a "dialogue." "Let's discuss things," he said, intending that someone from the audience take the floor and offer some comments which he would then respond to. No one came forward. He made another effort with his poem "The Sun." Though written ten years earlier than *At the Top of My Voice*, "The Sun" is relatively free of the deliberately anti-aesthetic, rough, and vulgar lexicon used to produce an aesthetic shock in his earliest poems and revived in his last major poem. It should have been a good choice for this audience, since it is very clean. The full title of the poem is "An Extraordinary Adventure That Befell Vladimir Mayakovsky at His Summer House" (*Neobychainoe priklyuchenie byvshee s Vladimirom Mayakovskim letom na dache*, 1920),[7] and it is a desolate man's dialogue with the sun, which dropped in on him one July day for tea and conversation.

The opening lines of the poem are a clownish expression of a despair over life which is an essential feature of Mayakovsky's poetry, forming a counterpoise to occasional bursts of poetic optimism. In his play *Vladimir Mayakovsky, a Tragedy* (1913) he had already taken upon himself the burden of human mutilation and human tears; in the poem entitled *Man* (*Chelovek*, 1917), he took leave of life because the bourgeois and money rule the world, then returned to earth again after an "avalanche of years," only to find that "nothing had changed"; in the poem *The Backbone Flute* (*Fleita pozvonochnik*, 1915) the lines occur: "Would

[5] Mayakovsky printed his poems either in complete lines, in phrase-lines taking a "ladder" form, or in phrase-lines in "staircase" form. Slashes are used to indicate the division of lines quoted in the text, and also to indicate phrase-lines that Mayakovsky had printed in staircase form. See "Introductory Remarks." The numerals refer to the lines of each poem cited, as numbered in *PSS*.

[6] We note that the language of the poem is still too strong for the Soviet editors, who print only the first letter of the words for "shit" (*govno*) and "whore" (*blyad*).

[7] *PSS*, II, 35.

it not be better/ to punctuate my line with a bullet?" "The Sun" holds special appeal because it states his despair and then overcomes it—all in the space of a brief encounter with the source of life.

When the poem opens he is in a state of revulsion at the changeless, predictable grind of day and night, and at the sun itself that disappears in the evening into a hole behind a roof-encrusted village, only to rise again all crimson-bright in the morning. He directs a shout at the sun: "Get down off of there! / You've moseyed enough times into your hot spot. . . / You parasite! There you are wrapped in soft clouds / while I have to draw my propaganda posters winter and summer" (29-34). He invites the sun to "drop down for tea," and the sun promptly obliges him. He is frightened at first, but soon feels warm and comfortable, and begins to chat with the sun about "this and that," about how fed up he is with producing posters for ROSTA [the Russian Telegraph Agency], and so forth. The poem was written during the period in his life when he was producing at a fantastic rate "windows" for the Telegraph Agency, placards and posters with drawings and agitational poetry that were hung in the empty display windows of city stores during the famine years. Says the sun:

> OK. But don't grieve!
> Take a simple view of things.
> You think it's easy
> for me to shine?
> You just try it!
> But once you've started out,
> you've taken the job on,
> you just go ahead—and shine real sharp! (86-93)

The poet draws not only light but courage from this conversation, and he feels at last that even though the sun, "a sleepyhead," may occasionally need a rest, the poet can still cast the great beam of his verses into the night:

> Always to shine . . . no matter what.
> That's my motto
> and the sun's! (127-132)

Obviously we can know very little about the nature of that "great beam" if we do not possess the language in which it is projected. What I have so far said about it has been said in English, and therefore represents either translation or paraphrase of various meanings. But the meanings we have found might very well have been presented in prose: disillusionment, whimsy, the sickness unto death, renewal of courage, humorous resignation—all these might have been the subject either of a sober essay or of a story about a visit with the sun intended for children and imaginative adults, and in either case written in prose. But Mayakovsky had said, "I'm a poet and that's why I'm interesting." If we take him at his word then we must pay attention to the fact that what he wrote is *in verse* and that it employs with casual assurance the entire compass of poetic tones.

Certain stereotypes concerning that verse are well established in Russian and non-Russian criticism. Mayakovsky has been labelled an innovator, a neologist, a breaker of canons, an experimenter, and so forth. The widespread notion of him as an undisciplined, emotionally errant personality is reflected in an equally widespread impression, buttressed by the work of certain scholarly investigators, that his verse, metrically "free" and unpatterned, is not measurable by the known poetic scales.[8] This impression was created in part by Mayakovsky himself, who wrote in his essay "How to Make Verses" that he had never had anything to do with "iambics and trochaics." But he was quite unreliable as a critic of his own work. Nearly everything he wrote is carefully organized as to rhythm and rhyme; the poem about the sun is written in pure iambic measure with alternating four-foot and three-foot lines, and alternating masculine and feminine rhymes. It is one of his best poems and it would be absurd to treat it as an anomaly. It is not even an exception. His first poems were written in conventional binary, or two-syllable, meters, and were less revolutionary in their metrical structure than the much earlier work of certain symbolist poets.[9] And yet the sense of something new is an inherent quality of the poem about the sun as it is of

[8] Such a viewpoint is explicit in the work of M. P. Shtokmar, "O stilevoi sisteme Mayakovskogo," in *Tvorchestvo Mayakovskogo. Sbornik statei* (Moscow, 1952). The same idea is implicit in many other works and also in the reaction of readers unversed in poetry who fail to find in many of the poems any clear pattern of scansion. The best summary of and commentary on recent studies of Mayakovsky's verse is V. Zhirmunsky, "Stikhoslozhenie Mayakovskogo," *Russkaya literatura*, No. 4, 1964.

[9] This is clearly established in recent studies of Mayakovsky's verse, and was pointed out much earlier in V. Trenin and N. Khardzhiev, "Poetika rannego Mayakovskogo," *Literaturnyi kritik*, No. 4, 1935.

all his best work, and the novelty is as much a matter of meter as it is of poetic vocabulary, imagery, or rhyme. The curious fact is that Mayakovsky has managed to use a "conventional" meter, the so-called syllabo-tonic meter, in which the poet works within a more or less rigid frame of alternating accented and unaccented syllables, to suggest the possibility, indeed the imminent likelihood, of escape from that format into free, conversational statement. Building his poem carefully according to the rules of literary artifice, he still has contrived its cadences so as to suggest the final abandonment of artifice, and, in Robert Frost's phrase, "the sound of sense."

He uses many devices to contrive this effect of freedom from device. Some of his most strikingly developed rhymes are not quite rhymes, but either truncated or merely assonant, for instance *pylál:plylá* (blazed:hovered). There is an occasional chiasmic internal rhyme that, suddenly breaking into, even though part of, the strict pattern of conventional end-rhymes, acts upon the latter both as contrast and support: *bylá zhará, zhará plylá* (there was heat, the heat hovered). Rhyming words or phrases often produce a humorous effect because they are so far apart lexically and grammatically that the near correspondence of sounds stirs unexpected incongruities of thought and language; thus the word for "propaganda posters" is rhymed with ". . . clouds thou," *oblaká ty; plakáty.* Alliteration is abundant and rich, done with infantile fascination at the possibilities offered by contrived coincidence: *krivílsya krýsh karóyu; dirévneyu dyrá; do dnei poslédnikh dóntsa.* The poetic devices are so casual that they seem a happy accident in the line.

Word play is unremitting, and puns, like rhyme and alliteration, are complex and rich; the word for "to drop in" happens to be the same as the word for "to set," which offers the intriguing possibility of having the sun "set" for tea, and since the word for "sit down" in Russian is *also* used of the sun's disappearance beyond the horizon, the poet may, Joshua-like, order the luminary not to "set" but to "have a seat by the tea."

But the most striking artifice Mayakovsky employs is also the most obvious one: the poem is a teatime chat with the daylight orb carried on in the unconstrained idiom associated with relaxation and a bit of the brew. This naturally involves colloquial cadences and a sub-poetic vocabulary, words not normally used for lyric purposes and regarded as unsuitable for poetic converse with the sun, the universe, or for that matter with the self. There is a perfect unity of opposites contained in lines that say with strict iambic beat and a regular rhyme scheme what it seems anyone might say without even trying. "Get down off of there!" a command to the sun, sounds like a maternal imperative shouted at some troublesome offspring who clambers all over the shed roof; the sun chattered "about this and that"; he (it) quite informally invites the poet to "spread the tea and jam"; the sun and the poet agree to "keep on shining, no matter what"; and of course it's not easy to come up shining every day, "you just try it! (*podi poprobui!*)."

The poem's power grows out of a startlingly original idea—to call it fantasy would belittle the poet's honest labor. Mayakovsky has produced a brief human drama in the form of a casual colloquy with the sun. The mood of the poem and the aspect of the world change imperceptibly in it: the disconsolate and hazy heat of the first lines gives way to friendly warmth and the "courage to go on." The miracle is accomplished by a pain-racked poet who really *means* everything he says, but who is at the same time a verbal artist playing a baroque improvisation on the complex instrument of human speech in its modern Russian variant. It may be that the verbal play itself is what comforted him. And he succeeds in turning upside down the old myth of sun worship: in his poem the sun becomes a comrade and collaborator.

When Mayakovsky had finished the recitation of this poem to the audience in the Plekhanov Auditorium, notes were again passed up from the floor. One of them presented to him the ghastly query, "What is the idea of the poem about the sun?" A shattering blow, but Mayakovsky answered it, quietly, literally. He said, "The poem is a kind of joke. Its basic thought is 'Shine on no matter how miserable reality may be!' " Another voice from the crowd, "What do you mean things are miserable?" Then Mayakovsky proposed to recite, no doubt in self-justification, the last part of his poem *Vladimir Ilich Lenin* (1924).[10]

Mayakovsky's *Vladimir Ilich Lenin* in many ways recalls the techniques of Sergei Eisenstein in the film *Ten Days that Shook the World*, and we must remember that Eisenstein was a friend and associate of Mayakovsky in the mid-twenties. Both artists use the most sophisticated techniques of their media to create a myth of the bolshevik revolution. Consider the treatment of Kerensky in

[10] *PSS*, vi, 33.

Ten Days: he is a poltroon, a popinjay, and a coward who sells out Russia to foreign capital. But then we look upon the bright aura of the revolution: the massed soldiers; the Winter Palace at night; the empty bourgeois coats in the chairs of the former ministers; the sharp, sudden forests of bayonets; the rhythm of excited movement; the multitude of faces, loyal, afraid, contemptuous, devious, utterly devoted; and dominating the great historical moment the immortal figures of the men who made the revolution. Similarly, Mayakovsky presents facts and events from a viewpoint that denies normal humanity to the enemies of Lenin and the bolsheviks. The brilliant democratic statesman Milyukov is characterized by a contemptuous epithet (1650-1660); the premier of the Provisional Government in 1917, Kerensky, is no better than a girl: "come and pet her!"; opposition parties hold a knife poised at the back of the working class; the mensheviks are weak and traitorous. The "other" side appears in the poem as unregenerated black; all the bright colors are reserved for the heroes of "our" side: Lenin, who figures both as prophet and savior; Stalin and Trotsky, his faithful disciples.

Lenin is elevated into an image that is essentially "religious" in the sense that greatness, goodness, and glory are his by native right, and there is no questioning the justice of his cause. For the conventional God we may substitute History, which in the fullness of Time brought Lenin to redeem the world and point the way to salvation: he is a kind of predestined savior who appeared according to history's law at the moment of capitalism's decline and violent fall. Critics of the poem complained that Mayakovsky was apparently not interested in the "real" Lenin, in his actual life or personal psychology or the nature of his political genius. The Lenin of Mayakovsky's poem is a myth. He is the messiah foretold in the scriptures of Marxist prophecy, and the story of his great deeds begins far back in human history (348). He was promised long ago; he came at the proper and inevitable moment and he acts in response to the eternal laws of history. And he was just "an ordinary fellow," unpretentious as the common human kind; he might even have been born in a stable.

Mayakovsky succeeded in consecrating a great poem to a political cause. It is anything but a propaganda pot-boiler. He worked on it for many months during 1924; he gave it everything he had, and as a verbal artifact it is not inferior to some of his best things. There are in it a satisfactory number of those verbal surprises that are characteristic of Mayakovsky, and that enable him to fix vividly an idea or a scene or a person. We see the endlessly moving line of mourners on that cold January day when Lenin lay in state: "It was as though/ Russia/ was again/ a nomad nation" (317-320). And the announcement that the true topic of the poem is the mythical Lenin, not the real person Ulyanov:

> Short / is the life / of Ulyanov
> Known / to its last syllable;
> But the long life
>   of Comrade Lenin
> We must tell / and describe once more. (338-346)

Or the delightful colloquial condensation of the Marxist view of capitalism: "Capitalism/ when he was young/ wasn't a bad sort/ —an ambitious lad" (508-510). Lenin's thought is "simple as bread/ straight as a rail" (900); and "the bourgeois are black, like crows in winter" (1351). The lines that describe the funeral procession are solemn, with a slow, funereal retardation. The great power of the poem arises from the pervading sense of grief that fills it; it is a hero's funeral march, and perhaps it should be read, not only as a march for Lenin, but for all leaders who have caught the devotion of a great mass of followers.

Even after the reading of that poem the heckling of Mayakovsky continued, and assumed a kind of organized menace. One of the hecklers decided to give some concrete examples of Mayakovsky's unintelligible verses. The heckler had obviously come prepared, and he read a number of things, all written before the First World War, when Mayakovsky was a young and irreverent futurist painter and poet. One of these was a poem entitled "But Could You?" (*A vy mogli by?* 1913), and this particular one Mayakovsky decided he must defend. He himself recited it again, in his own way, and then said: "Any proletarian ought to understand that poem. If he doesn't he's simply illiterate. You should study. I really want you to understand my things." Here is a more or less literal translation of the poem in question:

> I color-smeared the chart of everyday
> splashing paints on it from a drinking-glass;
> on a dish of fish aspic I showed
> the slanted cheekbones of the ocean.

On the scale of a tin fish
I read the message of fresh lips.
And you—
could you play a nocturne
on a downspout flute?[11]

There would seem at first sight to be some question as to whether the meaning of this poem should really be clear to any proletarian—or to a member of any other social class—and perhaps Mayakovsky was permitting himself an irony when he said that its meaning was obvious. But he did have a point. On one level perhaps anyone could understand it: the poem says that poetry, painting, art in general, while using the dull inventory of everyday reality, transforms it into new color, new form, new meaning, and even new music. That much is easy. Moreover, the images ought to be clear to a proletarian since they are drawn from city life: the tin fish is a reference to store-front street signs, and the murmuring downspout was a ubiquitous urban shape and sound. But the poem is actually rather complex and offers many possibilities of interpretation. It is clear that the poet takes the everyday grind and splashes his own color on it, but what of those "slanted cheekbones of the ocean on a dish of fish aspic?" One explanation is that the poem is a verbal realization of a still-life that Mayakovsky had been painting. Perhaps it was a table scene and one of the objects was a bowl of fish aspic which, in a cubistic displacement of shapes, may have looked like the waves of the ocean and at the same time like slanted cheekbones. The poem, then, may be a verse realization of a cubistic still-life, perhaps of more than one such painting.

The Soviet scholar Khardzhiev, writing in *Literaturnoe nasledstvo*, No. 65 (1958), maintains that there is another "level" of meaning here, and that "fish aspic" refers to the hardened stereotypes of conventional art, that he, Mayakovsky, has broken, thus obliging art to reveal new and unexpected reality, in fact a "raging" ocean of reality. The "tin fish" may be part of a cubist painting, or it may be an urban street scene with signs over stores: and the scales on the fish are lips that bear a message of the future calling to new things. Then in the last lines there is a shift to a new plane of apprehension, from the visible to the audible, and the poet's work, it turns out at last, is to make soft, tender music

[11] *PSS*, I, 40.

out of store signs, downspouts, and fish aspic. The poem is interesting also as an early introduction to the images of water and the sea that are recurrent and insistent in the major work of Mayakovsky.

After reciting the poem "But Could You?" Mayakovsky waited for more questions or comments, but the workers sat silent. "Why don't you say something?" he asked. There was no answer. "If you don't say anything it follows that the poem was understandable. Now I'll recite something from *Very Good.*"

Very Good (*Khorosho: oktyabrskaya poema*, 1927)[12] was written to celebrate the tenth anniversary of the October revolution and indeed bears the subtitle "An October Poem." Its nineteen chapters tell of the bolshevik seizure of power, the frozen and starving winters of the Civil War period, and recovery and rebuilding, and it ends with an affirmation of life, of Russia, and of socialism. It is a product of the era of the "literature of fact" in the poet's career, a time when he wrote under the influence of Brik, Kushner, and Tretyakov, theoreticians of Mayakovsky's Left Front of Art who had worked out a notion that writing is a craft not basically different from other socially useful occupations, and that the highest form of literary activity is factual reporting. In the poem he adopts the fiction that he is simply relating a series of events gathered up—"drunk up"—as he puts it, out of a "river by the name of fact." Soviet scholars have produced long and learned researches, really impressive of their kind, that show with meticulous certainty the documentary or eyewitness sources of everything Mayakovsky says in the poem. But like so much of Mayakovsky's life and work, his factography, as it is called, is a kind of literary fiction. Out of real names and events and actual documents he creates in the poem several kinds of myth. First there is a political myth: in the treatment of the liberal democrats who opposed the bolsheviks there is crude distortion of character and fact; the account of the taking of the Winter Palace is broadly oversimplified—perhaps falsified would be a better word. Just as he does in the poem *Vladimir Ilich Lenin*, Mayakovsky uses his poetic talent to create a contemporary myth of bolshevism. He solemnizes a myth of the "intervention" in which the poor and hungry, "with Lenin at their noggins and pistols in their hands," fight off the wicked forces of the western world, who advance to the strains of "Yankee Doodle Dandy" and "It's a Long Way to

[12] *PSS*, VIII, 233.

Tipperary." And in the same material there is myth-making of a purely literary kind. Read in abstraction from particular historical events and persons, the poem becomes a dramatic picture of how the downtrodden and oppressed, the poor, the naked, and the hungry at last asserted their humanity against the powers of this world, of how the not-so-meek at last inherited the earth; it draws the reader along even if he is aware that a certain violence has been done to historical reality.

But there is still another kind of myth-making in the poem, which was pointed out by the poet himself. In his autobiography he said of this poem that he had introduced in it, intersecting the historical plane, facts based on purely personal associations and experiences, and he mentions as an example of this his meeting with the poet Alexander Blok soon after the revolution, an event described in chapter 6. That is one of the most moving episodes in the poem, since it sums up Blok's personal tragedy as well as the tragedy of the Russian intelligentsia as a whole. "This revolution is all very good," said Blok—he sympathized with it—but he added: "On my estate in the village the peasants have burned my library." Chapters 13 and 14 describe the terrible winter of 1919, but deal with the cold facts in a personal and lyrical manner. They tell, not about great events, but about "Osip, Lily, and me," or "Olya, Mama, and me." Only during that winter, Mayakovsky said, did he come to understand "love and friendship, and families." The shape of the room where he spent the cold nights, the angle and position of a particular staircase, particular people and moments, the name of their dog, private rather than public events are the material of those exquisite chapters. "Love," he discovered, "is finding a carrot for a girl whose bright eyes are dimmed for lack of vitamins":

> I've / given presents / of flowers and candy.
> But more / than all / expensive gifts
> I remember / that precious carrot /
> and half / a log / of birchwood for the fire. (1991-2001)

In this poem, *Very Good*, as in so much of Mayakovsky, we have an alternation between the two Mayakovskys, the two poetic "personas," one lyrical and one political. The discovery of this is sometimes attributed to Roman Jakobson, but actually Mayakovsky himself is the source of the idea about the number and variety of his selves, as we shall soon see. The question remains how much of the poem he recited to the students in the Plekhanov Auditorium, and that is uncertain. But according to Pavel Ilich Lavut, the organizer of his recitals, he usually recited both the public and private sections of the poem.

Twice in the course of that last meeting Mayakovsky, as near to pleading as he could come, had attempted to win the favor of his "workers' auditorium" by reciting his political verses, and twice he failed. Even after the reading of *Very Good* the atmosphere was poisoned by complaints about another "unintelligible" poem, which when recited turned out to be the work of Khlebnikov. There was a brief barbed exchange between Mayakovsky and certain of his hecklers. Slavinsky wrote: "Mayakovsky in his indignation directed sharp comments at the slanderers and idiots, not all of which I managed to jot down. . . . A girl student jumped up and babbled something, grimacing the while. His rolling bass voice suddenly drowned out the confusion of noise. I looked up at the speaker, then down at the auditorium. I asked Bessonov what to do, how to quiet Vladimir Vladimirovich. . . . Meanwhile Mayakovsky was demonstrating the students' ignorance of poetry by citing statements they had made, and he took great offense at their reproaches: 'I'm astonished at the illiteracy of this audience. I didn't expect to find such a low level of culture among the students of a respected institution.' Someone in spectacles in the front row shouted, 'That's demagoguery!' Mayakovsky turned in the direction of the speaker, 'Demagoguery! Comrades, is it that?' The bespectacled person wouldn't give in, but stood up and shouted, 'Yes, it's demagoguery.' I was desperate. I grabbed up the empty decanter from the table and rushed toward the exit. Lavut stopped me. I took his word for it that this is the way it always was when Mayakovsky spoke, and that Mayakovsky always got the best of it. He leaned over the edge of the platform and stared at the screaming idiot with hatred in his eyes and with all the power of his awful voice ordered him to 'Sit down!' But the idiot wouldn't sit down. He kept on shouting. There was great confusion in the hall. Everybody was standing. 'Sit down! I'll make you sit down!' Then the noise subsided. They sat down again. Vladimir Vladimirovich was very tired. Staggering slightly he came down from the platform and sat down on the steps leading up to it. There was complete silence. He'd gotten the best of it."

The meeting soon ended, but only after Mayakovsky had been asked to recite "Left March" (*Levyi marsh*, 1918) and some anti-bourgeois Civil War jingles. He ended on a quietly sad note: "Comrades, we'll get together again in a few months. . . . You shouldn't hold a grudge against me." He tried to leave the hall alone and quietly, and a few minutes after he left Lavut returned to say that he'd forgotten his cane; Lavut added that that sort of thing had never happened before. Five days later he had shot himself.

It is especially revealing to begin the investigation of Mayakovsky's life and work by concentrating on this brief moment near the end of his life. Thanks to the devoted efforts of Slavinsky, the record of this incident in Moscow contains in little the full tragedy of a poet misunderstood and rejected during his own lifetime both by those he wanted to reject him and by those he wanted to accept him. And the unplanned program of his poetry reading, growing as it did out of the intense psychological pressures of the moment and as an answer to the attacks upon him, summed up his essential features as a poet, and constituted a kind of defense of himself. He gave his audience one of the best of his early cubo-futurist poems, a poem of the middle period where despair and hope are in hazardous balance, his great funeral ode to Lenin, his ode to the revolution, *Very Good*, and of course the poem that began the recital, his last appeal "at the top of his voice" to his ultimate judges, "the future." It was clear that his audience wanted none of it.

Chapter Two

THE REVOLUTION: POLITICS

1) Papa, Mama, Olya, and Lyuda

Whatever is close, intimate, and singular found its way into Mayakovsky's lyric poetry, and of course his own family has an important place in it. During an episode in heaven that occurs in the poem *Man*, his father suddenly materializes, perhaps in the place of God, but with the palpable form and motion of the old man himself:

> My father beside me.
> Just the same.
> Only a little deafer,
> and his ranger's uniform's
> a little more worn
> at the elbows. (635-640)

Staring down at the earth from heaven, Vladimir the elder offers the solemn comment: "It must be springtime in the Caucasus now."

In *A Cloud In Pants* (*Oblako v shtanakh*, 1915) when his girl deserts him, he telephones a frantic cry for help to his mother and sisters:

> Hello!
> Who's that?
> Mama?
> Mama!
> Your son is marvellously ill!
> Mama!
> He has a heart on fire.
> Tell Lyuda and Olya
> There's no hope for him! (162-170)

And in his suicide note, a prose poem of a special kind, he commends the "family" to the care of his "Comrade Government," listing them as "Lily Brik, Mama, my sisters [Lyuda and Olya] and Veronika Vitoldovna Polonskaya." The narrative will in due course reveal how Lily and Veronika gained adoption into the family; I have already commented on the appearance of the Briks in the intimate circle of sufferers during the 1919 winter of cold and hunger, where he speaks in the poem *Very Good* of "Osip, Lily, and me."

"I was born on the 7th of July, 1894 (or '93—the opinion of my mother and my father's service record do not agree. In any case it was no earlier). My home place is the village of Bagdadi, Kutais region, Georgia."[1] Though Mayakovsky's autobiography (*I Myself*) is a deliberate parody of the genre, it does contain snatches of childhood memory that may throw light on the mature poet. The father who contributed to *Man* that ruminant observation on the state of the seasons in the Caucasus was a forest ranger, though of noble ancestry, an official of the Russian government whose demesne of responsibility stretched out over a vast and primitive area of mountain and forest, and who was involved, so the memoirists tell us, with the magnificent beauty of the Caucasus, with its cliffs, torrents, and precipitous ravines. They tell us also that he loved nature, and "understood it with his whole being."[2] His son, however, demonstratively despised nature and all who celebrate it, and scenes of nature are almost totally absent from his poetry. Rejection of the paternal air and way of life is explicit in his account of a trip with his father over the mountains when the struggle with steep trails and resistant vegetation is suddenly interrupted by a distant view of a factory illuminated by electricity. "After electricity," Mayakovsky said, "I lost interest in nature. Too backward." Very little is known of Mayakovsky's relationship with his father, who died, when the boy was thirteen, of an infection caused by a cut on his finger, but the fact that Mayakovsky all his life dreaded infection, carefully cleaned and recleaned glasses, knives, and forks before using them, and was a compulsive washer of his own hands, argues that his father's death was a deeply traumatic experience, even that a measure of fear and guilt may have been associated with it. Mayakovsky unconsciously reveals a genuine affinity with his father when he

[1] *PSS*, I, 9. The records show that he was born July 7 (19, new style), 1893, in Bagdadi, now called (predictably) Mayakovsky, a village in western Georgia.

[2] A. V. Mayakovskaya, *Perezhitoe* (Tbilisi, 1957); as quoted in V. Katanyan, *Mayakovsky; literaturnaya khronika*, 4th ed. (Moscow, 1961), p. 9.

records a memory of the old man singing the *Marseillaise* in Russian sounds that imitated the sound but not the sense of the French words, an approximation of which in English might be: "A lawns on fundy lap a tree-ee-ee!"[3] Not only was the result an anticipation of the nonsense language (*zaum*) favored by certain of Mayakovsky's futurist comrades, it was also a preview of Mayakovsky's own procedure in his play *The Bathhouse* (*Banya*, 1930), where a British agent articulates Russian words that sound like English but add up to hilarious nonsense: "It is very well," for instance, translates into *i zver revel*: "and the beast roared." Mayakovsky's father in his ranger's uniform, tall and profoundly bearded, looks out at us solemnly from a 1905 photograph the center of which is a pensive twelve-year-old Volodya, circled by his mother and his older sisters Olga Vladimirovna and Lyudmila Vladimirovna.

Mayakovsky's autobiography offers other interesting nuggets of information, most of which have more to do with the concerns and conflicts of the twenties than with the actual experiences of the young boy. Lermontov's phrase "kindred hills," and his use of the word for "cliffs" in an archaic pronunciation irritated him as a boy, so Mayakovsky says, and when he learned that such things were "poetic" he says he came to hate them. Clearly the professional anti-poet and agitator of the twenties speaks here for the child.[4] On the other hand there may be important psychological evidence in the memory that the second book he read was *Don Quixote*, which he loved: "I made myself a wooden sword and wooden armor, and slashed about me."[5]

Mayakovsky was educated, he says, "by female relatives of every degree," using an untranslatable neologism (*vsyakoyurodnye sestry*) that gives proper emphasis to the important role played by his sisters in his early life. They introduced him to the revolution. When Lyudmila went to Moscow to study drawing, Olga and he both wrote her telling of their involvement—Mayakovsky was twelve years old—with the events of 1905 in Georgia,[6] and she brought back with her from Moscow "long sheets of paper" covered with revolutionary verses and songs. "Verses and revolution," said Mayakovsky, "somehow fused in my head." Rebellion in the high school had erupted in so serious a form

[3] *PSS*, I, 10-11. [4] *Ibid.*, p. 11. [5] *Ibid.*, p. 12.

[6] V. Pertsov, *Mayakovsky, zhizn i tvorchestvo* [I], *Do . . . revolyutsii* (Moscow, 1951), 22ff.

that the administration was obliged to meet with student committees and discuss their "demands." Olga proudly recounts her own election to one such committee, and Vladimir's letters tell of student strikes, singing the *Marseillaise* in church, cannons pointed at the school yard, and the sound of revolutionary songs coming from the streets.[7] Curiously enough, the earliest letter of Mayakovsky, a poet always concerned with the graphic aspect of his verse, is penned in a single spiralling line which moves out from a central point on the paper. And he provided an original pattern for the date: $19\frac{2}{2}05$.[8]

2) An Underage Revolutionary

The family had always lived in decent poverty—the elder Mayakovsky once described himself as a member of the "non-landed gentry"—but with his death in 1906 they began to know penury. On borrowed funds they removed to Moscow, where they made ends meet by letting out rooms to students. The food was bad, the rooms "miserable." The lodgers were inpecunious young radicals; one was arrested and executed, another committed suicide.

Time spent on the benches of the Moscow *gymnasium* only interfered with Mayakovsky's education. He reports that he got poor grades: "F's weakly variegated by D's and C's," to translate freely from his autobiography. But education of another kind proceeded through the reading of Marxist literature and frequent contacts with radical students. He professed a total indifference at this time to belles-lettres (not surprising in the future anti-poet), and a passion for Karl Marx (not surprising in the future bolshevik agitator). Another autobiographical remark under the heading "First Halfpoem" might serve as a definition of his career as a poet, and in any case offers clear support to the proponents of a "binary Mayakovsky":

> The third class of the *gymnasium* published an illegal newspaper, "Impulse" [*Poryv*]. I took offense. Other people write, and I can't? I began scribbling. What came out was incredibly revolutionary, and to the same degree awful. Something like our own Kirillov. Don't remember a line. I wrote another one.

[7] *PSS*, xiii, 7ff.

[8] *Ibid.*

What came out was lyrical. Not regarding such a heart condition as fitting my "socialist dignity," I gave it up completely.[9]

The dilemma stayed with Mayakovsky all his life and is the major theme of his last long poem, *At the Top of My Voice*. "Incredibly revolutionary" poems—better than Kirillov but not as good as Mayakovsky—alternate with lyrics, which he seems at times to have regarded as unworthy of his calling; but I am anticipating. Early in 1908 Mayakovsky joined the bolshevik faction of the Russian Social Democratic Party,[10] and was elected, at the tender age of fourteen (everyone agrees that he looked older), to its Moscow Committee. The "election" was much less formal than Mayakovsky's references to an "all-city conference" would lead us to believe. The revolutionary movement was at its ebb and the government, firmly in control for the moment, had filled the prisons with Party members. A few Moscow bolsheviks met secretly in the woods at Sokolniki outside Moscow and constituted themselves the city committee; Mayakovsky became part of it by virtue of his presence at that meeting. He took the Party name Comrade Constantine, no doubt in honor of his older brother, who had died at an early age.[11] He was arrested soon after this when, carrying a bundle of illegal proclamations, he walked into a trap set by the police in a house where his comrades had an illegal printing press. At his interrogation he concocted a transparent "cover story" to explain his presence at the apartment: the proclamations had been given to him near the Pushkin monument by a man whom he knew only as "Alexander," to be delivered to the apartment of another man with whom he was not acquainted at all. The examining magistrates were not deceived. In view of his youth he was released in the care of his mother.

Soon after his release Mayakovsky again came under the observation of the police, apparently as the result of frequent contacts with other persons whose activities interested them. The archives of the Third Section have yielded a rich harvest of the "diaries" kept by the plain-clothes operatives who watched him

[9] *PSS*, I, 16.

[10] Katanyan, *Khronika*, p. 17.

[11] On the "Moscow Conference" see V. Zemskov, "*Uchastie Mayakovskogo v revolyutsionnom dvizhenii*," in *Literaturnoe nasledstvo*, LXV, *Novoe o Mayakovskom* (Moscow, 1958), 451.

constantly and reported his every movement, every visit, every errand during the summer of 1908.[12] The detectives assigned to him, referring to him by their code name "the tall one," pedantically recorded visits to the grocer and the baker, streetcar trips, and excursions to the country. The resultant material is a curious exercise in futility, since the meticulous accounts of Mayakovsky's movements not only tell us nothing about what he was doing, but create an enclosed reality of their own within which a simple record that, for instance, "he came out of the house at ten-thirty, went to the bakery shop, and returned home carrying some kind of package," takes on an aura of suspicion. After a careful analysis of all the records V. Zemskov, an objective and admirable scholar, can only admit that we do not know exactly what Mayakovsky was doing during that summer.[13] However, the writers of memoirs and reminiscences assure us that he was engaged in "underground party work."[14]

Mayakovsky's second arrest took place in January 1909, when he fell into the net of a police operation aimed at forestalling the plans of a group of social-revolutionary "expropriators," who organized robberies to support their organization. It is clear that Mayakovsky had no connection with their plans, though he did have contacts with individuals involved in them. He was released at the end of February 1909.

His third arrest was also an accident, and this suggests the suspicion that he may have been prone to such accidents. It came about as the result of a jailbreak involving a dozen or so female political prisoners, magnificently planned and executed by a group of social-revolutionaries and social democrats working together. The story of the prison break on July 1, 1909 reveals imaginative daring and resourcefulness on the part of the thirteen female prisoners and their friends outside the prison, and ludicrous impotence on the part of the authorities. Most of those involved outside the prison were known to the police, and were in fact under secret surveillance while carrying out their project. The plot involved complex plans and preparations. The jail supervisor, who had recently suffered a painful personal tragedy and was on the verge of suicide, was won over to the side of the prisoners; she provided them with wax models of the vital locks

[12] See Zemskov, pp. 485-495; and also Katanyan, *Khronika*, pp. 22-26.
[13] Zemskov, p. 495.
[14] See Katanyan, *Khronika*, p. 17.

and brought in the clothing they would need, some of which, we are told, was made by the mother and sister of Mayakovsky. Powerful soporifics were procured and placed at the right moment in the food of the guards. Ropes were made and smuggled in. Activities inside the prison were carefully coordinated with preparations outside to receive and conceal the escapees. The plan worked to perfection in despite of a numerous and busy army of policemen, who no doubt were at that very time recording the observed movements of many suspicious characters. It is unlikely that Mayakovsky was directly involved in the actual break, though one imaginative and totally unsubstantiated account places him in a steeple ringing out the bells to signal the inmates that all was in readiness.[15] Learning of the project's success from the newspapers of July 2, he rushed to the apartment of one of the principal conspirators, I. I. Morchadze, where he was met at the door by the chief of police. Once again he had stumbled into a trap, and Soviet biographers have some difficulty handling this episode. Pertsov explains Mayakovsky's lack of circumspection (he does not call it that) by the jubilant mood he was in when he read of the escape, and by his eagerness to learn the details, to offer help, and the like.[16] He does seem to have been in a state of nervous exaltation that did not subside at least until after his first interrogation. Morchadze recalls that he arrogantly dictated to the examining magistrate what he should write, developing in the course of his statement a complex series of rhyming puns.[17] Morchadze suggests also that his career as a poet began at that police interrogation.[18]

His third arrest led to imprisonment for six months, five months of it in solitary confinement. Mayakovsky's account of this period is telegraphic in style, but charged with meaning: "I was taken in. I didn't want to stay in jail. Raised hell. Kept moving me from one station to another—Basmannaya, Meshchanskaya, Myasnitskaya—and finally the Butyrki prison, solitary cell No. 103."

[15] "Novye materialy o Mayakovskom," *Vechernyaya Moskva*, July 19, 1955.

[16] Pertsov [I], 108-109.

[17] The untranslatable puns are given to us by one of the participants: "Ya, Vladimir Mayakovsky, prishol syuda po risovalnoi chasti . . . a ya, pristav Meshchanskoi chasti, reshil, chto vinovat Mayakovsky otchasti, a potomu nado razorvat ego na chasti." In V. *Mayakovsky v vospominaniyakh sovremennikov*, p. 84.

[18] *Ibid.*, p. 85.

The precise nature of his insubordination in the police station is set forth in a secret report of the jail inspector Serov of Meshchanskaya station, and while its style lacks Mayakovsky's laconic force this document does have a kind of factual felicity:

> Vladimir Vladimirovich Mayakovsky's conduct stirs up the political prisoners to resist the police officers. He insists that the sentries grant him free access into any and all cells, since he calls himself the spokesman [*starosta*: "elder"] of all the prisoners; when he is allowed out to the latrine or the faucet he refuses to return to his own cell, but walks up and down the corridor; he pays no attention to my requests that he maintain order. . . . On the 16th of August at 7 p.m. he was let out to the latrine, whereupon he walked up and down the corridor, going up to other cells and demanding that the sentry open them. The sentry's request [*prosba*] that he return to his own cell, he refused, for which reason the sentry, since he had to let the others out to the latrine singly, began to ask him insistently to return to his cell, whereupon Mayakovsky called the sentry a "bastard" [*kholui*], and began shouting up and down the corridor, so that all the prisoners could hear him, saying "Comrades, this bastard is pushing your spokesman into his cell," which excited all the prisoners, who in turn began to raise a disturbance. In communicating this information to the Security Section, I humbly request that arrangements be made to transfer Mayakovsky to another place of confinement, and I would add in this connection that he was transferred to me from Basmannaya station by reason of his riotous behavior.
>
> Inspector Serov[19]

One of the prisoners confined in a cell near Mayakovsky recalled that the politicals had on one of their walks elected him as their "spokesman," and that his duties were to observe the feeding of the prisoners, maintain contact with "the outside" (*volya*), and gather information of various kinds. Letters in the police archives show that Mayakovsky, the fifteen-year-old "elder," did undertake to improve the lot of his jailed comrades, especially in the matter of food.[20]

Mayakovsky was soon transferred from inspector Serov's station to solitary confinement in the Butyrki, of which he later wrote:

[19] Quoted in Zemskov, p. 523.

[20] *Ibid.*, p. 520.

I learned to love
In Butyrki.
Who cares about the Bois de Boulogne?
Who sighs over seascapes?
You know
I fell in love
with a funeral establishment
through the peephole
of cell 103.[21]

A sign marking a "funeral establishment" was the one thing visible from his narrow cell.

During those five months a walk in the fresh air was a priceless favor, a patch of sunlight shining on a wall was worth "everything in the world." He was not quite sixteen at the time of his third arrest, and the effect of the long incarceration on his character and career was incalculable. After four months he wrote to the authorities claiming complete innocence of the charges against him and arguing for immediate release partly on the grounds of deteriorating health, with symptoms of "neurasthenia and anemia"; but no medical evidence for this was presented.[22]

What took place inside the young man is far from clear. Shklovsky, who was close enough to him to know, says that he emerged from confinement "deeply shaken" (*potryasyonnym*), that as a result of it he was reserved and secretive, and that for all his proliferation of poetry and talk, he "knew how to be silent."[23] It should be mentioned that his mother and sisters somewhat lightened the long incarceration by visiting him all three together whenever they were permitted, and that they contributed money out of their penurious earnings to have him served the "better" fare to which his noble rank entitled him, even in jail. He was released at last when the authorities, after an exhaustive investigation, determined that he had no direct connection with the jailbreak from the women's prison. In spite of the efforts of Soviet memoirists and iconographers to establish such a connection, no clear evidence for it has ever been found.[24]

The Butyrki prison marked a sharp turning-point in his life. We know that after his release he broke with the Party and Party

[21] *PSS*, IV, 87.
[22] Zemskov, p. 528.
[23] V. Shklovsky, *O Mayakovskom* (Moscow, 1940), p. 12.
[24] Zemskov, p. 524.

work, and we have his own account, written in 1922, of his reasons for considering the months in Butyrki prison to have been the most important period of his life. The vicissitudes of the time and his own family's misfortunes had made it impossible for him to receive any systematic formal education. The haphazard nature of his training and his interests is clear from the comments of contemporaries and from his own letters. He had acquired an accidental smattering of various things, but until after his third arrest he never revealed any firm interest in literature. Removed in 1908 from the *gymnasium*, which was the path to higher education, and destined for a career as a practical illustrator, he nonetheless developed some interest in philosophy, history, political economy, and the physical sciences. In a letter to Lyudmila during his second detention he asked for a number of books, among them Marx's *Capital*, and his varied desiderata suggest that he planned to try to satisfy the university entrance requirements through private reading. Among the many books he requested only two items had to do with literature: a *History of Russian Literature* and the works of "Tolstoy or Dostoevsky."[25]

His education as a modern poet began in cell 103. He "threw himself" upon belles-lettres, as he puts it, reading all the latest things. The symbolists, particularly Belyi and Balmont, struck him because of their formal innovation, but their imagery and themes had nothing to do with his life. He tried to apply their formal discoveries to his own subject matter, but what came out was radical sentimentality (*revplaksivo*). He offers as an example of the sort of thing he wrote four lines that tell of his "hundreds of desperate days" in traditional rhythms. "I filled a whole notebook with such stuff. Thanks to the jailers—they took it away from me when they let me out. Otherwise I might even have published it." Unfortunately the notebook has never been found, though Mayakovsky himself searched for it in the police archives in 1925.[26] That notebook, regardless of the quality of the verse, would have given a glimpse of his first attempt to face himself. Poetry begins when there are questions that transcend the plane of theory and practice, and such questions—susceptible of formulation but not of answers—thronged Mayakovsky's mind. His casually ironic comments in the autobiography do suggest such a state of mind. Mayakovsky's polemical position at the time he

[25] *PSS*, XIII, 10 (letter of January 1909).

[26] Zemskov, p. 534.

wrote *I Myself*, and the style he adopted in it, required that he take a lightly contemptuous attitude toward all things venerable, and that he refuse to be serious; his motto might be translated into the idiom as "What, me worry?" This assumed attitude has created difficulty for his biographer, Pertsov, who is at times irritated by the poet's flippant references to established divinities.[27] Tolstoy's *Anna Karenina*, for instance, was the last book Mayakovsky read in prison, but he says the reading was interrupted by his release: "So I don't even know how that affair came out with them, the Karenins."[28]

The section of the autobiography entitled "The So-called Dilemma," departs briefly from the nonsense style and conveys something of the real concern that occupied the solitary sixteen-year-old prisoner. I'm an ignoramus (*neuch*), he said, deprived of schooling and reduced to the dissemination of revolutionary ideas received at third hand and poorly understood. As a result of his long meditation in prison he decided he must "study." That section of his autobiography has special psychological interest:

> I came out of prison in a mood of great excitement. The ones I'd read were the so-called greats. But it would not be difficult to write better than they did. I already have a correct attitude toward the world. The only thing I need is experience in art. But where to get it? I'm an ignoramus. I need to get serious training. Kicked out of the *gymnasium*, even out of the Stroganov School. If I stayed in the Party I'd have to work underground. And as I thought, in the underground you never learn anything. The future—writing handbills and proclamations all my life, setting forth ideas taken from correct books, but not ones I thought out myself. Shake out of me everything I've read and what's left? The Marxist method. But hadn't that weapon fallen into childish hands? It's easy to use it as long as you deal only with the ideas of your own side. But what about when you meet with the enemy? After all I can't really write better than Belyi. He said his thing brightly: "Into the sky I released a pineapple," I said mine with a whimper: "Hundreds of desperate days." It's all right for the other Party members. They even had a university education. (Higher education—I didn't know yet what it was—I respected it!) What could I oppose to the old aesthetics that bore down upon me? Surely

[27] Pertsov [I], p. 123.

[28] *PSS*, I, 17.

the revolution demanded of me serious schooling. I went to see Medvedev, who was still a Party comrade. "I want to make a socialist art." Sergei laughed loud and long: "You haven't got the guts."

But I think he underestimated my guts. I cut myself off from Party work. I began serious study.[29]

A brief commentary is clearly in order. We note, in the first place, that the future perspective offered by Party work—the writing of ephemeral propaganda leaflets containing second-hand ideas—was one horn of the dilemma on which the poet deliberately impaled himself for many years; in fact, that dilemma may have been more vividly present to him in 1922 when he wrote those lines than it was in 1909. The reference to a line from Belyi tells us that he was impressed by the latter's book of poems, *Gold on Azure* (*Zoloto v lazuri*, 1904), and especially by a poem based on an audacious metaphor of the sun as a pineapple dragged up out of its underground hothouse, thrown in a deep arc through the sky and falling at last into the unknown. The reference to Belyi is very significant, since the sun was a frequent visitor in Mayakovsky's own verse, and its daily traverse of the heavens is the subject of one of his best poems. The reference is significant for another reason. In *Gold on Azure*, full of solemn incantation to the sun, Belyi often abandoned conventional stanzaic structure, arranging words and phrases according to a system of emotional emphasis, which resulted in many "lines" of only one or two words. This is so close to Mayakovsky's later practice that we may assume he is offering in this passage an oblique reverence to a teacher.

His comment on the university confirms us in the belief that he at one time planned to qualify himself for the entrance examination. It's most interesting, moreover, that he should report in that immediate context a conversation with Sergei S. Medvedev, a Party comrade who not only gained entrance to the university, but became a noted chemist and a member of the Academy of Sciences. Medvedev's recollections of this period were taken down from his own dictation in 1938, but when he searched his memory he could not recall any such conversation as Mayakovsky reported, or ever having made the remark that "he didn't have the guts." He did recall that he had said something to Maya-

[29] *Ibid.*, p. 18.

kovsky about the importance of a university education, advice which Mayakovsky's memory may have metamorphosed into a hearty laugh and a contemptuously vulgar phrase.[30]

The passage entitled "The So-called Dilemma," like the autobiography as a whole, is a complex mosaic of actual events and real situations, but shaped and patterned to fit the mature poet's created image of himself. His report that he "wanted to make a socialist art" amusingly characterizes both his vaulting ambition and his posture during the debates of the twenties, but it does not apply at all to the career in painting and poetry that he actually entered upon in 1911. On the other hand, the passage does reveal, for instance, Mayakovsky's admiration for the symbolists, whose influence on his early verse is incontestable. Perhaps most important, it underlines Mayakovsky's abiding concern about his own lack of education—a defect that, paradoxically, contributed to the idiosyncratic freshness of his early poetry. And of course the dilemma of which he speaks—the contrary pull of "Party work" and "art"—was in a sense the story of his life.

[30] S. S. Medvedev, "Iz vospominanii," in V. *Mayakovsky v vospominaniyakh sovremennikov*, pp. 68-75.

Chapter Three

THE REVOLUTION: ART

1) Among the Futurists

Mayakovsky had been sentenced to three years' exile from central Russia, but the sentence was rescinded as a result of his mother's connections and efforts, and also in consideration of his youth. Suddenly and unexpectedly he was released from his solitary cell and turned up on a bitter January day in 1910 in his mother's apartment, wearing no coat but only the school jacket he'd had on when they arrested him in July. (His first act upon entering was to wash his hands.) His friend and fellow-futurist Aseev recalled many years later Mayakovsky's account of that first day "in freedom":

> I remember a story of his about how when he was released from jail . . . he immediately rushed out to see Moscow. He had no money for a streetcar, no warm coat, only an enormous, undeniable, uncontrollable desire to see and hear the city again, the movement, the crowds, the noise, the horse-car bells, the lantern lights. And there he was in a short jacket and light shoes without galoshes . . . the sixteen-year-old Mayakovsky taking his first post-incarceration walk around Moscow, by way of the Sadovoe Ring.[1]

His verse experiments while in jail and even earlier seemed to him so pathetic that he decided to become a painter. He could turn out drawings on demand and on commission, and this was how he kept alive during the first months after his release. At first he entered Zhukovsky's studio, which threatened him with a more or less lucrative career as a producer of artistic designs for chinaware and the like, but in a few months he transferred to the studio of the artist P. Kelin, who prepared candidates for entrance into the Moscow Institute for the Study of Painting, Sculpture, and

[1] N. Aseev, *Krasnaya nov*, No. 6, 1924. On Mayakovsky's handwashing on this occasion see Lyudmila Mayakovskaya, *O Vladimire Mayakovskom* (Moscow, 1969), p. 149.

Architecture. After a year's preparation he was accepted by the Institute, and in August 1911 he seemed seriously launched upon a career as a painter.

He reports astonishment at the fact that the Institute was warmly disposed toward "imitators," but persecuted independent spirits such as Larionov and Mashkov. It was difficult for a candidate professing cubist views to gain admission to the Institute at that time.[2] However, one representative of the avant-garde, David Burliuk, entered the school of painting at about the same time as Mayakovsky, and the moment of their meeting was critical in Mayakovsky's life. Burliuk stood out from his environment by arrogance of manner and foppishness of dress. He carried and frequently used a lorgnette, he dressed in high fashion, hummed at his work, and as a cubist he invited hostile attention. The two men agree that their acquaintance began when Mayakovsky mocked and abused Burliuk, driving him almost to the extreme measure of physical retaliation.[3] We must remember that Mayakovsky himself affected at this time a demeanor and dress calculated to arouse comment: a wide-brimmed black hat pulled down over his brows, black shirt, tie, and trousers, long uncombed hair. "He looked," said Livshits, who met him in the northern capital, "like a member of the Sicilian Mafia, tossed up by fate into St. Petersburg." Burliuk's flamboyant bid for attention no doubt seemed a special challenge to Mayakovsky, which may explain the latter's initial effort to reduce his rival's size. But instead of coming to blows they became good friends, and Burliuk's influence on Mayakovsky's career was decisive.

David Burliuk (1882-1967) was already a professional painter who had participated in modernist exhibitions in Russia and abroad. He has a place of some importance in the history of modern European art, having participated as early as 1911 in the *Blaue Reiter* movement in Munich. He was an active member of the Russian avant-garde in painting, and he was a moving figure in arranging exhibitions which included the works of Larionov, Goncharova, and Aleksandra Ekster. In fact the extravagance in dress and behavior that later characterized the cubo-futurists began as early as 1910 at meetings of the group of painters known as the Union of Youth. Burliuk also had organized a group of innovative painters and poets under the name "budetlyane," a Russification of the western term "futurists," and he was the leading

[2] *PSS*, I, 19.

[3] *Ibid.*

spirit in the publication of the first futurist collection, entitled *A Trap for Judges* (*Sadok sudei*, 1910) and printed on the reverse side of ordinary wallpaper. In fact, the futurist group first called itself "Hylaea," the ancient Greek name for the area, famous as the scene of some of Hercules' feats, near Kherson where Burliuk's father managed an estate. Burliuk thus furnished a setting and a classical symbol for the early meetings of the futurists. Ten years older than Mayakovsky, well-informed on modern movements in literature and the arts, and in permanent rebellion against the "academy" in both painting and poetry, Burliuk offered his young friend ideas and a direction that he was ready to receive. The strength of Burliuk's influence is borne out by Mayakovsky himself, who calls him "my real teacher," the man who "made me a poet." He credits Burliuk with his elementary education in modern European poetry: "He read me Germans and Frenchmen." In fact Mayakovsky's contention in his autobiography is that Burliuk not only discovered and encouraged his first steps in the poet's trade, but disciplined and supported him: "He forced books on me. Paced and talked constantly. Wouldn't let me out of his sight. Used to give me 50 kopeks a day. So that I could write without starving. . . ."

The tribute paid Burliuk in Mayakovsky's autobiography is impressive. No other person is remembered at such great length in that curious document; no one else is honored as a "magnificent" friend and "real teacher," or thought of "with constant love."[4] Mayakovsky's laconic recollections convey a sense of Burliuk's restless energy and enterprise, and Vasilii Kamensky said of him that he had a great talent for "finding able pupils—poets and artists, singers, musicians, and orators"—and pouring into them his own avant-garde ideas. Another devotee, the futurist poet Benedikt Livshits, who dedicated a poem to him as a prophet in search of a "third terrestrial pole," has given us a vivid description of Burliuk on a train journey from Kiev to Chernyanka, pacing up and down the carriage jotting down verses and quoting Baudelaire, Verlaine, and Mallarmé.[5] Kamensky quotes from a letter supposedly written to him by David Burliuk:

[4] *Ibid.*, pp. 19-21.

[5] V. Kamensky, *Zhizn s Mayakovskim* (Moscow, 1940), p. 10. See also B. Livshits, *Polutoraglazyi strelets* (Moscow, 1932) for much interesting material on this period in Mayakovsky's life.

. . . Two new fighters have come and signed up—Volodya Mayakovsky and A. Kruchonykh. They're both very dependable. Especially Mayakovsky. . . . He's a crazy youngster (*vzbalmoshnyi yunosha*), a great tease, but he's quite witty, sometimes unusually so. A child of nature, like you and all of us. You'll see. . . . Mayakovsky's with me all the time and he's beginning to write good poetry. He's a wild natural genius and he glows with self-confidence. I've given him the idea that he's a young Jack London. He likes that. I've completely tamed him and now he minds: he's straining for the pedestal of the fight for futurism.[6]

Burliuk's initiative is evident in each of Mayakovsky's steps toward his new career. In December 1911 he drew Mayakovsky into an exhibition in St. Petersburg organized by the Union of Youth, where the future poet's canvases were viewed along with those of Goncharova, Larionov, Malevich, and Tatlin. Mayakovsky's first public speech was a commentary on Burliuk's report on cubism, delivered at a meeting organized by the painters' group, the Jack of Diamonds. Burliuk and Mayakovsky regularly appeared together to propagandize cubism in painting and futurism in poetry, and their activities aroused the opposition of the conservative directors of the Institute; these gentlemen passed a resolution to the effect that "Burliuk and Co." must desist from making public speeches, on pain of expulsion. The public speeches continued, and in February 1914 both were expelled.[7]

The "fight for futurism" was a deliberately outrageous campaign against contemporary art and literature initiated in Moscow and carried on in the provincial cities of Russia. To advertise their first appearance on October 13, 1913, the futurist comrades, Burliuk, Mayakovsky, Kamensky, and Livshits, gathered at a busy point in Moscow and at exactly noon set off down the street with a slow and solemn step, each in turn reciting his latest, most shocking "futurist" poems. Their mien as they moved was stern and serious and they didn't smile at all, though Mayakovsky was

[6] Kamensky, p. 8. Doubt has been cast by Soviet scholars on the authenticity of this letter, and Khardzhiev suggests that Kamensky invented it himself. But Burliuk never repudiated the letter, and even if it is an invention (which I doubt), it still tells us something about the relationship between the two men.

[7] N. Khardzhiev, "Mayakovsky i zhivopis," in *Mayakovsky, materialy i issledovaniya* (Moscow, 1940), pp. 337ff.

wearing an orange blouse (supposedly made for him by his mother and sisters), Burliuk was in a top hat and frock coat and had a dog with rampant tail painted on his cheek, Livshits wore an extravagant tie and handkerchief, Kamensky, who was an aviator, had an airplane painted on his face, and they all wore wooden spoons, instead of green carnations, in their buttonholes. Kamensky in his book describes the wild consternation of the crowds that gathered to observe this literary phenomenon. Amusement turned into outrage and even fear. Members of the crowd threatened to beat the poets. Someone called the police, who tried to break it up. A young girl offered Mayakovsky an orange, which he proceeded to eat. "He's eating! He's eating!" the whisper went up and down the street.

The public appearance in Moscow was followed by that tour of the provinces which Mayakovsky later described as his "Golgotha of auditoriums." The stations of his journey were Kharkov, Simferopol, Odessa, Kishinyov, Nikolaev, Minsk, Kazan, and some other towns—in all, seventeen. The chapter in his autobiography devoted to late 1913 and 1914, the time of the tour, is entitled "A Jolly Year," and in it Mayakovsky suggests that the enterprise was motivated by the need to propagandize a new approach and new ideas: "Publishers wouldn't print us. The capitalist nose smelled dynamite in us. They wouldn't buy a single line of mine."[8]

On their swing through the provinces the futurists aroused curiosity, amusement, anger, and some real interest; it is certain that they achieved their principal aim, which was to attract attention to their painting and their poetry through the device of affronting the public. Their performances were attended by large audiences in search of sensation, amusement, and the opportunity to abuse "those clowns." Newspaper accounts of the day all agree that their meetings were as a rule well attended. In a word, the tour was a success, though not necessarily one of esteem. Each appearance involved some outlandish pieces of stage business, a report by Mayakovsky or Burliuk on modern poetry and painting, recitations of poetry, and the projection of their paintings onto a screen, with commentary by Burliuk. Some of them appeared with painted faces; Mayakovsky at times wore a top hat pushed back onto his neck, and of course had on his famous orange-yellow blouse, described as follows by a journalist of the day: "It was an ordinary blouse without a waist, like a Parisian workingman's

[8] *PSS*, I, 22.

blouse, with a turned down collar and a tie. . . . It had alternating wide black and orange-yellow stripes. On the handsome, dark, tall young man it produced a very pleasant impression."

On some occasions they contrived an initial mystification by opening with a quiet tea party on stage. Arranging themselves at a table they sipped tea quietly and slowly, conversing the while in low tones just as though they were at home, and occasionally looking out at their perplexed and increasingly noisy audience. Once, a grand piano was suspended on cables over the stage, and remained there without explanation or comment throughout the recital. Intermissions in the recitals were announced as for fourteen minutes. A recital was often preceded by an appearance on the streets: in Odessa, for instance, Burliuk, Mayakovsky, and Kamensky, in top hats and frock coats, hired a carriage apiece and drove in single file about the streets, to the accompaniment of such comments from observers as: "The futurists! The futurists are coming." Often enough, Mayakovsky informs us, the police broke off their seances "in the middle of a word."

Clownlike antics, elaborate jokes, and a mock polemic with the audience tended to conceal the real—I might almost say serious—purpose of their provincial tour. Actually, their lectures offered some education in modern artistic trends, examples of modern art and poetry, the latter superbly read by Mayakovsky, and brief nuggets of futurist literary theory, as worked out, for the most part, by Khlebnikov and Kruchonykh. A fairly typical performance, described in great detail by Kamensky, was their appearance in Kharkov. Kamensky himself opened it with a talk berating contemporary critics as "anchors inhibiting movement and progress," and stating the futurist idea of the "word itself" as the end and aim of poetry: "Poetry celebrates the nuptial service of words." Burliuk then presented his lecture on "cubism and futurism" with illuminating remarks on post-impressionist painting, concepts of line, surface, and color, the concept of "texture" (*faktura*), cubism as a doctrine concerning surfaces, and concluded with an account of the tendencies in modern art represented by the Jack of Diamonds, the Union of Youth, and the Donkey's Tail. He offered a magic-lantern treatment of old and new painting, from Raphael, "a mere copyist," to the cubists and futurists with their manipulation of geometry and color. This was by all accounts the gayest moment of the evening, and Kamensky produced a vivid transcription of the audience reaction:

> David projected a dark cube and with it a cubistic representation of a head: "That's a portrait of Mayakovsky!" There was an explosion of laughter in the hall: "Serves him right! What a portrait! Nightmarish angles." He projected a figure consisting of broken lines: "Girl at a window." More laughter: "Which is the window and which is the girl? And why a girl?" Then came a "lady with a cat." "The poor thing! She's all cut up!" Burliuk explained: "Here you see a rendition in planes." "That's no rendition! It's an earthquake! . . ."[9]

Mayakovsky followed Burliuk with an attack on contemporary criticism and current notions of art that owed much to his early training in Marxism. He demanded a "scientific approach" and a "dialectical understanding" of history and of aesthetics, as opposed to the "metaphysical" view that aesthetic norms are fixed and unchanging. He attacked contemporary critics by name and devoted a large part of his report to derogation of established poets old and new. Older poets knew many tricks, he admitted; but the ancient Egyptians could produce electricity by stroking cats, and no one credits them with the discovery of electricity. The burden of his argument was that only futurist poetry was analogous, in its inventive departures, to modern science. The performance closed with declamations of their poetry in which all the participants joined. Afterwards there was a lengthy informal debate with members of the audience in the foyer of the auditorium.

2) The Ambience: European Affinities

The records of the time offer a surprisingly detailed picture of the futurist campaign to force their work on public attention, and to reform the aesthetic taste even of the deep provinces. But to understand the meaning of the movement in which Mayakovsky was a first cause and eager participant we must take into account the situation of the day in literature and art. Obviously the Hylaeans were not performing in isolation, but were a component part of an intellectual current that was running powerfully both in Europe and in Russia. What is perhaps most important, the literary movement we are dealing with was, as should now be

[9] The best sources for the futurist "tours" are Kamensky, *passim*, and N. Khardzhiev, "Turne kubo-futuristov 1913-1914 gg.," in *Mayakovsky, materialy i issledovaniya* (Moscow, 1940), pp. 401-427.

evident, deeply involved with the visual arts. This was a period when painters and poets worked closely together on aesthetic problems in many parts of Europe. In Russia the disputatious avant-garde groups included many young painters who were also theoreticians and practitioners of poetry. Almost all the early futurists came to poetry from painting, or practiced both arts simultaneously. In addition to Burliuk and Mayakovsky, Khlebnikov, Elena Guro, Kamensky and Kruchonykh occupied themselves with painting. Avant-garde painters produced poetry, and Malevich wrote a theoretical article, "On Poetry." Evidence of this clear connection appears in the tendency of futurist poets to use the terminology of painting, words such as "dislocation" (*sdvig*) and "texture" (*faktura*), in speaking of the poetic effects they hope to achieve.

Even after his expulsion from the Institute, Mayakovsky continued to produce cubist canvases, and as late as 1915 he took part in an exhibition along with Larionov, Goncharova, Lentulov, Falk, Tatlin, Malevich, Kandinsky, Chagall, and some others. To this exhibition he contributed his only surviving cubistic canvas, one with the characteristic title "Roulette" (he was a compulsive gambler) and bearing a close resemblance to modern abstract art. Larionov and Goncharova provided illustrations for the first collection of poems published by Khlebnikov and Kruchonykh; some of their drawings represented real objects, but deformed and dislocated, and others were done in an infantile style. Moreover, the futurist poets, when they theorized about their own verbal art, insisted on its close analogy with modern innovations in painting. Khlebnikov is quoted as saying, "We want the word to follow boldly after painting," and Mayakovsky in one of his earliest public statements emphasized the "analogical paths which lead to the creation of artistic truth in painting and in poetry." One of his "theses" in that statement, given in shorthand form, was that "Color, line, and surface . . . are the *end-in-itself* of painting: the concept of painting; the word, its outline, its phonetic property, myth, symbol: *the poetic concept.*" The last statement provides one key to the understanding of his own poetry, in which the liberated word, as we shall see, contains the principal poetic charge, but also develops both myth and symbol.[10]

It is interesting to note that in Paris at exactly the same time there was a similar interaction of poetry-making and painting in

[10] *PSS*, I, 365.

the group associated with Guillaume Apollinaire. Many of the poets belonging to that group were also painters, and in Paris, too, avant-garde poets propagandized cubism in painting: we may mention Apollinaire's *Les Peintres Cubistes* (1912). To move the analogy one step further, Mayakovsky and Apollinaire both are concerned with the graphic qualities of the printed page, and they often presented their poems as visual objects. Curiously enough Mayakovsky's first published poem, "Night" (*Noch*, 1912), which describes the interweaving and succession of sunset colors in city windows, seems almost an echo of Apollinaire's poem "Les fenêtres," published in the same month and year. And Apollinaire published in 1913 a "Manifesto-synthesis" which looks like a more elaborate echo of the famous "Slap at Public Taste" which in 1912 presented the program of the Russian cubo-futurists. In it Apollinaire (echoing Marinetti) called for the destruction, among other things, of syntax, the adjective, punctuation, the tense and person of verbs, and so forth. And he distributed a largesse of "*mer-de*" (the word was provided with musical notes and intended to be sung) to a lengthy catalog of traditional values, including critics, professors, museums, ruins, Venice, Versailles, Dante, Shakespeare, Tolstoy, Goethe, Montaigne, Wagner, Beethoven, and Edgar Allan Poe. A generous gift of "roses," on the other hand, went to the prophets of radical innovation: Picasso, Apollinaire (of course), Matisse, Braque, Salmon, Kandinsky, Stravinsky, and so forth.[11]

There is no proof of influence in either direction. What we observe is rather a parallel historical situation, a community of attitude toward the process and purposes of art, and violent rejection, in both cases, of the immediately precedent art—symbolism. Still another parallel with the French example—a sociological one—suggests an important factor in the noisy futurist rebellion. In Russia as in France "cubo-futurism" (the term was used only in Russia) was the product of relatively plebeian upstarts in the cultural world. The futurists almost without exception came from the less privileged, less aristocratic, less cultivated levels of society, in contrast to the symbolists, who were firmly domiciled at the very highest point of European intellectual culture. What could the former do but reject that culture, "throw it overboard from the steamship of contemporaneity" as the Russian

[11] Two pages of the Manifesto are reproduced in Francis Steegmuller, *Apollinaire: Poet among Painters* (New York, 1963), pp. 264-265.

manifesto suggested. And there is yet another parallel: while in almost all cases the symbolists were native to the metropolitan centers, Paris, St. Petersburg, or Moscow, their muscular rivals were young men from the provinces, who, like all such young men, proposed to take the "city" by storm. There is, moreover, a tenuous but perhaps helpful historical analogy with the Russian *raznochintsy* or "men from the lower ranks," who made their presence felt in various unorthodox ways in mid-nineteenth-century Russian literature and literary criticism. Mayakovsky, with his improper dress, his rudeness and lack of ceremony, his contempt for the older generation and their poetry, and his admiration for science, is the modern counterpart of the type represented by Bazarov in Turgenev's *Fathers and Sons.*

Another foreign affinity of the Russian futurists was the Italian futurist movement, and specifically Marinetti, who visited St. Petersburg and Moscow in 1914, giving public lectures intended to propagate the new artistic credo. The Russians had known of the Italian futurists since 1909, when Marinetti's manifestoes were translated and discussed in the Russian press, and because the Russian futurist literary collection, *A Trap for Judges,* appeared only in 1910, there arose a nice question of priority. The Russian futurists claimed a patent of priority in the invention of futurist ideas, and in order to support their claim they moved up the date of this publication from 1910 to 1908. In their manifesto *The Word as Such,* published in 1913, Kruchonykh and Khlebnikov not only moved up the date of their collection, but said that the Italian had been "sniffing the Russian air, and had begun to write interlinear translations, copybook cribs."[12]

The inane dispute over primacy probably helps to explain the unfriendly reception accorded Marinetti, during his visit to Russia, by the cubo-futurists, who were at great pains to establish the fact of Russian national autonomy and freedom from foreign influence.[13] And indeed the problem of Marinetti's "influence" is clouded and difficult. Many of his poetic procedures—the "liberation of the word," the breakdown of syntax, the cultivation of pure sound, elimination of the verb—run parallel to the experiments of Kruchonykh and Khlebnikov, a fact about which

[12] Vladimir Markov, *Russian Futurism: A History* (Berkeley, 1968), p. 135; and, by the same author, *Manifesty i programmy russkikh futuristov* (Munich, 1967), p. 59.

[13] Kamensky, p. 114.

they were very sensitive.[14] His glorification of the machine and the modern city as sources of virile power have a tenuous connection with Mayakovsky, though the latter, as we shall see, celebrated the city in his lectures and manifestoes, but grieved over it in his poems. Street-parading, the baiting of audiences, the invitation to catcalls and abuse—all these were devices of the Marinetti repertoire, and he had used them successfully long before the Russian futurists' first appearance on the streets of Moscow. The similarities in form and style are too numerous to be accidental, and the Russians, when they insisted on their own priority, were certainly protesting too much. The Russian press in the early part of the century was alert to every cultural wind that blew from the west, especially from France. Marinetti's first manifesto was published (in French) in *Le Figaro* on February 20, 1909, and a partial translation appeared almost immediately thereafter (on March 8, 1909) in the St. Petersburg newspaper *Vecher*. Obviously his words found eager listeners among Russian artists and poets who shared his antagonism to established canons and wished to throw off the weight of the past.

Nor was the content of Marinetti's program totally alien to the Russian futurists. Marinetti was an outspoken propagandist of Italian expansion, and an excited prophet of the wars that such expansion might entail. War he considered a necessary social hygiene, gladly to be embraced for the sake of recovering, say, the Italians under Austrian rule in the Alto Adige, or expanding Italian influence in Africa. Evidence of Russian chauvinism and the glorification of war is not lacking in the work of both Khlebnikov and Mayakovsky; the latter's jingoistic poems of 1914 are now a forgotten episode, but there were many of them, and they sound uncomfortably like Marinetti. The Italian futurist's contempt for women may be reflected in Mayakovsky's *Tragedy*, and Kruchonykh in one of his statements betrays an affinity with Marinetti when he announces that "out of base contempt for women and children our language will have only the masculine gender," and in his *Victory over the Sun* he attempts to force this principle on the language.[15] Marinetti on his part regarded the Russian cubo-

[14] Roman Jakobson in *Noveishaya russkaya poeziya* (Prague, 1921), p. 8, gives the viewpoint of a Russian formalist, to the effect that the Italians devised a new poetic form to express a new content, modern industrial life, but for the Russians the new form was invented for its own sake.

[15] See Markov, *Manifesty i programmy*, pp. 62, 63; also *PSS*, I, 70

futurists as savages and "pseudo-futurists," and would not acknowledge them as his pupils.

The two movements were very different in their genesis and in their social composition. Italian futurism, according to Marinetti, began among the gilded intellectual youth of northern Italy the night of a wild automobile ride that ended with his car in the ditch and himself soaked with the muddy offal of a nearby factory: at that moment, dumped into factory waste, Marinetti, by his own account, experienced a vision and a renewal. He awakened, in a word, to the astonishing new facts of modern industrial life.[16] None of this resembles closely the Russian experience.

It is clear, however, that the Hylaeans were part of a movement that was felt at the time throughout Europe. Strikingly similar tendencies can be observed among the group of English "vorticists" associated with Wyndham Lewis and the publication of *Blast.* As Professor Poggioli put it, the Russian futurists shared with the movement in western Europe the features of activism, antagonism to authority and convention, and nihilism in their attitude toward the established culture.

3) The Ambience: The Russian Environment

The futurists' immediate literary predecessors, the symbolists, had held themselves aloof from popular contagion in a "tower" which was literal as well as figurative; the futurists renounced the tower and exposed themselves to the urban masses in cafes, theaters, and impromptu street meetings.

Their announcement of a clean break with all past art and with the dominant tendencies of their own day has at times obscured their complex relationship to both. The classical tradition and symbolism receive almost equal abuse in their public statements, but they reserved the bitterest blows for the latter as a competing but already discredited form of modernism. Actually the futurists themselves grew out of symbolism, and the special virulence of their protest against it betrays the trauma of an adolescent recov-

("Mysli v prizyv"), and pp. 355-364. On Khlebnikov's Russian chauvinism see Markov, *Russian Futurism*, p. 193.

[16] For translations into Russian of several important Italian futurist documents see N. Osorgin, "Italyanskii futurizm," *Vestnik Evropy*, No. 2, 1914, pp. 339-357. See also Christa Baumgarth, *Geschichte des Futurismus* (Hamburg, 1966).

ering from his first love. Mayakovsky's urbanism had its precedent in Bryusov, Belyi, and Blok, and his use of anti-poetic themes and vocabulary derives in part from symbolist poetics. But symbolism seems to have run its course by 1910, and in that year (the year of symbolism's "crisis") opposition movements can be clearly discovered; in fact they announce themselves. The futurists were not alone. Mikhail Kuzmin's essay "On Beautiful Clarity," the manifesto of a brief movement known as "clarism," gave eloquent voice to a widely felt revulsion against the use of poetry as a surrogate for religious revelation, and against the conversion of poetic language into a luminous haze of suggested wisdom. Kuzmin spoke out loud and bold in favor of *clarity*: "If you are a conscientious artist pray that your chaos (if chaos is your thing) be clarified and organized, or else contain it within the clear contours of a form: in a story tell a story, in a drama act, keep lyricism for lyric poems, love the word like Flaubert, be economical in your means and miserly of words, be exact and real—and then you will find the secret of a marvellous thing: 'beautiful clarity,' and this I call 'clarism.' "[17]

Another and more viable aspect of the revolt against symbolism was the movement known as "acmeism" and associated with the work of Gorodetsky, Akhmatova, Gumilyov, and Mandelshtam. Gumilyov was the principal formulator of acmeist tenets, and his statements were directed against symbolism as a philosophical as well as a poetic movement. "To take symbolism's place there comes now a new movement, whatever its name may be, either acmeism (from the word *akme* signifying the supreme degree which a thing may attain, its peak or bloom) or . . . but which at any rate demands a greater balance of powers and a more precise notion of the tie between subject and object than was the case with symbolism." The phrase "subject and object" betrays concern over basic epistemological considerations and their relation to poetry. The acmeists reinstated in poetry precisely *this* world—the world of perceived impressions—as opposed to the *other* world. As Gumilyov put it, the symbolists had been concerned to penetrate the "unknown," but the "unknown," the Kantian "thing-in-itself," is by definition unknown. The universe is likely to keep its secret, and therefore the acmeists focused on the palpable and actual, giving up the effort to shadow forth in poetry what cannot

[17] As quoted in *Russkaya literatura* xx *veka* (Moscow, 1966), pp. 500-502.

be seen or plainly said. Robert Frost neatly pictured the dilemma: "We dance around in a ring and suppose,/ But the secret sits in the middle, and knows."

Gumilyov's statement on the relationship of acmeism to symbolism brilliantly summarizes the philosophical essence of the matter, and suggests important implications for poetic theme and style:

> Russian symbolism devoted its principal effort to the unknown. It joined forces with mysticism, now with theosophy, then again with occultism. Some of its searches in this direction approached the creation of myth. And it has a right to ask the new movement whether it (the new movement) can boast of any but animal virtues, and what is its attitude toward the unknowable. Acmeism's first answer to such a question would be to point out that the unknowable by definition cannot be known. . . . The unknowable provides us with a childishly wise, painfully sweet sensation of our own lack of knowledge—that's all.[18]

The signal feature of acmeist poetry was what Stender-Petersen called *dinghaftigheit*, a kind of saturation with the concrete objects of experience. A rose may be, for instance, treated in poetry as a symbol of transcendent beauty or emblem of love or devotion, but it may also be described and dealt with as a rose—something having a concrete olfactory and visual existence; acmeists tended to take the latter view of things. The formalist critic Zhirmunsky once pointed out that the difference between Akhmatova and Blok lay precisely in Akhmatova's facility for reconstituting in poetry the body and texture of particular things. A stylistic consequence of this is that nouns and nominal constructions predominate in her poetry, to the disadvantage of verbs.

The universe we do know, the world of sight and sense, may be only a kind of garment draped over the real body of eternal being, but the garment is the only thing we can describe. Gumilyov himself described that garment in a variety of shapes and forms and colors, in exotic examples gleaned from distant shores. Mandelshtam has been described as a Hellenist, and he was indeed a devotee of the classical world, especially its sculpture and

[18] As quoted in N. Brodsky, V. Lvov-Rogachevsky, and N. P. Sidorov, eds., *Literaturnye manifesty ot simvolizma k oktyabryu* (Moscow, 1929), p. 43.

architecture. The harmonious forms and colors, as well as the concepts and language of other cultures, are a chief concern of his poetry. I should perhaps remark in passing that, having abandoned the transcendent vision of the symbolists, these particular representatives of the acmeist school still search for the concrete and the real at a certain distance from the common experience, and that they discover in remote vocabulary a new source of poetic interest.

Acmeism and futurism were related currents in the post-symbolist world. Both movements reacted against the themes and the language of symbolism and both attempted to recover the consciousness of immediate experience—the isolated and intimate psychological event of a woman's emotional life as in the work of Akhmatova, the vivid optical reality of streets and store signs as in Mayakovsky, and, in the experiments of Khlebnikov and Kruchonykh, an intense awareness of the concrete material of poetry, language itself.

An activity that revealed the essential characteristics of the futurist movement was the production of "manifestoes" that condemned the past, and indeed the present, and proclaimed the future as the special province of the new movement. The cubo-futurists produced a number of such prose works, the most famous of which I have already mentioned: "A Slap at Public Taste." That manifesto appeared in 1912 as part of a collection of futurist prose and poetry bearing the same title. The earlier collection, "A Trap for Judges," as we have seen, had been printed on the reverse side of ordinary wallpaper. This one was printed on a kind of dappled brown wrapping paper, and bound in coarse cloth. The volume in its physical appearance and texture was a negative commentary on the fine paper and luxurious binding that often encased the work of established writers, and it called attention to the position of the authors as voluntary outcasts in the world of literature. In the manifesto the four signers, David Burliuk, Velimir Khlebnikov, A. Kruchonykh, and Mayakovsky, proclaimed themselves the most and only moderns and they consigned to oblivion, "threw overboard from the steamship of modernity," Pushkin, Dostoevsky, Tolstoy, "and so forth, and so forth." In a passage whose consciousness of infection suggests that Mayakovsky wrote it, we are told to "wash your hands, you who touched the filthy slime of the books written by all those innumerable Leonid Andreevs." We note here the "contemptuous" plural, a rhetorical device that suggests to the reader that the enemy to be discredited is indeed hydra-headed, but also despicable in his manifold and slimy proliferation. And the statement continues: "All those Maxim Gorkys, Kuprins, Bloks, Sologubs, Remizovs, Averchenkos, Chornys, Kuzmins, Bunins, etc. want only a country house on the riverside. This is the way fate rewards tailors."

The catalog of rejected writers is fairly complete, including representatives of classical realism and the leading writers of the symbolist school, as well as some who could not be classed with either. It even includes a few who were admired and imitated by the authors of the manifesto: Sasha Chornyi and Kuzmin were both highly regarded by Mayakovsky. The viewpoint of the authors is, of course, the future, and they would hurry forward time's work in decomposing the corpse of culture. The phrase "We look at their nothingness from the height of skyscrapers" and the program "to stand on the block of the word 'we' amid the sea of boos and indignation" are both recognizable echoes of Marinetti. The program for poetry was largely the contribution of Kruchonykh and Khlebnikov, whose poetic practice it expressed exactly:

> 1) to enlarge vocabulary in its *scope* with arbitrary and derivative words (creation of new words);
> 2) to feel an insurmountable hatred for the language existing before them. . . .
>
> And if *for the time* even our lines are still marked by the dirty stigmas of your "common sense" and "good taste," there tremble on them *for the first time* the summer lightnings of the New-coming Beauty of the Self-sufficient (Self-valuing) Word.

The "Slap at Public Taste," with its relatively simple program and its amusing hyperbolic statements, caught the attention of the literary public, and still stands as the emblem of the futurist movement. Though it was greeted with outraged or scornful ridicule, it has a quality of gay iconoclasm that appeals to the mute image-breaker in many of us. We still feel a kind of visceral content at the dislodgment of those gods and demigods from their awesome seats, and lingering admiration for the four little demons who did it.

There were a number of other manifestoes, some of which are more important for the futurist literary program, but they are rather technical in nature and less well known.[19] One of them, published without a title in *A Trap for Judges, No. 2* (1913), sets forth in declarative fashion a program that involved a radical operation on all aspects of poetic language, and spells out the linguistic reforms broadly stated in the "Slap." Though it was signed by all the leading members of the group, this declaration betrays the hands of Kruchonykh and Khlebnikov. Its chief points may be summarized thus: 1) grammar, conventional syntax, and spelling rules are to be rejected as shackles upon sudden, individual, and original linguistic insights; 2) the special role of prefixes and suffixes in Russian has been realized (in the work of Khlebnikov); 3) poems are to be made like objects of visual art and the hand of the poet himself must be visible (a reference to the handwritten hectograph publications of Kruchonykh and Khlebnikov); 4) vowels convey the feeling of time and space, consonants give us color, sound, and smell (such intuitive and unprovable notions about language were widespread, and may derive from Rimbaud or the French symbolists); 5) conventional rhythms are to be abandoned in favor of living colloquial speech; 6) innovation in rhyme should be cultivated (rhymes at the beginning or in the middle of lines and reverse rhymes have been worked out by Burliuk and Mayakovsky); 7) the word is the creator of myth (not an original idea, but one frequently used by Mayakovsky); and finally, 8) a point that seems out of tune with the spirit of the whole, and was, according to Livshits, the contribution of Kruchonykh, though it is in accord with the temperament of either Guro or Mayakovsky: "We are obsessed with new themes: futility, senselessness, the mystery of the potent nonentity—these things we celebrate."[20]

A number of manifestoes signed by Kruchonykh and Khlebnikov carry the device "the word as such," and these statements of poetic policy, far more radical than any so far mentioned, help to elucidate their own experiments in the area of "language creation." The essential idea that runs through those statements is that the futurist poet has acquired a new freedom, one previously unknown to poets, in the creation and manipulation of language.[21]

[19] All of the pertinent documents are published in Russian, with notes and commentary, by Vladimir Markov in his *Manifesty i programmy russkikh futuristov.*

[20] Markov, *Manifesty i programmy*, pp. 51-53.

[21] Valerii Bryusov argued at this time that there was actually nothing new

The extreme statement of the poet's right to neologism is Kruchonykh's pronouncement that "words die, but the world is eternally young. The artist beholds the world anew and, like Adam, gives to everything names of his own choosing. The lily is beautiful but the word 'lily' is shameful, it has been handled and raped. Therefore I call the lily '*yeoohi*,' and her pristine beauty is restored." Kruchonykh provides a motivation for "transrational," or "nonsense" language (*zaum*): ". . . the artist is free to express himself not only in the accepted language (concepts), but in a private (*lichnym*) language (a poet is individual) as well as in a language without definite meaning (not frozen), transrational (*zaumnyi*). The accepted language binds the poet, a free language allows him to express himself more fully."[22] And as an example of what he means Kruchonykh quotes some famous lines of his own: "go osneg kaid," and so forth. In spite of the deliberately irrational pose (the several points in the document, for instance, are not given consecutively: No. 4 comes first followed by No. 5, then No. 2 and No. 1; No. 3 is omitted), a real even if exaggerated aesthetic problem is the basis of Kruchonykh's program. By his flight into private language and nonlanguage, Kruchonykh would escape the "accepted" language of conventional poetry, which had become, as he thought, frozen and fixed in cliché.

The elucidation of Mayakovsky necessitates a brief consideration of the personalities and the poetic work of certain futurist colleagues, particularly Kruchonykh and Khlebnikov, both of whom, and especially Khlebnikov, had a demonstrable effect on his poetry. Aleksei E. Kruchonykh (1886-1969) was, like most of the futurists, a provincial. He was from Kherson in the southern Ukraine and he was of peasant stock. He was first a painter, as we have seen, but he gave up painting for literature, though he continued to work at illustrating futurist books. The most extreme of the futurists, Kruchonykh often seems to suggest that he never expected to be taken seriously. He had already published two or three little books before the appearance of the famous "Slap" in 1912, and these publications illustrate among other things the

---

in this, and that much of it could be found in Baudelaire, Rimbaud, and Mallarmé, and even earlier poets. See his "Novye techeniya v russkoi poezii: futurizm," *Russkaya mysl*, No. 3, 1913.

[22] Markov, *Manifesty i programmy*, p. 63.

concern of the futurists with poetry publishing as a visual art. Some were produced by hand and multiplied by a hectographic process. Occasionally the letters in a printed book came from various type fonts and were mixed together in a haphazard sequence. *A Game in Hell* (*Igra v adu*, 1912) was printed in letters that resembled Old Church Slavonic. Misprints were deliberate, and punctuation was as a rule abandoned. In appearance, in publishing technique, and in the materials he used, Kruchonykh's books reject the established habits, standards, and practices of the bookmaking profession. They are like the efforts of a child or an unversed savage to produce a book without instruction or practice and without access to proper materials; the epithet "primitive," used, in the technical sense, of Kruchonykh's poetry, may be applied also to his books.

In a tiny collection of poems entitled *Pomada* (1913) Kruchonykh published a work that has become the most famous example of "transrational" language, or *zaum*. It was made up of the following sounds (they of course have no meaning in Russian):

dyr bul shchyl
ubeshshchur
skum
vy so bu
r l èz

Kruchonykh later claimed that these lines had in them more of the Russian spirit than all of Pushkin, and this statement, usually taken as a supreme example of futurist *épatage*, actually has a germ of meaning. We note in these lines a crowded accumulation of hushing sibilant sounds, and repetition of the rather guttural back vowel *y* (ы), sounds that, though characteristic of Russian speech, have been regarded by some poets as too harsh for poetry. Thus the stone which the builders of Russian poetry rejected becomes here the head of the corner.

In his book *Explodidity* (*Vzorval*, 1913) Kruchonykh provides a key intended to unlock the riddle of his transrational writing. He likens his poetry to the recorded gibberish of a saintly flagellant in the throes of religious exaltation: "Nosoktos lesontos, Futr lis natrufuntru. . . ." and so forth, and argues that *zaum* is the speech one resorts to in the most serious moments of life. He then presents a poem of his which he claimed was written in the "universal language." It is made up entirely of vowels. Such experiments were not infrequent, and one of them suggests the vocal essentials of a slow religious chant:

i a o
o a
o a ye ye i ye ya
o a
e y i e i
i e e
i i u i e i i u.

Kruchonykh experimented with what might be called "writing in tongues," though he never claimed religious inspiration. He did profess to have suddenly mastered (at three o'clock one morning) Japanese, Spanish, and Hebrew, and provided examples of each in a transrational idiom.[23]

There is much in Kruchonykh that seems mad, but there is also method in him. Obviously *zaum* presents itself as a violent critique of the stereotypes of language, and its announced program is one of creative destruction. But it was also something else, and its real significance has been very little studied. Viktor Shklovsky, in an interesting defense of *zaum*,[24] points to numerous examples of meaningless language even in conventional poets and adduces many cases of infatuation with unintelligible sound: peasants listening to Slavonic prayers, sectarians speaking in tongues, and children engaged in play. But these cases are not analogous to the transrational language of Kruchonykh. The examples Shklovsky cites from poetry occur in contexts that presume meaning; sectarians are in a state of frenzy that Kruchonykh neither experienced nor induced in others; the illiterate orthodox listeners to the sound of prayers whose words they don't understand experience them in a total situation which gives them meaning. Finally, children's jingles may not have denotation, but they do have a conventional significance in the sense that they have a group function. They are repeated over and over again and passed on from one generation of children to the next; nobody knows their origin, and the first meaning of the words, if any, may have been lost, but, as with the Slavonic prayers, all members of the group know

[23] *Ibid.*

[24] V. Shklovsky, "O poezii i zaumnom yazyke," in *Poetika* (Petrograd, 1919), pp. 13-25.

when and how to use them. Kruchonykh's *zaum* is primitive and infantile, but it differs from children's jingles precisely in that it has no social existence. Evidence of its complete lack of function is the fact that Kruchonykh's most famous single poem, "Dyr, bul, shchyl," is frequently quoted inaccurately even by experts in the field. Kruchonykh's *zaum* is an experiment in which language dissolves in meaningless syllables and unaccountable sounds. Obviously it fails to communicate anything except a poetic aphasia induced by too close an inspection of the separate elements of speech. Kruchonykh is like Achilles in Zeno's paradox: because he must cover each unit of the distance separately, he cannot run the race at all.

An interesting suggestion that the word play of the cubo-futurists is related to the behavior of psychotic patients was offered by a psychiatrist, Dr. E. P. Radin, in a study entitled *Madness and the Futurists* (*Futurizm i bezumie,* 1914). Dr. Radin takes the much too literal approach of asking simply whether the futurists are really mad, yet the evidence he offers from the actual writing of acknowledged madmen is extremely suggestive. Paranoid persons have in common with the futurists (and, we might add, with other schools in modern art) the tendency to divorce form from content, to iterate meaningless verbal structures, to coin completely new words from existing roots (Dr. Radin gives among many examples the word "*smorkatel,*" a "nose-blower," invented by a patient to describe one of the people spying on him), and to use existing words in meaningless combinations (paraphasia). To say that such procedures are analogous to the futurist verbal experiments is not to suggest that the futurists were psychotic, though some of them may have been. Dr. Radin's evidence reveals that paranoid madmen, like the futurists, having detached verbal material from any connection with real things, manipulate that material so as to create new and self-contained verbal structures. What Dr. Radin neglects to point out is that the private language of madmen takes on for them a literal reality of its own, while the linguistic experiments of the futurists are offered as aesthetic experience. Yet his study is immensely interesting for its revelation of an essential kinship between the two.

Viktor Vladimirovich Khlebnikov (1885-1922), who later adopted the Slavic-sounding first name Velimir, was another young man from the provinces, having been born not far from Astrakhan. An abiding interest all his life was mathematics, a subject in which he specialized at the University of Kazan. He developed fairly early a kind of obsession with the mathematical aspect of history, and he tried to develop formulas that would express historical movement in mathematical terms; he did in fact predict that 1917 would be a year of great upheavals. In 1908 he transferred from the University of Kazan to the University of St. Petersburg, where he specialized in Slavic studies. His interest in poetry brought him into contact with the symbolists, and he was for a time a regular visitor at the Wednesday night meetings of Vyacheslav Ivanov's "Tower." Mikhail Kuzmin valued his work, and Khlebnikov had the highest regard for Kuzmin. He reported with some satisfaction that he had been recognized by Petersburg poets of both the symbolist and acmeist persuasions. In his experimentation with poetic language and rhythm, however, he was engaged in a highly idiosyncratic project, vitally different from the similar efforts of many poets of the day. He was probably more deeply immersed than any of them in Slavic languages, especially in the Russian variant of the Slavic family, and his mind was a rich storehouse of the vocabulary and idiom of Old Russian, Russian folklore, and Russian history, as well as the characteristic speech turns of various classes and professions. He was an expert in primitive Slavic history and mythology. The urban theme and Marinetti's "skyscrapers and steamships" play almost no part in his work. Khlebnikov might be described as a latter-day Slavophile, although Livshits coined a better term: "easternizer" (*vostochnik*).[25] Khlebnikov's chauvinism was a force equal and opposite to Marinetti's, and when the Italian futurist visited Moscow Khlebnikov composed, together with Livshits, a leaflet warning his Russian countrymen to reject the foreign influence. Khlebnikov was pathologically shy and retiring, but on that occasion he was moved to distribute his leaflets in the hall where the foreign guest was to speak, and was prevented only by the threat of force from the organizers of the meeting.[26]

Khlebnikov was in many respects an anomaly among the futurists. He was a quiet man and contributed almost nothing to the futurist noise of 1913 and 1914. He seldom joined their public parades and when called upon to recite his poems at their gatherings he did so in a disconcerting mumble, sometimes breaking off after a few lines with an apologetic "and so forth, and so forth." As

[25] Livshits, p. 218.

[26] Markov, *Russian Futurism*, p. 151.

we have seen, he looked for language and themes in the ancient past of Russia and was almost untouched by urbanism, virility, speed, the modern emphasis, and other futurist shibboleths. When we examine the manifestoes of the movement we find that his hand is prominent only in those statements that have to do with a revolution in poetic language; it was precisely as a bold experimenter that his comrades valued him. Benedikt Livshits reports a conversation with Marinetti in which he described Khlebnikov to his uncomprehending foreign guest as the "Pushkin" of his generation, and went on to say: "The most daring efforts of Rimbaud are childish babble by comparison with what Khlebnikov does in exploding the thousand-year-old stratifications of language and fearlessly plunging into the articulatory depths of the primordial (*pervozdannyi*) word." Livshits said that on first reading Khlebnikov, he "felt on [his] face the hot breath of the basic word. . . . The revelation of the roots of words was a kind of myth-making, an awakening of meanings dormant in a word as well as a birth of new ones."[27] Mayakovsky valued Khlebnikov as a kind of poetic laboratory, and there is no longer any question that he used the discoveries made in that laboratory.[28] "He is a poet," said Mayakovsky, "not for consumers but for producers of poetry." And Markov offers the startling judgment that in poetry "Khlebnikov is a king; Mayakovsky a vassal."

The essential feature of Khlebnikov's experimentation with language can be given in summary form, though it should be borne in mind that his intellectual purposes far exceeded the formal play, and that, as a matter of fact, he was behaving according to the premises of a philosophy of language which postulated a single, original, and universal tongue where protean riches lay concealed under the fixed habits of grammar, syntax, and conventional spelling. The linguistic validity of his theories need not concern us,[29] nor is it important to question the objective nature of his statement, for instance, that in *Devii bog* the linguistic principle is Slavic, in *Ka* African, and in *Deti Vydry* Asian.[30] What can

[27] Livshits, p. 227.

[28] See N. Khardzhiev, "Khlebnikov i Mayakovsky," in *To Honor Roman Jakobson: Essays on the Occasion of His Seventieth Birthday* (The Hague, 1969), II, 2301-2327.

[29] The linguist Baudouin de Courtenay sharply dismissed these notions about language. See *Otkliki*, Nos. 7-8, 1914.

[30] In V. Khlebnikov, "Svoyasi," *Sobranie sochinenii* (Munich, 1968), II, 8.

be observed and described are his experiments with the Russian language.

Roman Jakobson, whose study of Khlebnikov was the earliest and remains the most penetrating analysis of his verse habits,[31] examined concrete cases of his assault on accepted syntax. Khlebnikov often uses locutions that from the viewpoint of formal speech can only be called slips of the tongue. There are cases also of anacoluthon, or a sudden shift of construction, and of "incorrect" agreement of verb and subject:

> The fireflies' hovering swarm
> Seek to weave blue flax.

The abnormally frequent use of the adverbial instrumental case tends to diminish the role of verbs to the advantage of nouns and their qualifiers. Destruction of the verb was, as we have seen, a tenet in the program of the Italian futurists, and as a matter of fact the verb is greatly diminished in modern Russian poetry as a whole: Mayakovsky himself is a striking example of this. In Khlebnikov the device achieves a certain special effect. If the verb is the principal bearer of definite statement, then Khlebnikov's experiments in "verblessness" can be considered the poet's abdication of such statements, the formulation of which he leaves to the reader's imagination. In many of his lines the reader actively supplies the words of action or of state, and this is his contribution to the aesthetic whole:

> Hammer blows
> On the sea's grave
> On the water nymph's hill
> Along the rock's spines
> On the fingers of brass hands.

In general, Khlebnikov's innovations often have the effect of violating the precepts of *written* syntax, and injecting into poetry the usual habits—the rules, if you like—of conversational discourse. Many cases of anacoluthon or poor agreement in Khlebnikov simply reflect the imperfectly subordinated parts of a sentence spoken casually.

Khlebnikov's innovations in the poetic line were equally seminal. Dislocations of the normal word order or phrase succession

[31] Jakobson, *Noveishaya russkaya poeziya.*

is fairly common in poetry, but Khlebnikov "dislocates"—throws off balance—even the expected poetic phrase, leaving the reader only with a surprised sense of what it was he expected. His meters are usually free, but in the sense that they are unrecognizable as "meter"; instead they tend to reflect the rhythm of ordinary speech, but of a speaker who is touched by mental or emotional disturbance. The reader is curiously helpless before the phenomenon of Khlebnikov if his subconscious verse categories are limited to conventional iambs and trochees. His word order is whimsical and unpredictable, with a tendency to place auxiliary words—adverbs or prepositions—in a final or emphatic position: "I gallop aside and through" (*skachu ya vbok i cherez*). Rhymes are unschematic, often assonantal, and sometimes seem an accident in the line. At times, on the other hand they are elaborately playful, compound or palindromic. What we find in the formal structure of Khlebnikov's line is inspired play with all the elements of a poem, and with elements seldom used in poems. And an altogether original tension is set up by the use of colloquial phrase and rhythm to convey something either more or less than the meanings of ordinary speech.

Khlebnikov's creative play with language is best illustrated in his numerous experiments with roots and affixes. His most famous poem, and one that lends itself easily to approximate translation into English, is one called "Incantation by Laughter," based on an endlessly rich series of variations on the root of the word for laughter (*smekh*). The resulting poem serves as a working model of the Russian language, which grows in its infinite variety out of a relatively small number of basic roots by prefixing and suffixing. I offer the following translation:

O laugh it up you laughers!
O laugh it out you laughers!
That laugh with laughs, that laugherize laughily.
O laugh it out so laughily
O of laughing as laughilies—the laugh of laughish laugherators.
Laughterly, laughterly
Outlaugh, downlaugh, laughlets, laughlets.
Laughulets, laughulets
O laugh it up you laughers!
O laugh it out you laughers.

The verse is a charming poetic exercise in the communication of possible rather than real meanings. The "laugh," constantly reiterated, is thoroughly understandable, and the formal additions are understandable also as elements out of which sense may be constructed, though in the present case none results. To take one example, the form "laughlet" (*smeshik*), the word "laugh" (*smekh*) plus the suffix "let" (*-ik*), obviously means a miniscule laugh. And if this sudden neologism should prove difficult, we have the plural suffix "-s" (*-i*) which fully satisfies the strictest linguistic requirements. We may not accept or understand "laughlet," but there can be no misunderstanding about the form "laughlets": that clearly means "more than one laughlet." A somewhat similar operation was performed by Lewis Carroll in "The Jabberwocky," where "slithy toves" is obviously more than one tove, both partaking of the quality of slithiness.

We must distinguish still another method of word-building in Khlebnikov, according to which the suffix remains the same while the root changes. Naturally enough, the resulting series of neologisms may be rhymed: *letavu-metavu, zorir-gorir*. Another variation of this method involves the use of roots that are part of the understandable vocabulary: *grezogi-chertogi*, where *grez* means "phantom" and *chert* "devil." In all these cases the final syllables have the morphemic quality of an actual Russian suffix: the forms suggest, as I have said, the possibility of meaning. They consist of segmented and rearranged elements of the real language. Khlebnikov's procedure is analogous to the work of a cubist painter on the colors and shapes of the real world, or to that of the paranoid patients to whose written work Dr. Radin refers.

Other futurist poets deserve to be mentioned, and perhaps the most important after Kruchonykh and Khlebnikov were Elena Guro, Viktor Kamensky, Benedikt Livshits, and David Burliuk; I shall try to characterize them briefly.[32]

Elena Guro (1877-1913) was a contrast to her comrades as the only woman among them, as a senior poet (she was sixteen years older than Mayakovsky), and as a gently reared aristocrat. She is important as one of the influences that helped to shape Mayakovsky's own "myth" of the poet as a lonely and misunderstood

[32] Much material on each of these poets is to be found in Markov, *Russian Futurism, passim*, and selections from their work are given in D. Tschizewskij, *Anfänge des russischen Futurizmus* (Wiesbaden, 1963).

martyr. It has often been pointed out that the emotional apprehension of the city in her work is related to the young Mayakovsky's images of an urban inferno.[33] In addition to her poetry she wrote subjective, sensitive, and highly rhymical prose. The principal project of both her poetry and prose is the recapture of children's imagery, thought processes, and language. Through the device of infantile naiveté she endows the most ordinary experiences with freshness and novelty.

The poets Benedikt Livshits and Vasilii Kamensky were close comrades of Mayakovsky during the earliest period of his work, and each has left an important volume containing reminiscences of the period. Kamensky's *Life with Mayakovsky* we have already used extensively. It provides, along with vivid eyewitness accounts, much invaluable documentary material on the futurist activities of 1913 and 1914. Livshits' *The One-and-a-half-eyed Archer* (1933) is without question the best reminiscence of the period that we possess. Both books must, however, be used with circumspection, since their authors have an evident tendency not so much to embellish as to give artistic form to their experiences. Livshits presents with insight and irony the multitude of artists and writers who made up the Russian avant-garde of the early part of the century. He was a participant in the movement, and his perspective was broadly European; his first poetic models were the French moderns. A volume of Rimbaud, Livshits reports, accompanied him at all times, even in the army barracks when he served his time. He made sophisticated translations of the French moderns. His portrait of the young Mayakovsky is the only one we have from a Soviet observer that is free of any hagiographic embellishment.

Vasilii Kamensky was a genuinely gifted poet who wrote experimental verse that may have affected Mayakovsky, and who was in turn influenced by him. His rather considerable collection of verse, which includes two narrative poems on the peasant revolutionaries, *Stenka Razin* and *Pugachov*, tended to be overshadowed, in spite of their solid merit, by the poetic activity of his great contemporary.

Finally, a word must be said about David Burliuk. I have described him so far only in his role as the energetic entrepreneur of futurism and as the early "teacher" of Mayakovsky. There is an

[33] See N. Khardzhiev, "Zametki o Mayakovskom," in *Literaturnoe nasledstvo*, LXV, 405-406.

abundance of material on Burliuk, some of it written or inspired by Burliuk himself.[34] His life was long and very productive. His career as an artist began in 1904, when he was an art student in Munich and Paris, and ended with his death in the United States in 1967 at the age of eighty-four. During the latter part of his life he had many exhibitions, and was an important figure among a small group of experimental artists. *Color and Rhyme*, a magazine published by Burliuk and his wife Marussia at Hampton Bays, Long Island, developed and illustrated in successive numbers the major themes of David's life. One can find in it a wealth of information (not all of it accurate) about Burliuk as artist, innovator, organizer of art schools and promoter of movements, and as the intimate friend and occasional mentor of other great men. Mayakovsky and Khlebnikov enter its pages prominently, but largely because of the important role Burliuk played in their careers. Michael Gold, the prominent Communist editor of *New Masses*, produced a sympathetic sketch of Burliuk in 1945, done in Gold's characteristic style, which combines sentimental flourishes about "life," humanity, and a stylized Stalin, with hard implacable hatred of particular human beings.[35] His treatment of Burliuk is both worshipful and sentimental. We learn that the artist lived in moderate poverty, and for many years supported himself by working for the New York Communist newspaper *The Russian Voice* (*Russkii golos*). Gold also reported that Burliuk kept the prices of his paintings low so that workers could afford to buy them—on the installment plan if necessary.[36]

Burliuk was an organizer and inspirer of other men whose talent was in most cases far greater than his. His painting, as a whole, is an amalgam of many modern styles and does not offer any important original insights of its own. He once called himself a "primitivist," and many canvases suggest the influence of Goncharova, especially his peasant scenes; he produced many cubistic experiments, but these are usually a bit obvious in that they break up planes in such a way as not to obscure the "straight" drawing

[34] The most important of these are E. Gollerbakh, *Iskusstvo Davida Burliuka* (New York, 1930), and *Poeziya Davida Burliuka* (New York, 1931); Katherine Dreier, *Burliuk* (New York, 1944); Michael Gold, *David Burliuk, Artist, Scholar, Father of Russian Futurism* (New York, 1944).

[35] An anthology of Michael Gold's writings is available: *Mike Gold: A Literary Anthology*, ed. Michael Folsom (New York, 1972).

[36] Gold, *David Burliuk*, p. 10.

that serves as a base; Chagall is clearly present in some works; surrealism gets its due. Commentators have remarked on how difficult it is to "classify" Burliuk. His painting seems to sum up in an informed but unoriginal idiom the various movements in modern art in which he was a leading spirit, organizer, and mover. Much the same generalization can be made of his poetry, which is much less important than his painting. The critic Erik Gollerbakh wrote very perceptively that "in reading Burliuk you have the impression that his work is the creation of various authors, all quite different from one another in their philosophy, temperament, and style. Really, Burliuk had the faculty of getting into other men's skins."[37] The best of his poetry was written before the revolution, and in it he translates into Russian the themes and manner of the French *poètes maudits*, their anti-aestheticism, their deliberate use of vulgar vocabulary, and their shocking themes. He experimented with alliteration (one of his early poems contains only words beginning with the letter "l"), and with front and middle rhyme; and like Khlebnikov, he wrote palindromic poems. His poetry, like his painting, is a sophisticated reiteration of the main concerns of his contemporaries. We may deny him weight as an artist, but this does not in the least diminish his importance as an entrepreneur of modern art. And of course he was the organizer of those futurist publications in which Mayakovsky made his debut as a poet.

4) The Sense of Futurism

I have been trying to place in various perspectives the movement in which Mayakovsky took his first steps as a poet and in which he became a leading figure. The artistic and historical *sense* of that movement is elusive, and efforts to capture it have produced an array of contradictory statements. One of the most interesting of these statements is an impressionistic one by the poet Aleksandr Blok, who compared futurism to the contemporary acmeist movement: "Russian futurism . . . reflected in its foggy mirror a characteristic gay horror which is seated in the Russian soul and which many 'perspicacious' and very bright people had completely missed. In that respect Russian futurism

[37] Gollerbakh, *Poeziya*, p. 15.

is infinitely more significant, deeper, more organic, more vital than acmeism; the latter reflected nothing at all, since it bore within itself no 'storms and stresses,' but was an imported foreign object."[38] Blok's statement is unfair to the acmeists, and seems to ignore the "imported" character of much futurist baggage; but the phrase "gay horror" is an illuminating oxymoron if applied to the work of Mayakovsky, where irrational gaiety and horror verging on madness are in frequent contention.

Most other statements tend to generalize from a partial selection of facts; this is understandable, since we customarily place under the rubric of futurism such diverse and unhomogeneous phenomena as Mayakovsky and Khlebnikov, an urbanist and a Slavic primitivist. Vladimir Markov's statement, in his excellent study of futurism, attempts to include everything: the movement, he explains, "contained elements of impressionism, expressionism, neo-primitivism, constructivism, abstractionism, dandyism, theosophy, and so forth."[39] We can learn much from such a statement, but not what futurism was. A very broad definition was offered by Mayakovsky, who, writing in 1922, said that before the revolution the term futurist was used of all artists and groups that were considered avant-garde.[40] Futurism thus becomes a very rough equivalent of the Russian pre-war avant-garde. Roman Jakobson offered an even more interesting formulation when he said, "Khlebnikov is called a futurist. His poems are printed in futurist collections. Futurism is a new movement in European art. I will not offer here a more exact definition of that term. Such a definition could be arrived at only inductively, through analysis of a complex set of artistic phenomena."[41]

Perhaps the common denominator that constitutes the interconnection of so many seemingly disparate artistic phenomena is the fact already noted that, without exception, all the leading Russian futurists were revolutionary painters as well as poets, and that their first experience of innovation was in the medium of painting. Experimentation with visual objects suggested another

[38] Aleksandr Blok, *Sobranie sochinenii v vosmi tomakh* (Moscow, 1962), VI, 181.

[39] Markov, *Russian Futurism*, pp. 383-385.

[40] This statement occurred in a letter to Leon Trotsky, reprinted without the name of the addressee in *Literaturnoe nasledstvo*, LXV, 176.

[41] In his *Noveishaya russkaya poeziya*, p. 6.

possibility, experimentation with the aural materials of poetry. Painters of the avant-garde analyzed the objects of the real world as geometrical shapes in space and as bearers of color, and they arrived at a technique that treated space and color in abstraction from the practical objects. In Kandinsky's abstractions, as a matter of fact, bodies have disappeared and only the one attribute of color is left. The substance is gone, the accidents remain.

Similarly, in the poetic work of the futurists, meaning disappears and we have only linguistic forms that offer the possibility of meaning, formants that are in a sense the attributes of meaning. The futurists experiment with words and elements of words detached from their practical purpose. Interesting light is thrown on their procedures by the painter Kazimir Malevich, who hit upon the phrase "the body as such" (*telo kak takovoe*) to express the object of a cubist painter's creation: "The idea is to combine the variety and multiplicity (*raznoobraznost*) of lines, space, surface, and color with their mingled texture into one *body as such*" (my italics).[42] The play with roots, prefixes, suffixes, internal and external declension, syntax, grammar, rhyme, assonance, alliteration, and neologisms was a transference to poetry of the painter's search for the reality of "the body as such." Khlebnikov and Kruchonykh, as we know, were in pursuit of "the word as such."

The apperception of Khlebnikov's poetry, even when that poetry is completely unintelligible, provides aesthetic pleasure because it *reminds* the reader of intellectual processes as formed and delimited by language, at the same time suggesting to him the possibility of escape from any limitation of particularity and reference.

The philosophical derivation of the phenomenon of "modern art" is a fascinating problem, to which I can only allude in this chapter. It has often been suggested that the influence of Kant's *Critique of Pure Reason* was decisive in establishing the new direction for art. If the world as we experience it is shaped by our own minds, and the reality behind that world—the thing in itself—is unknowable, then an art that only imitates the forms we perceive (a "realistic" art) is useless to us, and the modern artist is actually engaged in a struggle, no doubt futile, to escape from the cabin and crib of his mind into contact with a more "real"

[42] K. Malevich, *O novykh sistemakh v iskusstve* (Vitebsk, 1919).

reality. But perhaps there is another way to explain what has happened. Since the only reality we know is the perceptive process itself, then perhaps the proper concern of the artist is with the elements out of which perception is made. Perhaps the play with color, line, form, space, time, and so forth is the artist's proper business.

Chapter Four

MAYAKOVSKY IN THE FUTURIST COLLECTIONS

1) The Earliest Lyrics

So far I have been attempting to reconstruct the historical ambience of Mayakovsky's early poetry. We have been locating and naming, in other words, those persons and situations and ideas that formed the mold within which that poetry took shape. Now we must shift the focus to the actual product of a poet whose stupendous genius had its own mark upon it and transformed all influences and anything already existing into something new and totally unpredictable. In Mayakovsky's poetry we witness the emergence from the futurist womb, so to speak, of a kind of monstrous birth, a poet who bears some of the characteristic features of his parent, but combines those with others that are passing strange. From the point of view of futurism, Mayakovsky as a poet had more than one pair of hands, eyes, and ears. He had two heads, and a forked tongue. The lessons he learned from Burliuk and Khlebnikov he made use of to create verses that *meant* something. Mayakovsky labored under a misapprehension that only a great genius could have turned to profit: the poetic devices of the futurists were only devices, but he took them seriously. He used their poetic system in order to express his own emotions, assert his own ego, create a myth of his own self. He made his futurist poems mean something, in fact, that was very important and very personal. Another eccentric feature of Mayakovsky's earliest poems is that they are almost all written in conventional syllabo-tonic verse meters and offer no evidence at all of innovation in the verse form itself.

In this chapter we will examine a number of Mayakovsky's earliest lyric poems, all first published in the series of collections produced by the futurist group between 1912 and 1914. An analysis of these poems will reveal certain features of the young Mayakovsky that developed and strengthened as he grew to maturity.

The collection of poetry and prose bearing the title *A Slap at Public Taste*[1] contained two poems by Mayakovsky. They were entitled "Night" (*Noch*) and "Morning," (*Utro*) and were offered as a two-part treatment of a city landscape at its moments of transition from light to dark, and back again. They were experiments in the reduction to poetry of that play with color, form, and line that intrigued the cubist painters. Of the four stanzas in "Night," the last has been pronounced totally unintelligible by one researcher,[2] and indeed certain lines are marked by a kind of Khlebnikovian detachment of words from meaning. Yet in these first poems Mayakovsky offers the visible world in forms that transcend word play and lay him open to insistent queries concerning meaning. In both poems there are two dimensions, one purely visual and the other personal. In the poem "Night" the poet appears as an emphatic "me" in the first line of the last stanza. That poem is divided into four stanzas; its meter is an amphibrach of surprising regularity, in other words a conventional beat; its rhyme scheme is a fixed and regular pattern: *abab/cdcd*, and so forth. It presents what we may metaphorically call an urban kaleidoscope of color and form, and the transition from one stanza to the next, like a sudden shift in the position of the framing box, drops the pieces of the picture into new patterns. Let us consider each stanza in turn.

1) Deep scarlet and white are crumpled and tossed aside; gamblers scatter golden ducats into the green of the sky, and glowing yellow window-cards are dealt to the black houses. Night approaching is seen in terms of the diminution ("crumpling") of certain colors and the emphasis upon others, and the process is boldly realized as a gambling metaphor. (Can I resist reminding the reader that Mayakovsky was an obsessive gambler?) We must also note that the metaphoric view of nature is expressed in the impersonal constructions: ducats are tossed (*brosali*), cards are dealt (*razdali*), scarlet and white are thrown aside (*otbroshen*).

2) Blue togas on the buildings hold no surprise for boulevards and squares, and the street lamps (or else the light from basement windows) cast bracelets of yellow wounds on pedestrian legs.

3) The street crowd is a quick cat with a pelt of many colors; swimming and twisting, it is drawn into doorways. Each member

[1] *Poshchochina obshchestvennomu vkusu* (Moscow, 1912).

[2] V. V. Timofeeva, *Yazyk poeta i vremya* (Moscow, 1962), pp. 50-51.

tries to drag along even a little bit the huge lump poured out of laughter. Admittedly the meaning here is obscure, but the final line of the third stanza prepares the entrance of the poet himself, since the "lump of laughter" would seem to involve a sudden emotional apprehension of the scene.

4) The final stanza introduces the poet's own "ego" and with it a grotesque fantasy which includes enticing paws of ladies' gowns (or, perhaps, ladies' gowns that entice the paws), black men laughing, and a parrot's wing blossoming above the forehead. The sudden intrusion of an animal image, with the suggestion of a splash of color, suggests something in the style of Chagall. The poet himself "feels the enticing paws of clothing, forces out a smile right into their [whose?] eyes." The black men (?) laugh at him and sound like blows on tin, frightening him. At this point we may boggle at the syntax; and heroic efforts have been made to construe the last stanza so as to make some kind of sense of it. Probably no logical meaning is either intended or decipherable from the words as given, but the emotional effect of the lines is immediate and in need of no elucidation. A poem that began as pure play with sound, color, and image has grown into an anguished personal vision by the end of the last stanza. The poet has, in all seriousness, introduced himself into the picture he is painting, and that self, even in this first poem, seems alone and anxious.

The poem entitled "Morning" presents a sharp contrast to "Night" in a number of ways. "Night" is divided into regular four-line stanzas, each one of which is a self-contained unit. "Morning" abandons stanzaic structure in favor of a division on the page into phrase units of varying length. The first poem was strictly conventional in its rhyming pattern; the second presents a complex experiment with rhyme. This suggests that the two poems are offered as an illustration of a verse canon, and its destruction. In the manifesto published in the collection *A Trap for Judges, No. 2*, the futurist leaders pointed with pride to Mayakovsky's rhyming experiments in this poem,[3] and he himself referred to it many years later in his essay "How to Make Verses," when he pointed out that end rhymes are not the only way to tie the lines of a poem together: "You can rhyme the beginnings of lines . . . and you can rhyme the end of one line with the beginning of the next."

[3] See above, Chapter Three.

The opening lines of "Morning" do create striking and original sound effects:

Ugryumyi dozhd skosil glaza.	The morose rain looked askance.
A za	Beyond
reshotkoi	The sharp
chotkoi	Grillwork
zheleznoi mysli provodov—	Of the wires' iron thought—
perina.	A featherbed.
I na	And on
neyo	It
vstayushchikh zvyozd	Lightly rest
legko opyorlis nogi.	The feet of awakening stars.
No gi-	But the per-
bel	dition . . . .

We note also that the poet rhymes a complete word at the end of one line (*nogi*) with identical sounds distributed over two words at the beginning of the next (*no gibel*), and that internal rhymes adorn many of the lines: "No gi- / bel fonarei, / tsarei / v korone gaza, / dlya glaza . . ." ("But the perdition of street lamps in their crown of gas, for the eye . . .").

The poem offers to the ear a variety of unexpected experiences in sound repetition, and yet it is still very conventional in its basic metrical pattern, which is a fairly strict iambic beat. Considered as verbal form and line, "Morning" is a versatile performance, but once again the lines suggest the haunting presence of a poet whose words are intended to "say" something. The stars are visible through a close grillwork of wires (a recurrent image in Mayakovsky's early poetry); light brings "perdition" to the street lamps; the morning reveals an "angry" bouquet of prostitutes; and suddenly the reddening east throws Moscow's many crosses, "suffering—quietly—indifferent," and her "coffins of houses" into one great burning urn. The lexicon of the poem has the ring of a personal desperation, intransigent and loud. Relief comes only in the last lines when the poet of urban themes ("a fine urbanist!" in Chukovsky's ironic phrase) looks beyond the "noise and horror" of the city to contemplate and metaphorize the red morning sky.

Perhaps the severest critic of these two poems was Benedikt Livshits, who tells of a long midnight walk with Mayakovsky ("the streetcars had stopped running") during which the not-yet-published poet recited his first efforts, obviously expecting praise and approval. Livshits claimed to have told him frankly what he thought: "A naive urbanism that echoed the Bryusov tradition, and a hardly less naive anthropomorphism, already thoroughly vulgarized by Leonid Andreev, could hardly be redeemed by a few surprising images, nor by those "reverse" rhymes that Volodya considered to be almost the lever of Archimedes, capable of moving all of world poetry from its axis."

Valerii Bryusov himself, a potent critic of the day, was almost equally disdainful of the two poems, though he did offer faint praise: "Even less satisfactory are the devices for finding new rhymes (and to tell the truth they are not new, since, even if we forget Tredyakovsky, we can still point to their very successful use by Edgar Poe), offered to us by V. Mayakovsky. . . . However in spite of these extreme manifestations, there remains something not devoid of value, a new attempt at expressivity in poetry."[4]

Scholars have demonstrated Mayakovsky's dependence—at second hand, since he knew no European languages other than Russian—on the *poètes maudits*, as well as on the symbolist poets who preceded him, in the treatment of urban themes. The urban theme had been fully developed by Blok and Bryusov before his debut; anti-aesthetic vocabulary was a commonplace in the work of Belyi, which Mayakovsky knew well; the symbolists had experimented with new rhymes and meters. And yet the aesthetic effect of Bryusov's or Blok's urban scenes, or the shock potential of Baudelaire or LaForgue (both of whom Mayakovsky knew in translation) are simply not related to Mayakovsky's purpose and performance in his early poems. This idea we will develop as we continue to analyze these poems, but the point should be made now that Mayakovsky's debt to other poets is not one that can be properly assessed. For Mayakovsky, to paraphrase T. S. Eliot's well-known phrase, *stole* their property from those poets and he used it—rather ignorantly—in an aesthetic project for which he is in debt to no one. What he took he translated from the language of sophisticated literary performance into the language of the self, and the notes of desperation plainly audible in both the poems we have seen are not literary but real. What appears in Blok or Belyi as a literary mode practiced by poets of high culture, Mayakovsky, perhaps because he lacked that culture, transformed into direct experience. His "urbanism" is quite naive, as Livshits long ago pointed out, but only because he took in

[4] Valerii Bryusov, "Novye techeniya," p. 34.

earnest what for other poets was already a somewhat worn literary fashion.

The collection of poetry and manifestoes entitled *A Trap for Judges, No. 2* contained three more poems by Mayakovsky: "Port," "Streetways" (*Ulichnoe*), and "From Street to Street" (*Iz ulitsy v ulitsu*).

Like the first published poem, "Night," the lyric "Port" is astonishingly conventional and regular in its metrical beat. The young poet whose public speeches excoriated conservatism in art produced in many poems of this period an iambic regularity and a simplicity of rhyme reminiscent of the eighteenth rather than the nineteenth century. The first five lines of the eight-line poem are absolutely regular iambic tetrameters in the sense that stresses occur on every syllable where the meter requires it:

> Prostýni vód pod bryúkhom býli.
> (The sheets of water lay under the belly).

The last three lines omit stresses only on the next to the last foot, which is statistically the most common variation in this meter:[5]

> Goréli sérgi yakoréi.
> (The anchor earrings glowed).

Rhymes have a kind of infantile simplicity, each one pairing identical grammatical categories: *byli / lili; zub / trub.*

The poem in its content is an extended metaphor of bed and love with a confusion of erotic and infantile images involving steamships on the point of departure (the poem was originally entitled "Sailing" [*Otplytie*]). A white tooth tears into waves the sheets under the belly. Love and lust pour out in the scream of the ship's siren. Boats in their cradles (*lodki v lyulkakh*) press to the nipples of their metallic mother. Anchor earrings glow in the "deafened" ears of the steamers. The poem is an effective mosaic of suggestive vocabulary and metaphoric play, but it carries a mark that we shall soon recognize as the signature of Mayakovsky: the coupling of love and lust with the scream (*voi*) of a siren. We have here an embryonic suggestion of the link in his imagination between love—or lust—and unendurable psychic

[5] V. Zhirmunsky, *Introduction to Metrics*, Edward Stankiewicz and W. N. Vickery, eds. (The Hague, 1966), p. 37.

pain. Scholars are able to point out that this poem bears a rather close resemblance to one by David Burliuk on a similar theme, written at the very moment when Burliuk was Mayakovsky's guide and teacher; although the general similarity is unquestionable, Burliuk's poem is of course devoid of Mayakovsky's characteristic "scream" of love.[6]

"Streetways" was actually "edited" by Burliuk, in the sense that he made certain changes in the text Mayakovsky presented to him.[7] The poem is, like many of Burliuk's poems, another attempt to translate a cubistic canvas into verse. The pattern of colors is particularly striking in the first of the three stanzas: the greenish black of damp mold, the red of cranberry juice, the bright green of a herring the color of moonstone, colored letters detached from any object. Once again the artist himself intrudes, in the second stanza, "pounding in the pilings of his steps," and with his appearance the "picture" takes on a specific emotional tone. Streetcars are *weary* as they cross their flashing spears. The *one-eyed* square lifts up its orb and *steals* closer. The sky looks into the white gaslight with the face of an *eyeless Medusa.* The metaphors are especially ambiguous and difficult, and the sense of the verse-canvas remains a riddle, but its "meaning" is perfectly clear; the emotional coloration is carried by a succession of distraught adjectives.

"Streetways" is conventional in form. The iambic tetrameters are regular except for occasional omissions of stress in the penultimate foot. The rhymes are as simple as those in "Port," except for two cases of "broken" rhyme (*tsvel gde/ selde* and *drob ya/ kopya*), which are neither original nor startling.

"From Street to Street" in its second publication carried the subtitle "I have a conversation with the sun near the Sukharev Tower." This places the scene of the poem—the "action," if we may call it that—on the Sadovoe Ring in Moscow, that portion of the Ring called Sadovo-Sukharevskaya Street.

The poem is intensely local as to both place and time. The procedures of the painter here transferred to a poem have an unexpected piquancy of effect, but this poem may also stand as an illustration of the reason for the difficulty Mayakovsky's work frequently causes. A painter dealing with this particular street scene had as the ingredients of his picture a tower, a church belfry, a

[6] Trenin and Khardzhiev, "Poetika rannego Mayakovskogo," p. 184.
[7] *PSS* (1935), I, 378.

sky spotted like trout, streetcar rails as seen from the rear platform of a moving tram, smoking chimneys, a street lamp. However realistic or impressionistic, surreal or cubistic these items may appear in a painting, they are in a sense motivated and justified by the painter's selection of a field of vision he projects upon a defined space, his canvas. Many of Mayakovsky's early poems offer obscurities which result from the circumstance that they project objects whose presence in the poem is motivated only by the poet-painter's selection of a field of vision.

Unlike the first three poems, "From Street to Street" is experimental in form. Malevich is reported to have said that he considered this poem the most successful experiment in "versified cubism."[8] That effect is achieved by the segmentation of words on the page, and by a succession of phrases that read roughly the same backward and forward:

U-
litsa.
Litsa
u
dogov
godov
rez-
che.
Che-
rez

This may be taken as pure word play, language made palpable for its own sake, as a formalist might say, and we need not trouble over those "faces of Great Danes sharper than the years." Mayakovsky provided some help with this poem in his essay "How to Make Verses" when he said that the images in it were suggested by a "streetcar ride from Sukharev Tower to Sretenka." Perhaps the repetition of meaningless sound in the opening lines imitates the metallic beat of wheels on rails. Perhaps. And if we take as our vantage point the rear platform of a streetcar moving generally south from the tower to Sretenka, certain images become measurably clearer. The "first cubes" leap from the windows of "houses rushing by." The "swan necks" of belfries are tangled in "nooses of wires." The "giraffe drawing" that suddenly variegates the sky

[8] Khardzhiev, "Mayakovsky i zhivopis," p. 398.

is the artist's inevitable projection of himself into the painting: Mayakovsky constantly and compulsively sketched giraffes in a variety of poses and expressions, and it is clear from some of the sketches that the giraffe (so tall, so handsome, so pathetic) is Mayakovsky himself. Nor is there great difficulty in understanding the "magician" who "draws the rails out of the streetcar's maw," once we have placed ourselves on the back platform of the moving vehicle.[9] Then very abruptly, with the announcement "We are overcome!" the tonality of the metaphor changes and various urban objects become involved in a violent sexual assault. "Hands burn the body. Cry all you like 'I don't want to.'" And the bald street lamp "lasciviously removes the street's black stocking." Erotic imagery, sometimes quite brutally clear, is fairly frequent in the early poetry of Mayakovsky.

The futurist collection *The Missal of the Three* (*Trebnik troikh*, 1913) included five poems by Mayakovsky, of which the most interesting was a brief study entitled "But Could You?" (*A vy mogli by?*), which we have already dealt with in the first chapter. "For Signs" (*Vyveskam*) and "Theaters" (*Teatry*) involve once again specific cityscapes; the first utilizes the technique, common in cubo-futurist paintings of the day (Goncharova, Malevich), of the street-sign montage: "iron books" of street signs with gilded letters, the "constellation" that was the trademark of a firm manufacturing bouillon, undertakers' wares, street lamps that "someone" (the subject, the actor, in many of his sentences is not named), morose and tearful, puts out. "Theaters" has been interpreted by one critic as an extended metaphorical treatment of the opening of a theatrical production.[10] We expect to find the poet himself in his verses, and his presence in "For Signs" is in the line "funeral establishment" (*byuro pokhoronnykh protsessii*). This image occurs again in the poem "I Love You" (*Lyublyu*), written in 1923, which I have already mentioned; there he tells of his five months in solitary confinement when the only thing he could see from his cell was a "funeral establishment." Both poems are written in conventional syllabo-tonic meters: "For Signs" is a quite normal amphibrach and "Theaters" is an iambic tetrameter. The rhymes are, once again, almost absurdly simple: *knigi / sigi; bukvy / bryukvy*.

[9] This is the eminently reasonable suggestion of G. S. Cheremin in his *Rannii Mayakovsky* (Moscow, 1962), p. 61.

[10] Timofeeva, p. 61.

"Something about Petersburg" (*Koe-chto pro Peterburg*) is a two-stanza study of metropolitan rain. It is saturated with metaphor: there are eight separately identifiable metaphors in the eight lines of the poem. The influence of Khlebnikov is clear in the suggestion of "poetic etymology" in the line "*slezayut slyozy s kryshi v truby*" ("the tears drip from roofs into gutter-pipes"), where a resonance is set up between *slez-*, "drip," and *slyozy*, "tears."[11] The poem also offers a set of richly emphasized alliterations: *sl / sk; k ruke / reki; bleshchet / blyudo,* etc. But the metric beat is again an unastonishing iambic.

"After a Woman" (*Za zhenshchinoi*) is structurally interesting in that the lines are arranged in rigid syntactical units, with proper subordination achieved through participles and gerunds. But the grammatical and syntactic forms of practical statement, which lead us to expect some weighty content, are filled instead with a series of obscure and outlandish metaphors. For instance: "having moved aside with an elbow the yeast of fog, strained whitewash from a black flask"; or, "having thrown slanted reins into the sky swung in the clouds, gray and grave." Each syntactically arranged sentence contains the possibility of meaning because the parts are properly disposed; but "sense" only teases the imagination. A series of erotic images can be deciphered without difficulty, and the poem almost certainly is meant to convey a lustful experience in terms of sunrise and the bursting forth of light over the city. "Excited by the red cloak of fornication, smoke pierces heavens like horns." There are "vulcan thighs" and "full ears of breasts ripe for the harvest," which are at first observed "behind the ice of clothing." "God is caught in a lasso and pulled in through the threshold crack." And at last "the east, observing them in a side-street, dragged the sun out of a black bag, and angrily struck the roof-ribs." The succession of strangely assorted metaphors all tending to the same purpose is something like the pictorial gibberish of an erotic dream. The meter is a completely regular iambic tetrameter with hypercatalectic caesura; the poem offers a piquant combination of perfectly normal form with weirdly surreal content.

In eight of the ten short poems so far examined Mayakovsky adheres religiously to the traditional syllabo-tonic metrical system. These poems are far less daring than some of the verse experiments of the symbolists. It was only with the cycle of poems

[11] See N. Khardzhiev, "Khlebnikov i Mayakovsky," p. 2306.

that appeared under the title *Me* (*Ya*) that Mayakovsky began the experimentation that would develop his characteristic accentual verse. The formal conservatism of his first printed poems argues that they were not really his first efforts, but rather the last in a relatively long series of poems written in a tradition different from that of the symbolists and alien to the futurists. During his period in solitary confinement he had filled a notebook with verses, which the jailers took from him; I have referred to the one example he gave of the poetry contained in that notebook. The Soviet scholar Timofeeva has pointed out that that four-line poem, with its traditional poetic vocabulary, its uncomplicated metrical system, and its intonation of unjust suffering, betrays the influence of underground political poets such as Skitalets or civic lyricists such as Nadson. For Mayakovsky the revolution had always been mixed with poetry; he wrote verse for the illegal student newspaper *Poryv* in 1907; and during his period in jail, probably still under the influence of the civic poets, he wrote many complaints over his "hundreds of desperate days." The rhythmic and rhyming habits he had formed in that school remained with him through his first poems as a futurist, and the result was the odd mixture we have observed of traditional form and "anti-aesthetic," urban, or cubistic content.

A thin book in lithograph form appeared in May 1913 bearing the title *Me* (*Ya*) and containing a "cycle" of three poems preceded by an introduction. The poems were called "A Few Words about My Wife," "A Few Words about My Mama," and "A Few Words about Myself." It was one of the best examples of the futurists' "self-published" books. Mayakovsky dictated the poems to the artist V. Chekrygin, who wrote them out for lithographing in a clear, sharp hand and also provided four black-and-white drawings having no clear relationship to the text of the poems. Another artist friend, L. Zhegin, produced three drawings and a portrait of Mayakovsky himself. The cover, done by the poet, is adorned by what seems to be a shapeless blob of ink, but is actually Mayakovsky's flagrant cravat, known as "the butterfly."[12]

In the poem that served as an introduction to the "cycle" Mayakovsky accomplishes a bold metaphoric leap and is himself the city. The poem then becomes a concretization of his own frantic sense of mutilation and misery: madmen's heels on the warm

[12] L. Zhegin, "Vospominaniya o Mayakovskom," in *V. Mayakovsky v vospominaniyakh sovremennikov*, p. 101.

pavement of his soul imprint a tangle of harsh words; hanged cities and tower-necks are in their noose of clouds; policemen are crucified at street-crossings. The poet alone "sobs" over all these things.

"A Few Words about My Wife" opens with two lines in an iambic meter with a singing lilt that suggests a parody of popular songs or conventional love lyrics:

> Moréi nevédomykh dalyókim plyázhem
> Idyót luná—zhená moyá.
> (Along the strands of undiscovered seas
> The moon, my wife, is riding.)

The fact that the poem is about the moon lends it a touch of the conventionally romantic. Moon, sky, and stars figure importantly in it, as they often do in Mayakovsky's work, but these items of sublimity are mingled in a close marriage with the vulgarly prosaic. "The moon, my wife, is riding along the strand of undiscovered seas. . . . Her carriage is shoutingly trailed by a many-striped throng of constellations." But then she is suddenly involved with a city garage and though her train is the Milky Way she is kissed by newspaper stands. The elevated image of the galaxy is abruptly negated in the very next line by the adjective "tinsel" (*mishurnyi*). The romantic thought of his "wife" the moon is immediately reduced by the line, "My paramour is redheaded" (*Moya lyubovnitsa ryzhevolosaya*). The poet himself, in a long and labored metaphor, weeps for his love: "And I? The yoke of my brows brings cold buckets from the well of my eyes." The distress of the poet abandoned by his love, an insistent theme of Mayakovsky throughout his life, appears for the first time in this poem. He "drowns in boulevards," and is "wafted with the melancholy of sands," but she "never throws a sparkling line into the realm of malicious roofs" where he makes his abode. And the "daughter" of himself and the moon is this very song that frequents the coffee-houses wearing net stockings. The moon herself is a strumpet who is kissed by kiosks, and her daughter, Mayakovsky's poem, is a whore.

This effort at translation, or paraphrase, or statement of meaning may seem slightly ridiculous because of the nature of the work. The idea of the word as "self-valuing" and in need of no denotational support, is basic to the poem. But the lines are packed with connotations, and the poem is not unrelated to the symbolists' efforts to reach, by other than logical means, a new level of knowledge. Mayakovsky has given us a succession of verbal stimuli—verse parodies, literary clichés, shocking associations ("tinsel Milky Way"), striking metaphors (the "malice of roofs"), whose total effect is sufficiently clear to the reader, though no logical statement can encompass it.

"A Few Words about My Mama" is a similar performance. Reality is vividly present in striking images: blue cornflower wallpaper, the Shustov factory, the window of the Avanzo store, which dealt in artist's supplies, the poet's felt hat, a window-frame at sunset. But the reality is strangely and unaccountably distorted, and the poetic cadences are like sweet bells jangled, out of tune and harsh. The clarity and tenderness of a conventional lyric are suggested but do not come through the dissonance. The lines "I have a mama on blue cornflower wallpaper, / but I pace about in peahen finery" may very well continue to defy interpretation. "Wallpaper" and "peahen finery" are partly motivated by the need to implement a startling rhyme—the first occurrence of the device in Mayakovsky—involving the echoing in one line of the final sounds of two preceding lines: *oboyakh* (wallpaper) and *pavakh* (peahens) in the first two lines rhyme with the *goboyakh rzhavykh* (rusty oboes) of the fourth line. Perhaps the poem will yield to an autobiographical interpretation; after all, we have already observed that the early lyrics, even when they are intended as urban still-lifes, manage to feature the soul of the poet himself.

"A Few Words about My Mama" is the first poem in which not only the soul but the physical person of the poet and his ambience become matters for contemplation. That he had a "mama" is one of the salient facts of his biography. Moreover, "Mama" was a special person, to whom he turned in imagined (and perhaps real) moments of desperation ("Mama! your son is beautifully ill!"), who loved and pampered him beyond measure, and who made him his yellow blouse. That he had a mama is clear; that she should be "on blue cornflower wallpaper" somewhat less so. Yet the line can be understood as metonymy: Mama stays at home; she is always there among the home things; she cannot be imagined apart from the wallpaper. The second line presents her son as an emphatic contrast: "But I pace about in peahen finery." Is it possible to miss Mayakovsky in that line? His friends insist that he never "walked," but "loomed" in the distance: "You could recognize him a mile off not only by his size but chiefly by his broad, uneven, and heavy gait."[13] The word *gulyayu*, which I have translated "pace about," suggests his daily traverse of Moscow's streets and boulevards. "Peahen finery" is nonsense unless it refers to his yellow blouse, long hair, broad-brimmed, flat-crowned felt hat, and of course his "butterfly," the flamboyant bow tie. The next line is more stubborn. "Shaggy daisies, measuring them with my steps, I torture," yields nothing at first except an interesting instrumentation (in Russian) of sound repetitions, though the daisy fits with the cornflower as a flower of sentimental association, the one whose petals when plucked tell whether "she loves me" or not. The next passage, "The evening strikes up a wail on rusty oboes [the translation is intended to convey, as the Russian does, the crying sound of the oboe] and I walk up to the window sure that I will see again a cloud sitting on the house," places the poet in a room looking out at the evening. Mama is sick, and a rustle of people rushes from the bed to an empty corner. But Mama is aware that there are heaps of mad ideas creeping from behind the roofs of the Shustov factory. Mama, perhaps the poet, perhaps the poet as a child, remembers a feverish hallucination which appears in the poem as an urban disarray of mad thoughts. The poem ends with a long sentence of regular and rather complicated syntax that says: "And when my forehead, crowned by a felt hat, the dimming window-frame bloodies, I will say, parting the wind's howl [a sound of oboes!] with my bass tones: 'Mama, if I come to pity the vase of your torment, smashed by the heels of the cloud dance, who then will caress the golden hands frantically twisted on the sign at Avanzo's window?' " The felt hat we recognize. It replaces laurel leaves as the poet's "crown."[14] The gradually darkening window at sunset throws its last scarlet upon the poet's brow. The "vase of torment," it has been convincingly demonstrated,[15] reached this poem from the French poet Sully-Prudhomme ("*Le vase brisé*") by way of a widely known Russian translation done by Apukhtin. The "broken vase" in that poem is equated with a "broken heart"; mama's vase of torment, therefore, is her poor heart, and we have here a parody of a sentimental metaphor. The final image, involving the display window of the Avanzo art supply store, is an evocation of hands wrung in agony, a recurrent image in Mayakovsky's early lyrics.

[13] *Ibid.*, p. 102.
[14] Cheremin, p. 61.
[15] In Khardzhiev, "Zametki o Mayakovskom," p. 402.

"A Few Words about My Mama" is a succession of strained but effective tropes carried by a complex sound system; the total effect of the poem is one of pain redoubled and inescapable. Mama's broken heart, perhaps her delirium, has resulted from her son's departure for the streets, the boulevards, the Shustov factory, and the Avanzo store. We have here the first suggestion of Mayakovsky's self-appointed vocation as a poet—to caress the sufferers in the city. For that he had to leave his mama. Like the young Jesus, he had work to do. The first two poems in the "cycle" express a double alienation—from love ("the moon, my wife") and from home ("Mama").

We must bear this in mind when we approach the opening line of the last poem in the cycle, "A Few Words about Myself," which has given rise to distress and consternation and has called forth heroic efforts on the part of some scholars. The line "I love to watch children dying" has been explained as signifying the poet's lack of enthusiasm for bourgeois family life with its burden of unwanted children, or as evidence of the baleful influence of decadent bourgeois poetics, or as a parody on some sickeningly sweet lines about "little children" (*detki*) by the French Catholic poet Francis Jammes, or as pure and unabashed *épatage.*[16] But the line, when read in context, and when taken in the context of other poems produced at about the same time, makes plausible psychological sense. Anything that suffers causes the poet pain, and innocent suffering, the quiet misery of a fallen horse, the "little tears" of helpless people (as in the *Tragedy*) carry a special weight of grief. The grief over little children, however, is so great that he cannot endure it, and to protect himself from the unbearable, he contemplates their suffering and death as an aesthetic matter, even learns to enjoy the sight. The key to the meaning of the first line is contained in what follows:

> I love to watch children dying.
> Have you ever noticed the misty crest of laughter's wave
> Behind the proboscis of melancholy?
> But I
> In the reading-room of streets
> So often leafed through the volume of death.

[16] See Lawrence L. Stahlberger, *The Symbolic System of Mayokovsky* (The Hague, 1964), p. 106; Pertsov, *Mayakovsky, zhizn i tvorchestvo* [I], 196-197.

The ready alternation of grief and laughter, and the conversion of unassuageable grief into laughter, either desperate or cynical, is probably the true sense of these lines. Grief may in a sense be softened if one puts on an analgesic cloak of indifference, and this psychological device may explain Mayakovsky's apparent lack of sympathy toward sufferers who, as he himself would ultimately do, found release in suicide: he spoke scornfully of the Moscow Maria who killed herself for love of him, and he harshly refused sympathy to Yesenin.[17]

Again, the poet's personal makeup intrudes upon his wordplay, and this is the point at which he departs from his futurist colleagues. The theme of the poem is his own alienation from home, hearth, and family; his own death, in other words, as a child.

Midnight with its wet fingers reaches out for *him*, and for a battered fence, a metonymy that associates the poet with a dilapidated city scene and a derelict situation. The mad cathedral, with drops of the downpour on its bald cupola, leaps up. Then for the first time Christ enters Mayakovsky's poetry in a series of religious images which foreshadow the personal Golgothas registered in many of the early poems:

> I see, Christ has escaped from his icon.
> The street-slush, crying, kissed
> The windblown hem of his garment.
> At bricks I bellow.
> The dagger of frantic words
> I plunge into the swollen flesh of the sky:
> "Sun!
> Father!
> At least thou have mercy and torment me not!
> My blood thou hast spilled pours down this nether road!"

These lines introduce a theme that will become a leitmotif in the work of the early Mayakovsky. The old Christ the Saviour is gone

[17] See Roman Jakobson, "Novye stroki Mayakovskogo," in *Russkii literaturnyi arkhiv* (New York, 1956), p. 200.

I will document later Mayakovsky's interest in Dostoevsky and affinity with him. It should be pointed out now that the line in question is strongly reminiscent of Lise Khokhlakova's remarks in *The Brothers Karamazov* on how she would enjoy watching the death of a crucified child: "He would hang there moaning and I would sit opposite him eating pineapple compote. I am awfully fond of pineapple compote." *Bratya Karamazovy*, Part IV, chapter 3.

from his icon-frame; the new Christ roams the city street, whose wet gutters, in search of healing, kiss the hem of his garment. That new Christ is the poet himself, and he is neither gentle nor forgiving but raises a fearful cry over his own and the world's suffering. Stretched from his gibbet (like the policeman in the introductory lines), his soul hanging like torn clouds on the rusty cross of the church tower, he echoes in a parodic paraphrase the words the Saviour addressed in his extremity to his Father in heaven. The cycle of poems thus begins and ends with a scene of crucifixion. The lines given above take up again the theme of children mutilated and dying; but now the child is the Son himself, Mayakovsky, and the one who "spills his blood" is his own Father. He addresses a plea to "time," whose slow passage and unsatisfactory work is suggested in the epithet "lame icon-dauber," to paint his countenance into the vacant icon frame, not as a proper Christ but as "the little freak of the times" (*urodets veka*). After a succession of extravagant images and jarring sound effects, the poem ends with two quiet lines that express an ultimate degree of loneliness:

I am alone, like the last eye left
To a man on his way to join the blind.

This series of poems marks a new level of maturation in Mayakovsky's poetic style, and the first appearance of the poet himself as a substitutionary sufferer. The city—some critics speak of the "myth" of the city in Mayakovsky—is now no longer a source of poetic *nature-mortes*, but the arena of a lonely crucifixion, and the poet feels a kind of cosmic obligation to take upon himself its ineluctable misery. We have noted that the city's gutters (the Biblical woman's "issue of blood"?) kiss the hem of his garment, and he is the only one who offers them a "cure"—through his verses. It is essential to Mayakovsky's "myth" that he—a Christ in motley and a poet—brings purification to a city steeped in human suffering. And it is necessary to point out that the vision of the city created in his poems dramatically negates his Marinetti-like prose statements on the modern metropolis and its "men of the future." At about this time he made a speech in Kishinev in which he said:

> Great cities have arisen with proudly soaring skyscrapers, great forests of chimneys, . . . netted bridges that leap over

rivers. . . . Expresses rush with mad speed, and not a spot of land is left that's free of the trace of automobiles. Like a graceful and light bird man has torn himself from the earth and hovers in the clouds in his aeroplane. . . . No, we don't need your poor old songs, capable only of making a man feel sentimental. . . . The man of the future should be hard, brave, daring, the master of life and not its slave.[18]

None of this ever appeared in any of his poems. But there were many Mayakovskys, and why should we apply to him the test of consistency? "Do I contradict myself?" he might have echoed Walt Whitman; "Very well, then I contradict myself. I contain multitudes."

Technically, the series *Me* represents an escape from the insistent iambic or amphibrachic measures of the early poems as well as a striking experiment with rhyme. The set of poems shows an effective mixture of conventional (syllabo-tonic) and modern (pure tonic) lines. Mathematical researchers offer us the bare statistical fact, however, that seventy percent of the lines are conventional.[19]

Continuing our examination of poems published in the futurist collections, we find that *The Croaked Moon* (*Dokhlaya luna*, August 1913) contained five new poems: "An Exhaustive Picture of

[18] Quoted in Kamensky, *Zhizn s Mayakovskim*, p. 103.

Concerning the last lines of the poem and the invocation to the sun, it might be pointed out that Freud has offered clinical evidence that the sun may stand as a father figure in cases of paranoid schizophrenia, and he reminds us of the widespread symbolism of the sun as father and "Mother Earth" as mother. One of the actual cases he describes involved a dialogue with the sun strikingly similar to the one reported in Mayakovsky's poem about the sun (see above, Chapter One) and in the last poem of the *Me* cycle: "Schreber has quite a peculiar relation to the sun. It speaks to him in human language, and thus reveals itself to him as a living being, or as the organ of a yet higher being lying behind it. . . . We learn from a medical report that at one time he 'used to shout threats and abuse at it and positively bellow at it . . . and used to call out to it that it must crawl away from him and hide.' He himself tells us that the sun turns pale before him." Freud's suggested interpretation is particularly interesting in view of the likelihood that Mayakovsky had experienced a measure of guilt and fear in connection with his father's death from an accidental infection that led to blood poisoning. (See above, Chapter Two). Sigmund Freud, *Complete Psychological Works* (London, 1958), XII, pp. 53-56, 80-82.

[19] N. Kondratov, "Evolyutsiya ritmiki Mayakovskogo," in *Voprosy yazykoznaniya*, No. 5, 1962, p. 105.

Spring" (*Ischerpyvayushchaya kartina vesny*), "From Weariness" (*Ot ustalosti*), "Love" (*Lyubov*), "We" (*My*), and "Noises, Noiselets, and Noisiks" (*Shumiki, shumy, i shumishchi*).[20] The first is a minor experiment in distributed rhyme. In "From Weariness" we have one of the rare occurrences of nature images in Mayakovsky's poetry, but they are used to create a graph of psychological pain. The poem is an invocation to earth, not as "mother," however, but as sister, as a feminine alter-ego, an "anima" figure in Jung's sense of the term, who embodies and shadows forth the poet's own suffering. The poet is a forlorn atheist, a brother orphan to his orphaned and wounded sister, the earth. Together, they are like horses whom death has saddled. He may find a mother some day, in the almshouse of the coming years, but for the moment he and his sister earth are entangled in ditches and muddy roads. In a remarkable line that recalls Khlebnikov's play with poetic etymology, the metaphoric structure is supported by a complex pattern of sound repetition: "*Dym iz-za doma dogonit nas dlinnymi dlanyami* (Smoke from behind the house catches us with its huge hands.)"

The brief poem "Love" is a succession of sexual metaphors—difficult to disentangle, but clear in their final import. "We" offers some unremarkable examples of phrases which reverse the order of syllables: *lezem zemle; doroga rog ada.* "Noises, Noiselets, and Noisiks" is an experiment in the verse rendition of the various noises of city life ("whisper of shoes, thunder of wheels"), and it recalls Khlebnikov in its manipulation of suffixes. Khardzhiev has pointed out[21] that both the ideas and the images of the poem are certainly connected with a manifesto published in 1913 (and immediately translated into Russian) by the Italian avant-garde composer Luigi Russalo entitled "The Art of Noise," in which he urged the importance of finding instrumental means for expressing in music the audible reality of the city: wagon wheels on pavement, streetcars, flags rustling in the wind, and so forth. Khardzhiev also quotes the composer Prokofiev on Italian instrumental innovations aimed at producing such effects.

Mares' Milk (*Moloko kobylits*, December 1913) contained the poem "The Huge Hell of the City" (*Adishche goroda*), a series of metaphors in four stanzas which adds further details to Mayakovsky's urban myth. Automobiles are "ruddy devils"; an old man

[20] The cycle *Me* was also reprinted here.
[21] "Zametki o Mayakovskom," p. 419.

weeps over streetcars; an airplane cries out and falls where the "wounded sun spills out its eye." And the last stanza sees the night in a sottish bed, drunk and obscene, its blanket of street-lamps crumpled up, while the moon, now feeble and unnecessary, has "hobbled off" (*kovylyala*) somewhere. This poetic vision of the city and of modern progress sharply contradicts, once more, the futurist mystique of mighty skyscrapers and bravely soaring airplanes.

"That for You!" (*Nate!*) and "They Don't Understand a Thing" (*Nichego ne ponimayut*) appeared in January 1914 in *Roaring Parnassus* (*Ryakushchii Parnass*). "That for You!" he had already introduced to the audience at the opening of a futurist cabaret, The Pink Lantern, in October 1913, and his reading of the poem created a public scandal. The four four-line stanzas at first sight seem no more than an extreme statement of the futurists' contempt for the bourgeois audience, and their routine invitation to catcalls and abuse. Written just before the start of the futurist tour of the provinces, it might be viewed as practice for that event.

Yet Mayakovsky has created in this poem an attitude and an image qualitatively different from that of other futurists, Russian, French, or Italian. Their baiting of the audience, their invitation to be hissed, was a public game whose rules both sides understood; the clamor that resulted was a source of amusement and satisfaction to everyone involved. But Mayakovsky in this poem, and in the poem "To You!" recited in February 1915 at the Stray Dog Cafe in Petrograd, abandoned the formal choreography of *épatage* to deliver a real affront, deeply serious and apparently intolerable, to his audience. The content of the poems and the audience reaction in both cases show that Mayakovsky had made a characteristic mistake: when he put himself and his own feelings of contempt into the poem, it became a real instead of a fictive insult. "The audience became furious. Deafening whistles could be heard, and cries of 'Down with him!' "[22] But Mayakovsky's mistake—his abandonment, at any rate, of the rules of the game—also made "That for You!" into a real poem instead of the formal exercise it might have been. For the first time Mayakovsky appears as the poet-martyr whose golden gift of words the bourgeois "mob" rejects, and whose tender heart (that "butterfly" [*babochka*]) they trample, "with boots or without." The audience

[22] Katanyan, *Khronika*, p. 49.

is a collective mass of ugly fat before which the poet vainly opens his treasure. He is a "coarse barbarian," who laughs at them and spits in their faces but at the same time wastes his gift upon them: "a spendthrift and wastrel of priceless words" (*beztsennykh slov mot i tranzhir*). The contrast of the poet, "whose only standard is his heart," with the vulgar philistine mob that reviles and persecutes him is an essential ingredient in Mayakovsky's image of himself and his destiny. The fact that he affronts them and invites their hatred is beside the point. They would not have understood him anyway.

"They Don't Understand a Thing" is similar in its emotional content, though it is a grotesque fantasy and not an address to an audience. Kruchonykh explained that it was "not a poem, but a trade signature appended to Larionov's picture 'The Barber.'" It may have been suggested by that picture, and its focus is visual as well as verbal.

> I went into the barber's and said, calmly,
> "Would you be so kind as to comb up my ears?"
> The smooth barber right away turned bristly,
> His face lengthened out, like a pear's:
> "Madman!
> Clown!"
> The words leaped out.
> Abuse hurled from squeal to squeal.
> And for a lo-o-o-ng time
> Somebody's head giggled
> Sticking up out of the crowd, like an old radish.

"They Don't Understand a Thing" is, like "That for You!" a statement of the poet's experience with the crowd whenever he tries a new phrase, or a new word, or a new idea. An effect of the grotesque is achieved by a series of vegetable similes: heads are pine cones ("bristly"), or pears, or old radishes. I shall have occasion later to point out certain affinities of Mayakovsky with Gogol. The device upon which this poem is structured recalls inevitably Chichikov's first impression of Sobakevich's head as a pumpkin, quickly transformed into a balalaika.

A teasing experiment first published in 1919 in the collection *Everything Written by Vladimir Mayakovsky (Vsyo sochinyonnoe Vladimirom Mayakovskim)* betrays a much earlier date of composition by the internal evidence of its broken rhymes, its "signboard" orientation, with detached and floating letters, and its effort, in imitation of certain contemporary painters, to convey in a poem a sense of movement against an urban background. "In an Auto" (*V avto*) motivates its broken rhymes by the passing snatches of conversation heard from a moving automobile. The total effect is not unlike that of Natalya Goncharova's "The Cyclist," painted early in 1913.[23]

"The Fop's Blouse" (*Kofta fata*), "Listen!" (*Poslushaite!*), "But Anyway" (*A vsyo-taki*), and "Petersburg Again" (*Eshcho Peterburg*), all written in the late winter of 1913, were published in No. 1-2 of the *First Journal of the Russian Futurists*, in March 1914. "The Fop's Blouse" presents one of the poet's self-images: stroller of city streets, fop, defiant rebel, lover of women, and bringer of verbal gifts both pretty and useful. In the first lines of the poem he converts into quasi-literal meaning—in the usual terminology, he "realizes"—the banal metaphor of the "velvety voice": "I shall make myself some black pants out of the velvet of my voice," and develops a new metaphor by extension: "and a yellow blouse out of three yards of sunset." The duality of Mayakovsky's character, a point upon which he himself insisted, is nowhere better illustrated than in this poem, with its high charge of courage and confidence. The city street, the scene of the poet's lengthy walks, receives a cosmic elevation: "Along the world's boulevards, down its smooth-polished strips I shall stroll along, Don Juan and fop."

The three other poems published in the *First Journal of the Russian Futurists* are important for a number of reasons, but chiefly because in them God the Father appears for the first time in Mayakovsky's poetry. Christ had entered the poet's city in the *Me* series, and the "Father" was also invoked as the cause of suffering; now the source of creation becomes a character in the story of the poet's life. The struggle with the idea of God grew into a major preoccupation of the young Mayakovsky, and we shall see that, just as there were many Mayakovskys, so there were many images of the deity in his poetry. Stahlberger offers the interesting thought that the young Mayakovsky rejected God the Father as the author of an intolerable world, but accepted and indeed

[23] *PSS* (1935), 390, and Camilla Gray, *The Great Experiment: Russian Art 1863-1922* (New York, 1962), Plate xx.

took unto himself the figure of Christ, who suffered and died for the world.[24] But as a matter of fact the Creator's image is not invariably a negative one in his prerevolutionary poetry. In these three poems he is a sympathetic, if sometimes pathetic, figure. "But Anyway" announces that Mayakovsky is the poet of the city's prostitutes and syphilitics, and that on the last day they will offer him, the poet, to God as their justification:

And God will cry over my book!
No words—just spasms all stuck in a knot;
And he'll run about heaven with the book of my poems under
his arm,
And, all out of breath, he'll read them to his acquaintances.

The deity is obviously a decent fellow, full of sympathy for his creatures and sensitive to poetry; given to rather ridiculous enthusiasms, however; possibly a bore.

"Petersburg Again" shows a different physiognomy of God. Its two four-line stanzas conjure up a fog hanging over the roofs of the city like a cannibal that devours unappetizing people. The sound of public clocks striking five and then six "hovers" (*navis*) over us like a rude word. And, in consonance with this gray misery of sight and sound: "From the sky some kind of trash looked down, / Majestically, like Leo Tolstoy." *Dryan*, which I translate "trash," would seem a negative, quite possibly a blasphemous, epithet if applied to the Creator; the Russian censors, divining this, required that the phrase "from the sky" be changed to "from the roofs," which actually improved the poem by introducing a metonymic contiguity of the Creator with his creation while there could still be no doubt, given the image of Leo Tolstoy, that the poem spoke of God. The final line, moreover, relieves the tension by introducing a venerable father image familiar to everyone: the gray-bearded didactic countenance of Leo Tolstoy, a somewhat ridiculous figure from the futurists' point of view, one already thrown overboard from modernity's steamship.

"Listen!" is one of Mayakovsky's finest poems, in both content and form. The form-content dichotomy is less than usually valid as applied to this poem, however, since its form—a broken rhythm of alarmed questions and agitated, half-spoken thoughts—carries the poem's sense of worried wonder about the origin of the world.

[24] Stahlberger, p. 69.

Listen!
You know—if they light up the stars—
That means—somebody needs them?
It means—someone wants them to be there?
It means—someone calls that spit pearls?
And struggling his way
Through the blizzards of noontime dust
Tears his way in to God
Afraid that he may be late,
Sobs
Kisses his veiny hand
Begs him
That there absolutely must be a star—there must!
Swears
That he can't bear this starless misery!
And afterward
He walks about anxious
But outwardly calm
And says to someone
"Well—it's all right now?
You're not scared?
OK?!"
Listen!
You know—if they light up the stars—
That means—somebody needs them?
That means it's necessary
That every night above the roofs
At least one star should shine?!

It is probably a mistake to read this poem, as Maurice Bowra does, as an ironic answer to the theological argument for the existence of God based on the evidence of design in the universe. The poem offers not an argument or the answer to an argument, but a set of questions. Why are the stars there? Who put them there? Does the fact that they exist mean that somebody had to want them? Did motive and purpose accessible to human minds or human hearts enter into their creation? Can you imagine a totally dark night sky, and wouldn't it scare you? Doesn't there have to be at least one? The final lines repeat the question with which the poem opens, and after his experience with the thought of a starless night, the poet is almost ready to convert his questions into statements. The form of the question is such that the conversion can be accomplished by a single shift of intonation, and the last lines seem to hover between doubt and conviction.

God's image here is infantile and appealing. You can rush in to see him—if the problem is pressing—without ceremony. His hand is like an old man's, with an intricate protuberance of veins and sinews, and you can cover it with tears and kisses. If things are really bad you can tell him straight out that you just can't stand it. That the infantile supplicant is the poet himself is strongly suggested in the line that pictures him walking about "anxious, but outwardly calm."

The stars are important in Mayakovsky's poetry. If there were no stars, *A Cloud in Pants, Man, About That,* "To Sergei Yesenin," "It's After One," and some others would have had to be different in crucial ways. A universe with stars in it, we may say, was a necessary design for the purposes of Mayakovsky's poetry, and this argues a kind of intimacy with and dependence on a natural phenomenon that had already impressed too many poets and ought therefore to be treated with contumely by a futurist. "Who needs those gobs of spit?" As a matter of fact, Mayakovsky in this poem is offering a correction to the anti-aesthetic blasphemies of Burliuk and the *poètes maudits,* who rejected such conventional poetic stuff. The stars are not "gobs of spit," or "pockmarks in the sky," but a mysterious mitigation of the night's darkness; and maybe necessary. Once again Mayakovsky's unlettered genius questions a literary pose as though it were meant seriously.

"Listen!" presents the basic metaphysical riddle in terms of a child's wonderment and fear. It is the first poem in which the lyric hero's suffering transcends his conventional urban stage setting, moving out into the universe itself in an infantile search for a father and first cause; in this the poem anticipates both *A Cloud in Pants* and *Man.* It does not have the effect of a satire on conventional religious belief; rather, it leaves the poet and the reader in a state of puzzled alarm, softened, it is true, by amusement at the translation into primitive terms of the causality argument.

The poem's complex and tight structure is concealed by Mayakovsky's characteristic device of breaking his lines into natural conversational phrase patterns that seem to, but do not, abandon the strophic system. Properly analyzed, "Listen!" is a poem of four stanzas of four lines each in a basically accentual meter, following the rhyme scheme *abab/cdcd/acac.* By dividing the lines into phrase patterns instead of stanzas, Mayakovsky achieves an effect of rising agitation over the questions posed by the universe.[25]

The poem "Listen!" marks a turning point in Mayakovsky's early career. He now moves out of the parochial self-publications of the futurist group to find acceptance in a number of journals: *New Life (Novaya zhizn), Virgin Soil (Nov), The Theater in Caricature (Teatr v karikaturakh),* and, most important of all, the journal *New Satirikon (Novyi satirikon)*, which published twenty-six of his satirical poems from 1914 to 1917. But before that important turn in his writing career, Mayakovsky produced a play that stands as a kind of summation of his futurist period, and at the same time points ahead to the principal concerns of his later work.

2) The *Tragedy*

The drama entitled *Vladimir Mayakovsky: A Tragedy* was produced in St. Petersburg in 1913. In the production of the *Tragedy* the arts of poetry and painting were in close collaboration. Its performances were sponsored by the avant-garde painters' organization, the Union of Youth, and one of the earliest statements about it came from the painter Kazimir Malevich, who wrote to Matyushin in the summer of 1913 that "Mayakovsky is producing such a drama that there'll be no end of enthusiasm."[26] Two artists belonging to the Union of Youth, Filonov and Shkolnik, provided the stage settings and the sandwich-board "costumes." The play was part of a joint futurist theatrical enterprise, since its performances (December 2 and 4, 1913) alternated with Kruchonykh's "opera" *Victory over the Sun (Pobeda nad solntsem),* for which Matyushin wrote the music and Malevich provided stage settings that are regarded as the germ of the new "suprematist" style in painting.[27] The music and settings had much greater interest than the near-nonsense of Kruchonykh's libretto on the conquest of the sun by the "strong men" of futurism.

Mayakovsky's work has many curious affinities with classical Greek tragedy.[28] The title itself, *A Tragedy*, immediately suggests such a connection. With the exception of the poet, all the actors

[25] G. S. Cheremin provides an excellent formal analysis of the poem in his *Rannii Mayakovsky*, p. 82.

[26] *PSS* (1935), I, 391.

[27] Gray, p. 136.

[28] See Stahlberger, pp. 20-43.

wear "masks"—cardboard signs—that mark their symbolic character and function in the play. Violent events take place off-stage and are reported in lengthy monologues. Many lines are spoken by all the characters together in a chorus-like recitation. An almost comic suggestion of the classical world is the appearance of the Poet—Mayakovsky—in the second act wearing a toga and crowned by a laurel wreath.

No information external to the play suggests that Mayakovsky was interested in the Greeks at this time, or that his intention was to model his work on Aristotle's formulas, but the play itself offers overwhelming evidence that Greek drama suggested to him a framework for the expression of the suffering and tragedy of modern man, trapped and mutilated in his great cities. Indeed, the play produced a kind of catharsis of emotion in some members of its first audience, one of whom reported:

> From the wings there slowly filed out, one after another, the cast of characters: cardboard, doll-like figures. The audience tried to laugh, but the laugh was suddenly broken off. Why? Because none of it was funny—it was terrifying. Hardly anyone in the audience could have explained why. . . . I had come to make fun of a clown, and when the clown suddenly started talking about *me* the laugh froze on my lips. . . .
>
> You couldn't understand anything. . . . The futurist group consisted of young people. . . . Of course they played poorly and pronounced their lines indistinctly, but they had something that came from the heart. . . . During the performance my eyes twice filled with tears. I was moved and touched.[29]

But Mayakovsky could follow Aristotle only part of the way. Greek drama takes for granted the existence of a world external to the poet, and of real characters in conflict. That world is the objective arena of a struggle which, though dominated by fate, engages a multiplicity of distinct beings who contend over mighty matters. But in Mayakovsky's play only the poet exists authentically, and the arena of conflict is his own mind. The separate characters, as we shall see, are that mind's detached fragments. In this respect, perhaps, Mayakovsky's *Tragedy* is closer to expressionist drama than to the Greeks. The psychic disturbance of

[29] A. A. Mgebrov, "Tragediya Vladimira Mayakovskogo," in *Mayakovsky v vospominaniyakh sovremennikov*, pp. 111-112.

the main character determined both the nature of the setting and the dreamlike quality of his other selves.

The author, producer, and director, as well as the central character for whom the play was named, is Vladimir Mayakovsky the Poet, who appeared against a backdrop which represented "a city with its spiderweb of streets." The painted scene contained the ingredients of a real metropolis—chimneys, houses, streets, signs—in a distorted chaos of color and shape. With the Poet was his "Acquaintance" (*Znakomaya*), a female figure twelve feet tall, who "has no lines," and whose unveiling in the course of the first act produces an effect of "terror." This female companion, a grotesque idol without worshippers, is the cardboard incarnation of that mystical feminine essence that figured in the thought of Vladimir Solovyov as Sophia, the Divine Wisdom, and in the poetry of Aleksandr Blok as, successively, the Beautiful Lady, the Unknown One (*Neznakomka*), and Russia herself. In his own lyrical drama *The Puppet Show* (*Balaganchik*), Blok had himself metamorphosed his "Beautiful Lady" into a cardboard doll; in Mayakovsky's gross female "Acquaintance" she is mute and mysteriously repellent, and is at last abandoned by the characters in the play.

The *Tragedy* is in two acts with a prologue and an epilogue, both spoken by Vladimir Mayakovsky. Among the cast of characters there is an old man with dry black cats; a man missing an eye and a leg; a man without an ear and a man without a head; a man with a long face; a man with two cardboard kisses; three women, one with an ordinary tear, another with a little tear, the third with a huge tear; in addition to all these there is "an average young man." The play is a "monodrama" in the sense that there is nothing in it that is not Mayakovsky himself. Both Livshits and Shklovsky have pointed out that there is only one "personage" in it, Vladimir Mayakovsky, and that he "dealt himself out" on the stage in the form of various doll-like bits of cardboard.[30] Livshits, who was his close friend at the time, described Mayakovsky's childish delight at his inventions and his possessiveness about them: "I understood only much later that there was something Hoffmannesque about this meeting of Mayakovsky with his own lyric images, embodied in concrete things."[31]

[30] Shklovsky, *O Mayakovskom*, p. 55.
[31] *Polutoraglazyi strelets*, p. 186.

Not only do the characters and their speeches reflect Mayakovsky, but many of the props and some of the sound effects were gathered up from his own lyric poems or from his speeches of the period. At the "beggars' holiday" that opens the first act, the assembled cripples eat iron herring off street signs, a huge golden bread loaf, and folds of that sunset yellow three yards of which had gone to make the poet's blouse. There is an old man who strokes dry black cats in order to produce electricity, an image repeatedly used in his speeches. At a high point of danger and alarm a downspout pipe plays a long, slow note, and sheet-iron roofs begin to howl. And Mayakovsky's self came accoutered in his customary yellow blouse with black stripes, and frock coat and top hat. The play is made of his life's external trappings as well as of his anxiety and frustration.

At the time he was writing the *Tragedy*, Mayakovsky produced three articles on the general subject of the theater; and while they offer no thoughts on Greek tragedy, they do express distaste for contemporary realism in the theater, and one of them offers the following recipe for a play that would combine the ingredients of ballet and trans-sense language. He speaks of that special art of the actor, wherein ". . . the intonation even of a speech that has no special meaning, and the invented but rhythmically free movement of the human body, give expression to powerful inner emotions (*perezhivaniya*)."[32]

This statement, together with references in the same article to the Shakespearean stage and the Oberammergau Passion Play, provides a slender programmatic link to the theatrical method of the *Tragedy*. The speeches he devised for it do, however, have meaning, a circumstance that elicited a mild futurist rebuke from Matyushin, who wrote that Mayakovsky "nowhere disjoins the word from sense, nor utilizes its self-oriented sound."[33]

The play does give expression to "powerful inner emotions." It introduces the motif of suicide, hereafter a recurrent one in Mayakovsky's poetry. In fact there is reason to believe that his conception of the *Tragedy* grew out of thoughts of suicide, since its original title, *The Railroad*, was probably connected with the death of a student lodger in the Mayakovsky apartment, who had

[32] *PSS*, I, 276.

[33] In *Pervyi zhurnal russkikh futuristov* (Moscow, 1914), Nos. 1-2, p. 15; as quoted in Pertsov [I], 214.

thrown himself under a train.[34] And the last lines of Mayakovsky's prologue announce the poet's intention to:

> Lie down
> bright
> in clothing made of laziness
> on a soft bed of genuine dung.
> And quiet,
> kissing the sleeper's knees,
> The wheel of a locomotive will hug my neck.

The play is about people who live in the city and are enslaved to objects, to "things" that have no mind or heart, though "they may have ears where people have eyes," or vice versa. These people are crippled, wounded, and afraid, and they bring to the poet their suffering, their fright, and their tears. The man with three dry old cats counsels rubbing such animals, for the sparks that these living creatures give out may run trains and light the cities of the future. God, he says, must be out of his mind with all his talk of vengeance upon human beings whose poor little souls wear only worn-out sighs. The earless man tells of cripples in the city (they develop from a woman's spittle) where legends of agony grow, where the chimney pots do a wild dance, where the side streets have their sleeves rolled up for a fight, where melancholy grows like a tear on the mug of a crying dog. The Poet then instructs his people that they are nothing but "bells on God's dunce cap" ("As flies to wanton boys are we to the gods; They kill us for their sport"), and he avers that though he has travelled much he has never found a soul to insert in the wound of his lips. (Once he thought he had found one. It wore a blue dressing gown and said, "Come in and sit down. I've been waiting for you. Won't you have a cup of tea?") A passage follows which presents in sharp form the psychological dilemma embodied in the line, "I like to watch children dying." The passage also underlines the method of the play, and the identity of the characters with their author:

> I am a poet
> I've erased the distinction
> Between my face and other people's faces.

[34] L. Mayakovskaya, "Detstvo i yunost V. Mayakovskogo," *Molodaya gvardiya*, No. 2, 1937, p. 91.

I sought my sisters in the decayed matter of morgues.
I have kissed the sick most gracefully.
But today
Onto a yellow bonfire
Hiding my tears deeper than the sea,
I shall throw my sisters' shame
And gray mothers' wrinkles . . . (203-212)

The sense of suffering and pain is so acute in the Poet that he hardens himself against it, prepares himself to be indifferent, even cruel.

When the Poet unveils his "female acquaintance," the huge woman, the effect on the stage is, as his direction indicates, "frightening," and he utters a desolate aside to the audience:

Ladies and Gentlemen!
They say
that somewhere
—maybe in Brazil—
there is one happy man! (215-219)

At this point another Mayakovsky enters the stage in the shape of "an average young man," who, not quite understanding what is going on, is horrified at the thought of destroying "mothers" and the accumulated culture of the ages. Things are not really so bad, for he himself has invented a machine to cut up chops automatically, and a friend is working on a trap for bedbugs. Moreover, he has a wife, who will soon have a son or a daughter. It's terrible to talk like this, he says. They should let things be as they are and should be, for he has a sister, named Sonya.

The average young man is the Mayakovsky who believes in love and family life and who made optimistic speeches on the megalopolis of the future with its express trains, airplanes, and skyscrapers. He will appear again in 1918 as the "very ordinary man" in the play *Mystery Bouffe* (*Misteriya-Buff*) who promises the proletarians miracles of production in the communist future.[35] In the *Tragedy*, however, *that* Mayakovsky suffers an absolute rebuff. "But," the Poet says to him, "if you had been hungry as I have been, you would devour the distant skies as the sooty mugs of factories devour them." The man with a long face says, "If you

[35] See below, Chapter Eight.

had loved as I have loved, you would murder love." The man missing an eye and a leg announces that "on the streets, where the faces, like a burden, are all exactly the same, old lady time has given birth to a huge, mouth-twisted rebellion! Before the snouts of crawling years, old residents of the earth have grown mute, and anger has blown up rivers on the foreheads of cities—thousand-mile-long veins. Slowly, in horror, the straight arrows of hair are raised up on the bald crown of time. And suddenly all things have shed the ragged habiliments of their worn-out names."

We note that a purely literary rebellion, the futurists' rejection of all outmoded vocabulary, takes metaphoric shape in the *Tragedy* as an uprising of the objects themselves against their status and definition, and as part of the general revolt against an unacceptable existence. The whole of the first act may be taken as an allegory of a revolution in the course of which even objects rebel: trousers run away from a fainting tailor; a drunken bureau tumbles out of the bedroom; and corsets climb down from the store-sign "Robes et modes." This is the clear mark of Mayakovsky: he metamorphoses the literary into the literal.

The second act reveals a post-revolutionary city, the pregnant stage direction for which is "boring" (*skuchno*). The Poet has been elevated to the status of a prince and appears in his toga and laurel wreath. The crowd presses in to worship him; the people are bearing gifts. A woman brings him a tear. A second whose son has died brings him another tear, which would serve, she says, as a nice silver ball for his shoe buckle. There is a man with two kisses, who tells how, in women's boudoirs, "factories without smoke or smokestacks," millions of little kisses are manufactured, "by the fleshy levers of smacking lips." In a surrealist scene a kiss grows ears and cries out "Mama," then in a moment grows huge and fat and furious. The man involved decides he must hang himself. Then a mass of children-kisses runs onto the stage and each deposits before the Poet—a tear. They depend on the Poet—"because he is the only one who can sing songs"—to take upon himself all their suffering, and he does. He gathers up their tears and packs them into his bag—the metaphor "to bear suffering" is realized in the pack of tears on his back. Then he announces that he must abandon the laurel wreath, his happiness, and his throne, in order to carry off these tears to the farthest north, where "in the vise of endless melancholy, with the fingers of waves, eternally, cruel ocean tears its breast. I will reach my goal, tired out, and in my last delirium will cast your tears to the dark god of storms, at the very source of beastly faiths."

The hopes of the revolution are frustrated, and so is the Poet's love. The sexual business of women is symbolized by gobs of spit that grow into cripples, or kisses that develop into fat beings. Women are odious and sad. The Poet's girl friend is a huge doll dressed in rags, who frightens all of his various selves when he tears the veil from her. Disdain for women was a fashionable futurist pose, but Mayakovsky's work reflects a real problem. Shklovsky offers a number of cryptic remarks on the meaning of the *Tragedy*:

> The poet himself is the theme of his poetry.
>
> The poet deals himself out on the stage, holds himself in his own hand, as a gambler holds cards. Here's Mayakovsky the deuce, the trey, the jack, the king. The stake is love. And the game is lost.
>
> The "man with a long face" says,
>
> Out of my soul
> You can also make
> Such lovely skirts!
>
> That's Mayakovsky's theme.[36]

Mayakovsky's major poems of the prerevolutionary period all deal with the disappointment of love. Shklovsky's comments on the play may be read as an encoded message to the effect that the *Tragedy*, too, grew out of revulsion at an amatory episode, possibly a triangular one in which the poet was an unsuccessful rival, as was usually the case. Shklovsky alludes to certain literary works in the passage from which the above quotation is taken, implying that they are somehow connected with the *Tragedy*, and all the works he mentions reflect the real experiences of their authors. Bryusov's *The Fiery Angel*, for instance, tells of the author's own contest with Andrei Belyi for a woman who in the novel takes the form of a witch.

Clearly the game of love is lost in the play, but the poet's biography yields no clear evidence as to any real episode that may lie behind it. A stern critic might object that such evidence would

[36] Shklovsky, *O Mayakovskom*, p. 56.

shed no real light on the play, and indeed it is true that the *Tragedy* stands by itself as an emotional statement. Yet in Mayakovsky's work the facts of the poet's life are the substance with which he works; his poems are confessionals, and their catalogue of sins and penances need not be sealed from the student concerned about the genesis and nature of his art. Reliable evidence on the sexual life of Mayakovsky during the period of the *Tragedy* is not easily available; we must be satisfied with reasonable conjecture based on cryptically worded information. The poet's friend and futurist associate Benedikt Livshits in his *One-and-a-half-eyed Archer*[37] provides the scholar with a puzzle in the following metaphorical and cryptic narrative. Mayakovsky, says Livshits, was fond of reciting Severyanin's lines, "Since the time that all men died / Women's pleasure is in war. . . ." Livshits goes on: "Why should a person so persistently savor the prospect of the disappearance of all males from the earth, I thought. Might this not be evidence of what Freud calls an 'inferiority complex,' a consciousness, no doubt only passing, of one's own insignificance?"

Livshits voiced his suspicion to Mayakovsky and was surprised to find that he had "hit the mark":

> It was as though he couldn't bring himself to disclose his secret in the city, where he was on intimate terms with every cobblestone and brick, so he impetuously carried me off to Sokolniki. There, at an already empty villa, in the abandoned house where we settled ourselves for the night, he confessed to me—what?
>
> A trifle. Something that wouldn't have worried a high-school boy of the fourth form.
>
> Unexpected combinations often produce an impression of supernatural depth and magical power. Faust's velvet blouse is replaced by Doctor Badmaev's Tibetan powders.[38]
>
> Isn't that why Mayakovsky was convinced that Rimbaud, blended with a rugged military barracks, should produce an astonishing curative effect?
>
> I didn't think I had the right to disturb his conviction, and so with a clear conscience I shared with him the pretended

[37] Livshits, pp. 161-162.

[38] Badmaev was a doctor who practiced "Tibetan medicine," and provided unorthodox and probably worthless remedies for all kinds of ailments. His pills and powders were much in vogue at the Russian court, and he even wielded some political power. See V. P. Semennikov, ed., *Za kulisami tsarizma* (*Arkhiv tibetskogo vracha Badmaeva*) (Leningrad, 1925).

experience not only of a veteran who had seen plenty, but of a habitual user of the diabolical *tisanes*, one who preferred a "season in hell" over a trip to the waters.

Livshits never provides a direct answer to the question "What was Mayakovsky's secret?" but he offers teasing hints. The fact that it wouldn't have worried a school boy suggests an adolescent sexual practice of some kind. The apparently far-fetched references to Rimbaud and a "season in hell" encourage the speculation that adolescent homosexual experiences might have upset Mayakovsky. "Badmaev's powders" and the search for some kind of "curative effect" remind us of what we know from other sources, namely that the poet was a hypochondriac, neurotically concerned about his health and fearful of infection. Other friends of the poet have suggested that his "secret" was a case of gonorrhea.

Of course, it would be absurd to suggest that Mayakovsky was a settled homosexual, though he had friends who were, notably the poet Kuzmin, to whom he wrote a hitherto unpublished couplet in the "album" of the artist Sudeikin:

> How pleasant at an evening on the Field of Mars
> To imbibe the heady rum of Kuzmin's talk.[39]

The treatment of women in the *Tragedy* strongly argues that he was at that time in violent recoil from boudoirs, dressing-gowns, and kisses, together with their consequences in pregnancy and procreation, possibly even infection. The "average young man" cherishes sister, mother, wife, and family, but Mayakovsky's other selves rebuke him, and they carry off the "enormous woman" on their shoulders and throw her away. Livshits' reminiscence, taken together with the *Tragedy*, throws new and unexpected light on Mayakovsky's psychic makeup. Perhaps he did "contain multitudes"; perhaps he was, in a manner of speaking, omnisexual.

In the *Tragedy* Mayakovsky gathered up in grotesque images the human pain that he found in the city and took that pain upon himself as a burden of suffering. The *Tragedy* continues the myth of Mayakovsky as Christ that emerged in the last poem of the *Me* cycle, where Christ fled from his icon-frame, and the Poet offers

[39] I am indebted to I. S. Zilbershtein for calling my attention to this couplet. The Russian original is "Priyatno v marsovom pole vecherom / pit Kuzmina rechi rom."

to replace him with his own image: "the little freak of our day." The *Tragedy* is replete with disturbed echoes of New Testament phrases which elevate the Poet to the status of teacher and savior. "Come unto me all ye who have shattered silence, who have found that the noose of days is tight"; "I see, on the cross of your [the Poet's] laughter a tortured shriek is crucified"; "Let us go to that place where for his holiness they crucified the prophet." The Poet even has his Gethsemane of doubt and fear: "Gentlemen, listen, I can't! It's all right for you, but what am I to do with all the pain!" And his journey to Golgotha: "I shall leave my soul on the spears of houses, shred by shred. . . . And with my heavy burden I shall go, stumbling." This startling analogy between the Poet and Christ is another link of the *Tragedy* to certain trends in German expressionist drama of the time.[40]

The image of the Poet as Christ reached its ultimate distillation in the poem *Man* (1916), where the stages of his life bear the titles "Nativity," "Life," "Passion," "Ascension," and "Return." Mayakovsky in the role of Christ is a dishonored prophet and teacher, but he is also, and primarily, one who suffers. His tender soul, hypersensitive to pain in both people and animals, can hardly endure the city-monster of his own times. Like the line "I like to watch children dying," the play offers an alternative to pain in images of harsh indifference: the cry crucified on a laugh, the shame of women tossed onto a bonfire. But in the end there can be no resolution except the poet's death.

The play is, moreover, a powerful initial statement of Mayakovsky's pessimism concerning humanity's estate and of the despair with which he viewed its prospects even after the violent revolutionary upheavals he anticipated and foreshadowed. The outcome of the revolution, in the *Tragedy*, as in *The Cloud, Man, The Bedbug, About That*, and indeed in his own life, is the recurrence of frustration in new forms. We note that the post-revolutionary city is "boring" (*skuchno*), and that its essential product is still human tears. Even before the revolution had occurred, Mayakovsky anticipated the revulsion at its final outcome so widespread among radical intellectuals in the west since the thirties. He was indeed a kind of prophet.

[40] On this aspect of German expressionist drama see Walter H. Sokel, *The Writer in Extremis; Expressionism in Twentieth Century German Literature* (Stanford, 1959), pp. 63-65.

Chapter Five

1915: THE CLOUD AND THE FLUTE

1) The Various Mayakovskys

That there were many Mayakovskys has now become a commonplace. There are two *loci classici* that elucidate the subject of his various and easily interchangeable selves, an article he wrote in 1915 entitled "About the Various Mayakovskys" (*O raznykh Mayakovskikh*), and a later statement as to the origin of the title *A Cloud in Pants* (*Oblako v shtanakh*). His explanation of the title is ironic and apocryphal, but it does reveal his view of himself:

> *A Cloud in Pants* was first called *The Thirteenth Apostle.* When I presented my work to the censor, I was asked, "What's the matter, do you want to go to jail?" I said, no, I didn't look with favor upon the idea. Then they cut out six whole pages, together with the title. That's how the problem of a title came up. They wanted to know how I could combine lyricism with coarseness, and I said, all right, if you like I'll be a madman, if you like I'll be most tender, not a man, but a cloud in pants.—Hardly anybody bought it, because the customers for verse in those days were mostly well-brought-up gentle ladies, and they couldn't buy it because of the title.[1]

The article elaborates on the nature of those "other" Mayakovskys who alternated with the tender lyricist.[2] There is a brash barbarian in a yellow blouse, a cynic who spatters people with grease spots, a "cabby" whose vocabulary shatters the calm propriety of decent houses, a literary huckster (*reklamist*) with his name in every paper, and—a cloud in pants.

Benedikt Livshits has left a vivid account of Mayakovsky's company behavior that bears out the self-accusation of barbarism and cynicism:

> At D.'s apartment on the Moika . . . we met several colorless young men and well-gotten-up young ladies. The latter Maya-

[1] Katanyan, *Khronika*, p. 77.

[2] *PSS*, I, 344-348.

kovsky treated, I don't know by what right, like the members of his harem, though he had met them for the first time. At table he peppered the hostess with cutting remarks, made fun of her husband, who was a quiet man and bore all of his insults without complaint . . . and when D., driven out of patience, dropped a remark about his filthy fingernails, he answered her with a frightful insult for which I thought we would all be asked to leave.[3]

Roman Jakobson has carefully analyzed Mayakovsky's dual personality as a poet, demonstrating in his work a regular alternation of lyric with political or historical themes: the lyric cycle of 1913-1915 is followed by *War and the Universe*; the long lyric poem *Man* (1916) by *Mystery-Bouffe* (1918) and *150,000,000* (1919); the tragic poem *About That* (1923) by *Vladimir Ilich Lenin* (1924). Jakobson's analysis perfectly fits the larger rhythm of Mayakovsky's work as a whole, but as we look closely we find a more rapid rhythm within certain periods in his writing career. During 1914 and 1915 Mayakovsky vacillated sharply between patriotic propaganda and topical satire on the one hand, and great lyric poetry on the other. While he was writing the *Cloud* and *The Backbone Flute* (*Fleita pozvonochnik*), poems not likely to achieve an immediate success, he offered his poetic gift for sale in the shape of jingoistic trash that he later tried to forget and would not republish in his collected works. This was his first brief venture into the production on demand of verse having an immediate and ephemeral purpose; in time this type of activity would consume a major part of his energy, and would even be dignified by a "theory."

His autobiography notes that he greeted the war in 1914 with great excitement. He was caught up in the mighty wave of patriotic and anti-German fever that infected all levels of Russian society in that year, although he later tried, in retrospect, to seem original and idiosyncratic:

War

I reacted with excitement to the war. First I only noticed its decorative and noisy aspects. Did posters on order, and of course very military ones. Then verse. "War Is Declared."[4]

[3] Livshits, *Polutoraglazyi strelets*, p. 124.
[4] *PSS*, I, 22.

August

First battle. War's horror came clear to us. War is repellent. The rear even more so. In order to talk about the war you have to see it. I tried to enlist as a volunteer. They wouldn't let me. An unreliable type.

So even Colonel Modle [chief of the Moscow Security police] did have one good idea.

Winter

Disgust and hatred for the war. "Ah, close them, close the eyes of the newspapers,"[5] and other things.

Totally lost interest in art.

Patriotic jingles to accompany propaganda posters occupied the poet from August to October 1914, and he even produced a number of drawings,[6] an enterprise in which he was joined by many artists of the Russian avant-garde: Malevich, Lentulov, Larionov, Burliuk, Chekrygin, and some others. The posters, called *lubki*, were primitive in content, and aimed at a wide and tasteless audience. The verses were on the same level: Austrians and Germans figure as repellent cartoon characters impaled on the bayonets or pitchforks of brave Russian soldiers defending the Slavic lands. The verses are a disgrace, but a disgrace shared by the literary elite of the day, most of whom—acmeists, symbolists, and futurists—produced during the early months of the war stirring calls to defeat the barbarians from the center of Europe; and when Ivan Bunin tells us that on the day war was declared Mayakovsky climbed up on the pedestal of the Skobelev monument in Moscow and shouted patriotic verse, we need not, even though the witness is prejudiced, be surprised or incredulous. Only very few held out.[7] To his credit, Mayakovsky felt from the very start of the war a secret horror at its blood and violence. Just as his Marinetti-like prose in praise of the modern city had been negated in his poems about the street and its people, so the jingoistic verse of 1914 is sharply contradicted in outlook and tone by such poems as "War Is Declared," and "Mama and the Evening the Germans Killed."

We note that he reported a sharp drop at this time in his interest in art. For a brief period at the end of 1914 he published in

[5] A line from "Mama i ubityi nemtsami vecher," I, 66.

[6] *PSS*, I, 451-452.

[7] I. Bunin, *Vospominaniya* (Paris, 1950), p. 240.

the liberal magazine *Virgin Soil* a series of articles on the war. These articles, like the posters, were agitational, but their level was markedly higher and they managed to propagandize not only the war but futurism, linking those two contemporary phenomena in curious ways. Three of the articles bore the title "Civilian Shrapnel"; the second was subtitled "Poets on Landmines," and the third, "To Those Who Lie with the Brush."[8] The point of those three articles is, briefly stated, that the futurists are more useful for the period of noise and war than are artists and poets of a calmer and more conservative stamp. He accepts the violence as a kind of Hegelian necessity in the movement of history toward perfection,[9] but offers the solemnly cynical thought that perhaps the war was invented just so that someone might produce a good poem. War is a "magnificent thing," because it threatens to dislodge the philistines who have dominated poetry and replace them with a poetic muse who "wants to ride the gun-carriage wearing a hat of fiery orange feathers" (of course we are reminded of a certain orange-yellow blouse).[10] The war will not only bury the old masters and the old poetry, but it will place a new stamp on the human psyche itself.[11]

The brief article "Now to the Americas!" calls attention to the prophetic utterances of Khlebnikov concerning the coming destruction of states, and his own *Tragedy*, which featured a "rebellion of things." Now, says Mayakovsky, life itself has legitimized us: "Under the yellow blouses of clowns were the bodies of healthy athletes, whom you need."[12] In the article "No Butterflies, but Alexander the Great" he attempts quite blatantly to capitalize on the war for the profit of his own group: "Of course what you consider to be poetry . . . should be forbidden in wartime, like night clubs and alcoholic beverages." A totally new cycle of ideas is invading the world, he says, and only words that are like shots can express them.[13] In the article entitled "Russia. Art. Us." he utilizes Khlebnikov's belligerent slavophile pronouncements and the primitivism of Goncharova to construct a specious case for futurism as pure Russian art unadulterated by the influence of "cultured" nations.[14] "War and Language" again draws on Khlebnikov's verbal inventiveness as evidence that the futurists foreshadowed catastrophic changes in the spoken language.[15] "The

[8] *PSS*, I, 302-308.
[9] *PSS*, I, 304.
[10] *PSS*, I, 307.
[11] *PSS*, I, 310.
[12] *PSS*, I, 311-312.
[13] *PSS*, I, 316-317.
[14] *PSS*, I, 319-320.
[15] *PSS*, I, 325-326.

Futurists" (*Budetlyane*) closely echoes Marinetti in its paean to war as "not senseless murder, but a poem about the free and exalted soul," and once again Mayakovsky argues that the new Russia will give birth to "futurist strong-men."[16] The articles in question assume an inevitable historical movement that will in the end justify the destructive nihilism of the futurists. A few years later, in 1918, he would claim the revolution as their literary patrimony, and attempt to exercise a kind of "dictatorship" over art.[17]

The journalist Mayakovsky seems shallow and self-serving. Sometimes his cynicism was open and vulgar, as in the poem "A Warm Word for Certain Vices" (1915) in which the "fast buck" is preferred over hard work, and the artist Vrubel is rhymed with "ruble," the only thing in which he supposedly (along with Pushkin and some others) believed.[18] That little poem celebrates the pure joy of separating acquaintances from their money at poker or some other friendly game, and it may commemorate the occasion on which he won those sixty-five rubles that took him to Finland and the resort area of Kuokalla in the summer of 1915.[19] There he visited and dined systematically with literary and artistic acquaintances, Kornei Chukovsky, the theater director N. N. Evreinov, the artists Repin and Puni. In the evenings he paced the seashore and, contending with the noise of the waves, composed *viva voce* his *Cloud in Pants*, usually scribbling the verses on cigarette boxes.[20] He made a special visit to Gorky at Mustamyaki in order to read him the burgeoning poem. This is what he wrote about that visit in his Autobiography (1922):

> Went to Mustamyaki. M. Gorky. Read him parts of the *Cloud*. Gorky was so deeply touched he cried all over my vest. My verses really moved him. I was a little proud. But I soon found out that Gorky sobs over any poetic vest.
>
> Anyway I still keep that vest. I could let somebody have it for a provincial museum.[21]

Gorky's own memory of that incident distributes the sobs differently. In a letter written to his friend and biographer Gruzdyov

[16] *PSS*, I, 332.

[17] See below, Chapter Eight.

[18] *PSS*, I, 86.

[19] *PSS*, I, 23.

[20] K. Chukovsky, *Repin. Gorky. Mayakovsky. Bryusov* (Moscow, 1940), p. 108.

[21] *PSS*, I, 23.

shortly after Mayakovsky's suicide, he described the visit and the reading of *A Cloud in Pants*:

> I liked his verses and he read very well; he even broke into sobs, like a woman, and this alarmed and disturbed me. He complained that a human being is "divided horizontally at the level of the diaphragm." When I told him that in my opinion he had a great but probably hard future, and that his talent called for a lot of work, he answered gloomily "I want the future today," and again, "Without joy I don't need any future, and I feel no joy." He behaved very nervously and was clearly deeply disturbed. He seemed to speak with two voices, in one voice he was a pure lyricist, in the other sharply satirical.—It was clear that he was especially sensitive, very talented, and—unhappy. . . .[22]

Of the two conflicting accounts Gorky's is the more reliable, since it is supported by other witnesses of Mayakovsky's poetic readings during the Kuokalla summer and by well-attested cases of emotional breakdown. The writer B. Lazarevsky gives a striking account of his Kuokalla poetry-reading, which he described as disturbing in its "sing-song style," and something like the performance of a "shaman engaged in incantation."[23] It was during this period, according to a number of knowledgeable reports, that Mayakovsky first attempted suicide.[24]

Gorky's statement regarding the "two voices" of Mayakovsky, the lyric and the satirical, was most perceptive. Shortly after the visit to Gorky the sixty-five rubles that financed his Kuokalla summer had been spent, as Mayakovsky put it, "without difficulty," and "in consideration of the need to eat" he began to write for the *New Satirikon* (*Novyi Satirikon*), a liberal journal of satire edited by the popular writer of very funny stories, A. Averchenko. He published altogether twenty-five short poems in that journal between February 1915 and February 1917, when new themes and new publishing outlets appeared. During the same period he labored over his four major poems, *A Cloud in Pants, The Backbone Flute, War and the Universe*, and *Man*, and

[22] *Perepiska Gorkogo s Gruzdyovym* (Moscow, 1966), p. 227.

[23] Katanyan, *Khronika*, p. 74.

[24] See Jakobson, "Novye stroki," p. 191. Soviet students of Mayakovsky are aware of these early episodes, but give no public attention to them.

produced a number of exquisite short lyrics, "How I Got to Be a Dog" (*Vot tak ya sdelalsya sobakoi*, 1915), "Lily-mine," "Fed Up" (*Nadoelo*), "To His Beloved Self the Author Dedicates These Lines" (*Sebe, lyubimomu, avtor posvashchaet eti stroki*, 1916), "To Russia" (*Rossii*, 1916), and some others, which we will examine below. In the pieces written for the *New Satirikon* Mayakovsky's characteristic voice and intonation can be clearly heard, but his metaphors are less bold, his syntax more nearly normal, and his rhythms not original; since money was a major consideration, these verses had to be reasonably accessible to the buyers. The experience was important in his development as a poet: he faced in writing those poems the problem of making himself understood to the general reader.

2) How the *Cloud* Was Made; and What It Said

The original title, *The Thirteenth Apostle*, and its subtitle, *A Tragedy*, hint that the poem was intended to develop the distorted religious theme of *Vladimir Mayakovsky, A Tragedy*, but the censorship inhibited the heterodox addition of a new apostle to the canonical twelve. In a preface to the first complete edition in 1918 Mayakovsky declined to restore the original title since he'd "grown used" to the new one,[25] but he had supplied a subtitle, *Tetraptich* (*Tetraptikh*), which still carries a religious overtone.

In that same edition, published soon after the revolution, Mayakovsky felt obliged to explain his poem: "I consider it a catechism of present-day art: 'Down with your love,' 'Down with your art,' 'Down with your society,' 'Down with your religion'—such are the four screams of the four parts." This exegesis is certainly ex post facto. The poem itself does not, as I shall try to demonstrate, offer any such clear-cut social message, and if we try to apply his catechism to the poem, we find it doesn't work. We must suppose that the poet re-interpreted his poem—and indeed it is rich with potential meanings—in the heat and exaltation of the revolutionary days. We shall see that the meaning of the four parts can be stated in terms of a different "catechism." The four parts can be said to be about love, art, revolution, and God, but the pejorative "your" doesn't fit them at all. The poet speaks rather with a certain inti-

[25] *PSS*, I, 441.

macy of "*my* love," and so forth, and what he says, if it can be reduced to prose, may be summed up as

My love is pain and frustration.
My poetry is a personal Golgotha, a crucifixion.
My revolution has been betrayed—and will be again.
My "father in heaven" doesn't exist—God is dead.

A curious revision in line 351 he made after the revolution and with the advantage of hindsight. He originally wrote that he could "see approaching in the thorny crown of revolutions, 'a *certain year*'" (*kotoryi-to god*, my italics). This he changed in the 1918 edition to "the year 1916"; since the revolution was already a fact, it was far better to have predicted its occurrence one year early than to let the record stand that he had only vaguely anticipated it. A prophet should try to be precise in his message, especially a futurist poet who had the example of Khlebnikov's predictions of disaster, based on mathematical calculation. If, on the other hand, he had inserted "the year 1917," this would have seemed suspiciously accurate, and no one would have been impressed.

The tragedy of which the poet speaks is love—or, more precisely, unsatisfied sexual desire, unrequited love: the enormous pain experienced by a huge sinewy clod, whose coarse bulk cries out for the soft and feminine. But the four parts extend the sources of his frustration to include his poetic career, his revolution, and his "father in heaven." In the poem he is a twice-rejected lover, a defeated revolutionary, an atheistic blasphemer whose curses are hurled at nothing at all, and a poet rejected by the mob. The fact that he is a self-conscious poet is always primary. The introduction to the poem is a programmatic announcement of his poetic style and a preview of his language, his imagery, and his rapid shifts of personality. He will taunt, wake up, insult (in the etymological sense—by stamping on it) the laggard thought of his readers; he will strike it with a bloody tatter of his own poet's heart. He is young, and there are "no gray hairs in his soul." A poet of the platform and the street, he "shatters" the world with the might of his voice. He moves serenely through the world, and in an echo of Walt Whitman, he "comes on handsome, twenty-two years old." Tough and hard, he pounds out his love on a drum. He says in line 8 that he has no tenderness; but in lines 21-26 he says:

If you like
I'll rage and roar on raw meat
—and then, like the sky, changing my hue—
if you like
I'll be unimpeachably tender,
not a man, but a cloud in pants. (21-26)[26]

The introduction is a prelude to the poem as a whole since it prepares the reader for a startling series of transitions from one emotional key to its opposite, from sinking despair to proud elation, from quiet reverence to fierce blasphemy. And the range of feminine objects who may learn love from his poem reaches the following contrasting extremes:

Come and study
you in cambric from a drawing room
proper little officer of the angels' league.
And you who calmly turn the leaves of lips,
Like a cook turning the pages of a cookbook. (16-20)[27]

The introduction also prepares us for the poem's imagery. Not only is the poet's love loud and raw and suitable for playing on a drum, but the poet himself is "all" love, if by love we understand carnal need. We shall examine in the body of the poem some remarkable cases of "realized" metaphor, a trope in which the poet naively accepts his own metaphoric assertion that A = B, and proceeds to describe B in literal detail. The introduction offers a remarkable example of what we may call a "realized" metonymy. The seething mass of flesh that "loves" is summed up in the lover's craving lips; his passion is such that *only* lips exist and the figure for a moment becomes a fact:

But you couldn't turn yourself inside out like I can
And just be pure lips and nothing else. (14-15)

Part I tells of his first rejection, by a "Maria" whom he met in Odessa. It may sound like raving, but it happened, it really happened—in Odessa. She said she'd come at four—but now it's eight, nine, ten. What we have here is a hyperbolized "stand-up." The evening moves away from the window, into the night's horror, morose, Decemberish. The candelabras laugh and neigh. He

[26] *PSS*, I, 175. [27] *Ibid.*

is nothing but a huge bundle of sinews, groaning and writhing. Of course it's well known that he's made of metal and that his heart is hard, but—and here another, deeper self speaks of what he really craves, alone with himself, at night:

> For one's self it's not important
> that he's made of bronze,
> that his heart is a hard iron clapper.
> At night what you want is
> to plunge your noise
> into something soft
> something feminine. (51-57)

Midnight is an assassin who caught up with him and cut him down. The scene is grotesquely distorted in sympathy with the man's inner misery, a device that once again marks Mayakovsky's affinity with expressionist poetry and drama. Gray raindrops, howling together, grimace hugely and frighten him—they look like the gargoyles of Notre Dame. Suddenly an irrepressible cry of hatred tears his mouth: "God damn you! Isn't that enough?" Then comes the first of the realized metaphors. Nervous agitation grows on him. A nerve moves very quietly, like a sick man getting out of bed; at first the nerve can hardly move, then he leaps up all excited; then some more nerves get up and do a tap dance; they dance so frantically that the plaster falls in the downstairs apartment; they dance until their legs give way under them.

The room, the objects in it, the hotel itself (for we learn that he is waiting for her in a hotel room) participate in the lover's desperation. Suddenly the door bangs, as though the hotel's teeth were chattering. In she comes at last, abrupt and cold as though to say, "*That* for you!" They have a brief conversation, outwardly matter-of-fact but covering a molten core. It is a shorthand sketch in which the whole scene and the history of the love affair is summed up in terms of its emotional highlights:

> "Look—
> I'm getting married."

(This while picking distractedly at her suede gloves.)

> "OK. Get married.
> That's all right.
> I can take it.

You see—how calm I am.
Like a dead man's
pulse." (117-124)

It is clear that she has been bought in marriage. She is conventional, obvious, perhaps cheap, a little vulgar, enamored of things (note the fine gloves). Her head is full of phrases:

Remember?
You used to say
"Jack London—
Money
Love
Passion"—
But I saw only one thing.
You were a Mona Lisa
that had to be stolen!
And somebody stole you. (125-134)

The shorthand account of old conversations reveals her flattery of the poet (Mayakovsky liked to think of himself as a Russian version of Jack London), as well as a mind circumscribed by cliché. Was such a type "worthy" of a self-acknowledged genius? That is part of his tragedy. That he should torture himself for *this*. Unaccountable! But such questions are clearly beside the point in the case of Maria, as of his other loves, all of whom are objects that excite an imperative carnal need.

The sense of abandonment and despair in love takes the form of another realized metaphor, rather, of a series of metaphors, one of them the elaborately developed figure of his poor miserable heart as a house on fire. The metaphors are intricate and rich; sometimes one leads into another and sometimes whole passages are implicitly metaphoric, or rather metaphoric by contagion with nearby metaphors that are quite explicit; sometimes a developed metaphor proliferates its own cluster of minor metaphors, each one triggered by a suggestion offered in the main metaphor. A case of lines that are metaphoric by contagion is the following:

Remember,
Pompeii perished
when somebody teased Vesuvius

Hey!
Ladies and gentlemen!
Admirers
of blasphemy,
crime,
and slaughter—
have you ever seen
the most awful thing of all,
my face
when I'm
perfectly calm? (143-156)

The explicit metaphor—he is a live volcano—governs the following lines: if he is a live volcano, then his moments of utter calm and quiet are the most fearful of all, because we know that there is a molten charge pent up in him, and unpredictable dangers are lurking there. The lines immediately following are also infected by the spreading volcano metaphor:

I feel
that "I"
am too small for my self.
Somebody keeps wanting to break out of me.
(158-161)

Those lines are especially moving in a larger context since they are prophetic of Mayakovsky's suicide; they are the lines that first occurred to Pasternak when he heard of the suicide. The important point here is that, once suggested, the image of bursting, tearing, leaping out of himself or his heart returns persistently.

Like the Homeric simile, Mayakovsky's metaphors sometimes draw so much attention to themselves that they tend to upstage his narrative. The poetic effect of "realization" is to breathe new life into a dead metaphor. He might have written that his heart was on fire, but such a line would hardly have been heard. What does he wish to convey? That his heart is suffering pain as the result of the frustration of desire. Emotional pressure is so great that it takes the form of physical symptoms. He feels a literal burning sensation where his heart is. He can hardly breathe. He's having visceral spasms. He can't stand it. Somebody had better do something: "Ma-a-a-ma! Call a doctor!"

No, not a doctor! The fire department. His heart is a building on fire. You hear the alarm bells and the apparatus and see the firemen in their gleaming helmets. You smell the fire (roast flesh?) and hear the prostitutes shrieking as they leap from the upper stories of this tall bordello. The firemen clamber up in their heavy nailed boots—but no:

> Don't wear boots!
> Tell the firemen:
> you climb a burning heart with caresses.
> I'll take care of it!
> I'll roll barrels of tears from my eyes.
> I'll brace myself against my ribs.
> I'll jump! I'll jump! I'll jump! I'll jump!
> Collapsed!
> But you can't jump out of your heart! (181-189)

The image of fire remains, but now it shifts to burning ships: the Lusitania sinking with no hope of rescue, its arms raised to clutch at deaf heaven; a ship on fire in a harbor, the glow from it reaching into quiet, respectable, bourgeois abodes. And Part I ends with a final cry—"to tell the ages that I am on fire."

Part II opens with the first in the series of sudden sharp shifts of mood upon which the poem is built. The hopeless creature who has just compared himself to a building in flames or a ship burned to the water's edge now trumpets his confidence:

> Praise me!
> I'm more than a match for the mighty.
> To everything that's been done
> I give the mark "nihil." (209-212)

The literary heritage in particular is of no interest to the young rebel, and here we have an echo of the futurist nihilism about culture and the "establishment":

> I don't ever
> want to read anything.
> Books?
> What good are books! (213-216)

The poem now provides relief from love in a practical discussion of poetry that dismisses its conventional subject matter, in particular, love. It is as a genius and radical innovator that the poet now contemplates himself. He claims the theme of the city as his own. As we know, this theme was not new: Mayakovsky had read Verhaeren and Bryusov and Blok, and he was well acquainted with Marinetti. But Mayakovsky adds a distinct note of his own to the treatment of the theme. Not only is the city street, with its beggars, prostitutes and consumptives and its weird cacophony, the source of much of his poetry, but it also figures in his work as one source of his suffering. And the suffering is original. The poet as such has taken on a function new to poets: he bears the modern city's burden of sin and misery, continuing his role as Christ-expiator. He weeps for and pleads the case of the legless and armless, and above all he pleads the case of the loveless. He hears the street's cry, "Help me!" to which other poets pay little heed. While poets work on their rhymes and rhythms: "The street writhes tongueless— / hasn't anything to shout or talk with" (231-232).

The poet of the second part scornfully rejects the gasping lover of the first, and all other poets who "boil up some kind of broth out of love and nightingales." His poetry is of and for the street. As in the poem *Me* the poet himself becomes the city: its throat is his throat, its streets are his body, and his chest has been trampled flatter than a consumptive's. The modern city is a new tower of Babel, and God punishes it by impoverishing its language. The harsh life of cobblestones and pavements has no poetry in it. God may advance in his wrath, but all the street can think of to say is "Let's go get something to eat!" Krupps and Krupplets have applied menacing grease paint to the city's face, but the mouth has only a few words, maybe two: "bastard, and borscht." Poets "soaked in tears and sobs"—and of course Part I has presented such a one—retreat from the city: "How can two such words sing of love and a lady and dewy flowerets?" And, bitter thing for Mayakovsky, the city's multitudes run after such poets begging them for their gift. Perhaps these lines were inspired by the popularity of Igor Severyanin, a matter that, as we shall see, caused Mayakovsky great pain. But the final sense of the passage is the rejection of poetry—"Books? What good are books"—in favor of gross reality, whether of a nail in one's boot, or of a factory. Mayakovsky admits that as a poet he himself is matchless: "The most golden-tongued . . . whose words give new birth to the soul and a birthday party to the body"; and yet he rejects his own gift: "The tiniest crumb of reality is greater than all I'll do or have done." Rejection of poetry, even its purest and best example, his own verse, goes beyond Marinetti and the futurist manifestoes in its sweeping rejection of all art, and foreshadows the nihilism of the twenties when he produced reams of stuff that did not even pretend to be art. In a strange travesty of Marinetti he sings the beauty of himself and all those like him who are prisoners of the "city-leprosarium," where money and filth ulcerate the body:

> We are cleaner than the blue air of Venice
> washed by both sea and sun.
> What does it matter
> that no Homers or Ovids
> knew of people like us,
> pockmarked with soot.
> I know
> the sun would dim, seeing
> the gold mines in our souls! (314-322)

Beggars though they are, they won't beg for alms. Each one holds in his own fist "the driving belts of this and other worlds." The latter image expresses limitless optimism regarding the human potential in the control of nature, and even of the universe itself, and suggests the possible influence of the philosopher N. F. Fyodorov, whose work, as we shall see, Mayakovsky knew.[28] By an arbitrary association, the poet is reminded of his "tour" of the provinces three years earlier. Once again a New Testament image carries the burden of emotion:

> That's what led me to my Golgothas
> on the stages of Petrograd, Moscow, Odessa, and Kiev.
> And there wasn't a one
> who
> didn't shout
> "Crucify him!
> Crucify him!" (329-335)

The "tour," then, was a futurist Golgotha in which the *outré* poet and irreverent innovator offered himself as a willing victim to the established literary priesthood. And they crucified him.

[28] See below, chapter 9. It has not heretofore been suggested that he knew Fyodorov at this early date.

But he also insists, given the context, that what made him go up the hill was not seeds to sow or sins to expiate, but his absolute belief in himself, his refusal to ingratiate himself or beg for mercy, his insistence on moving the levers of the world. He reaches out for transcendence and control.

The point is that poetry failed him. The crowd laughed at him and shouted him down. Beaten and kicked, he is like a dog once again. And Mayakovsky as a dog predictably has two personalities. In the very brief lyric "How I Got to Be a Dog,"[29] probably written early in July 1915, when he was finishing *The Cloud*, the poet reacts to the crowd's abuse with fang, claw, tail, and an angry bark. But here he is a dog that's all tongue, chastised and quieted by blows, dependent on his humans and ready to lick the hands that beat him:

> But for me,
> people,
> even those who hurt me,
> are nearer and dearer than anything.
> You've seen a dog
> Lick the hand that whipped it?! (336-341)

The failure of poetry leads to a sudden new change of key, a transition to thoughts of revolution, which he sees coming in a crown of thorns "in the year 1916." The biblical images now shift uncertainly. The poet is the harbinger of Christ, John the Baptist, and the Saviour himself is the revolution. But still the poet will not surrender the role of the crucified, and, as in the *Tragedy*, he suffers for the pain around him: "I am wherever pain is—anywhere; / on each drop of the tear stream / I have crucified myself." (353-355) But he is a Christ without humility, without gentleness, one who forgives nothing:

> I am wherever pain is—anywhere;
> on each drop of the tear stream
> I have crucified myself.
> Nothing must be forgiven any more!
> I've burnt out souls where gentleness grew.
> It was harder than taking
> a thousand thousand Bastilles!

[29] *PSS*, I, 88.

And when,
his advent
with riot proclaiming,
you come out to meet your savior—
for you I
will tear out my soul;
I'll stamp on it and trample it
till it spreads out big—
and I'll give it to you—a bloody banner. (353-368)

The lines hint at his besetting project, the sacrifice of his lyric self for the revolution, his "stepping on the throat" of his own song.

We note incidentally the recurrence of a favorite metaphor, with a new function. The soul of the poet becomes a banner for the revolution—in other words, a bit of textile is manufactured in the verse line out of something immaterial, a procedure analogous to the production of trousers out of the velvet of his voice, or a yellow blouse from a few yards of sunset. Note also that the poet's soul has a certain implied physical shape; it is bunched up, perhaps crumpled or tangled in itself; you have to stamp on it and straighten it out, and only *then* will it wave bright and bloody. The innocent-seeming lines offer a realized metaphor of the poet's own spiritual conflicts and inner entanglements, which he would overcome for the sake of the imminent revolution. Part II ends on this strong positive note: the poet's soul waving confidently in the wind.

But from the high elation of the revolution, Part III drops us suddenly into unmotivated thoughts of madness and images of despair:

Ah! Wherefore this,
whence this
brandishing of dirty fists
in the face of bright joy?
A thought of madhouses
came and curtained my mind
with despair. (369-375)

David Burliuk, who remarked quite correctly that everything in Mayakovsky's poetry is autobiographical, now appears in this poem. His one-eyed visage suggests the grotesque image of a man (Burliuk) scrabbling through the open hatch (his one eye) of a sinking ship. He crawled through, got up, approached, and said, with a gentleness surprising in a stout man, "Everything's fine!" Burliuk's encouragement had come to him as a word of hope escaping somehow from a total disaster, and the metaphor that transforms his eye into a hatch and has him literally crawl out of it is an example of how the poet uses a figure of speech to invent and concentrate upon a grotesque scene that contains elements of both dream and reality. But Mayakovsky treats the word of encouragement ironically:

> It's fine when the heart
> is shielded from inspection in a yellow blouse.
> It's fine
> when, in the teeth of the gallows,
> you cry out
> "Drink Van Houten's cocoa!" (390-395)

So the gaudy raiment of a clown-poet is actually a kind of armor, a shield behind which the sensitive heart hides itself. And he compares himself to the man who, according to newspaper accounts of the day, shouted an advertisement for a particular brand of cocoa just before his public execution, in return for which his family was given a tidy sum. Does this give us a view from within of the real emotional experience of those flamboyant appearances in the various cities of Russia? And yet in the next lines he *begins* to say that he would not exchange those bright and loud moments for anything in the world:

> And that second
> fiery-flashing
> loud
> I wouldn't exchange for anything
> I wouldn't. . . . (396-400)

But there is a nail in the boot, a grain of misery in his satisfaction. The phrase "I wouldn't" (*Ya ni na*) provides a negative association, since it rhymes with "Sever*yanina*":

> But out of the cigar smoke stretched
> like a long-stemmed liqueur glass
> the drink-sodden face of Severyanin.

How do you dare call yourself a poet
and grayly chirrup like a quail!
Today
you must
use brass knuckles
and cut yourself into the world's skull. (401-409)

A note is in order on Severyanin, whose face materializing in Mayakovsky's imagination poisons his memory of the "tour." Severyanin unquestionably had a talent for verse-making. An "ego-futurist," he celebrated in his skillfully turned poems the upper-bourgeois life of the cities: fine foods, expensive textiles for dress or decoration, dancing, riding, and the like. Mayakovsky admired and constantly recited Severyanin's poetry, but envied him his fantastic popularity, especially with female audiences. Undoubtedly the earlier lines about the street multitudes—students, prostitutes, businessmen—running after poets is a reference to Severyanin's eminently successful public recitations.

Livshits gives us a vivid sketch of Severyanin seated in state in his close, damp, and littered quarters in St. Petersburg, granting an audience to some female admirers, and he emphasizes that Mayakovsky was impatient to inherit all that.[30] He tells us also of a "duel" between the two in which they competed with their poems for the favor of an audience of ladies, but the duel, says Livshits, "ended in a draw." Moreover, on the futurists' "tour" of the provinces, Severyanin's recitations were greeted with favor by the provincial audiences, who could understand his verses but puzzled over those of Mayakovsky and Burliuk. But Severyanin broke with the group as a result of disagreement over the publicity-hunting antics I have already described,[31] and he continued with the tour of the provincial cities on his own. The abrupt outburst at Severyanin has a number of functions in the poem: it expresses Mayakovsky's discomfort at a memory of an unpleasant incident; it settles an old personal score against an envied rival; and, perhaps most important for the purposes of the poem, it confronts the elegant bourgeois lexicon of Severyanin's effete but eminently "singable" poems

[30] Livshits, p. 195.

[31] Khardzhiev, "Turne kubo-futuristov 1913-1914," p. 409. It should be noted that Severyanin had attacked Mayakovsky in verse, and that these and other references to Severyanin in Mayakovsky's poetry are items in a bitter polemic, the other side of which is usually ignored.

(indeed, he did sing them, sometimes holding a lily in his hand) with the linguistic resources of a "pimp and a card-sharp," and the brass knuckles of a street poet. Revulsion against Severyanin reaches a point of such severity in the following lines that Mayakovsky rejects emphatically *all* poets who are "damp with love"; and by implication he includes himself, who in the first part of the *Cloud* wanted to "groan out for the ages" that he is burning with love. In a megalomaniac image he now announces his mastery both of self and of the universe:

> You,
> damp with love,
> whose tears flow for the ages
> I resolutely leave,
> and in my wide open eye
> I place the sun,
> my monocle. (417-423)

The manic-depressive movement of the poem now hits upon an ultimate image of sexual satisfaction, an image that cancels out, even if only for a moment, the pain and loss of Maria with the ambitious day-dream of a man who would lie with his mother, the earth herself. In those lines the whole earth becomes a woman, her flesh quivering with the need to be taken; all things love him, and life is possible.

But suddenly (again, "suddenly") the sky darkens, rolls, and pitches. Thunder comes from the clouds and the sky takes on the metaphoric semblance of evil and monstrous characters: the "iron" Bismarck, and the general who liquidated the commune. If you think that's the sun "gently touching the café's cheek," don't be deceived: it's the monstrous murderer Galliffet! Once again horror lurks behind the world and its weather, even when the latter seems mild and gentle. So Mayakovsky must have a revolution. The call to revolution paraphrases the Saviour's words:

> Come, ye who are hungry,
> sweaty
> humble!
> . . . .
> Come!
> Mondays and Tuesdays
> We'll paint into holidays with our blood. (460-466)

His revolution can hardly be denied social content, given the presence of hungry masses, and the shadows of Bismarck and Galliffet as the enemy to be overthrown, but it is certainly in its basic quality Mayakovsky's rebellion against the earth, time (Mondays and Tuesdays are transformed into holidays), the sky, indeed the cosmos itself with its weight of reality.

The violent uprising reaches a rich verbal climax in the lines:

> Swore myself out,
> begged and pleaded,
> cut throats,
> slid up to someone
> bit into his flank.
>
> In the sky, red as the Marseillaise
> the sunset shuddered, dying. (476-482)

After the violent, orgastic discharge the poet picks up his madness again. There won't be anything left. Night will come, and tear you with its teeth and devour you. The poetic outcome of the revolution is no triumph, but another abrupt shift, after betrayal by a sky like Judas and a night "like the traitor Azef," to defeat and huddled despair. The red sky of revolution is totally suborned in the poem, purchased by a few pieces of silver—Judas's stars. Black night follows the brave red beginning.

After the fear and betrayal the poem moves easily and quietly into a moment of gentle melancholy and to thoughts suggested by the icon of the Virgin Mary which appears in the filthy tavern where the poet finds himself. She, the second "Maria" of the poem, penetrates his heart with her great round eyes. Why, he asks, do you grant this tavern crowd the gift of your painted gaze, when you know that once more they have preferred Barabbas to your son? There follow some curious lines in which the poet is once again quietly resigned, even submissive, as he contemplates the death of this generation, "mouldy in their joy," and the coming of new generations who will "grow the inquisitive hair of the wise men," will indeed be wise enough to christen their children with the names of his poems. His monument, like Pushkin's, is his verse, and the future is surely his. In the last lines of Part III he is tender again, as he wonders wistfully who he really is, and the problem of identity becomes explicit.

I, who sang the machine and England,
maybe I am just
the thirteenth apostle
in the usual gospel.
And whenever my voice
shouts bawdily—
then, from hour to hour,
all day long
maybe Jesus Christ is sniffing
the forget-me-nots of my soul. (524-533)

Part IV opens with a new access of pain, this time over his rejection by another Maria, the third if we count the Virgin, who appears near the end of the third part. The poem began with the refusal of his love—now it ends with another refusal. "It hurts! Maria, closer! Maria, give!" Not once had his heart ever reached the first of May—with him it's always the thirtieth of April. He's no Severyanin who could sing a sonnet to his Tiana, just a man of flesh and blood who needs her, and whose proposition becomes a prayer:

I just ask for your body
as a Christian asks:
"Give us this day
our daily bread." (620-623)

He reminds us of the tortured moment of his own poetic labor, to which he compares his present anguish:

Maria!
I don't want to forget your name
as a poet
who in the torments of night
gave birth to some word
as majestic as God
doesn't want to forget it.

Other similes he draws from the battlefield and the city:

I'll love and care for your body
as a soldier
mutilated in the war,
useless,
all alone,
cares for his one leg.

Maria—
You don't want to?
You don't want to!!
Aha—!
So—once again
dark and downcast
I take my heart,
washing it in tears,
carrying it
as a dog
takes back to his kennel
a paw run over by a train. (625-650)

The pathos of the first rejection was conveyed in images of fire and destruction, that of the second in the innocent mutilation of helpless creatures. But now the poet directs his attention to the root of the trouble, the core of existence itself, the true culprit, his father in heaven who created him a contradictory mass of insatiable needs and desires. Just as in the brief poem "Listen!" the puzzle of the world's existence is expressed in infantile images, so in *A Cloud* the metaphysical contradictions—time that must be eternal but can't be, space that is both infinite and limited, and, in human terms, desire without limit that cannot be satisfied—take on the imagery of unfulfilled sexual need:

Almighty one, you thought up a pair of hands,
fixed it
so that everybody has a head—
but why didn't you fix it
so that one could, without torment,
just kiss and kiss and kiss!? (693-698)

And now there is a second upsurge of violence. In Part III the violence was offered to the enemies of labor, but they took on cosmic proportions and were identified with sun, moon, and skies. Now in Part IV violence is offered to the source of it all, to the first and prime mover, who takes the form of an infantile worshipper's father image, and is even accompanied by angels.

You shake your head, old shaggy-hair?
Wrinkle your gray brow?

You think
that fellow behind you
with the wings
knows what love is? (683-688)

The frightened child who rushed in to God in the poem "Listen!" is now in full rebellion:

I thought—you were a great all-powerful god,
but you're a dummy, a little bitty god.
See me bend down,
get my knife out of my boot.

Look, you winged parasites,
huddle up in heaven there!
Ruffle your feathers and tremble.
But *you*—I'm going to cut you wide open,
with your smell of incense, all the way
from here to Alaska. (699-708)

The frightful lines contain a blasphemy that, in a universe endowed with order and a ruler, ought to end in the quick annihilation of the blasphemer. But nothing of the sort happens, and that is the final frustration, the unkindest cut of all. The poet's imprecations are answered by "silence." Old "nobodaddy" is a myth. There's no one there, and no one to blame for anything but only a huge indifferent being that hears nothing:

The universe is asleep
its huge ear
star-infested
rests on a paw. (721-724)

Mayakovsky's *Cloud* is a kind of confessional, a confession of the self to itself. Intensely autobiographical, it explores in a series of abrupt irrational shifts of mood the emotional tangle of the poet's life: his loves, his friends and enemies, his poetry, his revolution, and above all the insoluble riddle of his own existence. In its structure the poem is an externalized inner monologue, perhaps the only example in all literature of an inner monologue intended for public declamation. Pasternak observed a close affinity between Mayakovsky and Dostoevsky when he said that the early poems were lyrics that might have been written by one of Dostoevsky's young, rebellious characters.

3) The *Cloud* and "Reality"

If it is true that, as Burliuk said, all of Mayakovsky's poems are autobiographical, then we may be assured that the persons and events reflected in the poem are in some sense real, and it may be instructive and interesting to see what it is that the poem reflects. Kamensky has given us a circumstantial account of the poem's genesis as he observed the process during the futurists' stay in Odessa.[32] There was indeed a real Maria, he says, whose full name was Maria Aleksandrovna Denisova. They saw her first walking along the embankment with a middle-aged gentleman and another young lady. Mayakovsky abruptly left his companions and in a short time was observed riding in an open cab with the young lady herself. There is no explanation of how he managed to meet her and detach her from her escort. She was tall and stately, "with remarkable shining eyes, a real beauty." Burliuk christened her "Gioconda," which provided Mayakovsky with a humorous rhyme for "Jack London." After this first meeting he returned to the hotel "all excited, smiling to himself at something, very absent-minded, quite strange." Soon Mayakovsky, Burliuk, and Kamensky were invited to a dinner at the apartment of Maria's brother-in-law, where all three recited their poems and Mayakovsky held the floor with a seemingly inexhaustible store of anecdotes and wit. Kamensky maintained that the evening was a poetic triumph, though its results were devastating for Mayakovsky. When they returned to their hotel he nervously paced the room, could not sit still or concentrate, and gave every sign of being overcome with a great feeling of love. Burliuk was "portentously" silent. "Softly, like a child, almost helplessly he [Mayakovsky] said: 'I'm upset for some reason. Look, let's go to the seashore. I've never seen the sea at night. That must be marvellous.' "[33]

We should note in passing Roman Jakobson's reminder that water and the sea are vitally connected with the deepest experiences of the psyche.[34] At the end of the *Tragedy* he sets out

[32] *Op. cit.*, pp. 83ff. [33] *Ibid.*, p. 89.

[34] Jakobson, "Novye stroki," p. 197.

for the place where "cruel ocean tears its breast"; in *About That*, there is an ocean "as great as injury"; the final lines he wrote before his death mark the ebbing of a vital flow: "The sea draws back, the sea goes off to sleep." The series of water images, Jakobson believes, is linked with the motif of an "unrealizable, inexhaustible, impossible (*nebyvshei*) love." It is significant that at the onset of his first (as far as we know) great love, Mayakovsky turned to the sea at Odessa; and we know that he "wrote" *A Cloud* pacing the shores of another sea a thousand or so miles north of Odessa. Perhaps the sea symbolized for him also the limitless "ocean" of the visible universe upon which humanity "floats"; as we shall see later, the watery element does have such a function in "The Atlantic Ocean," a poem of the middle twenties.

But to return to Odessa and Mayakovsky's "Gioconda." He was restless and inconsolable. He talked of going to Siberia and taking her with him. He came late to recitals, something he had never done before. He kept delaying the scheduled departure from Odessa in the hope that "something" would happen. Finally he said: "Tomorrow at four she's coming. I'll tell her everything and I'm sure she'll agree, if only. . . . All right. Until tomorrow."[35] But he came back from the interview dark and silent. "Let's go," he said. Perhaps Maria had explained to him, "Look. I'm getting married." Once more, a "lovely skirt had been made out of his soul."

Maria Aleksandrovna figures in Kamensky's story as a rather pleasant young woman, certainly interested in poetry, adventurous enough to visit them in their hotel, and yet fully enclosed in a bourgeois environment. There had never been any real hope, we may gather. The author of a recent article on Mayakovsky in the popular journal *Ogonyok* (an article which, as we shall see, is disturbing in many ways) cites certain unnamed sources to the effect that "difficulties arose between Maria and Mayakovsky, the result of the social life of those days and a social system based on inequality, material considerations, or middle-class prejudice. In the poem all of this is summed up in Maria's words 'Look. I'm getting married.'" We also learn that Maria Denisova married a man who was later famous as a general of the Red Army, Shchadenko. Apparently she never forgot the furious young poet

[35] Kamensky, *Zhizn s Mayakovskim*, p. 98.

whose heart she had set on fire, since she made, soon after his death, what our source describes as "one of the first sculptural portraits of Mayakovsky."[36] Such is the generally accepted version of the "real-life" Maria.

Lily Brik has lent her authority to a version of *A Cloud's* heroine that calmly calls in question all of the evidence we have seen. In a letter to the Polish writer Woroczylski, she maintained that there never was a "Maria" and that the figure in the first part of *A Cloud* is only a generalized female portrait.[37] The brief affair in Odessa actually involved, according to Lily (who is no more able than her compatriots to abandon the notion of a "real-life" model) a seventeen-year-old girl named Sonya. If this is true, then both Burliuk and Kamensky have forced the facts of life into the mold provided by Mayakovsky's art, and the Soviet scholars we have cited may simply have invented for Mayakovsky a banal romance in which "true love" is thwarted by bourgeois circumstance. But the story fashioned by Kamensky and elaborated by Soviet students of Mayakovsky has an artistic form of its own,

[36] V. Vorontsov and A. Koloskov, "Lyubov poeta," *Ogonyok*, April 14, 1968. See also W. Woroczylski, *Życie Majakowskiego* (Warsaw, 1966), pp. 786-787.

A more recent investigation of the "real-life" Maria was undertaken by V. Makarov and V. Vorontsov: "Russkaya Dzhiokonda," *Poeziya*, No. 8, 1972, pp. 60-84. This is a detailed investigation of the life of Mayakovsky's early love which tells of her work as a sculptor, her participation in the Civil War and her marriage to the Red commander Shchadenko. The authors explain on grounds of practical good sense (what could the wandering poet have offered her at that time?) Maria's refusal to join Mayakovsky. They also offer a new interpretation of the lines concerning "Jack London, money, love, passion," based on a supposed conversation with Maria, the authenticity of which the article does not clearly establish. The pertinent passage from the article follows:

> During the conversation about literature there was a discussion of Jack London's heroes. One of the guests offered the opinion that their greed for money makes those heroes pathetic and insignificant. "What do you think?" he suddenly turned to Mayakovsky. Mayakovsky considered for a moment, but Maria came to his aid: "Of course that's so! Where there's money there's no love, no real feeling. Man is not born for money" (pp. 65-66).

If we are to acept this account Maria's comment not only suggested to him those lines in *A Cloud*, but gave him the approximate title of a scenario he would write several years later. In the absence of clear documentation one can only reserve judgment.

[37] Woroczylski, p. 126.

and, whether it is true or not, it will probably withstand Lily's hostile witness, especially since one may suspect an ulterior motive when she eliminates a rival from history's page.

Other items of Mayakovsky's biography, as we have seen, appear in the second and third parts of the poem, but in a highly emotional dislocation: Burliuk's encouragement, the tour of the provinces, his rivalry and conflict with Severyanin, perhaps also his early career as a revolutionist. Kamensky maintains that Severyanin actually entered into the early stages of the poem's composition, in that Mayakovsky used the first lines of one of the former's poems as a kind of "springboard" from which to develop the opening of the *Cloud*:

> He [Mayakovsky] looked out the [train] window at the panorama rushing past and kept humming the opening of Severyanin's famous poem:
>
> It was at the seashore—(*Eto bylo u morya*)
>
> He hummed it a number of times, to various tunes.
>
> And suddenly, smiling darkly, he began to repeat it, breaking it up rhythmically into separate words. We saw right away that Volodya had begun an important work and that the phrase "It was at the seashore" had served as a start, a kind of springboard.[38]

The Severyanin poem[39] is a melodious, eminently singable three-stanza treatment of a reciprocal seduction into which enter the seashore, a castle, Chopin melodies, shared pomegranate, seawaves of turquoise color, and a queen who becomes her pageboy's slave for a night. Severyanin's poem is a graceful pattern of seductive phrases having at its center a lady who "stormily surrenders." *A Cloud* is in every respect the negation and enemy of that poem and if Mayakovsky's work "took off" from it, we have a paradoxical study in attraction and repulsion.

Part IV begins with the poet's supplication to another "Maria," as to whose identity there has been some speculation. According to Roman Jakobson the second (third, as we've seen, if we count the Virgin) or Moscow Maria was T. Gumilina, an artist "all of whose painting is connected with Mayakovsky, as was her un-

[38] Kamensky, p. 99.

[39] I. Severyanin, *Gromokipyashchii kubok*, 3d. ed. (Moscow, 1914), p. 58.

published prose lyric *Two People in One Heart*."[40] According to this hypothesis Gumilina takes over in the poem the name of the first girl, and also her function, to reject the poet's love. Since the actual Moscow Maria was apparently in love with Mayakovsky and wholly fascinated by his personality and the business of his life, we must conclude that life's raw material has been transformed here for the uses of art.

4) Verses for Her: *The Backbone Flute* and Some Others

A Cloud is dedicated "to you, Lily" (*tebe Lile*). By the time of its first publication Mayakovsky had divested himself of all his Marias in favor of his ultimate and always love, the woman to whom his important work was to be inscribed, Lily Brik. His meeting with the Briks, Lily and her husband Osip, is noted in his autobiography under the heading "A Joyous Date," with the simple statement "July 1915. I meet L. Yu. and O. M. Brik."

Yurii Aleksandrovich Kagan, a Moscow lawyer, had two beautiful daughters, Elsa and Lily. Elsa first engaged Mayakovsky's attention when he visited their house to sell them copies of what she remembered as "his first long poem, *The Revolt of Things*," which was of course the original title of *Vladimir Mayakovsky, A Tragedy*.[41] He paid vigorous court to Elsa, who was seventeen at the time, taking her for long walks in the woods and frightening her parents, who did not trust "the futurists." Both Elsa and Lily tell of his visits and of the yellow calling card he left, as huge as a store-front sign and with his name on it in large block letters.[42] Elsa introduced Lily, who was already married to Osip ("Osya") Brik, to Mayakovsky. Lily tells of the night in the summer of 1915 when Mayakovsky first read them *A Cloud in Pants*. At first they were disinclined to listen to such outlandish verses, and begged Elsa not to ask him to read. But then:

> He read magnificently. We were all simply stunned. It was exactly what we'd been waiting for for so long. . . . Osya took the notebook with the poem in it and wouldn't give it up all

[40] Jakobson, "Novye stroki," p. 200. My own researches and inquiries in Moscow could unearth no trace of Gumilina's paintings, nor of her prose lyric.

[41] Elsa Triolet, *Maiakovski, poète russe* (Paris, 1945), p. 17.

[42] Lily Brik, "Iz vospominanii," in *Almanakh s Mayakovskim* (Moscow, 1934), pp. 59-79.

evening long, he kept reading it. Elsa was triumphant. And after that evening Volodya never went back to Kuokkala—he left there the mistress of his heart, his underwear at the laundress' and all his things, and on that very evening he dedicated *A Cloud* to me.

From that day forward Osya was in love with Volodya. . . .[43]

Lily's reminiscences offer at that point no statement to the effect that *she* had fallen in love with "Volodya." They digress instead into the details of her own life, the intellectual concerns of Osip and herself, and the many interesting people they knew. The list of books that Osip and she had been reading at the time reveals a remarkable catholicity of interests: "*Crime and Punishment, The Brothers Karamazov, The Idiot, War and Peace, Anna Karenina, Zarathustra,* Kierkegaard's *In Vino Veritas, The Cat Murr* . . . not to speak of some trifles." They were already acquiring the reputation of patrons of young literary men: "We once even took a certain poet to Turkestan simply because he very much liked the east." They collected a variety of curious characters: a famous actress "who was the most amusing and the most talented woman in the world," and whose amorous adventures were the source of many anecdotes and even some private family proverbs; a rich and eccentric family who collected unusual things—one of the first automobiles in Moscow, a bulldog, a snake, and a monkey; a young girl whose succession of "enthusiasms" included Freud, and whose last affair in Russia was with a woman who wore trousers and a pince-nez and always used the masculine gender when referring to herself. ("Osya saw that woman not long ago on the street, and she was pregnant. It frightened him.") Lily's own feminine charms are often the subject of her reminiscences; she tells, for instance, of a train ride during which she flirted with a tall, black-bearded fellow with "gay blue eyes" who turned out to be the powerful and sexually active monk, Rasputin. He insisted that she come to visit him, but "Osya" would not allow such a thing.[44]

Mayakovsky's efforts to find a publisher for *A Cloud* had met with no success until Osip Brik read it. He published the first edition at his own expense, and the poem, dedicated to Lily, came out in a mutilated version—for instance, the censorship replaced almost all the lines of Part IV, the blaspheming section, with long

[43] *Ibid.*, p. 62.

[44] *Ibid.*, p. 70.

rows of dots—in September 1915. By November, Mayakovsky had moved from his Petrograd hotel and installed himself in the Briks' apartment on Zhukovsky Street, thus establishing a triangular relationship and a new "family" that held together loyally until his death.[45] The arrangement was a marriage of both convenience and love: Osip became his publisher and agreed to pay him fifty kopeks a line for his poems, many of which were inspired by Lily and written for her. It is possible that this happy arrangement literally saved Mayakovsky's life, since he was in a state of suicidal depression during the immediately preceding period.[46]

Under Lily's gentle guidance, Mayakovsky soon acquired the outward appearance of bourgeois respectability. She had him cut his hair, wash himself, and dress decently. He took to carrying a heavy cane.[47] With the Briks he found, everyone agrees, a refuge, a congenial home with two friends, one of whom, Osip, was deeply interested in literature and could write shrewdly and perceptively on problems of literary form; with the other he had fallen in love at once and finally, and for the rest of his life. Shklovsky's description of Lily is brilliant and beautiful: "She could be sad, feminine, capricious, proud, vacuous, fickle, loving, clever, and indeed anything you like. That's how Shakespeare describes women in one of his comedies."[48]

The Backbone Flute was not only written for her and dedicated to her; she was the daily auditor of its impassioned verses as Mayakovsky labored to extract them (in his own words) "from the ooze of his heart":[49]

> *The Flute* was written very slowly, and each verse received a triumphant reading aloud. The verses were first read to me, then to me and Osya together, and then to the others. That's the way it always was all our lives with everything Volodya wrote. . . .
>
> I promised Volodya I'd listen to each verse of *The Flute* at his place. [At this point he had not yet moved in with the Briks.] For tea there was always a fantastic quantity of things

[45] *PSS*, xiii, 24 (letter to his mother).
[46] See Triolet, pp. 51, 63.
[47] Shklovsky, *O Mayakovskom*, p. 81.
[48] *Ibid.*, p. 82.
[49] From *A Cloud in Pants*, l. 226.

I like. There were flowers on the table and Volodya wore a very becoming tie.[50]

Beauty in Mayakovsky's poems eludes translation and deceives the conventional taste; thus his wonderful song about love, which, though dedicated indeed to Lily Brik, is probably meant for all women—or at least for all those in "the inexhaustible ranks of his own loves"—has passed unnoticed outside Russia. *The Backbone Flute* is a male lyric on the theme of love's madness and pain. The poetic figures that carry the burden of desire neither chasten nor sublimate the poet's love, but present it in terms of delirium. The "her" to whom the verses are offered is a thing of hellish fantasy, invented by some heavenly E. T. A. Hoffmann; the poet's thoughts are clots of blood, issuing from his skull. He may be a miracle-worker (as a poet) and a maker of holidays, but since he has no one to share his holidays with, he will dive down and brain himself on the pavement of the Nevsky Prospect. He has blasphemed, he's roared out his atheism, but now God brought her up out of the hot depths of hell, and, so that no one would guess who she was, gave her a human husband, and human music to set on her piano; if one should make the sign of the cross above the quilt that covers her there would be at once a smell of scorched wool and sulphurous fumes. He doesn't need her! He doesn't want her! And anyway he knows he'll soon croak. He begs God to pass judgment on him, set up a gallows on the Milky Way and string him up; he's ready to take any punishment, if only the Almighty will remove that woman. Even in drunken battle the words of love are not obsolete. The German speaks of Goethe's Gretchen, the Frenchman dies with a smile, remembering La Traviata, but the source of Mayakovsky's hell is no conventional literary type; she is a redhead with a painted face. When the centuries have whitened beards, only she will still be left—and he, rushing after her from city to city; in London fogs he will imprint on her lips the fiery kiss of street-lamps; in Paris, when she wanders onto a bridge and looks down, it's him she will see, pouring himself out Seine-wise, and calling to her; when she rides out with another man in Sokolniki Park, he will rise over the trees, naked and expectant, a moon to torment her. Should he be a czar he'll mint her pretty face on all his coins; should he be a convict

[50] L. Brik, *op. cit.*, p. 72.

he'll scratch the name "Lily" on his chains and kiss and kiss them. But the lady's virtue is as cold as monastery rock; the husband asserts his rights, and oh, that night! He tightened despair about his throat, and at his howls and laughs the smug mug of his room twisted out of shape with fright. He surrendered her; and King Albert of Belgium, all his towns surrendered, was a happy birthday boy by comparison.

This is admittedly a pale paraphrase, but it may give some notion of how Mayakovsky consciously employed near-psychopathic imagery to convey the intense force of sexual passion. Such poems certainly reflect his own nature and his experience in love, though it must be remembered that in them he is also a conscious poetic craftsman experimenting with the linguistic means for the expression of violent passion. The passion he expresses is male and physical. Quite unashamedly he celebrates *eros*, whose all-encompassing demand appropriates the whole psyche, and indeed is so exigent that it transcends *agape*. Flesh burning with such bright light becomes spirit.

We must be wary, in the case of a literary craftsman like Mayakovsky, when searching his work for a guide to his biography. Yet we have seen clear evidence that Mayakovsky himself experienced and acted out the kind of irrational attacks of wild emotion that his best poetry describes. His close friends have left the record of a number of incidents in which he displayed either manic elation or sudden weeping despair. Lily Brik relates that at the very time when he was writing *The Flute* he was asked to give a report on futurism to a group of friends that included Shklovsky, the Briks, Gorky, Kulbin, and a few others. He worked hard at preparing it, but when he realized that he was speaking to a small group of friends instead of to a packed auditorium, he broke down and wept, refused to continue, and went off into another room. Only with some difficulty was he calmed down and persuaded to return to the assembled and expectant guests and read some of his poetry.[51] Shklovsky, who also tells of this incident, reports that Gorky was at that time very fond of Mayakovsky and that he considered *The Backbone Flute* to be "the vertebral string, the very essence of lyric poetry, its spinal cord."[52]

In late 1915 and 1916 Mayakovsky produced a number of brief lyrics on the theme of love's disappointments. "To all" (*Ko vsemu,*

[51] *Ibid.*, p. 77.

[52] Shklovsky, *O Mayakovskom*, p. 84.

1916)[53] is a bitter cry for vengeance against those who hurt him, first of all, and primarily, the woman he himself loves:

> No.
> It can't be so
> No.
> Not you too?
> My sweet.
> But why?
> What did I do?
> All right—
> I made visits,
> I gave flowers,
> But I didn't steal the silverware! (1-11)

He is Christ, bearing his cross, to whom the mob gives no rest. He's had enough of it from everybody. An eye for an eye! If he finds another young and pretty girl he'll just rape her and then laugh at her. An eye for an eye! He's a mad dog ready to bite, a white bull with his neck chafed and sore under the yoke and bitten by flies, a moose with his branched head caught in wires. He'll paint the savage Razin's face on the icon of the Lord. His revenge is holy, and again he pours out his full heart in a poetic confession for posterity:

> People of the future!
> Who are you?
> Here am I
> all wound and pain.
> I will to you the orchard
> of my great soul. (126-132)

The magnificent little love poem "Lily-mine: Instead of a Letter" (*Lilichka: vmesto pisma*, 1916)[54] was written in 1916 as a private and personal missive, and published only in 1934 when Lily Brik included it in her reminiscences along with her many anecdotes and some excerpts about animals from Mayakovsky's letters—the latter, no doubt, because Mayakovsky employs some effective animal imagery in the poem.[55]

The poem concentrates in a few telling images the moment of terror when the hopeless lover, having somehow incurred Lily's

[53] *PSS*, I, 103.
[54] *PSS*, I, 107.
[55] L. Brik, *op. cit.*, p. 75.

disfavor (did I steal the silverware?), dreads her impending decision to send him away. In a day or two she'll curse him and throw him out, and

> In the dark entryway for quite a while
> my trembling arm
> can't get into the sleeve of my coat. (13-15)
> . . . .
> Don't do that,
> my dear,
> my sweet.
> Let's just say goodbye now.
> Anyway
> my love
> will hang
> like a weight on you
> wherever you run to. (20-28)

Once again the poet associates himself with images of hurt animals, who are nonetheless far better off than he. An overworked ox, for instance, can splash himself in cool waters, but without her love there is no sea for him, and with it there is no rest. A tired elephant majestically rolls in the sun-hot sand, but without her love he has no sun: "And I don't even know where you are / or who you're with." (43)

It should be pointed out that in all the love poems, including the poem *Man*, which we shall deal with in the next chapter, the love object, whether Maria or Lily, is shown as superficial and conventional. Maria talked of "Jack London, money, passion"—and at last got married. Lily in *The Backbone Flute* is a "red-head with a painted face," who has a conventional husband. In this poem her philistine character becomes explicit:

> Tomorrow you'll forget
> how I crowned you queen,
> how I burned my blossoming heart with love.
> The whirling carnival of vanities
> will mess up the pages of my little books. (56-60)

Needless to say, the pain of love is never assuaged by the thought that the object of love may not be deserving; on the contrary, the lover may become even more abject in his need: "Just let me / Spread one last tenderness / Before your departing steps." (64-66)

The third short poem that we consider in this context is entitled "To His Beloved Self the Author Dedicates These Lines" (*Sebe, lyubimomu, avtor posvyashchaet eti stroki*, 1916);[56] in it Mayakovsky condenses into a few striking images the paradoxes of his own existence. Earth provides no lair for one such as he—where is he to put himself? This is the question with which the poem opens, a question that echoes the line "He has no way out," repeated with only slight modifications in *A Cloud*, in *About That*, and in his suicide note. Possible answers to the question are framed in a series of conditional sentences which state the poet's insatiable need. For example:

> If I were
> small
> like the Pacific Ocean
> I'd stand on the tiptoes of my waves
> and at my flood offer caresses to the moon.
> But where can I find a love
> such as I am?
> Such a one wouldn't fit into the tiny sky. (8-15)

In each conditional statement a belittling epithet is applied to something huge or rich or brilliant: if I were *poor*, like a billionaire; if I were *tongue-tied*, like Dante; if I were *quiet*, like thunder; if I were *dim*, like the sun. The conclusion supports the shocking epithet, since in each case the scope of the poet's desire ranges beyond what is conceivable for a billionaire, a Dante, the thunder, or the sun. The gold of all the Californias is not enough for him; the words inspired by his love are a triumphal arch under which pass the paramours of all ages, "leaving no trace"; if he roared the full thunder of his voice, comets would hurl themselves down in terror, wringing their burning hands; the blinding rays of his own sun would devour night. Greater than the ocean, richer than Croesus, more eloquent than Dante, louder than thunder, and brighter than the sun, yet weighted down with that heavy love of his, he feels so huge and useless:

[56] *PSS*, I, 126.

I'll move on
dragging along my big love.
In what night,
delirious,
sick,
and what Goliaths begat me
so large
and so unnecessary? (50-57)

Chapter Six

1916: "IN MY HEAD, *WAR AND THE UNIVERSE*, IN MY HEART, *MAN*"

1) War Service, and a War Poem

When the war broke out in 1914, Mayakovsky was at first eager to experience the noise, color, and glamor that enveloped "the front," in the eyes of noncombatants. He tried to volunteer but was turned down because of his record as a subversive element. As we have seen, he contributed to the war effort verses that breathed the fire of conventional patriotism. His initial enthusiasm for the war was widely shared, and we find that Shklovsky volunteered and that Pasternak, too, considered volunteering at the very same time. Disillusionment set in when news returned of the front's bloody misery, and Pasternak reports how he was dissuaded from entering the war: "Shestov's son, a handsome ensign, made me swear to put this idea from me. With a sober positiveness he described the front to me, warning me that I would find there the precise contrary of what I expected. Shortly afterward he fell in the first engagement which took place after his return from leave."[1]

Mayakovsky was called up when his turn came, in October, 1915, but by that time his ardor had cooled: "Drafted me. Now I don't want to go to the front. I pretended to be a draftsman. At night I studied with an engineer how to make blueprints of automobiles. . . ."[2]

The poet's laconic account of his call into the army is somewhat misleading, since it tells nothing of the "ordeal" he experienced in his successful effort to arrange an agreeable assignment in the rear. About this he did report to his family in a letter written about October 8:

[1] Boris Pasternak, *Safe Conduct* (New York, 1949), p. 100.
[2] *PSS*, I, 24.

Dear Mama, Lyuda, and Olya!

Only now has my ordeal with regard to my summons ended, and I hasten to write and reassure you.

I've been taken in and sent to the Petrograd auto school where I've been assigned to the drafting department as a skilled and experienced draftsman.

There's absolutely no need to worry about me. After my work at school I can carry on the same activities as before.

My address is the same. Write about yourselves. How are things? . . .[3]

Most accounts agree that Maxim Gorky's connections secured Mayakovsky's assignment to the auto school, where he not only had light duties, but was able to maintain his own private quarters and continue his literary associations and activities. According to Pertsov, the sister of M. F. Andreeva, Gorky's agreeable companion, was the wife of one of the officers in charge of the auto school, and it was through his influence that Mayakovsky received his assignment.[4] The auto school, moreover, was a natural refuge for educated men with some technical training, and in 1915 it sheltered, in addition to Mayakovsky, the artist Radakov, Shklovsky, Osip Brik, and many others.

At this time Mayakovsky was close to Gorky, who invited him to participate in a journal he started in 1915, *The Chronicle* (*Letopis*). He was a frequent visitor at the editorial offices of the journal. He read a part of *War and the Universe* to the editorial staff, and it was scheduled for publication in 1916 but was eliminated by the censor. Part V of the poem, which contains no hyperboles of violence and blood but a utopian dream of man's perfection, was published in *The Chronicle* in February 1917.[5]

Mayakovsky's brief association with Gorky was an important factor in the creation of that poem. The political position of Gorky at the time—and it was shared by many members of his staff—was "defeatist": the war was a monstrous evil for which the Russian government together with the other capitalist powers was responsible, and it must be ended at any cost, including even the defeat of Russia. Indeed, the total defeat of the tsarist regime was

[3] *PSS*, xiii, 23.

[4] Pertsov, *Mayakovsky, zhizn i tvorchestvo* [i], 330.

[5] *PSS*, i, 443.

a consummation devoutly to be wished, since it would be followed by a revolution and the establishment of democratic socialism. These ideas, current in Gorky's circle, Mayakovsky adopted and translated into a system of poetic images in which the grinding of human beings into blood and dirt suddenly stops at the poet's command, those that were killed rise from the dead, and a time of great peace and perfection comes to humanity. There is no political terminology or overt socialist propaganda in the poem, and Pertsov is of course unhappy with the "abstract" nature of this utopia, but the poem is nevertheless a conscious reduction to metaphoric statement of a widespread mood of discouragement and defeat, as well as of the growing hope for revolution. And Mayakovsky's revolution is, naturally, final, absolute, and universal. Everything is forgiven; murderers give up their black thoughts, and "Cain plays checkers with Jesus Christ." The strong anti-war message of the poem is perhaps best expressed in the lines:

> Nobody asked
> that victory
> be guaranteed.
> What the devil good would it be
> to an armless stump
> left over from the bloody banquet?! (550-554)

The poem is divided into a Prologue, a Dedication (of course to Lily) and five parts.[6] The printed text is variegated with bars of music: in Part I the music of a tango popular in 1914, in Part III, interspersed with the martial beat of drums, the Orthodox hymn for the dead.

The Prologue sets, in a few short stanzas, the sense of the poem: the poet might be better off dead, but he must, through the ranks, through the racket, carry his love to the living, and now his love is neither selfish nor carnal: "If I trip— / the last crumb of love / drops forever into the smoky lake." (13-15) He is a prophet like the biblical ones, and the only one who speaks not only of present sin but of the justice to be, and like a prophet he expects persecution:

> All right!
> Shoot me.

[6] *PSS*, I, 211-242.

Tie me to a post!
I won't flinch!
If you like
I'll paste an ace on my forehead
so the target will burn brighter. (53-60)

In Part I the new Jeremiah lashes out at those Babylons and "hundred-housed Sodoms" (*stodomym Sodomom*), the cities of 1914, the poison of whose vice had infected even the countryside. The "fat ones" (*zhirnye*), the frequent object of his contempt in the early poems, here receive the full fury of a prophet's scorn. But his scorn is modulated by the grotesque comedy of the images he presents:

They gorge themselves
and after
in night's blindness
tumbling their flesh in thick wooly down
they crowd on each other to sweat.
And the towns shudder
from the creaking of the bedsprings. (153-159)

After this picture of urban gluttony and lust comes a passage of nostalgic regret, rare in Mayakovsky, for pastoral innocence spoiled by what we might call "the urban sprawl":

Innocent ones!
They didn't have it for long.
Right away
iron rails oozed urban
infection into the village sunburn.
Where birds sang—plates clank.
Where the forest was—a square with its hundred-
  housed Sodoms.
Brothel after brothel,
fauns six stories high break into their dance. (179-187)

Mayakovsky makes the universe itself a participant in this human orgy, as the sun "hoists its hot body" onto the whorish night, who's hardly had a chance to rest in the shade (poor thing!).

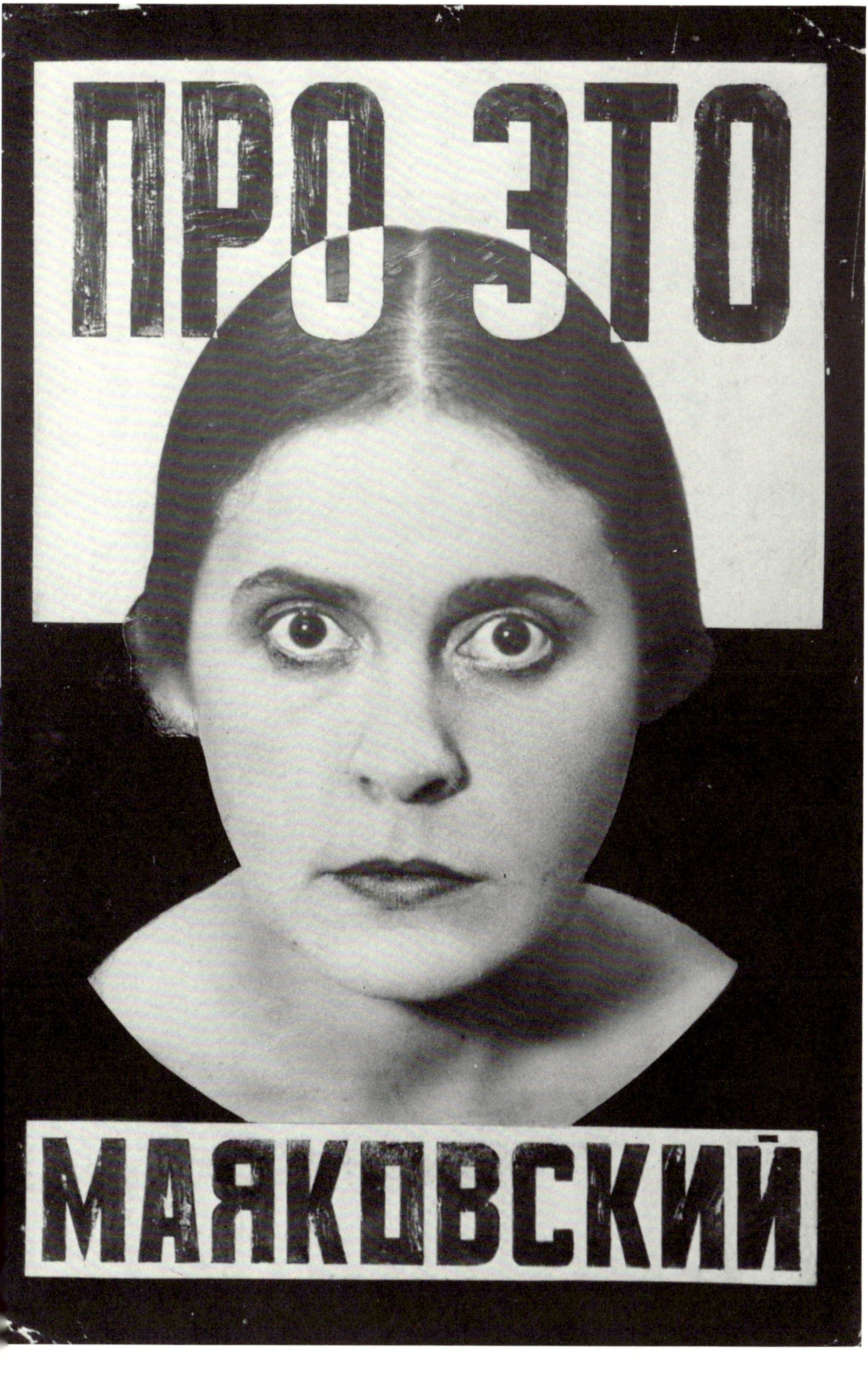
ПРО ЭТО
МАЯКОВСКИЙ

These illustrations, created by the constructivist Rodchenko for the first edition of the poem *About That*, deal with matters that were central to Mayakovsky's life and art. Lily Brik, whose great round eyes are a recurrent image in his poetry, appeared on the front cover of that edition, which is reproduced on the previous page.

Upper left: On the bridge over the Neva, to the far left a tiny helpless figure, but then in his dream fantasy a gloomy giant, the poet thinks of suicide. Rejected and resting on the ice, he tries to close his ears against the sound of his own groans; and in order to bemoan his lost love honestly and without affectation he transforms himself into a bear.

Lower left: Precariously balanced on the tower of Ivan the Great in the Kremlin, Mayakovsky looks down upon Moscow, New York, modern technology, and the "masses." Lily is splendid but indifferent, and a part of her seems to merge with the crowd. A heavy gun ("every Mauser and Browning," he wrote) is trained upon him.

Lower right: Brought back to life in the thirtieth century, the poet at his own request is appointed a zoo attendant. He had always loved animals, who offer poets both moral analogies and metaphors. We see him outside the cage looking at himself inside as a polar bear. He thinks maybe he will meet "her" there ("they'll surely resurrect her, she was so beautiful")—she liked animals, too.

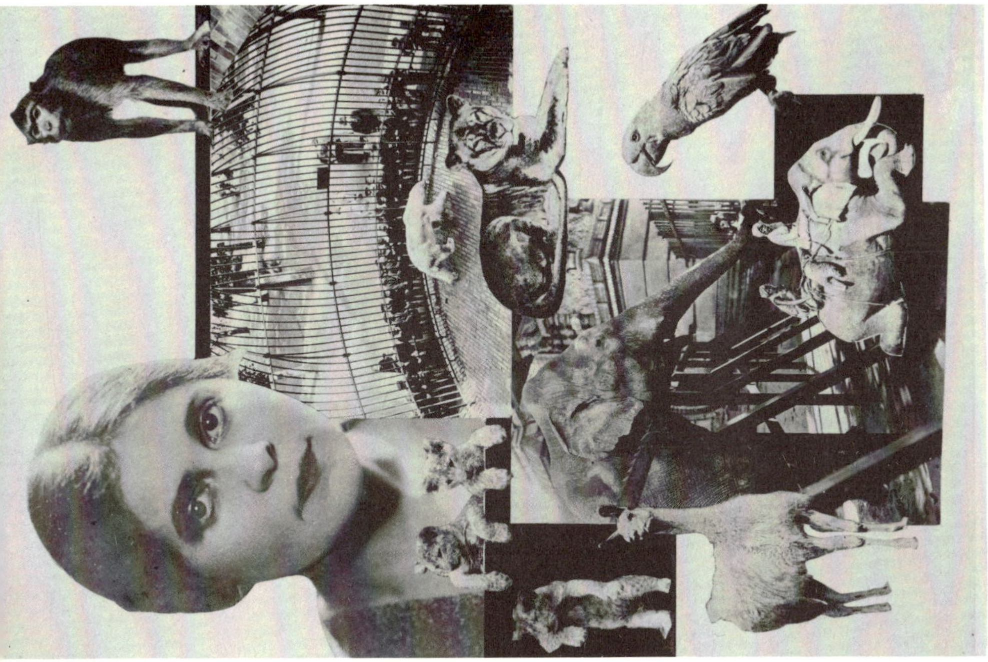

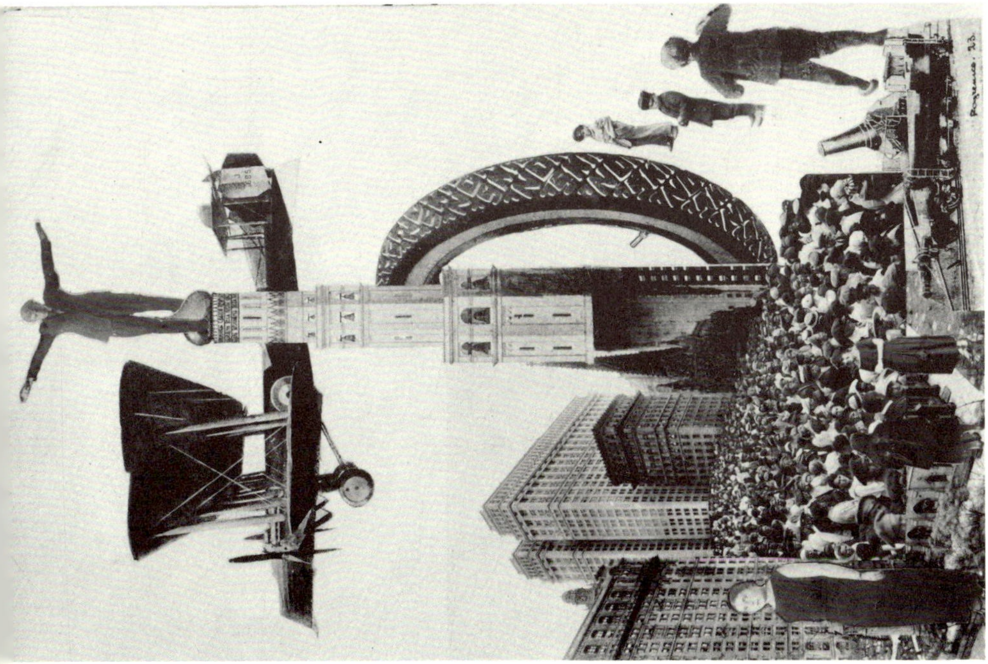

Left to right: David Burliuk, the painter Abraham Manievich, and Mayakovsky. The poet Alexander Alland is standing behind Burliuk. Taken at Rockaway Beach in 1925.

Left to right: Mayakovsky, Rafaele Carrillo, Secretary of the Communist Party of Mexico, Comrade Moreno, 1925.

Mayakovsky, probably taken in 1926 in Moscow.

Part I ends on this note of metaphoric horror at the guilt of men and of all creation, and thus the prophet has prepared us for retribution—the outbreak of the First World War, which happens "in one of the autumns" (in Part II). Guilt easily introduces a metaphor of disease, and it became "unbearably clear" that if you don't "take and open the veins of the people" the infected earth itself will die—all the Parises, Berlins, and Viennas will "simply croak." In a succession of invocations addressed to the nations, the compelling urge to war of each one is characterized: the Italian king sees the Germans "hovering over Venice"; Germany's museums, thoughts, and books disappear into gaping muzzles; Russia's blood, like the Tartar horde, seethes with desire; France has forgotten the tender love-whispers of boulevards and finds it good to burn and rape to the music of machine guns.

In Part III all Europe becomes an arena for a bloody gladiatorial battle among the sixteen states, and the whole world is a pagan Colosseum. The war is a vast spectacle of death, and the poet calls upon the "property man" to bring on the hearses and more widows: "not enough widows in the crowd": "And into the heavens / soars / a fireworks display of facts / each more monstrous than the last." (387-390)

The struggle against God, who caused it all, or at least allows it, takes the direct crude form of an attack on heaven, as in *A Cloud*, and, again as in that poem, heaven turns out to be empty:

> The angels tremble.
> You could even feel sorry for them.
> Oval faces whiter than their wings.
> Where are they—the gods?
> They've run away
> all of them
> Sabaoth
> Buddha
> Allah
> Jehovah. (529-538)

Part IV puts an end to the bloody show, and the poet as prophet now alters his message. Having witnessed the utter confusion of humanity in "madness and death," as Leonid Andreev put it, having seen through to its most awful the dire retribution of which he was the herald, Mayakovsky now recoils from wrath and foresees a day of reconciliation and perfect harmony. But before that vision takes shape he must (in Part IV) settle the question of blame for mankind's present misery. "I am wherever pain is—anywhere," he said in *A Cloud* and in many of his early poems, but it is not enough now to *feel* another's pain: he is also *responsible* for it:

The dead—
it makes no difference
who killed them,
me or him. . . . (611-614)

The universe will bloom again
joyful—and fresh.
And so there won't be any silly lies about it,
I confess,
that I alone
am to blame. . . . (656-662)

The message at this point reminds one strongly of Dostoevsky's "brothers," all of whom were in a sense guilty of their father's murder, and it seems certain that this passage, with its frantic cry to be forgiven for all murders, reflects the influence of the great novelist. The poet catalogs history's great crimes: a child sacrificed to an idol, a Christian thrown to the lions, a heretic torn on the rack:

That was me,
Mayakovsky,
who offered
the beheaded infant (669-672)

. . . .

That was me
Mayakovsky,
Vladimir,
taking in the circus with drunken eyes. . . . (679-682)

. . . .

Mayakovsky
in a basement of Seville
tore loose the joints
of heretics. (688-691)

Indeed there is not a drop of blood in the day's carnage for which Mayakovsky, Vladimir, is not guilty, and it would seem to follow at this point that his father in heaven, so roughly assaulted in Part III, must be absolved of the blame. It is only for himself that he asks absolution:

People!
Dear ones!
For Christ's sake
for the sake of Christ
forgive me! . . . (725-729)

But this vile and evil era of Vladimir Mayakovsky will pass, and then there will be no one to torment human beings: "And people will be born, / real people / better and more merciful than God himself." (752-754)

Mayakovsky in his assumption of universal guilt goes far beyond the Christ myth of the cycle *Me* and the *Cloud.* Christ is a scapegoat who cleanses by his atonement, but no theological opinion has ever held that the gentle Saviour carried any guilt within Himself. What Mayakovsky suggests is a collective guilt, a universal human involvement in the suffering of all men (even of animals, as we shall see), and if all men are guilty then each one can say "I (Mayakovsky, Vladimir!) did it." Placed in the context of 1915, the lines may also be taken as a valid statement of a real psychic experience. Mayakovsky had welcomed the war, tried to join the killing himself, and when rejected wrote vile propaganda urging others to kill. He may very well have developed guilt feelings under the influence of Gorky and his "peace" group.

Part V presents Mayakovsky's personal utopia, and like everything personal in Mayakovsky it takes on universal dimensions. His own lyric problem, the love of Lily, is beautifully solved in the poem:

Hello my sweet!
Every hair I caress,
so curly
and golden.
O what zephyr
from what south
worked this miracle upon my buried heart?

Your eyes are full of blossoms
like two green meadows.
And I tumble around in them,
a happy boy. (955-965)

Can we resist contrasting Lily's eyes in this happy metaphor with the frightening apertures of *The Backbone Flute*: "Two open graves / are the eyes dug in your face." (228-229)

But the personal lyric is subordinated in this poem to a utopian scheme that embraces all humanity and indeed brings together in childish play old enemies such as Cain and Jesus Christ. Everyone must be happy:

And all around!
Laughter.
Flags flying.
All colors.
They pass by,
Rising high.
Thousands of them
. . . .
every young man has Marinetti's fire,
every old man has Victor Hugo's wisdom. (966-976)

And not only humans:

And beasts in great style grow curly fleece;
the seas,
so stormy yesterday,
lie down at your feet
and purr. (1000-1004)

Dreadnaughts that once brought destruction now carry into quiet harbors sheaves of all kinds of things, and cannons are used to trim the grass. And of course

That free man
of whom I shout
will appear
believe me he will!
Believe me! (1050-1056)

2) On *Man*

a) *In General*

It has been said that the poem *Man*[7] is the crowning point of Mayakovsky's prerevolutionary poetry,[8] and there is no question that in it the motifs and methods of the early Mayakovsky rise to a climax of luminous energy. The poem offers a proper conclusion to the obsessive thematic concern with the self and its frustrations that we find in Mayakovsky's earliest work. The frequent appearances of the poet in the early poems as Christ or as savior have their final distillation in *Man*, where the stages of Mayakovsky's life bear the titles "Nativity," "Life," "Passion," "Ascension," "In Heaven" and "Return." His frequent poetic incarnations of the deity—as an old man with "veiny hands" ("Listen!"), or as something "majestic, like Leo Tolstoy" ("Petersburg Again" [*Eshcho Peterburg*]), or as someone who "runs about in heaven with a book of my poems under his arm and recites them, all excited, to his acquaintances" ("But Anyway" [*A vsyo-taki*]) —reach a high point of irony in this poem in the endless philistine bliss of the heaven He has prepared for us.

In its thematic content and in its linguistic virtuosity, the poem is indeed a kind of summation of Mayakovsky's prerevolutionary poetry, but in one respect it stands apart from that work as a whole. His poetry tends to be intensely local and particular. His earliest lyrics betray the immediate concerns of a painter who works at poetry. The painter's studio and its materials, as we have seen, enter into many of these lyrics; some of them appear to be verse realizations of urban scenes or cubistic still-lifes on which the poet was working. Even in the *Cloud* there are verbal pictures of real places, however distorted their shapes may be. *War and the Universe* has a specific date, 1915, and addresses itself to a particular event, the war in Europe. But the poem *Man*, though it was written during the period between the February and October revolutions, is an abstraction from immediate and topical reality. Somewhat like his *Tragedy*, it is about Mayakovsky, but also about man in general; the characters that appear in it—Mayakovsky, the Ruler of All (*Povelitel*

[7] *PSS*, I, 445.

[8] Z. Papernyi, *Poeticheskii obraz u Mayakovskogo* (Moscow, 1961), p. 35.

vsego), the girl, Nikolaev the engineer—invite symbolic interpretation; one may think of them as Man, his enemy, the eternal feminine, perhaps the eternal husband. Man's fate is the poet's theme, and that fate is shown as total, or, in Stahlberger's phrase, "cosmic" alienation.[9]

Mayakovsky himself suggested that *Man* should be considered as a companion piece to *War and the Universe*. One of the items in his autobiography,[10] speaks of the period during 1916 when he was a recruit behind the lines and the two poems were taking shape in his imagination: "A most miserable time. I draw officers' portraits (getting out of things). In my head *War and the Universe*, in my heart *Man*." The first of these, which Mayakovsky indicates was a cerebral exercise, expresses keen disgust with humanity in its present state, using the evidence of the cruel warfare of 1915, but it preaches perfectibility and prophesies a time of deep peace when, as we have seen, Jesus Christ "will play checkers with Cain." The movement of Mayakovsky's heart, however, did not accord with the bright prophecies of that poem. *Man*, which he finished "soon after"[11] *War and the Universe*, is a poetic refutation of the earlier poem, and its pessimism concerns not only the human state but the nature of existence itself. The close juxtaposition of these two poems, a procedure suggested by Mayakovsky himself, is a convincing illustration of the duality in the poet's nature. In his work despair forms an almost equivalent counterpoise to great bursts of poetic optimism, and the outcome is always in precarious balance.

b) Earlier Criticism

Before offering an interpretation of the poem *Man* it may be helpful to review briefly the most important criticism of that work. Such a review will place in focus the principal critical approaches to Mayakovsky's work as a whole. We shall examine

[9] Stahlberger, *Symbolic System*, p. 63.

[10] *PSS*, I, 24.

[11] It is not certain exactly when the poem *Man* was finished. The best evidence indicates that it was begun before the events of February 1917, and finished between February and October 1917. See Cheremin, *Rannii Mayakovsky*, p. 107. See also *Literaturnoe nasledstvo*, LXV, 556. The most interesting treatment of the problem is offered in Jakobson, "Novye stroki," pp. 108, 203. Jakobson's evidence indicates that the poem must have been written, in part at least, during the period between the February and October revolutions, and that it may not have been finished until the end of 1917.

first the most recent Soviet criticism of the poem, then move to earlier criticism, and end with the work of émigré and western critics. This procedure has the advantage that it will reveal the present state of critical thought on the poem and at the same time trace important divergences in method and approach between certain contemporary Soviet scholars, on the one hand, and other critics, both Marxist and non-Marxist, on the other.

Among recent Soviet studies of Mayakovsky, G. S. Cheremin's *The Early Mayakovsky* (*Rannii Mayakovsky*, Moscow, 1962), holds special interest as an effort to explore objectively the work of the poet's "cubo-futurist" period. Cheremin has much to offer on Mayakovsky's relationship to the futurist movement, and especially on the differences between Mayakovsky and his futurist colleagues. He firmly dismisses the thesis frequently advanced in earlier Soviet criticism that Mayakovsky was never "really" a futurist.[12] He deals directly with the evidence as to the poet's aesthetic ideas and behavior during the period before the revolution. Concerning the poem *Man*, he maintains that it "synthesizes and generalizes the ideas, themes, and motifs of the poet's earlier work."[13] Mayakovsky's comment as to the origin of *War and the Universe* in the head and *Man* in the heart referred, Cheremin believes, to the difference in method between the two poems: the former is oriented toward certain external facts, the latter is told, so to speak, entirely from within. The basic satirical thrust of the poem is, for Cheremin as for nearly all the more recent Soviet critics of Mayakovsky, against bourgeois society. In contradistinction to other works of Mayakovsky, in which the critique of bourgeois social relations is directed at Russian reality, the poem encompasses the same theme "on a world-wide scale." The poet's imprisonment on earth with the twin weights of Law and Religion holding him down symbolizes "the contradiction between the poet, who bears love to all people, and the oppressive force of the bourgeois city."[14] The Ruler of All is an abstract creation which underlines the "general, absolute, and complete sway of capital." The gloomy fantasy of the poem's conclusion seems to Cheremin to express not hopelessness in the face of the anti-human principle in the world but rather hatred for the devotees of ready profits and cash in hand. The point of the poem is not that the poet is unable to go on living but that

[12] Cheremin, pp. 47ff.
[13] *Ibid.*, pp. 108ff.
[14] *Ibid.*, p. 110.

he refuses to live "in this kind of world."[15] Only a radical change in reality itself can overcome the inconsolable loneliness and alienation the poem expresses; only a revolution can revive the poet's spirit. Cheremin means, of course, a revolution of the oppressed masses against the power of capital, the "October revolution," which did indeed take place at the time when the poet was completing *Man.*

An extended discussion of the poem is offered by A. Metchenko.[16] He interprets the lyrical hero as a Promethean figure who, though bound, blinded, and chained to earth by the "bankers, tycoons, and doges," preserves his hatred of those enemies into eternity. The biblical form and terminology of the poem Metchenko explains as parody, and the heaven described in it seems to him intended to satirize the various religious fictions as to a life after death. The Ruler of All is "a personification of the world of property," and Metchenko compares the poem to Gorky's "City of the Yellow Devil" as "one of the most powerful exposures of capitalism in prerevolutionary literature." Money has the power even to corrupt the girl, though in the end she hears the voice of her heart and leaps to her death out of pure love: "There is a legend: / she leaped to him / out of the window. / And they just lay upon each other, / body to body." (I hope to show that there is another possible interpretation of those lines.) Metchenko finds that Mayakovsky makes an attempt in this poem to be precise about the kind of revolution needed. "Not every revolution will do away with the power of money personified by the Ruler of All"; that is how he explains the lines "No rebellion ever touches thee, uncrowned master of our hearts." The poem, according to this interpretation, is a reaction to the "bourgeois democratic" revolution of February 1917, and strikes a sharply dissonant note amid the chorus celebrating the arrival of "bourgeois" freedoms.

Mashbits-Verov, in his *Mayakovsky's Long Poems,*[17] develops a very similar interpretation of the poem but adds some interesting refinements of his own. Complaining that earlier critics, especially those who wrote during the twenties, overemphasized the darkness and despair in the poem, Mashbits-Verov seeks "life-

[15] *Ibid.*, p. 112.

[16] A. Metchenko, *Mayakovsky, ocherk tvorchestva* (Moscow, 1964), pp. 78ff.

[17] I. Mashbits-Verov, *Poemy Mayakovskogo* (Moscow, 1963), pp. 236-257.

affirming" notes and succeeds in finding some. The clear affinity of the poet with the sun (in spite of the graveyard darkness at the poem's end) he regards as a bright, positive note: "Though night still rules, though the sun has turned away from its herald, the poet ineradicably believes that it nevertheless will return to him . . . and that the rays of dawn will overcome the darkness."[18]

The hopeless lines that announce the eternal sway of the "contented and well-fed," Mashbits-Verov explains, reflected a time of tragedy for Mayakovsky and marked a spiritual crisis from which he emerged with increased strength and maturity and after which he made greater demands on himself and on life. After passing through "the dark night of the soul" in 1917 Mayakovsky grew to an understanding of the real nature of the power exercised by money, and he therefore expected more from the revolution: nothing less than the complete abolition of the exploitation of man by man. "Objectively, then, the poem is a sentence of death upon capitalism. Subjectively, as a stage in the poet's development, it is a work in which the artist faced a task toward the resolution of which his whole life had led him."[19]

Papernyi's comments on the poem are acute and arresting.[20] They depart somewhat from the pattern we have so far observed in that they give attention to the poem as a literary structure. Papernyi is able to distinguish between the poet's life and his literary production, between his politics and his poem. He maintains that the loneliness the early poems express does mirror certain facts concerning the poet's psychological condition, and that the revolution did indeed free him from his isolation and give him a sense of belonging to other people.[21] But he does not confuse these observations about the poet's biography with poetic analysis; indeed his book demonstrates an awareness of the distinction between the two.

Papernyi finds in the work of the early Mayakovsky a quality he calls "bi-tonal," a shift in tone arising from a contrast between opposing sets of poetic images: "On the one hand we have an image which expresses the view of the poet himself; on the other a grotesquely parodied 'answer' from the real world." In the poem *Man* the poet's hymn to the human hand, heart, and mind is overbalanced by a series of "contrasting images." The human

[18] *Ibid.*, p. 255. [19] *Ibid.*, p. 257.
[20] Papernyi, pp. 35, 63, 76, 112, 225.
[21] *Ibid.*, p. 35.

hand is made to hold a gun, the heart is chained by "religion," the mind is locked by "law." This poem, and much of Mayakovsky's early work, is built upon a series of such contrasts, Papernyi suggests: "The poetic and the spiritual, everything connected with the life of the heart, with dreams or song, is locked in mean and vulgar forms, is contained in reality as in a jail."[22] The special relationship of the poet in *Man* with the sun has often been pointed out, and Papernyi illustrates how the shifting role of the sun fits into Mayakovsky's system of contrasting images. The poem opens with a singing anticipation of dawn, but the bright promise ends in darkness and in the conviction that life is barren and pointless.[23] Papernyi's analysis throws great light on the nature of the poem, and, by extension, on the psychological condition of the poet, perhaps even on his social and political position.

The comments of V. Pertsov, who has produced a three-volume study of Mayakovsky,[24] are a sharp contrast to those of Papernyi. His interpretation is a conscientious effort to place Mayakovsky in the proper literary pantheon. He regards it as significant that the poem completed just before *Man* was entitled *War and the Universe* and thus betrays the poet's affinity with Leo Tolstoy (since the words for "peace" and "universe" are homonyms in Russian). And since Gorky wrote a prose poem entitled *Man* (it was published in 1904 and nothing in it but the title is like Mayakovsky's work), it follows that the two great writers were "ideologically close." Pertsov does recognize the vast difference in idea and methods between the two works, but his apparent purpose is to force Mayakovsky's poem into a respectable frame of literary reference, where, flanked by Leo Tolstoy and Maxim Gorky, it would seem to be adequately protected against formalist and futurist associations, as well as against any imputation of philosophical pessimism. The poem he interprets rather simply as a representation of the tragic hopelessness of the contemporary human situation, where man is drawn into "the abyss of declining capitalism"; he finds in it also a contrasting picture of the great possibilities the "dream of socialism" places before human society. The figure of the Ruler of All is a personification of capitalism, analogous both to Woodrow Wilson in Mayakovsky's *150,000,000* and to Gorky's "Yellow Devil." He concludes, finally, that the "objective meaning of the poem is that only revolution

[22] *Ibid.*, p. 96.

[23] Papernyi, pp. 225, 226.

[24] Pertsov [I], 394ff.

can save man and his society from destruction." There is nothing like that in the text of the poem, but of course the qualification "objective" rescues Pertsov from total fatuity: we may understand him to mean that such an idea may be deduced from the poem quite apart from the author's intention. And he is able to support this interpretation of *Man* by quotations from *another* poem, written at least five years later.

Shortly after Mayakovsky's suicide in April 1930 the Marxist literary critic Vyacheslav Polonsky, who had often engaged in literary polemics with the poet, published an important book about him in which a number of pages are devoted to *Man.*[25] He finds that *Man,* like Mayakovsky's other poems of the pre-revolutionary period, is saturated with pessimism. The theme of frustrated love that runs through the early poems reaches here a high point of tormented misery. Polonsky shows convincingly that in poems such as *War and the Universe* and *Man* the protest against war or against the world is not a social protest at all. The poet is alone; he suffers alone; upon him alone rests the burden of responsibility for the war and human suffering. Nor is there in those poems any sense of proletarian class-consciousness or any tidings of impending revolution. Mayakovsky was a pessimist, says Polonsky, right up to the eve of the revolution, and death, specifically death by suicide, was one of his most prominent themes.[26] Contemporary Soviet critics would of course not agree with him in this, and it may be that Polonsky is bending the stick too far. The poem *War and the Universe* can hardly be described as pessimistic in its final effect, and everyone remembers the prophecy of revolution "in the year sixteen" contained in the *Cloud.* Yet it is significant that Mayakovsky's early dreams of world-wide peace, or of a revolution coming like Christ in his glory, end in huddled despair or the rejection of life.[27]

An earlier Russian Marxist critic, Alexander Voronsky, takes a view of *Man,* and indeed of all Mayakovsky's work, that is at sharp variance with the interpretation espoused by almost all contemporary Soviet critics.[28] Voronsky singles out for special attention those passages in his work, both before and after the

[25] V. Polonsky, *O Mayakovskom* (Moscow, 1931).

[26] *Ibid.*, pp. 37ff.

[27] See *A Cloud in Pants,* ll. 480-500, in *PSS,* I, 189, and also the last lines of *Man.*

[28] A. Voronsky, "Vladimir Mayakovsky," *Krasnaya nov,* No. 4, 1925, pp. 249-277.

revolution, which reveal the poet's obsession with the thought of suicide. He is somewhat disturbed, moreover, at Mayakovsky's relative "illiteracy," and at his contempt for culture and its representatives. The poet's hero, Man, is an artless being made of "meat" who possesses hands and arms, a brain, and great appetites. He is "as simple as mooing." He is coarse and greedy, he sinks his teeth into whatever he wants, he is both a child and a savage. Kant, Hegel, Tolstoy, Rousseau, Christ, Socrates, all subtle philosophical systems, Christian culture—none of this means anything to Mayakovsky's Man. His needs are limited and his horizons narrow. He despises anything spiritual or intellectual. For his love's embrace he is willing to sacrifice not only philosophy but literature and art. Mayakovsky's socialism seems to Voronsky to have little in common with Marxist scientific socialism. His ideology is more like that of the frustrated bourgeois whom more agile competitors have deprived of the world's goods. The city is a place of torment for Mayakovsky, in Voronsky's opinion, simply because the "ownership of goods is in the hands of his enemy." Mayakovsky's essential estrangement from proletarian themes is borne out, moreover, by the complete absence from his poetry of the productive center of modern life: the factory.

Soviet interpretations of *Man* have, since 1934 at least, repeated with only minor variations a stereotyped formula that places the poem in the context of proletarian struggle against the oppressive force of capital. Papernyi's work is an exception to the rule, but no doubt only because he directs his attention in the main to the imagery of the poem rather than to its ideological message. Marxist critics who wrote during the twenties were free of the stereotypes and could examine Mayakovsky's work from many points of view. They were under no compulsion to explain away the poet's pessimism, or to gloss over his obsession with suicide, and they recognize the special significance of *Man* in his prerevolutionary work.

Turning now to criticism of the poem outside the Soviet Union, we find that a number of important insights into its meaning have been contributed by Roman Jakobson.[29] In his article on "a generation which wasted its poets" he deals with Mayakovsky's life and with his work as a whole. Though he does not analyze

[29] R. Jakobson, "O pokolenii, rastrativshem svoikh poetov," in *Smert Mayakovskogo* (Berlin, 1931).

Man separately, much of his article is concerned with themes, images, and attitudes expressed in that poem, placed in the context of the poet's life and work and in illustrative juxtaposition with lines from a number of other works. Jakobson makes the very important point that Mayakovsky's final letter and his suicide can be understood only in the context of his poetry. Unlike many poets, Mayakovsky's own life did indeed form the subject of his poetry, and his suicide is foreshadowed a number of times. Jakobson reminds us of the term coined by Trotsky, *Mayakomorfizm,* to express the poet's view of all existence. The poet's ego is in a constant struggle with the forces of *byt,* the established, static, and habitual. The Ruler of All is one of many forms assumed by *byt* in Mayakovsky's poetry. His enemy is a "universal" figure and "natural forces, people, metaphysical substances, are only the episodic masks he wears." There are two irreconcilable forces in Mayakovsky's world, *self* and *non-self.* It follows from this that the terms Mayakovsky borrowed from the Marxian intellectual environment, such as "bourgeois" and "proletarian," are only conventional symbols: "bourgeois" standing for static, satisfied, conservative, and "proletarian" for dynamic, striving, radical.

An attempt to apply to Mayakovsky's early work critical concepts and methods developed in recent years in the United States is Lawrence Stahlberger's book *The Symbolic System of Mayakovsky.*[30] The method of the book is in polar opposition to much of the earlier work on Mayakovsky. Stahlberger works in almost total abstraction from the man, the milieu, and the historical moment, searching in Mayakovsky's early works for parallels or affinities with archetypal situations or philosophical and religious ideas recurrent in world literature. The poem *Man* offers many possibilities for this kind of investigation. Stahlberger finds that its dominant motif is that of *bondage,* expressed by a group of related images in conjunction with the "I" of the poet.

> The poet ("I") is "driven into the terrestrial pen," pulls the "daily yoke," has a "chain, religion" on his heart, is "fettered" by the earth, has the globe of the earth "chained" to his feet, and is "enclosed" in a meaningless tale. This and similar symbolic complexes in Majakovskij's poetry which express motives of bondage, torture, and aloneness, may be summed up under

30 Stahlberger, p. 63.

> the term "martyrdom," and build up the "I" as the symbol of the martyr. The linkage to both Prometheus and Christ (culture-heroes) is apparent: Prometheus is fettered and staked to the rock, Christ is imprisoned and nailed to the cross, the poet is locked up in a meaningless tale, and man is bound to the earth (confined within space and time). The "I" of the poet also appears as martyr (or scapegoat) in *Vladimir Majakovskij, A Cloud in Trousers, The Backbone Flute, War and the Universe*, and other poems.[31]

Stahlberger points out that the imagery used in the passage that presents the earth as a prison shows a striking resemblance to that employed by the Gnostic sects. According to the Gnostics, the world is the creation of a demiurge or evil god. Man is imprisoned in the earth; he is also imprisoned in the flesh and in darkness; the planets or stars are watchers who guard his imprisonment, and "his appeals for help are answered with derision." It can easily be shown that images having some affinity with the picture of the world drawn by the Gnostics are embedded in Mayakovsky's poem, and in calling attention to this Stahlberger has thrown light on the nature of Mayakovsky's imagery and revealed in him a recurrent pattern of human thought.

Stahlberger offers other stimulating suggestions as to the meaning of the symbols in *Man.* The "anaesthesia" Mayakovsky experienced in heaven may be related to, possibly even influenced by, Kierkegaard's protest against the notion of heavenly bliss and of "eternity as the longest and most wearisome of all days. . . ." And Mayakovsky's return to earth, Stahlberger suggests, may be a poetic modification of Nietzsche's concept of "eternal recurrence." These suggestions are very plausible, since there is reason to believe that Mayakovsky had become familiar with both Kierkegaard and Nietzsche at about the time he was writing *Man.* We have already seen that among the books Lily Brik mentioned that she and Osip were reading aloud together at the time Mayakovsky entered their lives were Nietzsche's *Zarathustra* and Kierkegaard's *In Vino Veritas.*

This excursion through the criticism of *Man* has revealed a basic dichotomy in approach and method. Soviet critics as a rule read the poem as an episode in the poet's political biography

[31] Stahlberger, p. 14.

and attempt to throw light on it by consulting historical or ideological evidence. Mashbits-Verov, Metchenko, and Pertsov are examples of this method. Others attend either to the poem's structure or to motifs, images, and ideas in it, without reference to historical facts. Stahlberger, Jakobson, and perhaps Papernyi belong to this group. Neither approach is necessarily inappropriate. It is understandable that in the Soviet Union, with whose tragic and moving history Mayakovsky's work is saturated, critics should pay attention to evidences of his involvement with the revolutionary struggle. Although Stahlberger's book offers a great many new insights into Mayakovsky's work, it presents hardly any information concerning the poet's social or political position, and indeed Stahlberger may have given little attention to such things. Mayakovsky's life is as remote from Stahlberger's field of vision as is the life of Sophocles or the authors of the Gnostic texts echoed in *Man.* Stahlberger has posed questions that can be answered without reference to particular and local matters.

c) An Exposition of the Poem

The poem *Man* occupies a central point in the literary career of Mayakovsky. Not only does it provide a résumé of the themes and motifs of his early poetry, but it points ahead to the resumption of those themes—with an altered modulation—in the poem *About That* (*Pro eto*, 1923) and in some of the last lines he wrote.[32] In *About That* the intransigent hero of *Man* reappears to query the poet as to whether he has succumbed to the philistine temptations of property and family happiness,[33] and the tragic ending of the later poem, with its invocation to the Big Dipper, echoes these final lines of *Man*: "What heaven now?/ To what star?" It is important to recall that Mayakovsky himself and the audiences to whom he addressed the poem in 1918 treated it with high seriousness. The memoirs of the poet S. D. Spassky provide a vivid account of the effect on the hearers of Mayakovsky's poem, with its complex system of transitions from solemnity to casual humor and on again to deep tragedy. Spassky states that during the early months of 1918 Mayakovsky read the chapters of the poem *Man* almost every evening in the Poet's Café. He describes Mayakovsky at one such reading of this period:

[32] Roman Jakobson, "Za i protiv Viktora Shklovskogo," *International Journal of Slavic Linguistics and Poetics*, Nos. 1-2, 1959.

[33] *PSS*, IV, p. 151.

"He read in a low voice and very pensively. He hardly moved—it was as if he were holding a conversation with himself. And he seemed very large in the rather small room. He seemed morose and somehow lonely in the dim warmth and comfort of the place."[34]

The poem offers many possibilities of structural analysis, one of which will be suggested here. We may consider it as consisting of a three-part antiphonal series, in each of which strong major chords are answered by lines in the minor mode. In three quasi-religious episodes, to phrase the same idea in another way, faith is answered by unbelief and there follows in the end the darkness of despair. The opening section, entitled "Mayakovsky's Nativity," celebrates the hand, brain, and heart of a human being as a major miracle. A man's tongue, moreover, can make remarkable music:

> "O! ho! ho!" I sing
> And the high notes pour forth.
> "O! HO! HO!" I sing
> and my voice—
> the poet's obedient falcon—
> gently glides down low. (106-111)

This section of the poem contains a hymn to labor. Man as creator is revealed in a number of lowly activities: laundering, baking, shoemaking. When the poet raises his own heart to wave like a flag, "an unheard-of miracle of the twentieth century," the effect is one of elation at the richness of possibility resident in man's nature. But we remember that once before, in the *Cloud*, he had waved his heart "as a banner."

The transition in the second part of the poem, "Mayakovsky's Life," to a new thought and a new mood is marked by a deep-throated introductory line heavy with the vowel "o":

ryovom vstrevozheno logovo bankirov, velmozh i dozhei. (162)
(A roar troubles the lair of bankers, tycoons, and doges.)

Aroused and angered by the poet's joyous tidings, the powers of the real world emerge from their lair to proclaim another, their own, reality. Money is the essential thing, not the poet's heart waving on its eminence. Who, they ask, gave anyone the right to

[34] *V. Mayakovsky v vospominaniyakh sovremennikov*, p. 174.

sing? Who ordered the days to blossom with July? Tangle the sky in wires! Wind the earth in a maze of streets! Hands? Put a gun in them! A tongue? Poison it with rumor!

The disappointment of hope is immediate and sharp. The earth caught in a net of wires and streets is a distracted urban image reminiscent of many earlier lyrics.[35] The poet is "penned up" in the world; he bears his yoke of days. Law and Religion weigh him down. Images of constraint and containment dominate this part of the poem. A jailer whose thousand eyes are city street lights stands watch over him. The earth is a shackle on his feet. The ocean of his overflowing love is held fast by houses, and he is enclosed forever in a tale signifying nothing.

Reality has become a foaming vortex of money. Money in the poem stands as a symbol of the alien element (at times Mayakovsky calls it *byt*) in which the poet, whose vision is personal, subjective, and arbitrary, becomes encrusted. It stands for "hard" objective reality, for quantification and generalization. It is the antithesis of poetry. It is pure abstraction; it "doesn't smell," nor does it possess contour or color. Its value is not attached to particular persons or objects but applies equally to all things, without taste or judgment: books, houses, labor, bric-a-brac, art, and purchased love. Its various guises—dollars, francs, rubles, crowns, yen, marks—are not really distinct from one another: one can be converted into another by a simple quantitative operation. It is the negation of the heart. It is the enemy of metaphor in that it establishes between unlike things a *tertium comparationis* that is purely quantitative. It is the universal without concreteness. It swallows everything without discrimination: "Geniuses drown, and hens, horses, violins, / elephants drown in it / little things drown." (237-239) It seems to symbolize in the poem the totality of that impersonal objective existence before which the poet feels mixed revulsion and despair.

The Ruler of All appears, occupying a spot in the center of the money vortex. The poet's rival and invincible enemy, he takes the form of the conventional cartoon image of the greedy capitalist, a circumstance which, I believe, has misled some Soviet commentators. He is an inveterate philistine (*meshchanin*) in his tastes and in his attitude toward art and science. He reads

[35] See *PSS*, I, 38. Compare: "Lebedi shei kolokolnykh gnites v silkakh provodov."

cheap bourgeois novels of love and intrigue. Humanity may stand in wonder before the work of the sculptor Phidias, but it was actually the Ruler in one of his incarnations who ordered those statues: "I want some plump babes made out of marble." It was he who ordered God, "his artful cook," to fashion a pheasant out of clay for his appetite's sake. He needed a gather of stars for the delight of his female, so a legion of Galileos crawled all over the heavens with their telescopes for him. And he is immovable. He is the uncrowned master whom no revolution touches.

Like the "Maria" in the *Cloud* who leaves the poet for marriage, the girl in *Man* too is drawn into the vortex of the enemy's plenty. She whispers to the Ruler the names of Mayakovsky's poems: "His little flute, His little cloud" ("Fleitochkoi," "Oblachkom"); thus Mayakovsky's works of art, like those of the sculptor Phidias, are appropriated, used, and vulgarized by the enemy of all artists.

Clearly the Ruler in this poem does not fit any simple symbolic scheme. To speak of him as a "personification of capitalism" narrows the poem unduly, although Mayakovsky would no doubt have considered the contented capitalist as one version of the Ruler. He stands, rather, for something in the nature of existence that seemed to the poet recurrent, pervasive, and inescapable. It may be that, as Voronsky maintained, the enemy discerned by Mayakovsky was simply the successful bourgeois, the owner of goods inaccessible to poets; if that is so then the "bourgeois" is only one of his many masks. For the "same old baldhead" appears later in the poem in the guise of an "idea," or as religion, or even as Satan.[36] It seems clear that he resides also in the poet himself, and we may suspect that we have here that "other Mayakovsky," the one who was tempted by fine clothes, little French automobiles, and good food—who was, indeed, not strong against the allurements of material bliss. Finally, the poet would no doubt have recognized another version of the "old baldhead" in those contemporary Soviet commentators who force his honest lines into a preconceived pattern of their own.

The second exploration of faith and hope takes place in heaven. In the section of the poem called "Mayakovsky's Ascension" the poet's thoughts turn to suicide. In a passage of singular power which he recalled five years later in the poem *About That* he develops images of cold despair:

[36] *PSS*, I, 266.

> The soul shivers.
> She is fast in the ice
> and cannot move!
> That's how,
> under a spell,
> I'll walk the Neva embankment. (377-382)

He seeks a chemist who will sell him a draft of poison, but since man is immortal he has no need of the drink. Mayakovsky simply ascends into heaven and the promised bliss while pedestrians look on in stupid amazement. Over the churches with crosses burning in the light, over the forests filled with a "crowish cawing," Mayakovsky soars into the infinite. Now, indeed, he is everywhere, and he calls upon the poets to sing about the new "demon" in an American suit and shiny yellow shoes.

The section of the poem called "Mayakovsky in Heaven" is an answer to the traditional hope for happiness beyond the shackles of earthly life. Throughout this section there is a marked contrast between the lofty subject and the casual colloquial idiom in which it is treated. Having arrived, he puts down "his things" and relieves himself of the "load" of his tired body. Looking around, he finds that the much-admired heaven is nothing but a kind of "polished smoothness" (*zalizannaya glad*). Angels among the clouds are singing an aria from *Rigoletto*: "They have a fine life, these angels, a fine life." At first he found things difficult. Earthly philistinism was not at home with the celestial variety, and here we have a glimpse of the philistine in the poet himself. It was irritating, for instance, that no one had a "corner" for himself, that "there was no tea-time and no papers with the tea." But he got used to it. With all the others he would go out to stare at new arrivals and greet his newly deceased friends, then show them around the "central station of all phenomena," take them for a guided tour of the "chief warehouse of all possible rays," or show them an "ancient blueprint, no one knew whose, the first unsuccessful attempt at a whale."

In Mayakovsky's poem the notion of a transcendental being whose realm exists beyond the given world is reduced to infantile concreteness. His pictures of cloudland are like those of an urban child who is fascinated with science and technology, who figures the metaphysical first cause in terms of the levers, plugs, and handles that control all reality, and who sees the endless process of evolution as blueprints and charts of projects tried and rejected.

But the poet's disappointment is inescapable in heaven as well as on earth. The celestial realm has its own rigid organization. Everything is busy and serious. The bodiless beings are decent and workmanlike. They scold the poet for "lying around idle." In fact bodiless beings "have no heart." He proposes that he take on in heaven the role of poet, thinker, and observer, that he simply "spread himself out on a cloud and contemplate everything," a proposal the heavenly powers firmly reject. He falls at last into a deep ages-long sleep, one lasting sixteen thousand—or million—years.

The promise of earth is disappointed by the reality of "money" and its power over life; the promise of heaven is disappointed by heaven's "reality," in other words, by the nature of the human intellect itself, which inexorably defines and categorizes with a view to controlling external reality. The blessed ones in heaven have each an assigned task to perform, be it repairing clouds or firing the sun, and everything is done in "frightful orderliness" (*v strashnom poryadke*). The poet's special calling is no more honored in heaven than it is on earth. This suggests the possibility of a return to earth after "an avalanche of years" and an exploration of the planet's own potential for paradise.

The poem reaches a third climax, a final turning point, in the section called "Mayakovsky's Return." The thought occurs to the poet that after the lapse of millions of years earth must be quite different. No doubt there is "fragrant springtime" in all the villages, and the cities are full of light. Perhaps humanity is now a singing family of red-cheeked and happy people. I should point out, incidentally, that the sudden appearance of Mayakovsky's father at his side emphasizes again the childlike nature of his celestial images. The old man is just the same as he was, "only a little harder of hearing," and his ranger's uniform is a little more worn at the elbows. "It must be spring in the Caucasus now" is his prosaic comment, and for a moment in the poem the "father" seems to stand in the place of God himself. It is to him that Mayakovsky complains about the boredom of heavenly life and announces his intention of returning to earth, where time and progress must surely have wrought a change.

The third disappointment is the sharpest of all. The myth of heaven man can lose if he can still accept the idea of progress and believes in the possibility of an earthly paradise. But if man's promise is not realized on earth, if life after death is a childish dream and progress a myth, what is man to do with himself (*kuda devatsya*)? This is precisely the problem Mayakovsky poses in the third climax of the poem. Nothing has changed on earth since he last saw it. The human throng is still tied to "business" (*v povodu u dela*). The "same old baldhead" presides over the terrestrial "can-can," sometimes in the form of an "idea," sometimes as a kind of devil, sometimes like a god, hidden in the clouds. The disappointment of man's life on earth had been summed up earlier in the frustration of love and the pang of jealousy. After his return to earth it is "the same old thing." The thought of love offers itself and the poet "welcomes his madness back." He searches for his old love on Zhukovsky Street, where he had once lived with Lily and Osip, and finds her after all those years, but in the lawful bed of *another*: "I'm Nikolaev, an engineer. Why are you bothering my wife?" Disillusionment is complete when the poet learns that a legend has grown up around his own name. Thousands of years ago the name of "Zhukovsky Street" had been changed to "Mayakovsky Street," because, as a pedestrian explained, the poet had shot himself here at his loved one's door. And "she leaped to him out of the window, and there they lay upon each other, body to body." Thus humanity manages much as before. A foolish legend adorns the harsh inescapable reality. Love is not satisfied, but tales are still told in its honor.

The foolish story connecting his name with mutual "love unto death" is the final and sharpest wound the poet receives. The "future" has failed its prophet. Not only is the Ruler still enthroned and money dominant, but—what is infinitely worse—cheap fiction and verbal claptrap have vulgarized and dissipated the poet's tragedy. Mayakovsky realizes now, it would seem, that neither time nor distance will ever bring a change, and that even beyond the farthest cluster of nebulae that the most powerful telescopes will ever reveal there can never be any Elysian Fields, nor any place for the poet to rest. With mounting despair he wanders the emptiness of interstellar space.

The poem *Man* is a philosophical meditation on the nature of man, his present condition, and his promise for the future. The "man" involved is Mayakovsky himself, a poet. The basic idea, a not unfamiliar one in the work of the early Mayakovsky, is that the poet has "nowhere to go" (*emu nekuda detsya*). The force that dominates objective reality, represented in childlike images as the Ruler of All or as an angelic band busily managing the heavenly realm, or as the bald head of a lawful husband and father, allows no place for the man whose only banner is his heart. Man appears in the poem as a creator. Whether in the guise of baker, shoemaker, or poet, the important thing about him is his urge to make beautiful shapes or sounds or to think beautiful thoughts. This urge is frustrated by the invincible enemy in this world, in the next, and indeed "for ever and ever, Amen."

Chapter Seven

FORM, IMAGE, AND IDEA IN THE EARLY POEMS

1) Meter and Rhyme

Critics have occasionally compared Mayakovsky to Whitman in the supposed "freedom" of his verse lines, but the comparison is largely unwarranted, in spite of occasional echoes of Whitman in the early poems. Mayakovsky's verse is as a rule carefully structured as to rhyme, and falls into more or less regular patterns of accentual meter. We have already observed the subtle stanzaic structure and rhyme scheme of the poem "Listen!,"[1] in which the breaking up of lines into conversational phrase units conceals but does not destroy a complex poetic artifice. And we have also observed that the earliest poems, those written in 1912 and 1913, perfectly fit the conventional syllabo-tonic system. Beginning in 1913 with the cycle *Me*, Mayakovsky developed his characteristic verse style, in which the organizing element is the heavily accented syllable, usually occurring three or four times per line and with no strict requirement as to the number of unaccented syllables between the accents: these may vary from none to six.

The most interesting work on Mayakovsky that has appeared in the Soviet Union in recent years is the mathematical analysis of his verse forms undertaken by Professor Kolmogorov and a group of statisticians at Moscow University.[2] They are quite modest in their claims and they do not offer literary judgments, but the raw material of their studies makes it possible for literary scholars to speak with authority as well as judgment on Mayakovsky's behavior as a poet. Kondratov's study,[3] for instance, reveals that a

[1] See above, Chapter Four.

[2] See V. M. Zhirmunsky, "Stikhoslozhenie Mayakovskogo," *Russkaya literatura*, No. 4, 1964, pp. 3-26, for a commentary on recent work concerning Mayakovsky's metrical system and an examination of the major statistical studies of the early sixties. Full bibliographical reference to a series of articles that appeared in *Voprosy yazykoznaniya* will be found on page 9 of that article.

[3] Kondratov, "Evolyutsiya ritmiki," pp. 101-108.

quarter of the lines in the *Cloud* are conventional syllabo-tonic lines, but also that such lines almost never occur in close succession—in other words, there are no "stanzas" made up of them.[4] This leads to the question of the function of conventional lines in the context of accentual verse, and this is a question for literary scholarship. Sometimes such lines have the effect of parody, as in the lines referring to Severyanin,[5] or the line referring to the "proper little officer of the angel's league."[6] At one point the regular beat has the effect of a revolutionary marching song: "Cóme you stróllers, hánds out of póckets nów." (*Výnte gulyáshchie rúki iz bryúk.*) The conventional lines do not organize any part of the poem; they are used rather for incidental rhythmic effects that reinforce meaning.

Kondratov's statistics also reveal that the *Cloud* is organized in four-line stanzas, that the great majority of the lines have four or three accented syllables, but that there may be only one accented syllable in a line or as many as nine (this occurs in only one line).[7] And of course the rule in Mayakovsky's accentual verse is that the number of unaccented syllables between the accents varies.

A meter constructed in this way would seem to be rather free, and some scholars have questioned whether it can properly be called a "meter." The answer to such a question is that the lines are so structured that the ear experiences the regularity of four- or three-accent lines as the *expected* rhythm of the poem, and that the line with *one* accent or with *nine* accents (like the occasional syllabo-tonic lines) are experienced as a rhythmic variation. Take, for example, the second stanza:

Vót i vécher / v nochnúyu zhút	(four accents)
ushól ot okón, / khmúryi, dekábryi.	(four accents)
V dryákluyu spínu khokhóchut i rzhút	(four accents)
kandelyábry.	(one accent)

(Then the evening, in nighttime horror
Went away from the window, morose, Decemberish.
At my broken back neigh and guffaw
The chandeliers.)

[4] *Ibid.*, p. 103.
[5] *PSS*, I, 187, ll. 404ff., and p. 193, l. 616.
[6] *PSS*, I, 175, ll. 17-18.
[7] Kondratov, p. 106.

We note here the essential beat of the poem: a basic four-accent line "surprised," so to speak, by a sudden violent break in the rhythm, which in this case accords with the frantic emotional state of the speaker.

We have already pointed out that Mayakovsky printed these verses in the so-called ladder form, and that each phrase unit appears as a separate "line"; in the example above, slashes (/) indicate the phrase units into which the poem is broken on the page. This treatment of the lines is a consequence of the fact that the poems are intended for *declamation,* and a break in the line indicates a syntactic or emotional pause. The readers thus become participants in the process of declamation.[8]

Rhyme is a factor of prime importance in organizing Mayakovsky's lines. At times it seems that rhyme is more important than accentual beat, and one critic, Shtokmar, maintains that rhyme is the essence of the matter, and that Mayakovsky's verse should be called "rhyming" (*rifmovannaya*) rather than accentual.[9] The line and stanza boundaries are marked by rhymes, the sense of things is tied into firm knots by rhymes, rhymes are often a source of punning amusement, and Mayakovsky himself, in "How to Make Verses," offered evidence that *without* rhyme his verse would be virtually formless:

> Maybe you could leave the verse unrhymed. Impossible. Why? Because without rhyme the verse will fall to pieces.
>
> Rhyme returns you to the preceding line, forces you to remember it, holds together all the lines that form a single thought.

And again:

> Rhyme ties the line together, and therefore the rhyming material must be even stronger than the verbal material that goes into the rest of the poem.[10]

[8] In addition to the works already cited, two additional articles devoted to Mayakovsky's verse system have appeared: B. P. Goncharov, "O pauzakh v stikhe Mayakovskogo," *Russkaya literatura,* No. 2, 1970, pp. 47-62; and A. L. Zhovtis, "Osvobozhdyonnyi stikh Mayakovskogo," *Russkaya literatura,* No. 2, 1971, pp. 53-76.

[9] M. P. Shtokmar, "O stikhovoi sisteme Mayakovskogo," in *Tvorchestvo Mayakovskogo,* p. 292.

[10] *PSS,* XII, 105-106.

Moreover, Mayakovsky's notebooks offer ample evidence that for him "gathering material" for poems was to a large extent the invention and listing of possible rhymes.

The question is which is more important as an organizing factor in Mayakovsky's poetry, rhythm or rhyme, and the answer can only be that they are almost equally important; the regularity of accentual beat is supported and emphasized by rhyme schemes which are often very regular: in the *Cloud* there are only minor variations from the pattern *abab*, however concealed the pattern may be by Mayakovsky's heavily accented "phrase lines." For example:

> Voshlá ty
> rézkaya, kak "náte!" a
> muchá perchátki zámsh b
> skazála:
> "Znáete— a
> yá vykhozhú zámuzh." b

> You came in
> abrupt as "take it or leave it!"
> Fussing with your suede gloves
> you said:
> "Look—
> I'm getting married."

Mayakovsky's rhymes seem a clownish play with sound and sense, and it is obvious that, by preference, they violate the classical canons of nineteenth-century rhyme. But once again we must be wary of supposing that the violations are formless and arbitrary. There are clear rules for rhyming in Mayakovsky's verse, and the rules are based on the fundamental fact that his verse is meant to be declaimed, loudly, to an immense audience. The rhythm is the rhythm of *shouted* remarks, and each accented syllable carries such a heavy weight of vocal energy that unaccented syllables nearly disappear and it's quite possible to rhyme *shagóv mnu* (steps crumple) with *Góffmanu* (to or for Hoffmann). It should be said that the writer E.T.A. Hoffmann entered *The Backbone Flute* at that point chiefly because the name in rapid colloquial delivery fortuitously, and humorously, rhymes with a Russian verb form in which the root vowel (*m[?]nu*) has disappeared. Thus the reader's legitimate amusement at a funny rhyme is mingled with subconscious awareness of linguistic processes. Similarly the phrase *lzhi za nei* (lies about it) and the word *zhiznei* (of lives) are perfect rhymes given a declamatory emphasis in which the unaccented syllable *za* is slurred over, and may not even be heard in some parts of the vast auditorium which the reader must imagine as the setting for Mayakovsky's poems. Indeed these poems are so made that even a single reader alone in his room experiences the lines as a rolling and resonant "oration."[11]

One of the earliest analyses of Mayakovsky's rhyming habits was made in 1923 by Zhirmunsky,[12] who maintained that Mayakovsky offered in his "approximate" and "innocent" rhymes nothing that had not already been done by his predecessors Blok and Bryusov. V. V. Trenin[13] takes the contrary position that Mayakovsky's rhymes cannot be characterized simply as "inexact" according to the rules of conventional rhyme, but that they conform to a set of "rules" that arise from the declamatory nature of the lines, linked to the fact that in spoken Russian the word accent is strong and heavy. Trenin attempts, even, to set up new criteria for Mayakovsky's rhyming practices: classical rhyme is based on the correspondence of the accented vowel, as well as of the vowels and consonants in the syllable *following* the accent; Mayakovsky's modern rhyme requires that the accented vowel and the consonant immediately preceding it correspond, though the vowels and consonants following the accent need not. In other words, classical rhyme calls for correspondence at the end of the word, modern rhyme (in the Mayakovsky example) at the beginning. Trenin offers an impressive amount of material to support his position, and examples from other modern poets which indicate that they tend to follow the same rhyming practice. He finds also examples of experiments with rhyming possibilities, consonantal rhymes, for instance, in which not the vowels but the preceding and following consonants correspond: *slushat'-loshad'*, for instance.

Mayakovsky's rhymes are in their form and effect a kind of "unity of opposites." Just as his images combine the base and the

[11] A linguistic analysis is to be found in Roman Jakobson, *O cheshskom stikhe, preimushchestvenno v sopostavlenii s russkim* (Prague, 1923; repr. Providence, 1969), pp. 101ff.

[12] V. M. Zhirmunsky, *Rifma, eyo istoriya i teoriya* (Petrograd, 1923).

[13] V. V. Trenin, *V "masterskoi stikha" Mayakovskogo* (Moscow, 1937), pp. 101ff.

lofty, the serious and the comic, gutter diction and philosophical discourse, so the rhymes he uses, broken, distributed, assonantal, and so forth, are devices of comic poetry, which he uses to convey solemn and important thoughts. The Russian critic Dmitrii Mirsky suggested that an English equivalent of a Mayakovskian rhyme would be Browning's "ranunculus" rhyming with "Tommy-make-room-for-your-uncle-us."[14] Another affinity of Mayakovsky is Ogden Nash (Miriam-delirium; epidermises-kermises; honest-harnessed; red wagon-pet dragon, etc.), but we may doubt that either Browning or Nash would use such rhymes in lines that express anguished frustration or total alienation from God and the universe. The tantalizing quality of Mayakovsky's prerevolutionary poetry is that in it he succeeds in speaking of his soul's desolation using hyperbolic images and "funny" rhymes. His voice has a humorous inflection even when his subject is the mass slaughter of 1915 in Europe, or his own suicidal thoughts. And, paradoxically, the comedy in his verse underscores its deep solemnity.

One of the most interesting studies of the sources of Mayakovsky's verse forms is Trenin and Khardzhiev's "Mayakovsky and Satirikon Poetry,"[15] which names and briefly considers the principal writers of the *Satirikon*, a journal of humor and satire. Mayakovsky himself in his autobiography acknowledged a special debt to one of these writers, Sasha Chornyi: "My honored poet—Sasha Chorny. I liked his anti-aestheticism." The article I have mentioned considers the *Satirikon* writers Chorny, Potemkin, Goryansky, from the viewpoint of their influence on Mayakovsky's verse. Sasha Chorny, in his low diction and easy conversational idiom, as well as in his broken and combination rhymes, bears an unmistakable resemblance to Mayakovsky. But the difference between the two is vital: Mayakovsky uses low diction and off-beat rhymes not to amuse or satirize or even primarily to shock, but rather to vent his own malaise:

> Ulýbku *uberí tvoyú!*
> A sérdtse rvyótsya k výstrelu,
> a górlo brédit *brítvoyu.*

[14] As cited in Patricia Blake, *The Bedbug and Selected Poetry* (New York, 1960), p. 23.

[15] V. Trenin and N. Khardzhiev, "Mayakovsky i satirikonskoe poeziya," *Literaturnyi kritik*, No. 4, 1934, pp. 117-139.

(Get rid of the smile!
The heart yearns for a bullet
and the throat dreams of a razor.)

War and the Universe and *The Backbone Flute* both conform fairly closely to the accentual pattern of the *Cloud*, with few significant variations. The poem *Man*, however, presents a rich variety of metrical and rhyming effects, which have been studied in meticulous detail by V. V. Ivanov.[16] Indeed that poem, in its dazzling succession of shifts from one rhythmical pattern to another, presents the young Mayakovsky's full poetic range. The poem opens with a solemn invocation to the day and the night in long lines of free verse that, like certain other lines in the poem, are reminiscent of Walt Whitman. A substantial number of lines (100, according to Ivanov) are rhymed iambics. We find amphibrachs (˘ ´ ˘), and "pausative" verse forms characteristic of Blok, but with great variety in the length of the lines, some of which are hexametric in form, as well as the four- and three-accent tonic (accentual) verse that is the dominant pattern in the *Cloud*. The versatility and freedom of its forms reinforces the power of the poem's imagery and idea. We have seen that conventional meters, iambic or trochaic, often have the function of stylization or parody. They also produce in the reader a kind of ambivalence: when the regular cadence of iamb or trochee breaks into the pattern of accentual verse it seems to increase the sense of auditory variety, and piques curiosity as to meaning as well as form.[17]

2) Idea and Influence

The four long poems and some of the shorter ones written between 1913 and 1916 are the record of a young man's dispute with a world he never made and where he does not fit. The principal party to such a dispute, naturally enough, is God, and we have seen the various shapes the deity takes in some of the early poems. He is a kindly father in "Listen!" (but one who insists you have to be on time!); an enthusiast for Mayakovsky in

[16] V. V. Ivanov, "Ritm poemy Mayakovskogo 'Chelovek,'" in *Poetika* (*International Conference of Work-in-Progress*) (Warsaw, 1966), pp. 243-276.

[17] See Zhirmunsky, "Stikhoslozhenie," p. 20.

"But Anyway!"; majestic, like Leo Tolstoy, in "Petersburg Again." In the *Tragedy* he is a senselessly cruel being who talks of punishing little people who know nothing but pain and tears. In *The Backbone Flute* he is a "celestial E.T.A. Hoffmann" whose insane imagination invented the accursed woman Mayakovsky loves. What's more, he has punished the loud atheist who cried out "There is no God" by calling this Lily up out of hell and ordering him to love her. There too, as in the poem "Listen!" he proposes to visit God, if he exists, to plead his case, and promises again to be prompt. God may hang him from the Milky Way, draw and quarter him, do anything he pleases, if only he will take away that damned woman. In both the *Cloud* and *War and the Universe* the poet at first blames God for the personal and general misery, but both poems in the end find that God is dead and heaven empty: in the *Cloud* the universe is a huge sleeping animal indifferent to suffering or blasphemy; in *War and the Universe* all the gods have fled, and the transformation of human life is brought about by "a free human being." In *Man* God never appears, though his heaven is a place of blissful—and dull—satiety, and at the conclusion of the poem we are again left alone in a desolate universe without divinity or hope. When Mayakovsky announces himself in the *Cloud* as a modern "Zarathustra," the reference may be to Nietszche rather than to the Persian prophet. *Thus Spake Zarathustra* was widely read among the Russian intelligentsia just before the First World War, and, as we know from Lily Brik's reminiscences, it was a favored item in the milieu Mayakovsky entered in 1915.[18] Zarathustra's message that God is dead is deeply embedded in the early work of Mayakovsky, if we take it as a whole. In the *Cloud* the fact that heaven is deaf comes as a sudden surprise at the very end of the poem, and we are left, after a riot of wild emotion, with a quietness, the stars, and a question. In *War and the Universe* the flight of the gods is a kind of climax to the poem; but the restoration and repair of the world is to be the work of man, and Mayakovsky's "free human being" may very well be an ideological relative of Zarathustra's Superman. The poem *Man*, on the other hand, leaves us once again with the sky, the stars, and the same old query; the "free human being" has failed to appear, even after an "avalanche" of years. I have already had occasion to

[18] See above, Chapter Five.

mention that the stars and the universe are matters for contemplation toward the end of the poem *About That* (1923) and in some of the last lines Mayakovsky wrote, but in these later works the state of mind and the poetic intonation are altogether different.

In Mayakovsky's early poetry infantile images of the creator and his plans at last give way to a sense of loneliness in infinite space. God the father has disappeared and will not again enter Mayakovsky's work until after the revolution, when the poet contributed verse and drawings to the campaign of the "godless" against religion; but in those works he is nothing but a vicious invention of the priests and the exploiters.

Yet Mayakovsky was fascinated with the story of Christ, and we have seen the frequent appearance in his early poetry of New Testament texts. The poet is himself a new Christ, who bleeds for his humans, those who inhabit the "city-leprosarium." In an unpublished essay[19] Natalya Tarasova suggests that the god Mayakovsky rejects is the deity of the bourgeois, of the fat and contented ones who view suffering and sin without mercy; the compassionate Christ is a different matter, and indeed a different "religion." Miss Tarasova reminds us of a parallel with Belinsky's letter to Gogol. Belinsky wrote: "That you should support such a doctrine by reference to the Orthodox Church I understand. . . . But why do you mix up Christ in all of this? What does he have in common with any church, much less the Orthodox Church? He was the first who announced to men the teachings of freedom, equality, and brotherhood, and in pain and torment he affirmed and impressed upon us the truth of his teaching. . . ." This affirmation of Christ by the irreligious was taken up again by Dostoevsky in *The Brothers Karamazov.* Miss Tarasova mentions the adolescent Krasotkin, who is against God and religion but who says: "If you like, I'm not against Christ. He was a purely human personality, and if he had lived in our time he would certainly have joined the revolutionaries, and would have played an outstanding part." We may remark here that Ivan Karamazov, too, rejected God—or at least his creation—but that Alyosha reminded him of Christ as a justification of the world. Mayakovsky as Christ, we have observed, forgives nothing, in

[19] Natalya Tarasova, "Tema bogoborchestva v poezii Mayakovskogo" (unpublished manuscript, 1962).

fact has "burned out" the place where tenderness grew, reminding us once again of Ivan Karamazov when he speaks of a mother whose little son has been tortured by a sadistic landowner: "She doesn't dare to forgive him! If she wants to, let her forgive him for herself alone, let her forgive the tormentor for her boundless maternal suffering: but she doesn't have the right to forgive him for the suffering of her mutilated child. . . ."

The tradition of denying the orthodox God but accepting the figure of Christ is continued, with important modifications of the Christ figure, by Mayakovsky. We need not argue any specific influence of either Belinsky or Dostoevsky, since the idea is deeply embedded not only in the Russian tradition, but in the Christian religion itself: the Christ who saves men from suffering and damnation is a reproach and a correction of the Old Testament God. Mayakovsky says of God in the *Tragedy:*

> He's God
> and screams for a cruel reckoning,
> while in our poor souls there are only
> worn-out sighs.

Dostoevsky's influence is clear, however, in the passages of *War and the Universe* that assert Mayakovsky's guilt for all humanity's sins, and beg for forgiveness. I have already suggested *The Brothers Karamazov* as an important source for those passages, which may be a direct echo of the Elder Zosima's story about his brother. Just before his death the young man gained faith in God, and became convinced that he was guilty in the eyes of the whole world: "Even if I am guilty before all yet everyone forgives me, and that is paradise. And am I not in paradise now? . . . And I want to tell you, mama, that each of us is guilty before everyone else, and I more than any."

Dostoevsky's prose translates into the sharp, simple lines of *War and the Universe*: "I confess / that I alone / am to blame."

The problem of Mayakovsky's debt to Dostoevsky is complex and subtle, but there is no doubt whatever that the novelist, a spokesman for conservatism and the orthodox, fascinated the atheistic young rebel. Lily Brik maintained that Mayakovsky loved to read Dostoevsky, and in 1966 she produced an article entitled "A Proposal for Researchers" which is a kind of preliminary statement on some specific echoes of Dostoevsky in

Mayakovsky's early poetry.[20] She finds a number of passages in *About That* (1923) where there are clear echoes of *Crime and Punishment*, both of mood and of specific events. These we shall examine later. She mentions also the derivation of the guilt feeling in *War and the Universe* from *The Brothers Karamazov*, and a number of other curious coincidences, some important, others probably not.

Lily assumes a certain "community of feeling" between Dostoevsky and Mayakovsky, and at that point problems arise. Her statement is true to the extent that Dostoevsky himself can be identified with certain of his own characters. V. Kozhinov, in an article that accompanied Lily Brik's in the magazine *Problems of Literature*, quotes the comment of Pasternak that we have already seen, to the effect that the early work of Mayakovsky is "a kind of continuation of Dostoevsky. Or rather, it is lyric poetry written by one of [Dostoevsky's] young, rebellious characters."[21] Pasternak's insight is immensely illuminating. The "lyric hero" of the *Cloud* and *Man* is a tormented Karamazov—a mixture of Dmitrii and Ivan—whose love of life and rage against God appear, not in rational discourse, but in a wild mélange of metaphors.

I have already remarked in passing on a certain affinity of Mayakovsky with the French *poêtes maudits*—and perhaps even a debt to them. Baudelaire, Corbière, Laforgue, and Rimbaud were available in Russian translation, and they, no doubt, were the "Frenchmen" to whom Burliuk introduced Mayakovsky. Rimbaud, of whom Bryusov said that "he might be called the first futurist," was particularly important in the Burliuk milieu. The young Mayakovsky had some things in common with those poets: 1) the use of images and themes from a lower, "unpoetic" universe; 2) grotesque "realization" of abstract notions; 3) the unrelenting egoism of the lyric hero; 4) degradation of the matter of high poetry: the stars, the moon, and so forth. But in spite of these clear parallels Mayakovsky's originality is not in question. Mayakovsky was ignorant of the French language and not versed in the traditions of French poetry. His appropriation at second

[20] Lily Brik, "Predlozhenie issledovatelyam," *Voprosy literatury*, No. 9, 1966, pp. 203-207.

[21] V. Kozhinov, "Dostoevsky ili geroi Dostoevskogo," *Voprosy literatury*, No. 9, 1966, pp. 208-209.

or third hand of their motifs and methods is a curious demonstration of genius linked to ignorance. He knows the poetic mechanisms, but does not seem to know that they are literary poses, an episode in the long dialogue of modern French poets on the nature and purpose of poetry. He therefore uses the procedures inappropriately, for the purposes of his own ego, and in the interest of celebrating his suffering heart. Taking his departure from the *poêtes maudits* he moves off from them at an unpredictable tangent, and creates out of their effete materials, as we have already seen, a perfectly serious statement about his own self.[22]

A more complicated matter is his relationship to Whitman. We have already seen that Mayakovsky's carefully organized rhythms and rhyme schemes are quite unlike Whitman's freely surging lines. Chukovsky, whose translation of Whitman Mayakovsky read, maintained that Mayakovsky was interested in the American poet as an innovator, and as an enemy of "philistinism." At another point Chukovsky reported that Mayakovsky, even though he knew no English, had sufficient insight into Whitman's poetry to correct one of Chukovsky's own translations.[23] Many lines in the *Cloud* and in *Man* are clear echoes of Whitman and give evidence that Mayakovsky had read him attentively. We have already seen that in the *Cloud*, "Shattering the world with the might of his voice, / he comes on handsome, / twenty-two years old," and we have heard him say, with Whitman, that he "celebrates himself." In *Man* there is a series of lines that seem for a moment to breathe the spirit of Walt Whitman. "Walk around and look at me on both sides. On both sides you will be astonished at seeing a center with fine rays coming out. They're called hands, a pair of marvellous hands. Look! I can move from right to left and from left to right. Look! I can pick out the best possible neck and drape my arms around it!"

Notwithstanding echoes of Whitman in Mayakovsky's work, the two poets are almost polar opposites, and no light whatever is thrown on either by these accidental and superficial similarities. Whitman's poetry expresses a kind of joy at the sheer fact of existence—his own and that of everything else.

[22] On the general subject see A. V. Fyodorov, "Mayakovsky i literatura zapada," in *Vladimir Mayakovsky; sbornik statei* (Moscow, 1940), pp. 94ff.

[23] K. Chukovsky, "Mayakovsky," in *V. Mayakovsky v vospominaniyakh sovremennikov*, p. 122.

It's true that he "celebrates himself," but the celebration is not exclusive:

> I celebrate myself, and sing myself,
> And what I assume you shall assume,
> For every atom belonging to me as good belongs to you.

And again, of the man given up as dying:

> I seize the descending man and raise him with resistless will,
> O despairer, here is my neck,
> By God, you shall not go down! hang your whole weight upon me.

And of the "other," the "not-I": "Clear and sweet is my soul, and clear and sweet is all that is not my soul." And on death:

> Has anyone supposed it lucky to be born?
> I hasten to inform him or her it is just as lucky to die, and I know it.

Whitman is, like Mayakovsky, a kind of solipsist, but unlike Mayakovsky he includes in himself as real the multifarious items of the universe that his poetry catalogues with such an ebullience of joy. Mayakovsky's poetic genius, on the other hand, sets the ego of the poet at odds with the external world. Rain, clouds, sun and moon, the streets and structures of the city, prostitutes and lovers—all these things are denied autonomous existence in the *Cloud* and are forced to undergo a metaphoric process of identification with the poet's own emotional states. In *Man* external reality is admitted as autonomous and everlasting, but it affords the poet neither joy nor love. Mayakovsky could never have written the innocently worshipful lines of Whitman's preface to the 1855 edition: "The known universe has one complete lover and that is the greatest poet. He consumes an eternal passion, and is indifferent which chance happens and which possible contingency of fortune or misfortune and persuades daily and hourly his delicious pay. What balks or breaks others is fuel for his burning progress to contact and amorous joy. . . ."[24]

[24] For a study of Whitman and Mayakovsky see Dale Peterson, "Mayakovsky and Whitman: The Icon and the Mosaic," *Slavic Review*, XXVIII (1969), 416-426.

3) Imagery

We have observed in some detail the operation of Mayakovsky's image-making apparatus as we studied each of the poems; it remains to sum up and to generalize. The image of the poet's heart is a kind of red thread—if we may attempt to revive a figure of speech—that runs through the four long poems. In the *Cloud* his heart suffers a variety of metaphoric vicissitudes: at first it is a bloody tatter, then a bloody banner for revolutionaries, and finally a poor dog's bloody paw run over by a train. The successive metaphors of the heart register the shifts in shape and tone that the hero himself, the cloud in pants, undergoes in the course of the poem. In *Man*, we recall, the poet's heart is again a banner, and his only one. Papernyi has pointed out similar shifts in the images of heaven and earth. Heaven ranges from a place of "strikes" and "uprisings" to the "night of reaction," and earth is at one point a panting woman, at another Rothschild's whore; finally she perishes "at the knives" of the revolution. The sun as the source of life is a frequent visitor in Mayakovsky's poetry. We recall that in the last poem of the cycle *Me*, the sun is addressed as a kind of heavenly father to whom the crucified son turns for mercy. In the *Cloud* the sun is General Gallifett advancing to mow down human beings; the last rays of its setting are the death of the revolution; or it is Salome dancing a thousand times around the earth, John the Baptist's head; then again it is Christ betrayed by a Judas-like night for a scatter of silvery stars. *Man* opens with a joyous, almost religious, greeting to a new sun and a new day, but that very greeting anticipates the betrayal that underlies the poem. Night is a traitor, an assassin always lying in wait. Mayakovsky's imagery in the prerevolutionary poems allows the imagination no illusions of permanent light or peace. Only the stars (when they are not pieces of silver) hold a measure of comfort: they stand in the poet's imagination as a symbol of the mystery of creation itself, in the early poem "Listen!" (1913), in the *Cloud*, in *Man*, in *About That* (1923), and in some of the last lines he wrote:

> Just see how quiet the world is!
> Night has laid a heavy tax of stars upon the sky.
> In hours like these you get up and you speak
> To the ages, to history, and to the universe.[25]

[25] *PSS*, x, 287.

It is important to note also that the aspect of the sun changes crucially in the poem "The Sun," written in 1920, after the revolution; this alteration of a recurrent image may offer a clue as to the psychological effect of the revolution on the poet. When the sun visited Mayakovsky at his summer place in 1920 it was transformed in the course of that poem, as we have seen, from a dully repetitive purveyor of heat and haze into a source of light and confidence. We will deal later with the problem of the revolution in Mayakovsky's verse and in his psyche.

4) Animals

Mayakovsky constantly and compulsively drew giraffes—in a variety of touching, innocent poses. He identified himself with the great, long-necked creature, timid, relatively defenseless, both ungainly and graceful in stance and movement, and we should not overlook the irony inherent in this identification: the poet, self-proclaimed as "golden-tongued," chose as his preferred metamorphosis a totally mute beast. This poet was articulate, quick and devastating in repartee, even eloquent when the need arose, and he was always in brash contention with crowds; but a part of him would have preferred to be dumb and shy.

The giraffe was his favorite beast-double, but there were many others: dog, bull, elk, elephant, ostrich, bear, and, of course the most important one, the horse. Mayakovsky's animals are all alter egos of the poet himself, and each one expresses some aspect of his own alienation. Often he appears as a dog, the first time telling of how he grew canine tusk and tail, got down on all fours and barked at the huge crowds that pressed around him. We have seen him in the *Cloud* as a whipped dog licking the hand that beat him. In the poem "To All" (*Ko vsemu,* 1916), tormented by abuse and frustration, he is suddenly a mad dog under the bunks of a barrack, lashing out at fat legs; and we recall that, in the *Cloud,* at the climax of revolution he "slid up to someone— / bit into his flesh."

The dog in Mayakovsky snarls, yelps, and bites at his oppressors, though he may also lick their hands. The bull roars, "his neck an ulcer under the yoke, / a swarm of flies about it." In *The Backbone Flute* he is again a bull:

> You set a smile on your lips.
> Look.

What a handsome toreador!
But that's me
throwing a jealous look into your box
from my dying bull's eye. (154-159)

The elk has his branchy head caught in wires (the wiry net of the city?) and his eyes are charged with blood: "A trapped heart, I rise above the world." As an elephant Mayakovsky is tired and in need of a roll in heated sand. And one of the most touching of his transformations is the "ostrich from over the seas," wearing feathers of "stanzas, meters, and rhymes." The loneliness of the poet among philistines, Mayakovsky's persistent theme, receives its most effective bestiary symbol in the great bird who is out of place in Russia—"that snowy horror," who must "bury itself deeper" in poetic feathers, who dreams of another homeland, and whose true nature is a puzzle to ordinary humans, some of whom inquire simply as to its use value:

People shrink away—
Shouldn't we leave,
doesn't it bite?—
Others are bent in humble flattery.
"But mama
O mama,
does it lay eggs?"—
"I don't know, honey.
Maybe it does."[26]

If we pass over for a moment the bear, the shape he takes in the poem *About That* (1923), Mayakovsky's most poignant animal double was the horse, and "Be Better to Horses" (*Khoroshee otnoshenie k loshadyam*, 1918)[27] is one of his most beautiful short poems. In its emotional rhythm the poem bears a striking resemblance to "The Sun," and the fact that both poems were written *after* the revolution and during a period of feverish involvement in revolutionary activity suggests that an important—even if temporary—psychological change had taken place in the poet as a concomitant of that activity. We shall presently see other evidence, also poetic, of this change in emotional outlook.

Like "The Sun," "Be Better to Horses" at first balances precariously between despair and hope, but at last courage moves

[26] *PSS*, I, 130-131.

[27] *PSS*, II, 10-11.

the scale with absolute certainty. The subject is a common street occurrence of the war and famine years—a half-starved and overworked horse falls and cannot rise; this was no light matter for the horse, who might be butchered on the spot. Curiously enough Maxim Gorky published a prose sketch of just such an occurrence in the very issue of *New Life* (*Novaya zhizn*) that carried Mayakovsky's poem. In Gorky's sketch a huge Negro undertakes to comfort the horse by adjusting his body on the cobblestones, but does not succeed in encouraging the horse to rise and walk.[28] Mayakovsky brings the animal to its feet and to willing acceptance of its hard lot.

The poem is a technical masterpiece. Its opening miraculously imitates the sound of a horse's hoofs as it plods dispiritedly along a paved street. The words used include the basic vowel sounds of the Russian language given in series from front to back, each one preceded by a gutteral "gr" and followed by a labial stop "p." The words themselves carry meanings totally independent of the action, which lends emphasis to the onomatopoeic device.

Bili kopyta	Hoofs beat
Peli budto:	As though singing:
Grib.	Mushroom.
Grab.	Plunder.
Grob.	Grave.
Grub.[29]	Coarse.

The poetic projection of the subject's experience upon the outside world, a favored device in the *Cloud*, reaches a point of perfection in this poem when the street, drunk on wind and booted with ice, "slips and slides," and again when the same street, reflected in the eyes of the fallen horse, "is overturned, and pours away." The crowds that pressed upon Mayakovsky as a dog, the flies that tormented him as a bull, the good people who shied away from him as an ostrich, reappear in this poem as a gang of idlers who gape at the hapless beast and laugh:

"A horse fell down
Look it fell down—a horse,"
Kuznetsky[30] laughed.

[28] V. Katanyan, "Otnoshenie k loshadyam," in *Mayakovskomu; sbornik vospominanii i statei* (Moscow, 1940), pp. 65-70.

[29] The final "b" in Russian is devoiced to "p."

[30] A street in Moscow.

I was the only one
who didn't join in the howl.
I came up.
And I looked into
those horsey eyes . . .
I came up and I saw
great drop after tearful drop
roll down that big mug
and hide in the hair.

And the poet is overwhelmed by a kind of universal animal melancholy that pours out of him in tender speech:

No, horse, don't!
Look, horse!
Why do you think you're any worse than they are?
Honey!
We're all horses, kind of,
each one of us in his own way is a horse.

Perhaps the speech helped, perhaps the old horse was in no need of a nurse, but in any case it leaped to its feet, neighed and moved on, waving its tail a bit. And it seemed to the horse:

He was a colt again
and it was worthwhile to live
and work was worthwhile.

(i stoilo zhit
i rabotat stoilo)

Mayakovsky's horse symbolizes the poet himself in contention with the vulgar philistines of the street, but in this poem the animal symbol for the first time includes more than Mayakovsky. Not the poet only but all sentient beings suffer under the weight of their lives, and the poet suddenly realizes the community of his own suffering with the general "beastly" misery: "we're all horses, kind of." Moreover, the poem is a little fable whose moral point is that one dispirited being can perhaps help another if he gives him love and encouragement. This may seem an elementary and certainly an unremarkable thought, but for Mayakovsky it is an enormous stride beyond exclusive concern with the self and its frustrations. The final lines are echoed many times in Mayakovsky's post-revolutionary verse: in the close of "The Sun," with its call to "shine on, no matter what," and in those stirring lines near the end of *Very Good* (1927):

> I've been over the globe
> almost—
> and life is good
> and it's good to be alive
> and in this struggling seething
> mess of ours it's the best.[31]

Those, and other lines of a similar tenor, entered Mayakovsky's poetry only after the revolution, which he proclaimed as his own.

[31] *PSS*, VIII, 322.

Chapter Eight

THE POET ENGAGED

1) *Art of the Commune* AND *Mystery-Bouffe*

The revolution of February 1917 found Mayakovsky in Petrograd occupied with the not too onerous—and safe—duties of the auto school, duties which had nonetheless won him a medal "for devotion."[1] Caught up in the elation of the moment at the overthrow of the monarchy, Mayakovsky was for a time in sympathy with the aims of the Provisional Government, a fact that has been a source of embarrassment to some Soviet historians.[2] During those turbulent days he was one of the most active and articulate figures in the organizing of artists and writers to defend their own interests. He was elected, for instance, along with Punin, M. A. Kuzmin, and Alexander Blok, as a member of the executive board of a newly formed Provisional Committee for the Union of Art Workers,[3] and he spoke often and well on the need for the freedom of artists from government control. His defense of "freedom" in those days was apparently motivated by the fear that figures hostile to the futurists, Benois and his World of Art (*Mir iskusstva*) group, for instance, might gain a measure of control in the new government. We shall soon see that his fears were unfounded.

The turn of events in October 1917 changed all literary perspectives. Mayakovsky recorded that he had offered himself to the revolution, and that he was willing to "do anything." The chronicle of his life during that year reveals a variety of activities, most of them in some way connected with the new government. During the year he appeared frequently in the Poets' Cafe to read his poems, and his letters to Lily Brik convey an alternating elation and disgust at these activities. He was involved also in what he calls "*Kinemo*," the cinema, and he wrote a scenario, *Not Born*

[1] Katanyan, *Khronika*, p. 82.

[2] There is an excellent and apparently exhaustive piece of research on this topic: E. A. Dinershtein, "Mayakovsky v fevrale–oktyabre 1917 g.," in *Literaturnoe nasledstvo*, LXV, 541-576.

[3] *Ibid.*, p. 544.

for Money, based on Jack London's novel *Martin Eden*. In his own words, written to Lily Brik:

(Moscow, First half of March, 1918)

Write me, Lily dear!

Things are to a considerable extent repulsive. I'm bored. I'm sick. I'm sore. My only amusement (and I wish you could see it, you'd be terribly amused) is that I'm playing in the "cinema." I wrote the scenario. I have the principal part.

I gave Burliuk and [Grinkrug] parts.

I'd like to see you.

I can't write, my mood's miserable.

I've begun to read French—for kicks.

I kiss and embrace you and Osip.

Your Volodya[4]

The letters of the period are first-hand evidence of rapid changes in his mood. Another letter, written shortly after this one in answer to a letter from Lily, is full of good spirits, telling of the publication under his editorship, along with Burliuk and Kamensky, of the *Futurists' Newspaper* (*Gazeta futuristov*), of which the only issue appeared on March 15, 1918, and the poems, "Our March" (*Nash marsh*) and "Spring" (*Vesna*), that he had written for it. He wrote a scenario for a second film, *The Young Lady and the Hooligan* (*Baryshnya i Khuligan*), and in that film also he played the principal part. In May of the same year he produced a third scenario, *Held Fast in Film* (*Zakovannaya filmoi*), leading parts in which were taken by Lily Brik and himself.[5] He was involved also in the organization of a fictive "publishing house," ASIS (Association of Socialist Art), actually a venture supported by money borrowed from his friends, under the imprint of which the *Cloud* and *Man* appeared in uncensored versions.

The first overt effort to claim a special place for the futurists in the revolutionary state was the newspaper already mentioned, the *Futurists' Newspaper*. In the one issue that appeared Burliuk, Kamensky, and Mayakovsky boldly identified themselves as the true revolutionaries of art, and Mayakovsky addressed an "Open Letter to the Workers," in which he expressed his amazement that old-fashioned "Aidas and Traviatas" are still heard in theaters

[4] *Ibid.*, p. 107.

[5] For a detailed account of these matters see William Rudy, "Mayakovsky and Film Art" (unpublished Harvard dissertation, 1955).

conquered by the working class, and his hope that a "revolution of the spirit" may once and for all clear away the "ragged vestments" of the old art. It is impossible to foresee the magnificent life that future art will bring to mankind, he said, "but one thing is clear—the first page in the history of modern art was turned by us."[6] The letter reads uncomfortably like a document in the more recent Chinese "cultural revolution," with its call for a complete break with the "bourgeois" in art; yet its principal point is that the futurists are "revolutionaries of form." Such documents actually represent an attempt of the innovators in art to gain wide and official recognition; the time seemed to them ripe to "crash" the art business, and to dispossess the conservatives, who were still in favor with the public. In the same issue of that newspaper there is an editorial article complaining that although Mayakovsky's *War and the Universe* and Kamensky's *Stenka Razin* were among the earliest revolutionary poems, yet the futurists are still persecuted and driven from the public presses, even as they were "in czarist times."

The brief and stormy history of the journal *Art of the Commune* (*Iskusstvo kommuny*), the weekly paper published by the Fine Arts Section (*Izo*) of the People's Commissariat of Education, is extremely revealing as to the difficulty Mayakovsky and his futurist friends experienced in their effort to be recognized as the true "proletarians" of art. The one literary group whose members as a whole welcomed and supported the bolshevik revolution were the Moscow futurists, and the result of this was an adventitious and short-lived alliance between futurism and bolshevism. The futurists, who were installed as editors of *Art of the Commune*, attempted to assert themselves as the semi-official leaders of artistic and literary life. In flamboyant pronouncements they claimed to be the original revolutionaries in art and to speak in such matters for the proletarian state. Their intransigent nihilism and their policy of a "clean sweep" for the old order of things seemed *at the moment* to be in line with official policy. The idea of radical, absolute solutions permeated the air, and the futurists, having appropriated an eminence as friends of the new regime, spoke of a "proletarian dictatorship" in the arts. Mayakovsky's statements of the artistic program, usually in the form of brief poems printed as editorials, betray the strident emotional extremism that characterized both him and his times. His "Order to the

[6] *PSS*, XII, 8-9.

Army of Art" (*Prikaz po armii iskusstva*), which appeared in the first number of the paper (December 7, 1918) called his futurist comrades to the "barricades of heart and mind":

> Out with cheap truisms.
> Erase the old from hearts.
> Streets are our brushes,
> squares our palettes. . . .

The poem entitled "It's Too Early to Rejoice" (*Radovatsya rano*), published as an editorial statement in the second number (December 15, 1918), calls for an attack on "Pushkin, and those other generals of classicism":

> You catch a white Guardist—
> Up against the wall!
> But what about Raphael?
> Have you forgotten Rastrelli?
> It's time
> for bullets
> to pepper museums. . . .[7]

"The Poet Worker" (*Poet rabochii*) attempted to refute the widespread notion that poets are useless fellows who never work:

> Who is greater—the poet
> Or a technician who
> leads people to material profit?
> Both.
> Hearts—are also sources of power.
> The mind—is also a cunning motor.[8]

Several other short poems—"Left March" (*Levy marsh*), "Astonishing Facts" (*Potryasayushchie fakty*), "On That Side" (*Toi storone*), "With Comradely Greetings, Mayakovsky" (*S tovarishcheskim privetom, Mayakovsky*)—first appeared in *Art of the Commune*; they all took the general position that the art of the past is of no use to the factories, the streets, and the working-class quarters of the city, and therefore should be eliminated. Occasionally the paper carried editorial articles on the problems of modern art, and one of these expressed a pathetic confidence in the "proletariat" as an "advanced" class able to understand and appreciate the "advanced" art of the futurists: . . . "They are not

[7] *PSS*, II, 16.

[8] *PSS*, II, 18-19.

children, but quite grown up, as is evidenced simply by the fact that they have made their own an economic theory which leaves in the shade all the economic "sciences" of the bourgeoisie. . . . There's no point in trying to teach [the proletariat]. It will do the teaching itself."[9]

Some articles signed by Kazimir Malevich breathe the spirit of Marinetti. One of these, entitled "Architecture, as a Slap at Steel and Concrete," is a plea for a style in architecture that is proper to modern life, and a rejection of the "arteriosclerized" forms of ancient Greek architecture. He finds that the new Kazan railway station in Moscow is an example of the latter: "The locomotives will blush with shame, when they see they have to enter an almshouse."[10] Another, "About the Museum," a fierce rejection of the heavy weight of the past concentrated in the museums, appeared at the height of a government campaign to persuade the "intelligentsia," who had been responsible for the museums, to go on working hand in hand with the new regime. "Do we need Rubens or the Pyramid of Cheops?" Malevich asks. "We would rather complain about a broken nut than about the dilapidation of the Church of Basil the Blessed. . . . Is it worthwhile to pay attention to the dead?"

Curious evidence of the difficulties encountered by the new art was "Letter from Vitebsk" written by Marc Chagall and published in an early number of the journal.[11] The letter tells with some astonishment of what happened when futurist artists attempted to decorate the city of Vitebsk for the first festival of the revolution:

> . . . I must confess with some pain, that even advanced revolutionary comrades, even they, foaming at the mouth, showered us with bewildered questions: "But what the devil is this?"; "Please explain!" . . . "You mean *that's* proletarian art?" . . .
>
> Well, let this petty philistine malice seethe all around us, we still have hope that very soon new artists—proletarians—will arise from the ranks of labor.

Not infrequently articles and editorials in the paper throw light on the harsh realities of political power and the efforts of the editors to hold and manipulate it. There is evidence that Osip Brik

[9] *Iskusstvo kommuny*, No. 12, February 23, 1919.
[10] *Ibid.*, No. 1, December 7, 1918.
[11] *Ibid.*, No. 2, December 15, 1918.

was not only a perceptive publisher and brilliant formalist critic, but also a shrewd organizer of literary affairs and a man with a taste for power. Some first-hand accounts of the period identify him as in some sense an associate of the Cheka, one of the radical intellectuals who, like Babel, had been drawn into the rough business of "defending the revolution." According to one reliable story he actually did serve at one time as a legal consultant for the secret police organization.[12] One of his signed articles in *Art of the Commune* was a bitter and scornful attack on "bourgeois" artists who complained that they received only "3rd category rations," and a firm reminder that adequate nourishment would only go to "proletarians": "The answer is very clear. The proletarianization of all labor, including artistic labor, is a cultural necessity. . . . And no amount of tears shed for their supposedly vanished creative freedom will help in this matter."[13]

Evidence of the debate taking place among the editors concerning the harnessing of art to the wheel of politics was Shklovsky's now famous article "On Art and Revolution," which contains many Shklovskyesque *mots.* In it Shklovsky rejected the efforts of the futurists to link their art work to the Third International, since the function of the futurists was precisely to liberate form from content. "Art," wrote Shklovsky, "has always been free of life, and its color never reflected the color of the flag flying over the city's fortress."[14]

The hopes of Mayakovsky, Brik, Chagall, and Kamensky were deceived. They soon found themselves not only out of step with the proletarians, whose taste in literature, if it existed at all, tended to favor the classics and to reject the sophisticated linguistic contortions of the futurists, but sharply at odds also with the leaders of the Party-State. It is well known that Lenin regarded Mayakovsky's work with frank distaste. Somewhat later, during the controversy over the Proletcult, he inadvertently revealed his hostility when he linked the futurists with "decadents, partisans of an idealistic philosophy hostile to Marxism, and simply ne'er-do-wells from the ranks of the bourgeois publicists and philosophers."[15] Of Mayakovsky himself he said: "Pushkin I understand

[12] The idea that Brik was associated with the Cheka is hinted at by Nadezhda Mandelshtam in her reminiscences, *Hope Against Hope* (New York, 1970), pp. 172-173.

[13] *Iskusstvo kommuny,* No. 4, December 1918.

[14] *Ibid.,* No. 17, March 1919.

[15] *Pravda,* December 1, 1920.

and enjoy . . . Nekrasov I acknowledge, but Mayakovsky—excuse me. I can't understand him." During the period of *Art of the Commune* the concern of Lenin and other party leaders for what they called the "cultural heritage" led them to stern disapproval of the futurist attack on the art of the past, and Lunacharsky himself intervened to correct the editorial line of *Art of the Commune.* Mayakovsky's poem "It's Too Early to Rejoice" moved him to write a rejoinder entitled "A Spoonful of Anti-Toxin" (*Lozhka protivoyadiya*),[16] whose principal target was Mayakovsky's announced program for dynamiting old monuments and shooting up museums, and in that article Mayakovsky's methods received a measure of rebuke.

It is symptomatic of the times that Lunacharsky himself had some sympathy with the futurists—he had appointed many of them to leading positions in the Commissariat of Education—and that, as a matter of fact, a lively controversy developed around his own critique of Mayakovsky. The main burden of his published article was a defense of the "cultural heritage" against extremist attacks, but in it he also cautioned the futurists against the mistake of imagining that they were a kind of state-sponsored school of art. They constituted one particular group in the world of art, he insisted, and they did not speak in the name of the government. It has recently come to light that not all of what Lunacharsky wrote was published in *Iskusstvo kommuny.* A concluding section sharply critical of Mayakovsky himself was not published:

> But actually Vl. Mayakovsky worries me very much.
>
> He's very talented. It's true that within his new forms, coarse but tough and interesting, he conceals essentially very old-fashioned thoughts and an old-fashioned taste. . . .
>
> However, he's a talented man. With the passage of time one may expect him to display greater maturity of mind and heart, and he has already achieved a high level of originality in formal mastery.
>
> But then what frightens one is his boyhood, which has continued too long. Vladimir Mayakovsky is an adolescent. . . .
>
> One may forgive, a little bit, such a young fellow when he envies his older brothers on Parnassus and finds it impossible to speak of them without hatred, when he thinks that the mighty

[16] *Iskusstvo kommuny,* No. 4, December 1918.

> corpses . . . interfere with the success of his own handiwork, and when he wants to see himself the first and foremost artist on a denuded earth and among people who have forgotten the past: it's better that way, without competitors. . . .[17]

Lunacharsky's attack was answered in the same number of the paper by an editorial statement and by Mayakovsky's poem "On That Side." The editorial statement twitted Lunacharsky with being a poor reader of poems, since his criticism of "It's Too Early to Rejoice" was based on a literal understanding of that poem's figurative language concerning the necessity of "shooting" the classic generals. "No modern critic would assert that Pushkin in the line 'Set fire to hearts with your word' is inciting poets to use combustible materials and burn the hearts of his neighbors." But the argument of the editors is actually a sophistry: Mayakovsky's poem did call for relegating the classics to an inferior position, and Lunacharsky's article is an answer to *that* program. The poem "On That Side" reiterates and reinforces the nihilism of Mayakovsky's earlier statement, though it does add the idea that once the innovators have established their art in "battle," they will spread out all ornaments, and "you can like whichever you like."

Lunacharsky's intervention is clear evidence of unhappiness with the futurists at the highest level, and their journal *Art of the Commune* was discontinued early in 1919; but before its demise the journal had become the arena for arid and scholastic discussions of such questions as the relationship of new art to old, who is and who is not a revolutionary artist, what art ought to be, and so forth and so on. This insistent polemic made *Art of the Commune* a dull paper, and in spite of the few sharply penetrating articles it carried, no one could have greatly regretted its passing.

The most important factor in the low official estimate of Mayakovsky was the "difficulty" of his poems, and however radical the futurists claimed to be, their message was lost, not only on Lenin, but on proletarian readers who knew nothing about the "old" culture of the nineteenth century or the futurist rebellion against that culture. As Trotsky put it: "The futurist break with the past is, after all, a tempest in the closed-in world of the intelligentsia which grew up on Pushkin, Fet, Tyutchev, Bryusov,

[17] *Literaturnoe nasledstvo,* LXV, 571-573.

Balmont, and Blok. . . . The futurists have done well to push away from them. But it is not necessary to make a universal law of development out of the act of pushing away."[18]

Mayakovsky's most important revolutionary effort of 1918 was the verse drama *Mystery-Bouffe*. In October 1918, he sent to the Central Committee for the Organization of the October Celebrations a brief outline of his revolutionary "spectacle and extravaganza," in which Mayakovsky, the poet heretofore of his own ineffable self, removed himself into the background in favor of the "masses." The play, a modern variant of the mediaeval mystery with added ingredients of farce and blasphemy ("bouffe"), was presented in its first version in 1918 on the anniversary of the October revolution under the direction of Vsevolod Meyerhold. The play faced difficulties from the start, and throughout its history. Experienced actors were unwilling to perform in it. An advertisement in the Petrograd papers announced preparations for the staging and called upon actors wishing to take part in it to present themselves in a certain place at a certain hour. The advertisement rang with revolutionary fervor: "Comrades Actors! You are under obligation to celebrate the great anniversary of the revolution with a revolutionary production. You must present the play *Mystery Bouffe*, a heroic, epic, and satiric portrait of our era, written by Vladimir Mayakovsky. . . . To work, everyone! Time is precious."[19]

The plot, if sensational, was very simple. After the earth has been destroyed by a flood there remain, seeking refuge at the North Pole, "seven pairs of clean" and "seven pairs of unclean." The "clean" are various bourgeois figures such as Lloyd George, Clemenceau, and a Russian speculator; the "unclean" are proletarians: a miner, a carpenter, a laundress, and so forth. The unclean are deceived by the clean, whom they throw overboard from the ark. The settings where the action takes place are various: the universe, the ark, hell, heaven, the cloud country, the promised land. After overthrowing the clean, the unclean visit hell, where they deposit the clean, then a traditional heaven which they leave in disgust, and finally they return to earth and the promised land of the Communist paradise.

[18] L. Trotsky, *Literature and Revolution*, Rose Strunsky, trans. (New York, 1925), p. 131.

[19] *PSS*, II, 506.

The play is a kind of working model of the flamboyant revolutionary literature of the moment, and it succeeds in conveying the spirit of that moment, as Mayakovsky felt it. It contains the elation of victory that the bolsheviks and their close sympathizers felt on the day after the revolution, and it contains also an ingredient of revolutionary ethos common to the writings of Gorky and Lenin: contempt and black hatred for the "clean" world. It has a sense of the future and of historical movement. Mayakovsky speaks in it of the storming of the planets by "airships of the commune, fifty years hence"; and the "very ordinary young man" in the play speaks of a time when the "sun will perform such tricks . . . that pineapples will yield two crops a year from pickle shoots." The play is blasphemous: Jehovah himself—the old institutionalized religion—is conquered by the unclean, who, Prometheus-like, steal his lightnings from him and use them for "electrification." It is frankly topical and ephemeral, and includes not only persons but phrases and ideas that were alive to the spectators of 1918 but that have only historical interest today. Mayakovsky, in his introductory remarks to the second variant, produced in 1921, advises his posterity to introduce new topical material for each future performance—material significant for *their times*. Thus the individual ego of the author seeks to screen itself behind the mass, the Party program, and political matters of the passing moment.

The characters of the play are conventional puppets, manipulated by Mayakovsky to illustrate a Marxist political cosmogony. The seven pairs of "unclean," the workers of the world, conquer every hazard: capitalists, liberals, vacillating intellectuals, menshevik "compromisers," and Jehovah; they journey through economic chaos and hell itself in order to emerge as their own masters in their own earthly heaven. The play touches on topical matters, echoes disputes of the period, propagates political myths, speaks out in favor of terror ("either them or us"), and talks of the future in prophetic tones. It has bright word play and broad comedy, and, in the 1921 version produced by Meyerhold, with the focus of action moved from the stage to the center of the auditorium, it was a daringly conceived spectacle. A special performance was given for the delegates to the Third Congress of the Comintern. The play illustrates and celebrates the partial fulfillment of prophecy the bolsheviks and their sympathizers saw in the revolution, and conveys their faith in history's final vindication. There may be some still left whose faith is so naive that they would find Mayakovsky's "mystery play" a moving experience. But it must be said that, in spite of occasional flashes of Mayakovsky's poetic genius in it, his "heroic, epic, and satiric" extravaganza is quite dead. The modern reader requires a detailed commentary in order to follow its topical matters, and the journey, except as a historical exercise, is hardly worth the effort.

The play is interesting, nonetheless, as a study in the transformation for revolutionary purposes of certain recurrent and characteristic imagery. The persistent water images of the poems flow together in the *Mystery* and, breaking free of all constraint, emerge as the "world revolution," a flood that encompasses and cleanses the globe itself. The "slanted cheekbones of the ocean" that once appeared on a dish of fish-aspic, the "ocean-monster" of the *Tragedy*, the "ocean of love" that in *Man* is "encircled by a barrier of houses"—indeed all the oceans of Mayakovsky's poetry—contribute their energy in the *Mystery* to forming the great flood that wipes out the past.[20]

Some years later, in the poem "The Atlantic Ocean" (*Atlanticheskii okean*, 1925) written on shipboard during his journey to America, Mayakovsky once again identified the ocean with the revolution. In that poem, however, the revolution ceases to be a violent and destructive force, but has been domesticated, and indeed performs useful tasks. I have suggested above[21] that the sea symbolized for Mayakovsky the boundless "ocean" of reality upon which humanity "floats." Some of his early poems are philosophical meditations, through the medium of fantastic imagery, on the nature of that reality. "The Atlantic Ocean" is another such meditation, and it too begins in a mood of fear and frustration. The "ship" may be tossed on the waves, shaken from mast to keel, shattered, overturned. Sometimes the ocean is a peaceful, decent fellow, but at other times he's a dangerous drunk and unpredictable. As for the tiny ship with its human passengers, the ocean has this comment:

> If I like I'll sink it.
> If I like I'll bear it along.

[20] See Papernyi, *Poeticheskii obraz*, p. 179.

[21] See above, Chapter Five.

(*Khochu toplyu*
Khochu vezu.)

Like the universe of the *Cloud*, the ocean is at first indifferent to human beings:

We don't need people,
they don't make much of a meal.
I won't touch them—all right . . .
let them go. . . .

But here there is a sudden change of key. Mayakovsky merges the image of the stormy, strange, indifferent sea with the revolution, and the watery element, after a brief and decisive uprising, becomes an almost cozy and comforting presence. As the revolution is accomplished

Small meetings of the last waves
make noise
about something
in an elevated style.

And then the business of organization takes over:

. . . in the ocean's factory
a wavy local committee
sweats / over a problem . . .
And underneath / quiet and business-like,
a weave of coral / grows into a palace,
so that life may be better
for the toiling whale wife
her whale mate, and their
pre-school whale child.[22]

In Mayakovsky's imagery the universe, instead of grudgingly enduring human life, is now part of it. The sea of reality, tamed and directed by the revolution, has become a friendly element. "The Atlantic Ocean" should not be dismissed as propaganda. That poem, along with *Mystery-Bouffe* and a number of other things, reveals that the revolution and the Soviet power have a function in Mayakovsky's psychology as well as in the structure of his poetry. That function is to reconcile the bruised "ego" of the

[22] *PSS*, VII, 15.

poet, frustrated in love, in war, in poetry, even in blasphemy, with the world. We note that the place of action of *Mystery-Bouffe* is the whole universe; in other words its setting is the same as that of the *Cloud, War and the Universe*, and *Man*. But in the mystery play the universe, like the sea in *The Atlantic Ocean*, has grown gentle, and even hospitable to the human project.

Mystery-Bouffe is replete with the image material of the early Mayakovsky, altered to fit the new outlook of a revolutionary poet. Mayakovsky-Christ is present, but now he is simply a *man*, and his kingdom is on earth. He walks over the waters to reach the ark that carries the unclean, some of whom would reject him. He is no longer a crucified or a suffering Christ, but a prophet of the future who has come to fire their spirits; and the suicidal Mayakovsky of the early works reveals himself in the comment, "For I know / how hard it is to try to live." (1129-1130) He offers the new gospel of material plenty here on earth, and he reverses the beatitudes of the Sermon on the Mount:

My heaven is for everyone
Except the poor in spirit . . .
Come unto me
you who calmly sink a knife in
and walk away from your enemy's body with a song. (1162-1170)

This "very ordinary man" carries a complex of Mayakovskian roles. Not only is he the new Christ, he is also the "average young man" from the *Tragedy*, who, we remember, invented a machine to cut up chops automatically, and whose friend was working on a trap for bedbugs.[23] In the *Tragedy* he is a ridiculous figure firmly rejected by the very movement of the play; in *Mystery-Bouffe* his prophecy of superflux is the highest point:

In my heavenly house are many mansions—
crammed with furniture—
and the elegant comforts
provided by electrical services. (1148-1151)

Can we forbear the observation that those "baths, elevators, showers" that violated the soul in the early poem "From Street

[23] See above, Chapter Four.

to Street" now figure as valued accessories in an American heaven? We recall in the *Tragedy* the malaise that overcame "things," and their rebellion against their own names. *Mystery-Bouffe* reconciles "things" with their own existence and with man. A locomotive and a steamship have speaking parts. Mayakovsky's own urban dissatisfaction disappears when he contemplates the communist city of the future in the following stage direction:

> The gates open and a city is revealed. But what a city! The lattice-like forms of transparent factories and houses tower toward the sky. Trains, streetcars, automobiles are wrapped in rainbows. In the center is a garden of stars and moons, crowned by the brilliant corona of the sun. Out of the display windows the finest *Things* come forth, with the hammer and sickle at their head, and move toward the gate, offering bread and salt.

Chernyshevsky's Crystal Palace is the forerunner in Russian literature of those transparent factories and houses, but the main trappings of the scene are drawn from Mayakovsky's own early poetry: automobiles, however, are no longer red devils, nor do the "tired streetcars cross their flashing spears." The sun is no longer wounded, nor is the moon "unwanted, flabby."[24] And "things" of every kind, under the new Marxist dispensation, serve their creators with no thought of existential rebellion. The revolution would seem to have set all things straight; but what if it hadn't?

It should be pointed out that the play was coolly received, and that Mayakovsky was obliged on several occasions to defend it against the argument that it was pointless, and unintelligible to the masses, opinions that revealed the conservative theatrical tastes of many Party leaders, and probably also of the "toiling masses." Mayakovsky's report of his experience with *Mystery-Bouffe*, entered under the date October 25, 1918, in his autobiography, reveals a large measure of chagrin over the episode: "I finished the 'Mystery.' Read it. A lot of talk about it. Meyerhold and K. Malevich produced it. There was a great howl about it. Especially among the super-communizing intelligentsia. A cer-

[24] These phrases are from the poems "Streetways" and "The Huge Hell of the City," both written in 1913.

tain Andreeva did plenty. To interfere with it. Shown three times, then smashed. Various 'Macbeths' again."[25]

2) *150,000,000*

The poem *150,000,000* was written in 1919 and published, after long epistolary haggling with the State Publishing House, in April 1920.[26] In his autobiography Mayakovsky wrote for the year 1919: "My head full of 150,000,000. Started agitational work in ROSTA" (Russian Telegraph Agency). The juxtaposition is not accidental. *150,000,000* is frankly propagandist, just as were the cartoons and posters he produced for ROSTA. And both varieties of propaganda were, in the poet's intention, anonymous. He goes on to say about the poem: "Finished 150,000,000. Published it without my name. I wanted anyone at all to add to it and improve it." But the device did not work, since the hand of Mayakovsky was clearly visible: "But no one did add to it and anyway everyone knew who wrote it. What's the difference. Publish it now under my name."

Not only were the masses—150,000,000 Ivans (the 1919 population of the USSR)—the hero of this poem, but the opening lines announce that the masses are also its author:

> 150,000,000 is the name of the creator of this poem.
> Its rhythms—bullets,
> its rhymes—fires from building to building.
> 150,000,000 speak with my lips. . . .
> Who can tell the name
> of the earth's creator—surely a genius?
> And so
> of this
> my
> poem
> no one is the author. (1-17)

However, just as the poetic concepts, the characters, the rhythms and profoundly self-conscious rhyming devices employed in *Mystery-Bouffe* clearly revealed the hand of the author, so in *150,000,000* the exclusive personal authorship of an intensely original individual, Mayakovsky, was immediately obvious.

[25] *PSS*, I, 25.

[26] *PSS*, II, 115-164.

Ostensibly the poem's hero is one "Ivan," who stands for the oppressed people, rather than Mayakovsky himself; but the poet's own hand is obviously manipulating his puppet-like figures. Considered as a literary production the poem is in part a sophisticated parody of the ancient folk epic, the *bylina.* There are two figures of heroic proportions in the poem: Wilson, the defender of world capitalism, and Ivan, a thoroughly Russian champion of the downtrodden. Wilson is located in Chicago, a city that stands on a single screw and is completely "electro-dynamo-mechanized." Even when a Chicagoan lifts his brow, the work is done by electric power. Wilson has pistols with four triggers and a saber bent into seventy sharp blades. Ivan has only "a hand and another hand, and that one stuck in his belt." But as in the Russian folk epic Ilya of Murom vanquishes the frightening enemy without serious difficulty, so here there is never any doubt that Wilson, "whose drawers are not drawers but a sonnet," who eats and grows fat "adding one floor after another to his belly," will succumb to the Paul Bunyan-like Ivan. In the *bylina* the heroic *bogatyrs,* when sliced in two by their enemy's blade, do not die but have their numbers exactly doubled; similarly Ivan, when cut open by Wilson's sword, emits multitudes through his open wound, a conceit that combines material from the folk epic with the modern collectivist mystique. Wilson is of course no real figure but a literary symbol of evil power modeled on the Tatar enemies with whom the Russian folk heroes in the *bylina* regularly do battle. The faraway mysterious capital from which those enemies usually issued forth has become a certain "Chicago," and their devilish magic is nothing but "mechanization." Viewed as a literary production the poem is a triumph of sophistication and verbal skill; read as political commentary or propaganda it is nothing at all; taken literally—and some contemporary critics did so take it—it is of course a cheap attempt at political mythmaking.

Party leaders reacted to both these works with a kind of obtuse, instinctive hostility. Lenin wrote in a note to Lunacharsky: "Aren't you ashamed of yourself for voting to publish '150,000,000' in 5000 copies? Nonsense, stupidity, double-dyed stupidity and pretentiousness! In my opinion only about one in ten such things should be published, and in editions of not more than 1500 copies—for libraries and eccentrics." Trotsky, though somewhat more perceptive than Lenin, still could find no good use for Mayakovsky's agitational pieces: "How out of place and how frivolous do these primitive ballads and fairy tales sound when hurriedly adapted to Chicago mechanics and to the class struggle!"[27] In short, Mayakovsky's brave beginning as a propagandist of the new regime ended in failure. The futurist "ego" of the poet, his ever restive imagination, his instinctive iconoclasm of imagery and diction, seemed to Lenin a kind of literary "hooliganism." Such people could not be trusted.

Concerning *Mystery-Bouffe* and *150,000,000* it might be said that both are sophisticated literary parodies, but that the form chosen in each case was ill-advised if Mayakovsky's purpose was to influence any large segment of the working people. The mixture of mystery play and vulgar comedy in the *Mystery* would probably not appeal to any worker sufficiently educated to be interested in a *play* about the world revolution; and the *bylina* echoes in *150,000,000* would certainly not impress workers or even urbanized peasants of the twentieth century. They reacted, we may be sure, with a mixture of amusement and contempt. We must conclude that Mayakovsky made a gross mistake in these two works. For instance, it was one of the conventions of the *bylina* that the tale told was not a present fact but a true happening of the deep past. Transference of the content of the *bylina* to present time and actual people destroyed its effectiveness except as parody addressed to a sophisticated audience.

3) The "Windows"

A major part of the poet's energy during 1919, 1920, and 1921 was lavished upon propaganda posters produced on commission for ROSTA (The Russian Telegraph Agency), and called "Windows," or, more fully, "Satirical Windows," a designation they acquired because most of them were displayed in the empty store-windows of urban centers. The posters (*plakaty*) thus served the double purpose of concealing from the pedestrian's eye the evidence of an economy in ruins while turning his thoughts to the struggle against enemies of the revolution and to the great hope of the communist future. At first the procedure was to make one poster for one window, but as time went on as many as three hundred stencilled copies of a single poster were produced.[28] The third volume of Mayakovsky's collected works

[27] Trotsky, p. 153.

[28] *PSS*, III, 475.

contains 634 windows in which the hand of Mayakovsky is identifiable as both artist and versemaker, and he asserted in his autobiography that during this period his "days and nights were spent with ROSTA. All kinds of Denikins were advancing. I write and draw. Made about three thousand posters. . . ."[29]

The initiator of the project was Mayakovsky's old friend the painter Chekrygin, whose idea was to provide in each poster several cartoon-like drawings accompanied by brief versified captions. Chekrygin's first posters each carried drawings and verses on many topics. When he entered the project, Mayakovsky, with an artist's sense of form, hit upon the idea of producing windows with several drawings structured around a single versified "text," a few lines of which would belong to each of the drawings. For example, window No. 409 has four drawings, the first of which shows a bayonet-studded road leading toward a bright red sun, and under it the lines: "Comrades! Thorny is the road / to the commune." The second drawing shows a Red Army man donning heavy boots: "The advance guard of the commune / must be well shod." The third shows a heavily booted leg breaking up the bayonets, and in the fourth a workingman strides confidently toward the bright sun:

> The Red army man's foot
> breaks the thorns—
> and then without hindrance
> you'll make it to the commune.

The propaganda message is clear: everything for the army during the hard days of the civil war, but afterward, comrades, life will be beautiful. The typical window is clear, sharp, and simple in form, exhibiting a felicitous marriage of visual and verbal message.

The great majority of the verse jingles Mayakovsky wrote himself, or else he supervised the poetic efforts of others involved in the project, and he came to be regarded as the moving spirit of the whole enterprise. Yet here too, as in the cases of *Mystery-Bouffe* and *150,000,000*, he maintained the fiction of anonymity. He claimed later that "nearly all the slogans and verses were mine," yet not a single one carried his name as the author.[30]

Labor on the windows was hectic and feverish and totally subordinated to the propaganda needs of the Party, but the poet

[29] *PSS*, I, 26.

[30] *PSS*, III, 473.

in Mayakovsky asserts himself in a variety of ways. Some of the verse texts are parodic imitations of certain classics of Russian literature, and many imitate the form of the *chastushka,* a kind of folk song with a simple, monotonous metrical beat. Pushkin's line "I pace the shore, the sky I scour,"[31] is used of the bourgeois refugees, thousands of whom were supposedly awaiting transportation on Princes' Islands near Constantinople. An early window depicting a bourgeois baffled by the problem of opening a small casket imitates in form and content Krylov's fable "The Casket Is Easy to Open" (*Larchik prosto otkryvaetsya*). After the bourgeois smashes it with a sword and pokes at it with a key, the workers, needless to say, can open it without difficulty. Kozma Prutkov's amusing fable "The Shepherd, the Milk, and the Reader" is converted to the use of a window on the defeat of the white general Yudenich.[32] A deft parody of the first stanza of Zhukovsky's ballad "Svetlana" reveals the bourgeois seeking to learn his future, and expiring at the thought of what is in store for him:

> Once
> on Epiphany evening
> the bourgeois were telling fortunes:
> When will we
> make the red one knuckle under? . . .[33]

Krylov's fable "The Elephant and the Pug-dog" provides the title and the verse form for a window predicting the inevitable crushing of the Poles by Russia.[34] And a number of windows utilize rhythms and phrases from popular songs of the period as well as revolutionary songs.

The verse form of the windows reveals the versatility, inventiveness, and verve of Mayakovsky the poet, but their content offers no more than a running paraphrase of articles and editorials he found in the current numbers of *Pravda, Izvestiya, Gudok* (*The Siren*), and other official publications of the day. Seldom has so much talent been expended on necessarily ephemeral matter, and it is not difficult to understand the onset of depression at this time that the poem "The Sun" records.[35] The cynic who wrote jingoistic propaganda in 1914 is once more in evidence as an employee—on commission—of the proletarian

[31] From *Eugene Onegin,* I, 50.
[32] *PSS,* III, 40.
[33] *PSS,* III, 53.
[34] *PSS,* III, 76.
[35] See above, Chapter One.

state. The newspapers *Pravda* and *Izvestiya* reviled white generals, or lampooned western politicians, or castigated menshevik "renegades," or called for volunteers for the war fronts, and Mayakovsky's pliable muse bent herself willingly to each project in turn. Soviet scholars point out quite correctly that no undue pressure was ever brought to bear on the poet, and that if he "stepped on the throat of his own song" he did so of his own volition and with conviction. He himself once clearly said that he provided his own motivation: "It may be true," he said at a meeting where the role of the poet was being discussed, "that you can't force a poet, but he can force himself."[36] And indeed during those years he forced himself so successfully that "his own song"—the love lyric—could hardly even be heard: apart from "The Sun" he wrote hardly anything but agitational verse during 1920 and 1921, until at last the silence was broken by the lyric poem "I Love You" (*Lyublyu*, 1922).

Mayakovsky rationalized his work on the windows as an important step in the direction of involving literature with the working class, the proletarian state, and thereby with humanity's future. In the preface to a collection of windows reprinted in 1929 he observed:

> These are not just verses.
>
> The illustrations are not intended as graphic ornamentation.
>
> This is a continuous record of the most difficult three-year period in the revolutionary struggle, conveyed in spots of paint and the sound of slogans. . . .
>
> Let lyric poets recall the verses to the music of which they fell in love. We're happy to remember also the lines to the accompaniment of which Denikin fled from Oryol.[37]

4) The Left Front of Art

The principal purpose of the organization called *Lef*, the Left Front of Art, was to institutionalize and rationalize the alliance of the former futurist avant-garde with the proletarian state, and to motivate the production of art forms that would serve the revo-

[36] Pertsov, *Mayakovsky, zhizn i tvorchestvo*, II (Moscow, 1958), 141.

[37] For a thorough study of Mayakovsky's work on the "windows," see V. Duvakin, " 'Okna Rosta' i ikh politicheskoe i literaturnoe znachenie" in *Tvorchestvo Mayakovskogo; sbornik statei* (Moscow, 1952).

lution while at the same time utilizing in a journal called *Lef* the formal experiments that had been the principal contribution of the futurists. Mayakovsky's description of these events in his autobiography is exaggerated and polemical:

> We organize "Lef." "Lef" may be defined as the encompassing of the social theme by all the instruments of futurism. This definition of course doesn't exhaust the question. Anyone interested should look at the issues of *Lef*. We closed ranks firmly: Brik, Kushner, Aseev, Arvatov, Tretyakov, Rodchenko, Lavinsky.
>
> I wrote *About That*. About the general way of life but on the basis of personal experience. I began to contemplate the poem *Lenin*. One of the slogans, and one of the great aesthetic achievements of "Lef," was the de-aestheticizing of the productive arts, constructivism. Poetic supplement to the magazine: agitational pieces, and also commercial agitation: advertisements. . . .[38]

These are rather cryptic remarks, and in need of some exegesis. The persons mentioned were all active figures in the futurist movement and some of them had been associates of Mayakovsky before the revolution. Osip Brik was one of the leading critics of the formalist school, and his two essays "Sound Repetition" (*Zvukovye povtory*) and "Rhythm and Syntax" (*Ritm i sintaksis*) are neglected classics of Russian criticism. He was erudite and fecund of ideas. Some of those who knew him closely described him later as the most intelligent man they had ever met. His genius expressed itself, however, not in critical or scholarly production but in brilliant talk, and in literary projects and undertakings of various kinds. One such project was Mayakovsky, whose early patron he was. He also served the poet as a source of information and ideas, and he was an indispensable adjunct to the household of a great poet who cared little for reading. An associate of the group once compared Brik's position to that of the "learned Jew" in the entourage of provincial governors of the nineteenth century, whose sole function was to keep the governor abreast of culture. Osip Brik was a kind of "learned Jew attached to Mayakovsky."

The others mentioned were all important members of what might be called the Mayakovsky entourage of the twenties, and

[38] *PSS*, I, 26.

all were major contributors to *Lef*. Boris Kushner was an acute critic who had been a frequent contributor to *Art of the Commune*, and became a specialist during the *Lef* period in the literary "sketch." N. N. Aseev was an original poet and a devoted follower of Mayakovsky; Sergei Tretyakov was a playwright, poet, and critic whose most famous work is the anti-imperialist propaganda play *Roar China!* (*Rychi Kitai!* 1926); Rodchenko was an artist and photographer, and was responsible for many innovative cover creations used by *Lef* and *New Lef*; Lavinsky was also a contributing artist; Arvatov was an acute literary theorist who attempted to integrate the formalist and sociological critical methods. Other prominent contributors to *Lef* were Skhlovsky, Eikhenbaum, and Tomashevsky, all formalist literary scholars and critics, and of course Kruchonykh, who occasionally contributed his characteristic word play. The early stories of Isaak Babel and Valentin Kataev appeared in *Lef* and later *New Lef*.

One very important name is missing from the list given by Mayakovsky when he wrote those lines in 1928: N. F. Chuzhak-Nasimovich, perhaps the most dogmatic theoretician of futurism and the "new art" during the period of *Lef*, was a member of the editorial board of the magazine. Chuzhak was a bolshevik journalist to whom journalism seemed the highest order of creative activity under the new order of things, and his notions as to the function of literature in "building" life rather than "palely reflecting" it received prominent space in *Lef*. Mayakovsky no doubt omitted his name because of the unpleasant memories it conjured up for him, and also no doubt because Chuzhak tended toward that polemical writing—ill-mannered, scholastic, and arid—that eventually came to characterize the journal and converted large sections of it into dull and disagreeable reading matter. Chuzhak believed in a strictly disciplined approach to the work of creating a magazine in the spirit of futurist art, and regarded such poems as Mayakovsky's *About That*, published in the first number of *Lef*, as romantic "junk" unworthy of the enterprise. The interminable arguments with Chuzhak seem to have poisoned the deliberations of the editorial board.[39]

The platform for *Lef* which was developed during this early period stated the following purposes:

1) To aid in the discovery of a Communist path for all varieties of art.

[39] See V. *Mayakovsky v vospominaniyakh sovremennikov*, pp. 662-663.

2) To re-examine the theory and practice of so-called "left" art, freeing it from individualistic distortions and developing its valuable Communist aspects.

3) To struggle against decadence and aesthetic mysticism, as well as against self-contained formalism and indifferent naturalism, and for the affirmation of tendentious realism, based on the use of the technical devices developed in all the revolutionary schools of art.

Like so much of the "manifesto" literature of the twenties, this statement sounds to the modern reader something like a formal prayer addressed to a God whose character and attributes have been forgotten. Yet these formulas can be translated into simple prose. Most important is the promise to "re-examine" the position taken in the recent past by the futurists and condemned by the party. "Individualistic distortion" refers to Mayakovsky's besetting sin, of which he must purge himself. "Decadence" echoes a phrase by Lenin in his public letter on the Proletcult, in which he linked futurists with "decadents of every stripe." To struggle against "self-contained formalism" means simply to dissociate oneself from critics such as Shklovsky and others of the formalist school who studied literature as form and device rather than as social evidence. Note, however, that the qualification "self-contained" leaves the way open for any of these people to purge themselves of sin without giving up their basic heresy. The "affirmation of tendentious realism" is a retreat into the past and implies a condemnation of the "epic and heroic" style of both *Mystery-Bouffe* and *150,000,000.*

The Left Front of Art was doomed from the start to controversy both within itself and with other literary groups, since it harbored personalities, theories, and programs that could not live together in peace; indeed, the disharmonies produced by the editorial board of the magazine seemed to reflect Mayakovsky's own besetting conflicts. Chuzhak, when he maintained that the poem *About That* should not have been published in *Lef*, was simply applying the stern revolutionary standards of Mayakovsky's own "Order No. 2 to the Army of Art." Sometimes the journal gave promise of drawing into its pages the best artistic and critical talent to be found; at other times it seemed caught in the snare of politics and propaganda.

Mayakovsky and some other members of the editorial board seem to have thought of their enterprise as a weapon in the struggle against *byt*, by which they meant the already advanced petrification of political life into fixed hierarchical forms and the revival of materialistic incentives and petty-bourgeois economic and social "virtues." It is no accident that *About That*, a personal lyric and a cry of protest against the seemingly indestructible massif of established custom and prejudice, was published in the first number of *Lef*. The futurists connected this phenomenon with the relaxation of Communist aims during the period of NEP, but hindsight tells us that what struck them with such terrible force was the realization that the revolution, for all its surface destruction, had not altered the internal structure of the petty-bourgeois mass. An article by Sergei Tretyakov in the first number of *Lef*, which urges a rational approach to the problem of literature, is also a kind of programmatic announcement of the struggle with *byt* in the form of established and conventional literary taste.[40] The second number of *Lef* devoted several pages to bourgeois *byt* in its American manifestation, Babbitry, and thus identified the problem as one having worldwide dimensions. A translated excerpt from George F. Babbitt's depressingly cheerful remarks to a real estate dealers' convention[41] was included as concrete evidence of the philistine values dominant in the American business community, and no alert reader could miss the implication that Soviet society, many years after the revolution, still offered examples of analogous characters, values, and attitudes. The revolution had scotched the snake, not killed it.

The fact that language itself had fallen into fixed cliché formulas is the argument of an article by G. Vinokur, "On Revolutionary Phraseology,"[42] whose purpose was to demonstrate that the excessive repetitive use of revolutionary phrases and slogans had eviscerated them all and left them hollow and meaningless. "Really," he wrote, "all I have to see is a title like 'Greater Attention to Agriculture!' . . . and I know I will probably not read the article." Vinokur's statement, like Mayakovsky's own poetic language, strikes a blow against linguistic *byt*. Vinokur would break the bonds of the obvious and easy phrase, renew language and stimulate thought. The real danger, he says, is that minds may become so accustomed to "sloganized" thought that they will lose the habit of thinking and forget that words must mean something. He suggests that if he were a worker and such phrases were ad-

40 "Otkuda i kuda," *Lef*, No. 1, 1923.

41 *Lef*, No. 2, 1923, pp. 58-61.

42 *Lef*, No. 2, 1923, p. 104.

dressed to him, he would be insulted. In this of course he probably speaks only for himself and for other intellectuals. Indeed, emotionally charged phrases, repeated often enough, may very well have the effect on the mass mind of preventing thought by a kind of hypnotic process.

Boris Arvatov, an extremely gifted critic and theorist of literature who was sometimes known as "*Lef*'s Saint-Just," and who soon went mad, published a number of acute articles in the early issues of *Lef*. One of these is an effort to free Marx himself from stereotype and cliché,[43] and to try to establish what he actually said or thought about the problem of contemporary art forms. The fiercely logical "*Lef*ist" would put an end to the repetitive citation of Marx by ignorant "authorities." But this project, too, was doomed to frustration.

A number of formalist critics and linguistic specialists who had been close to the futurist movement from the start continued to have a prominent place in *Lef*. Shklovsky once pointed out[44] that the nucleus of the "Society for the Study of Poetic Language" (OPOYAZ), which consisted of critics and philologists with a special interest in new trends in poetry, joined the *Lef* group when it was formed in 1923. A natural affinity existed between poets, who were themselves laboratories of linguistic experiment, and scholarly specialists in the study of poetic language. We have seen that Roman Jakobson's essay *Contemporary Russian Poetry* is a perceptive linguistic analysis of Khlebnikov's work, with many comments on Mayakovsky.[45] Articles in *Lef* tended toward the formal or linguistic study of literature, and some of them were acute and penetrating. G. O. Vinokur published in the first issue an article entitled "The Futurists as Builders of Language" (*Futuristy stroiteli yazyka*), which is an early and neglected classic on the linguistic "inventions" of Kruchonykh and Khlebnikov. Osip Brik published a number of important critical articles and one piece of experimental prose fiction, "Not a Fellow-Traveller" (*Nepoputchitsa*),[46] which deserves special attention. That story is fascinating in form and puzzling in content. Brik's narrative technique recalls the movie scenario in its total emphasis on action and dialogue: the telling is reduced to essential statement as to location and movement of characters and notation of the words

[43] "Marks o khudozhestvennoi restavratsii," *Lef*, No. 3, 1923, pp. 76-96.

[44] Woroszylski, *Życie Majakowskiego*, p. 428.

[45] See above, Chapter Three.

[46] *Lef*, No. 1, 1923, p. 109.

they speak. The dialogue itself is simple, effortless, and nearly perfect—a casual rendition of actual speech, pregnant with situation, suspense, and character. Brik's genius apparently reached also into the area of *belles-lettres*; there, as well as in criticism, he was fertile but unproductive. The brief plot concerns a Party official who becomes infatuated with a beautiful bourgeois female, the wife of a Nep-man doing business with the state. His own wife and a Party rival slanderously accuse him of shady dealings with the Nep-man, and he is soon in trouble with his Party cell. At that point the *Cheka* intervene to examine the evidence, see through the deceits of the jealous wife, and sort out the right from the wrong. The head of the *Cheka* in this story figures as a benign Big Brother, possessing both power and wisdom. Internal evidence indicates that the author had some connection with the *Cheka*, of whose operations we receive a very favorable picture. The story's message is heavily pro-Party, anti-Nep-man, and anti-bourgeois, but with a prescient warning as to the mischief that would eventually be caused by malicious denunciations. In his article "The So-Called Formalist Method" (*Tak nazyvaemyi formalynyi metod*) Brik entered a defense of the formalists and of OPOYAZ,[47] and propounded the idea that a poet is a "craftsman and nothing else," a notion that led ultimately, as we shall see, to the theory of "literature as fact" and to the anti-poetic platform espoused by the *Lef* group.

In spite of the originality and high quality of much of the material it carried—especially in the section called "In Practice" (*Praktika*), where prose fiction and poetry were to be found—the journal *Lef* was a depressing publication, full of resounding dogmatic statements on the new role of art in "building life," constantly engaged in sharp polemical actions, either offensive or defensive, and always strident and stentorian. Those conservative forces in the Party that had always regarded the futurists with alarm, or contempt, or amusement now turned their fire on *Lef*, whose enemies included powerful figures: Polonsky, editor at one time of two magazines, *New World* and *Press and Revolution*, and Sosnovsky, a party journalist with easy access to the pages of *Pravda*.[48] Voronsky, the critic and editor of *Red Virgin Soil*, never a fully convinced admirer of Mayakovsky, rejected the no-

[47] *Lef*, No. 1, p. 213.

[48] See Sosnovsky's article "Litkhaltura," *Pravda*, December 1, 1923, and the answer to it, "Kritkhaltura," *Lef*, No. 4, 1924.

tion propagated by Brik and *Lef* that the artist was a "craftsman and nothing more."[49] As time went on the editorial board of *Lef* found itself at odds with the powerful Russian Association of Proletarian Writers, whose literary precepts demanded "imitation of the classics"—in other words, a return to the realism of the nineteenth century. In a word the climate was bitterly hostile to Mayakovsky's project, and *Lef* never prospered. After only seven numbers it ceased publication in 1925; it was revived as *New Lef* in 1927 and finally disappeared at the end of 1928.

The quarrel with Chuzhak concerned the relative value of literature as "production" and literature as individual expression.[50] The stated program of *Lef*, largely Chuzhak's construct, placed exclusive emphasis on the former, but in practice the journal in its section devoted to *belles-lettres* favored lyric poetry (Mayakovsky, Pasternak, Aseev), "trans-sense" verse (Kruchonykh and Khlebnikov), experimental satiric prose (Brik's "Not a Fellow-Traveller"), and stories of the wartime period in which the key element was individual emotional apprehension (Babel). The steady readers of *Lef* (surely there were some) would carry away the distinct impression of a schizophrenic division between the editorial board's theoretical position and its editorial practice. Chuzhak was of course aware of this, and very soon he left the editorial board, announcing his resignation in *Lef*.[51]

During the journal's final year its small body of theoreticians developed in radical form the notion of the literary man as a craftsman and of literature as a craft not basically different from other socially useful occupations. The highest form of literary activity, in this paradoxical theory, and the most useful "in the epoch of socialism," was factual reporting: the writing of topical sketches (*ocherki*), biographies, diaries, travel notes, and the like. The concern of the writer should be with *facts*, rather than with his own invention or fantasy. The fixation of objective fact was to be required of him, rather than the creation of artistic wholes, which tend to "destroy or disfigure the *fact*" in accordance with a subjective purpose. The activity of the craftsman-writer, moreover, should be determined by the *demand* of his client, who is, "in the epoch of socialism," the proletarian state. Since literary production is by its nature no different from other kinds of pro-

[49] See his "Ob iskusstve," in *Literaturnye zapisi* (Moscow, 1926), pp. 36ff.
[50] See his article on the subject in *Pravda*, July 21, 1923.
[51] *Lef*, No. 4, August, 1924.

duction, the writer, whatever his class origin or orientation, is simply a producer working for the state. Implicit in this theory is the tenet that the writer's ideology is not of crucial importance. Though their theories have the ring of dogma and the limits they suggest for the new "Literature of Fact" seem straitened and confining, yet it is clear that the ideas they developed would, if accepted, have had the effect of liberating the writer from the much more confining demand that he *interpret* reality in the light of dialectical materialism. To fix the writer firmly on the ground of *fact* meant to free him from the obligation to produce ideologically tendentious "imaginative literature." The Marxist opponents of *Lef* did not "expose" them in this, but they left no doubt that the "factual" emphasis of the Left Front of Art would deprive the state of a useful propaganda weapon.

The alliance between formalist critics and futurists continued in *New Lef*. Shklovsky published there his article "Tolstoy's *War and Peace*: a Formal-Sociological Study." Osip Brik's "The Rout of Fadeev" (*Razgrom Fadeeva*), a shrewd attack on the proletarian writers as poor epigones of nineteenth-century realism, appeared in 1928; Mayakovsky's irreverent letter in verse to Gorky was published in the first issue. Boris Kushner's travel sketch of Western Europe, one of the finest things in the genre of the sketch, was published in an early number of *New Lef*. In general, *New Lef* represented a definite improvement over *Lef*: the material published was interesting and original, even when its purpose was agitational. In an article entitled "For Innovation" (*Za novatorstvo*), Osip Brik wrote that since Soviet literature ought to have something new to contribute to world literature, the experimenters should not be hampered in their laboratory work by the requirement that the work be intelligible to millions of new readers: "It is a mistake," he said, "to demand that every cultural work be multiplied and distributed in the hundreds of thousands."

New Lef was published for a select few in a small edition. It received no warm reception either in government offices or among the "reading mass." Even its emphasis on agitation and propaganda was suspect, since those functions were carried out in its pages by iconoclastic literary critics such as Viktor Shklovsky and futurist artists indifferent to conventional standards of taste. As a result of pressures that have never been wholly explained, Mayakovsky resigned from the editorship of *New Lef* in July, 1928, after the seventh issue of the magazine had appeared. He explained later that "tiny literary fractionlets have outlived themselves, and instead of organizing groups literary men should transfer their activities to mass organizations carrying on agitational work: newspapers, 'agitprops,' commissions, etc. . . ." In 1929 Mayakovsky and those comrades who together with him had abandoned *Lef* formed a new organization which they called REF, the Revolutionary Front of Art. At a public meeting in October of that year, he explained that the new organization was needed to carry on the struggle with "apolitical tendencies." From this must follow, it might seem, rejection of the theory of the "bare fact," and the demand for tendentiousness and ideas in art. That organization too, as we shall soon see, he abruptly abandoned shortly after, to join the "proletarian" writers' group, RAPP.

The contention with cliché and moribund tradition that *Lef* and *New Lef* represented met with final defeat in the demise of those publications. Mayakovsky thereafter abandoned any organized challenge to conventional literary standards. *Lef* and *New Lef* were, in effect, his last "slap at public taste"; and "public taste," as we shall see, now tended to assume the aspect of official and rigid legislation. These publications are memorable for the critical work that appeared in them, but the literary high point of their career was reached very early with Babel's stories and Mayakovsky's poem *About That.* For a number of reasons that poem deserves special attention.

Chapter Nine

ABOUT THAT, AND ABOUT SOME OTHER THINGS

1) Preparatory

Mayakovsky's poetic "recapitulation" of his principal concerns and the leading motifs of his work has been pointed out in the case of the *Tragedy* and *Mystery-Bouffe*. The poem *About That* is another effort at summing up his past, but at the same time it points ahead to a future which the poet impatiently demands to see. The poem speaks of love, indeed the same old love for Lily Brik that inspired his earliest work. Just as in *The Cloud, The Backbone Flute*, and *Man*, love is defeated by the indestructible philistine who narrowly concentrates on personal and family happiness, and in this poem the suspicion grows that the enemy of *Man* and "ruler of all," the arch-philistine, has a firm seat in the proletarian state and in the poet's own self.

About That is a clear reminiscence of the earlier *Man*. The "Mayakovsky" of that poem is directly recalled as "the man from seven years ago" whose soul is "held fast in the ice," and who stares downward at his own death from the bridge over the Neva. The Ruler of All is not present in *About That*, but the acquisitive egos that insult the poet are the servants of the Ruler in the new society. *About That* is reminiscent of *Man*, but it purports to be an answer to *Man*, even a correction. The endings of the poems are in striking contrast. In both the poet takes leave of earth for the stars, but the ending of *Man* is disconsolate and hopeless: there is no refuge for the poet in a universe just as cold and hostile as the planet he has left behind. In *About That* his starry destination is the Great Bear, a near relative of the poet himself, since the bear has served in the poem as his metaphor and symbol. The constellation, moreover, is both a dipper and an ark, a nice conceit suggested by the assonance that links the two words in Russian (*kovcheg-kovsh*), and as an ark it will carry the poet through night's flood to harbors of daylight and sunshine:

Now!
Now!
Now!
Out into space!
Straight and sure!
The sun gilds the mountains.
Day smiles from the harbor. (1550-1556)

The strong major note in these concluding lines is reached only after a tortured progress through the poet's tangled emotional life. Like the *Cloud*, this poem too explores the poet's love, his friends and enemies, the abhorrent "fat ones" (*zhirnye*) in a new guise, his revolution in a new and "higher" phase, and the cruel paradox of certain death in despite of an absolute demand for immortality.

The poem *About That* may be broken down into three basic motifs—tragic love, the philistine, and the future—that are mingled in many ways. Before analyzing the poem itself, it would be well to place it in the context of a number of shorter pieces that served as practice and preparation.

Between 1920 and 1922 Mayakovsky's talent was almost totally devoted to the production of agitational verses. Those verses, written during the years of hunger and civil war, reflect for the most part the bolshevik concerns of a particular moment, and Mayakovsky wrote them as an employee of the state. Even during this period, however, there are occasional glimpses of an authentic poet: the poem about the sun, for instance, was written in 1920; some other poems of a lyrical or humorous cast were produced about the same time and published in a collection of poetry and prose whose title, *Liren* (1921), suggests that it was a partial outlet for dammed-up lyrical energies. One of these, whose title may be translated "What to Say to a Girl" (*Otnoshenie k baryshne*), is slight and cute with some characteristic phrase play at the end:

This night decided it—
Shouldn't we be lovers?
It's dark—no one would see.
I bent over her, really,
and as I bent I,
really,
said like a good father:

"Passion's precipice is steep—
Be so good,
as to leave.
Leave—
be so good."[1]

"Heinesque" (*Geineobraznoe*) and "Grief" (*Gore*) also offer interesting though unremarkable word play; the latter, a brief choreography of playful rhymes,[2] strongly recalls some of Mayakovsky's early contributions to the futurist anthologies. "A Cigar-Case into the Grass" (*Portsigar v travu*)[3] is a miniature confrontation of nature and technology, in which technology—the cigar-case—comes out far ahead.

The short piece entitled "About Some Trash" (*O dryani*, 1921)[4] is the earliest and probably the most potent of Mayakovsky's attacks on the philistines now panoplied in the red flag of revolution. Mayakovsky's old enemy, the *meshchanin*, is shown weaving his parasitical existence among the bric-a-brac of communism. Catlike, he purrs behind the back of the Russian Socialist Federated Soviet Republic:

From the wide expanse of the Russian soil,
from the day of the revolution's birth,
they came thronging in,
easily changing their color,
and settled down in all the offices.

The philistine is defined by his overweening interest in comfortable apartments, pianos and piano lessons, higher incomes, and showy uniforms (*tikhookeanskie galifishcha*). He has a picture of Marx on his wall—in a pink frame—and a canary-cage hanging from the ceiling. His comfortable cat is curled up sleeping on a copy of *Izvestiya*. This former hero turned solid citizen is a threat to the vitals of the revolution: Marx observes all this from his place of honor on the wall, and he fairly howls: "More frightening than Wrangel / is the philistine's life style." "About Some Trash" not only anticipates the warning against that life style contained in *About That*, but is a kind of preliminary sketch for the picture of neobourgeois contentment worked out much later in *The Bed-*

[1] *PSS*, II, 39.
[2] *PSS*, II, 40, 41.
[3] *PSS*, II, 42. This poem was not published until 1929.
[4] *PSS*, II, 73.

bug, the main character of which is a "former worker," and "former hero" who has lived down both his calluses and his wounds. Finally, we must note as a matter of some interest that the poem "About Some Trash" was published in the satirical periodical *Bov* on the same page with a eulogy of the heroes who had taken the Perekop peninsula in the Crimea from the White armies,[5] and that the last line of that eulogy—"Glory! Glory! Glory!"—is picked up in the opening line of the poem "About Some Trash":

> Glory, Glory, Glory to the heroes!!!
> Anyhow, they've had their full due.
> Now let's talk
> About trash.

During 1921 and 1922 Mayakovsky produced a cluster of short poems depicting scenes from contemporary Soviet life, with appropriate, sometimes biting, commentary. To this brief series of poems, published in various places, he gave the general title "Our Way of Life" (*Nash byt*). The series included "A Muddled Scene" (*Nerazberikha*, 1921), "A Verse about Myasnitsky Street, about a Woman, and about the All-Russian Scale" (*Stikhotvorenie o Myasnitskoi, o babe, i o vserossiiskom masshtabe*, 1921),[6] and the poem that attracted Lenin's favorable attention, "Lost in Conference" (*Prozasedavshiesya*, 1922).[7] Some others not expressly included in the series do nonetheless fit into it—for instance, "Bureaucratish" (*Byurokratyada*, 1922),[8] and "Comrades, Let Me Share with You My Impressions of Paris and of Moné." (*Tovarishchi, razreshite mne podelitsya vpechatleniyami o Parizhe i o Mone*, 1923).[9]

The experience of Soviet life that gave form and content to the poem *About That* accumulates gradually in these brief vignettes. "A Muddled Scene" is a poetic reflection of Moscow street life in 1921. The juxtaposition in it of violent contrasts gives a vivid impressionistic picture of the strange combinations produced by the revolution. The street scene is an unholy jumble that includes speculators, beggars, a chapel with worshippers fragrant of incense and unction, urchins and hooligans, and a political policeman (*chekist*) whose sudden appearance strikes fear into them all: "The devil only knows what a muddled mess! / And how many they are, / these muddled messes?!"

[5] "Poslyednyaya stranichka grazhdanskoi voiny," *PSS*, II, 71.
[6] *PSS*, II, 76, 83. [7] *PSS*, IV, 7. [8] *PSS*, IV, 20. [9] *PSS*, IV, 56.

The "Verse about Myasnitskaya Street . . ." works out a contrast between the inflated cosmic rhetoric cultivated by the state and the miserable reality of everyday life. The arithmetic of official articles and speeches knows only millions and trillions, but pays no attention to one old woman dragging her poor possessions along the muddy holes of Myasnitskaya.

"Lost in Conference" neatly characterizes the Soviet bureaucracy, which already exhibited features that would sooner or later become firmly fixed: insistence on routines along with brutal indifference to people, ritualistic jargon, and constant, interminable meetings. The poem is a powerful expression of the ordinary citizen's exasperation at the pompous inaccessibility of those minor bureaucrats with whom he must deal. Lenin's comment, contained in a speech he delivered at a meeting of metalworkers, is forthright in its revelation of the reasons for his changed evaluation of Mayakovsky:

> Yesterday I happened to read in *Izvestiya* a poem by Mayakovsky on a political theme. I don't consider myself an admirer of his talent, though I fully realize my lack of competence in the literary field. But it's a long time since I experienced such pleasure and satisfaction, from a political and administrative viewpoint. In his poem he utterly derides conferences and makes fun of the Communists because they're always conferring and re-conferring. I don't know whether it's good poetry, but I guarantee you it's absolutely right from a political point of view.[10]

"Bureaucratish," as the title suggests, is another attack on the impregnable paper fortress of officialdom, and it ends with a concrete proposal:

> I, as you know,
> am not a responsible official.
> I'm a poet.
> I have no office talent.
> But I think we should
> quite simply
> grab the office by its chimney
> and shake it out.

[10] V. I. Lenin, *Sochineniya*, XXXIII, 197-198.

And then sit quietly
over those we've shaken out,
pick out one and give him an order:
"Write!"
Only we'll ask him,
"For God's sake comrade,
don't write much!"

"Comrades, Let Me Share with You My Impressions . . ." expresses a poet's exasperation with the bureaucratic apparatus of the Moscow Section for Popular Education (MONO), for which he produced propaganda posters. The lengthy and complicated process of certification and approval of projects always repelled him, and it is difficult to say whether these poems reflect real inefficiencies in the bureaucracy or only the poet's impatience with any kind of organized procedure.

The resurgence of the philistine under the aegis of the hammer and sickle is a principal concern of the poem *About That*, and of two other long poems that he worked on during 1922 but never finished, *The Fourth International* and *The Fifth International*. This was clearly a period of troubled concern over the direction taken by the revolution. *The Fourth International* is in the form of an open letter to the Central Committee of the Russian Communist Party, whom it honors for their long and patient work "in the underground," then for their resolution and courage in "taking in their iron hands the fiery and fearful reins of the revolution." While it offers praise to the makers of the revolution, it raises in powerful images the specter of the philistine who threatens the revolution and all its champions. The most telling, and at the same time amusing, image—one that delivers a sharp satirical thrust at Mayakovsky's literary enemies, the proletarian poets—is a picture of the "proletcultist" of the future on a pleasant lawn in front of the building of the Soviet of Deputies, playing croquet.[11] This poem contains one of Mayakovsky's earliest statements on the takeover of the symbols, the slogans, and the martyrology of the revolution by a new class intent on creating itself as an establishment. Mayakovsky appeals for a "renewal of youth" and a new rebellion against the coming "communist satiety."[12] He will reject

[11] *PSS*, IV, 101.

[12] *PSS*, IV, 102. It is significant that those lines were cut from the version of the poem published in *Krasnaya nov* in 1922, No. 3.

the titles and honors the revolution bestows, and will retire to his garret, there to celebrate uprisings still to come. His function is to install poetic motors of a hundred horsepower in the Marxist dialectic and to prepare for a third revolution, the revolution of the spirit.[13] It is indeed fascinating to find in lines written early in the Soviet period the ideas of many young revolutionaries who came into prominence in western Europe in the sixties and who exhibited a basic revulsion at the very phenomenon registered in 1922 by Mayakovsky: the capture of the revolution by the Party bureaucracy. To be finally effective, the revolution must be not just an exchange of power, but rather a change in attitude and spirit that will do away with the old system of values. Mayakovsky in 1922 could see such a development only in the remote future.[14]

The Fourth International was actually intended as a kind of prologue to the poem that in its unfinished state now bears the title *The Fifth International,* planned as a poem about "life in the commune in five hundred years." The original title was *Three-times-ninth* (*Tridevyatyi*) *International,* and that fairy-tale expression for something in the far distant future is in close accord with the fantastic quality of the images in the two parts (out of a projected eight) that we have. For reasons not entirely clear, Mayakovsky dropped that title.

The poem is more than a utopia. It is a fantastic allegory on the nature of the poet, his peculiar virtues and strengths, and his sometimes repeatable experiments in the sphere of imagination. It offers also an explicit statement on the role of the poet in foreseeing the future and assisting at its birth. Characteristically, he rejects poetry that "sniffs roses" and then sings of them:

> For me
> it's an unbearable thought
> that roses were not invented by me.

[13] *PSS,* IV, 103.

[14] It should be noted that some Soviet commentators explain such poems as a reaction to the "bourgeois" revival that took place under NEP, and as a revulsion against the reappearance of successful NEP "businessmen," etc. That explanation simply does not square with the facts of the poem. We note 1) that proletarian writers are depicted as the carriers of philistinism, and 2) that the official honors Mayakovsky refuses are typical Soviet "titles."

For 28 years I've been cultivating my mind
not to sniff roses,
but to invent them.[15] (18-23)

Once again he insists on the superiority of human technology to nature's blind caprice, and he goes on to say that poetry should have the precision of mathematical formulas—certainly a surprising stance for the author of the *Cloud* and the *Flute*. But this is a rather obvious effort to associate poetry with the exact sciences, and a few lines later he insists that he wants to be a poetic "Einstein." We may be tempted to read these lines as whimsical self-parody.[16]

The basic conceit of the poem is the poet's own neck, which he can screw out or in, in order to raise himself to a higher vantage. This unscrewing of the neck is the special quality of a poet who is curious about everything, and especially one whose vision and purposes are planet-wide, indeed universal. This conceit places him in the blue and cloud-or-star-speckled heaven, whence he takes in the whole earth—and here there reappears that "planetarity" of vision that was central to *Man, War and the Universe*, and *Mystery-Bouffe*, and figured to some extent even in the *Cloud* and *The Backbone Flute*. I have already suggested that, however it be motivated, this is the technique of a film artist whose camera is completely free of any spatial or temporal unities, and who may radically shift scenes whenever his scenario demands it.

We note that in *Man* the same superterrestrial effects are used, but as a means of achieving detachment from the earthly "can-can"; in the *Fifth International* the purpose is to propagate and prophesy a revolution. The old means are made to serve the new purpose, and the world under the poet now seethes with the fiery birth of soviets. This poem is an oblique answer to *Man*. As in that poem, Mayakovsky leaves earth and hovers in the sky, observing the planet in its various shapes, contours, and aspects. And as in that poem, he returns to earth after a period of years, but he doesn't find "the old bald one" still in charge; he finds instead the

[15] *PSS*, IV, 107.

[16] Jakobson, in his article "On a Generation That Wasted Its Poets," tells us of Mayakovsky's interest at this time in Einstein's theory of relativity, and his intention to reduce poetry to "mathematical formulas." When Jakobson objected to this idea, Mayakovsky replied that of course he was referring only to trans-sense poetry. R. Jakobson, "O pokolenii," p. 25.

"life that had been dreamed of from the days of Fourier, Robert Owen, and Saint-Simon." The time lapse required for this to come about runs well beyond the span of a single human life, and we shall see that in *About That* the time distance is so great that special arrangements must be made for his resurrection if he is to see the brave new world. As for the prospect of the poet's own lifetime, he might well have said with Pasternak's Hamlet: "Everything is sunk in pharisaism" (*vsyo tonet v fariseistve*).

I have suggested above that the poem is concerned, like so much of what he wrote, with the nature of the poet and his work. Not only is the poet equipped to see beyond the normal ken, he is also preternaturally sensitive to sound. A strikingly beautiful exercise in hyperbole expresses the idea that the poet's ears are as potent as his eyes are:

> It's quiet as anything.
> Can't hear a thing.
> But my ears hear—
> my ears are used to it.
>
> First I couldn't even tell one note from
> another
>
> . . . .
>
> How can you tell the difference
> when somebody is cursing somebody out
> quite loud and with the usual obscenities.
> But now
> it's not just that my ears can pick out a
> fly's flight—
>
> I can hear
> the pulsebeat on every little fly paw . . .
> But what's a fly—a fly is nothing.
> I can hear,
> because I've got a kind of telescopic ear,
> how the millstones of the world
> produce a deep major note. (364-381)

We note in this poem a shift in the conception of the poet's role from that of the early period. We have seen that in the *Tragedy* and many other early things, the poet is a kind of *crucifixus*. But in *The Fifth International* the poet is hypersensitized, and his sight and hearing, linked to imagination, catch the very pulse of the future.

A section of the poem entitled "For the Not Fully Literate" is a proud statement of his purpose to remain the poet of his own ego, even though that ego, with all its senses sharpened, is in full focus on the socialist future. He says that a question is often put to him: "Forgive me, comrade Mayakovsky. Here you're always shouting about 'socialist art, socialist art.' But in your poems there's nothing but 'I . . . I . . . I . . . I'm the radio, I'm a tower, I'm this, I'm that.' Why is that?" And he answers the question:[17]

> The Proletcultists never speak
> of "I"
> or of the personality.
> They consider
> the pronoun "I"
> a kind of rascality.
> . . . .
> But in my opinion
> if you write petty stuff, you
> will never crawl out of your lyrical slough
> even if you substitute We for I. (496-511)

And the authentic voice of Mayakovsky in his chosen role of the "bogatyr" who will create the great epic (*bylina*) of the future can be heard in the lines: "If the world / under me / Is less than an anthill (*muraveinika menee*) / Then what matters it which pronoun I use (*mestoimeniya*)." (521-524)

The theme of love, which came as such a surprise in *About That*, had actually reappeared in a poem entitled "I Love You" written early in 1922, almost a year before he began work on *About That*. The inspiration and recipient of this poetic gift was of course Lily Brik, and the poem reflects a relatively happy and stable period in their relationship; it is his only poem about love that sounds a note of quiet contentment and as such it is a curiosity that repays study, as well as a masterpiece of the genre. The poem is divided into ten brief titled parts, each marking a stage in the passage of the poet's life, the climax of which is his meeting with "her," followed by the sober "conclusion" that this love will

[17] *PSS*, IV, 122.

be faithful and forever. It has an allusive relationship to both "Lily-mine" and "To His Beloved Self the Author Dedicates These Lines"; as in those earlier poems the poet's love is an enormous problem and a great weight, but in the earlier poems he bears his burden without relief. In "I Love You," on the contrary, Lily has taken the heavy thing from him and tosses it up like a toy or a child's rubber ball.

Let us consider the ten sections of the poem. The first section, "That's the Way It Goes" (*Obyknovenno tak*), tells us that everybody is granted some love, but that, what with business and incomes and the like, the soil of the heart dries out.

> The heart wears a body,
> the body wears a shirt.
> But that's not all!
> One fellow—the idiot—
> fixed up false cuffs
> and starched his shirt front.[18] (7-12)

When they begin to get old, people think of what they're losing, but it is too late then. The section entitled "A Kid" (*Malchishkoi*) and indeed all the sections devoted to the stages of Mayakovsky's life emphasize the poet's separateness from ordinary creatures; he is a special case. People are trained from childhood to do some kind of work, but he used to run off to the riverbank and loll about (*shlyalsya*) not doing a damn thing. "And mama got mad at me: / 'You're a bad little boy!'" (30-31) As a boy he only wanted to lie about and contemplate things. We recall that as a visitor in heaven in *Man*, he expressed the same simple need for which the "busy beings" in that realm had no sympathy at all. But the sun (a frequent confidant) understands him, and says:

> You can hardly see the fellow
> but he has a heart / too.
> He does the best he can.
> But how / can there be room
> in the little space / that's him
> for me,
> and the river,
> and a hundred miles of cliff?! (43-53)

[18] *PSS*, IV, 85.

"A Young Fellow," the next section, stresses the difference between Mayakovsky and other young fellows in the matter of education. Every idiot of either sex has learned his grammar, "but I was kicked out of the fifth class and they kept tossing me into various jails." Comfortable apartment-house lyrics he can hardly appreciate:

I learned about love
In the Butyrki prison.
What's the Bois de Boulogne to me?
What do I care about sighing and seascapes?
You know / I fell in love
with a "Funeral Establishment"
through the peephole of cell 103. (64-71)

"My University" recounts the poet's experience of higher education, which was very different from that of his beloved:

You know French.
You can divide.
And multiply.
You decline beautifully.
Well, go ahead and decline!
But tell me—
Can you sing a duet with a house?
Do you know streetcar language? (82-89)

And there follows a brief recapitulation of his early poetic intimacy with the city's streets and houses: "But I spoke / Only with houses. / Water-towers were my company." (123-125)

"Grownup" once more underlines his special nature and his difference from others in the matter of love. Most grownups have businesses, and rubles in their pockets. Love has its price and its purpose:

But I,
no roof over my head,
stuck my big hands
into my torn pockets
and just strolled around—
wide-eyed.
It's evening.
You put on your best clothes.

Relax with wives or widows.
But me,
Moscow crushed me in its embrace
with the endless noose of its Sadovayas.[19] (139-150)

He tried to catch the very heartbeat of the city, opening himself to all passion, to the sun and to puddles. Most people have their hearts in their breasts, but not him: "But my anatomy has gone mad. / I'm all over one solid heart / Pounding everywhere." (166-168) In the *Cloud* he had announced that he was "all lips and nothing else," and the fact that now he is "all heart" has certain serious consequences. Far more than possible, far more than necessary, the heavy lump of his heart has grown to a huge bulk of love and of hatred, and his body is crushed under the burden and yoke he must bear. Swollen with the milk of his own verses, he still can find nowhere to pour it out. In the section "A Cry" (*Zovu*) he tells of raising his burden like a weight-lifter and carrying it along like an acrobat. Like an alarm bell summoning the populace to a fire, he cries out: "Here it is! / Here! / Take it from me!" (207-209) But all the nice ladies shy away from him: "We'd like something a little less. / We'd like a little tango maybe. . . ." (219-220) But then "you" came! The lines that tell of Lily's approach, her business-like (*delovito*) inspection of him, and of how she saw, in spite of his size and his roar, that he was just a little boy, are certainly unique because of the startling childlike images that communicate the delightful onset of pure love:

You took and
snatched my heart away
and you just started to play with it.
Like a little girl playing with her ball.
. . . .
And I was so full of joy!
I don't feel it any more—
that yoke!
I forgot myself with the sheer delight,
and I skipped about
like an Indian at a wedding.
I was so happy,
I felt so good! (234-254)

19 The Sadovaya Ring is a boulevard that encircles Moscow.

The three final parts drive home the point that this love is reciprocal and final, and the poem ends with a solemn vow: "I swear— / that I love you, / faithfully and forever." (314-316)

2) Part I: The Prisoner

That was the moment of which Mayakovsky might have said, paraphrasing Goethe, "Stay as you are, never move, never change," and indeed the poem "I Love You," like Keats's "sylvan historian," fixed a transient moment and held it fast in spite of the cruel changes that occurred in the poet's own life. The poem *About That*, to which we now turn, explores and examines a bewildering complex of emotional vicissitudes, and some comment is necessary on the circumstances of its composition as well as the "idea" of the poem.

It is noteworthy and perhaps not surprising that Mayakovsky in his public statements tended to minimize the significance of the love story, directing attention instead to matters of social import in the poem. It is true that his first announcement of the idea of the poem spoke of love and nothing else. In the earliest version of his autobiography, *I Myself*, published in 1922, under the section for that year he said, "Thought of an idea: about love. A huge poem. I'll finish it next year." But in the 1928 edition there is no mention of a poem about love under that year, but under the year 1923 he says: "Wrote *About That.* About our way of life in general but based on personal material."[20] And when in April 1923 he recited parts of the poem he emphasized once again the social rather than the personal component: ". . . in those parts of the poem that I've read [to you] the crucial thing is: *our way of life* (*byt*). And by that I mean a way of life which hasn't changed at all and which is now our vilest enemy, and turns us into philistines."[21]

We might argue that this shift in his idea of the poem, and perhaps even in its content, was conditioned by the political and social environment, by the expectations of his colleagues (at least some of them) in the *Lef* milieu, by the exigencies of his own reputation as a propagandist and poster-writer who had forgone, it seemed, the theme of love. The social pressures upon him were so complex that no simple statement can be made about them.

[20] *PSS*, I, 374 and 26.

[21] *PSS*, IV, 436.

The foot that trod upon the "throat of his song" was certainly his own, though his motivation was meshed with the demands of the government, the society, and the times.

Papernyi's[22] fascinating study of the manuscripts reveals that as Mayakovsky worked on the poem, he consciously softened its pessimism, emphasized positive notes, and confuted his own individualism by insisting that happiness can be found only in the collective. For instance, the suicide motif is vividly present in an early version when the gun-muzzle (*dulo*) appears as a possible anodyne for the poet's pain, but that word was removed in later versions, and Papernyi demonstrates that in his work on the poem Mayakovsky regularly muted the tragic notes.[23] In other words, a kind of self-censorship was at work, though it was only partly successful; there still remains in the poem a heavy weight of tragedy. Mayakovsky's revisions in the course of working on it were probably conditioned by the demands of his milieu, and it may be that the earlier and more "tragic" variants were nearer to his real meaning. Nevertheless the only complete poem we have to work with is the version he published.

It is important to note that Mayakovsky wrote *About That* during a period of seclusion and self-examination and the poem is a record of a kind of psychic self-communication. It belongs among the long poems beginning with the *Cloud*, each of which is a kind of lyric monologue that explores the distressful pendulations of the poet's own ego. The occasion for his withdrawal at this time was a temporary misunderstanding, to put it mildly, with Lily Brik, who found that she could not endure the excessive demands of her great lover (we must recall and emphasize that there is no

[22] Z. S. Papernyi, "Mayakovsky v rabote nad poemoi 'Pro eto,'" *Literaturnoe nasledstvo*, LXV, 217ff. Three manuscripts of the poem were preserved: a rough draft, a clean copy with corrections and additions, and a clean copy with a few corrections. They were preserved only by accident; Mayakovsky had actually thrown them away, but Lily Brik herself, with an eye to future value, recovered them and asked Mayakovsky to make her a gift of them. An incomplete version of the manuscript variants appeared in the first *Complete Works* (*PSS*) published under the editorship of Lily Brik herself (1934-1938). Nikolai Aseev published in that edition a long and perceptive essay that traces the growth of the poem as Mayakovsky worked on it: "Rabota Mayakovskogo nad poemoi 'Pro eto'" *PSS* (1934), v, 21. Another analysis of the same material is V. V. Trenin and N. I. Khardzhiev, "V masterskoi stikha. Zametki o rabote Mayakovskogo nad poemoi 'Pro eto,'" *Literaturnyi kritik*, No. 7, 1933.

[23] Papernyi, "Mayakovsky v rabote nad poemoi 'Pro eto,'" pp. 228-230.

evidence that she loved him), whose alternating fits of jealousy and depression made him a difficult companion. They agreed on a separation of two months, though perhaps it should be put somewhat more bluntly: she threw him out (*prognala ego proch*).

The poem was written, then, during a period of voluntary seclusion from December 28, 1922, to February 28, 1923, when he seldom left his room and met with friends and associates only when absolutely necessary for business. The isolation may have been, as he himself suggests, a period of self-examination, a struggle with his "old" self out of which he would emerge "a completely new man." According to this interpretation the poem is a kind of therapeutic objectification of his inner problems.[24]

The circumstances of its composition explain many otherwise puzzling matters in the poem itself, and the difficulties with Lily occasioned the production of a number of letters that are masterpieces of direct, uninhibited poetic prose, and that reveal as biographical fact the emotional state that took literary form in the poem *About That*. These letters, published in *Literaturnoe nasledstvo* in 1958,[25] are insistent and importunate cries for relief and sympathy.

(End of December, 1922)

Lily Dear,

I see you've decided. I know that my pestering is painful to you. But, Lily sweetheart, what happened to me today is so awful that I can't help grasping at a final straw, this letter.

It's never been worse than this—really I must have grown too much. When you threw me out before, I believed we'd meet again. Now I feel I've been torn away from my life, that there'll never be anything any more. Without you there's no life for me. I've always said that and I've always known it. Now I feel it, I feel it with my whole being. Everything that used to give me satisfaction is worthless now—repulsive even.

I'm not threatening, I'm not imploring forgiveness. I'll never, never do anything to myself—I'm much too much afraid for Mama and Lyuda. I've also reached a kind of sentimental adulthood. . . .

Yet I can't help writing, I can't help asking you to forgive me for everything. . . .

[24] *Ibid.*, p. 228.

[25] *Literaturnoe nasledstvo*, LXV (1958), pp. 128ff.

But even if you don't answer, you alone are in my thoughts. The way I loved you seven years ago I still love you this very minute. Whatever you want, whatever you command I'll do right away, and I'll do it with joy. How terrible it is to part when you know you're in love and when you know you're to blame for the parting.

Here I sit in a cafe and groan. The waitresses laugh at me. What a terrible thought that from now on, this is my life. . . .

If this letter makes you feel anything but pain and distaste, then answer me, for Christ's sake answer me right away. I'll hurry home and I'll wait. If you don't my grief will be terrible, terrible.

I kiss you and I'm all yours,
Me.

It's ten o'clock now. If you don't answer by eleven, I'll know there's no point in waiting.

Lily did answer. What she said has not yet been revealed, but Mayakovsky's next letters are calmer and more hopeful. The epistolary evidence is crucial to any critical evaluation of the poem. The extravagant and desperate demand for his woman, so beautifully expressed in the letter, is realized in the poem in the image of a disconsolate and roaring bear.

Though he insisted in public on the poem's social significance, the introduction, which purports to answer the question "About what, about that?" announces unmistakably that it is about love. A succession of original and powerful images conveys the imperative force of love and the absolute necessity to speak of it. This theme is a prayer to Buddha, and it sharpens a black man's knife against his master. If there's anything human on the planet Mars, it is scribbling about love too. Love will make a poor cripple soar like an eagle and dazzle the sun with verses. When it comes, its command is *truth* and *beauty*. Even if your arms are stretched out on the cross, when it comes you will hum a waltz softly. It dives deep under the daily routine and hides in the recesses of instinct, but don't dare forget it or suppress it! It will erupt and tear your heart out of your hide! Thus Mayakovsky insists in the introduction that the theme of love ("so petty, so personal") is inescapable, that in spite of his involvement with the daily routine of the revolution, he had to return to it once more. And yet the word "love" is never used: the poem speaks of "that," or "that theme," or "it," and only in the very last line of the introduction is a blank space left where the reader himself must supply the word "love" (*lyubov*) in order to make a rhyme with "foreheads" (*lbov*).

The poem consists of an introduction, two parts, and a conclusion, and is further subdivided into a number of titled sections, the last three of which are "Faith," "Hope," and "Love." Part I is called "The Ballad of Reading Gaol"; the reference to Oscar Wilde's work is richly suggestive of the poem's outward and inward meanings. Obviously it refers to his voluntary confinement during the period of writing, to the jail without bars where he suffered over the poem. But we must remember also that the prisoner of Wilde's "Ballad" is a man condemned to death because he killed his beloved—condemned, that is, because of a fatal overflow of love. And Wilde's prisoner is emphatic as to the close intermingling of love and hate, and the issue of both in death.

For each man kills the thing he loves
By each let this be heard
Some do it with a bitter look
Some with a flattering word
The coward does it with a kiss
The brave man with a sword!

Mayakovsky's lover is likewise condemned because he loved too much, because in his savage jealousy he was ready, like an animal, to devour his beloved, and in his animal fury "scratched the floor of his den with all twenty claws." Wilde's ballad is about a man condemned to death; in its original conception the death of the lover was also a central theme of the poem *About That.* We have already seen that direct references to suicide were present in early drafts and that the work on the poem would seem to represent, as Aseev put it, a "victory over thoughts of death and of suicide." But the victory was not total; the poem is deeply concerned with the theme and the thought of suicide, and there is a clear reference in it to "healing death." Mayakovsky's "Reading Gaol," his apartment on Lyubyansky Lane, is the cell where he awaits execution.

The thematic function of Part I is to affirm the Mayakovsky of the earlier poem *Man*, the frustrated lover and defeated human being, as a fact that still exists. The prosperous propaganda poet of the twenties cannot escape him. He still stands on the bridge over the Neva, still unreconciled to the earthly "can-can" and to "middle-class happiness," still loving and unloved, still an enemy of the comfortable life. This Mayakovsky needs help, he begs to be saved, he demands that the Party and the state, with which Vladimir Vladimirovich is now so intimate, "confiscate" and annul his grief.

The only real event in the fantastic world of the poem is a telephone call from Mayakovsky to Lily's apartment, where he speaks only with her housemaid, Annushka, whose drowsy voice and sloppy bedroom slippers we hear over the wire. The housemaid is the second in a deadly love-duel, but she is yawningly indifferent to the whole business. Time is the "physician" who stands on the sidelines, but the only bandage he brings—an endless one—is "healing death." The mechanical reality of the telephone (which bears the lightning-bolt trademark of the Swedish company that manufactured it), its receiver, its wires, and the cables underground are the subject of an amusing hyperbole: the voltage of the poet's emotion burns the underground cable and causes an earthquake remembered for many years by the inhabitants:

> An old resident lived on Myasnitskaya—
> a hundred years later he lived there—
> and a hundred years / later
> that's the only thing
> the old fellow used to tell the kids about:
> "Once—it was Saturday—Saturday night
> I went out for a hambone—
> I was looking for a bargain—
> when something hit!
> An earthquake.
> It scorched my feet—the soles of my shoes!"—
> The kids couldn't believe it.
> That happened? / —there?!
> An earthquake / in winter / at the Post Office?? (167-184)

In the *Cloud* the fire in his heart became a literally burning building with firemen and hoses and helmets; in this poem the electric shock wave of his emotion gives rise to a legend about some unbelievable natural phenomenon. We note that the fantastic hyperbole is couched in the homeliest phrases, in talk about a hambone and a bargain and Saturday night on Myasnitskaya.

Full of primitive, savage jealousy, the poet turns into a bear so that he may properly howl his rage and grief. In a passage that miraculously imitates the clipped phrases of sobbing speech, Mayakovsky tells us how a bear would weep:

> I don't know / whether they cry
> or not,
> bears.
> But if they do cry, then that's just how.
> That's the way: without any false sympathy
> they just moan, pouring out
> long ravines of howling.
> And just so that bearish Balshin
> awakened by my howl
> growls on the other side of the wall. (354-364)

An intimate detail of Mayakovsky's housekeeping, so to speak, is introduced in the figure of the neighbor who slept next door to him behind a thin wall, whose name was indeed Balshin, and who did insist on his right to peace and quiet.

In the section of the poem entitled "A Room That Floats Away," a dream suggested by the infantile sensation of a cold wetness in the bed, the result, however, of his flooding tears, grows into an authentic nightmare in which the room and everything in it suddenly flows into the night, becoming nothing less than the Neva itself. From this point forward, a dream reality dominates the whole movement and all the images of the poem. We have already noted the frequent occurrence of water in the poetry of Mayakovsky and suggested the symbolic connection of that element in his imagination with love, with death, or with the universe. The whole world "sort of floated away" in *Mystery-Bouffe*, and here too his firm four-cornered room with its solid furniture liquefies in the poem and carries him off, a sad, white bear pillowed on an ice floe in the Neva River. The dream fantasy maintains a tenuous connection with the prosaic reality of bed and sleep through the pillow on which the poet-bear floats, and the bedstead which may be a bridge:

> A white bear / I've crawled onto an ice-floe,
> and I float on my pillow-floe.
> The banks rush by, / one view after another,
> under me the ice of my pillow.

There's a breeze from Lake Ladoga.
The water rushes.
And my pillow-raft flies along.
I float,
feverish on my floe-pillow

. . . .

And I had to float / under an arched bedstead—
or maybe it was a bridge.
And that's the way it was: / just me and the wind. (428-445)

The last two lines attempt to convey the sense of a purely animal state of being in which the bear stands alone in comradeship and contention with nature. But the bear's journey is not aimless. His progress down the stream does indeed take him to a bridge, where he finds the *man* from the poem *Man* who stood on that very spot seven years ago and thought of his own death. The man needs help, and he suspects that Vladimir Vladimirovich, his other self, has betrayed him by worming his way into the conventional world of tight houses, marriage, family happiness, and satisfied paunches. The old Mayakovsky utters a plea to the new one not to sell him out, not to accept the banality of material bliss, not to become reconciled to the "system." The real self still stands on the bridge, still suffers, still needs help, still wants love. Vladimir Vladimirovich will never be loved or be happy until *this man* is saved.

Vladimir! / Stop! / Don't abandon me!
Why didn't you let me throw myself down then?!
Smash my heart out with a single stroke against the piers?

. . . .

Don't try to run away—
It's me / calling you!

. . . .

Pass an executive resolution!
Confiscate my pain / annul it. (498-538)

And Part I ends with the desperate cry:

Save him! Save him! Save him!
There, on the bridge, over the Neva
there's a man!

3) Part II: The Eve of Christmas

The title of Part II, "The Eve of Christmas" (*Noch pod Rozhdestvo*) also involves a literary reminiscence, this time of Gogol, with whose story of almost the same name (*Noch pered Rozhdestvom*) Mayakovsky deliberately associates his own work. The association of Part I with Oscar Wilde's poem, as we have seen, pointed to the poem's inner meaning; it is simply impossible that the title of Part II is an accident or an aberration. Moreover, Gogol was one of Mayakovsky's favorites among the classics, and the only one among them whom he never abused nor ever cast overboard from his steamship. Andrei Belyi pointed out the close relationship between Mayakovsky's hyperbolic images and Gogol's, and offered numerous examples of verbal experimentation that are basically similar in the work of both writers.[26] The Soviet scholar N. Khardzhiev has located additional thematic, figurative, and verbal correspondences that could not be accidental.[27] The Gogolian title of Part II underlines the element of fantasy that the work shares with Gogol's short story, and prepares the reader for a series of strange metamorphoses. The title has also suggested to some a possible religious significance in the poem, though that aspect is certainly not developed.[28] The direct reference would seem to be, rather, to the cozy Yuletide scenes from whose false warmth both the man on the bridge and Vladimir Vladimirovich exclude themselves. And of course there is an autobiographical reference to the season during which the misunderstanding with Lily and the poet's own solitary confinement had begun.

Part II describes the poet's futile effort to engage his family and friends in the project of saving the man on the bridge. In his bear's guise he returns to Moscow, and (we recall that this always happens to Mayakovsky in his various animal transformations) the passersby buffet him, ridicule him, and abuse him with mother-oaths. The man on the bridge needs a savior and thinks that he sees one approaching, but the apparition before him is a second transformation of his own self—there are now three selves

[26] A. Belyi, *Masterstvo Gogolya* (Moscow, 1934), in the chapter entitled "Gogol i Mayakovsky."

[27] N. Khardzhiev, "Zametki o Mayakovskom," pp. 397-401.

[28] M. Nag, "Fantastical Realism; the Problem of Realism in Mayakovsky's 'Pro eto,' " in *Scando-Slavica*, IV, 1959.

in the poem. At first he thinks it may be the "Saviour" himself, Jesus:

There's the Saviour! / Looks like Jesus.
Quiet and good, / with a crown of moonlight.
He's closer. / A smooth young face.
But it's not Jesus. / This one is gentler—and younger. (651-659)

Who could be gentler than gentle Jesus if not the poet himself, who had of course already established his own role as Christ and Saviour. The boy he sees is a young Communist who seems now to pray, and now to wave his arms as though addressing a meeting. The prayerful attitude may not suggest Mayakovsky, but the arm-waving is an unmistakable characteristic, and a clear signal that we have to do with one of the poet's "doubles," one that encompasses two aspects of his character. Certainly there is an echo of Blok's *The Twelve* in the sudden association of a revolutionary with Jesus Christ; even the crown (*venchik*) that adorns the figure of Christ in the last scene of that poem reappears in this passage. (654) But the boy, caught up in a tragic love story, is intent on suicide, and again there is an echo of Blok's technique in *The Twelve* when Mayakovsky's lines suddenly take on the rhythm of a sentimental love song (*romans*):

> The boy walked on, his eyes fixed on the sunset.
> And the sunset was matchlessly yellow.
> Even the snow was yellow near the Tver gate.
> But the boy walked on, seeing nothing. (676-680)

The "gypsy love song" abruptly breaks off and

> He walked on.
> Suddenly / he stopped.
> In the silk / of the hand
> cold steel.

Then the song resumes, the wind picks the boy's pocket, and we learn that the young suicide had penned a simple farewell note:

> Farewell . . .
> I'm ending it . . .
> Please don't blame anyone. . . . (695-697)

"How much like me," is the poet's comment, and it has often been pointed out that the phrase in *About That*, "Please don't blame anyone," is prophetic of the poet's own suicide note, written seven years later: "Don't blame anyone for my death. . . ." This strange and touching incident, which the poet treats with gentle irony, may actually describe one of the known occasions on which the young Mayakovsky himself attempted suicide.[29] This conjecture would seem to be suggested both by the clear identification of the young Communist with Mayakovsky himself ("How like me / that is! / Awful"), and by the definiteness of the locale of the fictional suicide: Petrovsky Park, just beyond the Tver gate. Thus the incident of the young boy's suicide may point to the past as well as to the future, and he may have used the phrase "Don't blame anyone" in more than one note. In any case, that phrase in both contexts is another literary reminiscence, this time of Dostoevsky's *The Possessed*, where the suicide Stavrogin leaves the unbearably laconic note "Don't blame anyone. I did it myself." ("*Nikogo ne vinit. Ya sam.*") The source of Mayakovsky's phrase in Dostoevsky is very clear from the earliest variant of that line in the manuscripts of *About That*, which corresponds word for word with Stavrogin's message.[30] We shall soon find other striking reminiscences of Dostoevsky in the poem.

He turns next to his family, particularly to his mother. The poem he wrote in 1913, "A Few Words about My Mama," reflects the severe wrench he felt at leaving Mama to do his own work on the streets of Moscow; Mama was the one to whom he turned in an extremity of suffering in the *Cloud*; it is not surprising that she should once again be his first recourse: "Instinct drew me to the family burrow," he says. Was Mayakovsky mother-fixated? Possibly. It is clear in any case that Mama and his sisters were a problem. As he enters Mama greets him with the conventional phrases proper to the season:

> "Volodya! You're home!
> For Christmas!
> Oh what a joy! What a joy this is!" (728-730)

The frenetic lines in which he begs her to help the man on the

[29] See Jakobson, "Novye stroki," p. 191.

[30] *PSS*, IV, 339, variants to ll. 695-697. Svidrigailov in *Crime and Punishment* leaves behind a similar suicide note.

bridge she answers with a trite exhortation to compose himself and calm down. Clearly there's no help for him in the family burrow:

> What do you mean then?!
> Do you exchange love for your afternoon tea?
> Is love's place taken by the darning of socks? (775-777)

In the section entitled "A Journey with Mother" he makes the point that the whole universe is spotted with philistines and families. Even in Africa the black man treats his little family to the afternoon tea, something that has now, for Mayakovsky, become a final symbol of middle-class happiness. The old and stereotyped values and virtues have even found comfort and repose for themselves under the terrible wing of the revolution:

> October thundered through.
> It judged / and punished
> and under its fiery-feathered wing
> you / made a place, / and laid out the chinaware. (805-811)

Next he turns for help to his friends, and there ensues a scene of ineffable satiric comedy in the Yule-warmed apartment of one Fekla Davidovna, her husband, and their family, where there is an assortment of verminous party guests rendered loud and silly by liquor. The details of Soviet *byt*—moustaches, cockroaches, mice, spider-webs, canaries, geraniums and family pictures—are vividly present. The adaptation of old religious symbols to the ideological and practical exigencies of the new order is illustrated in the transformation of protective fairies and spirits into a new variety of guardian angel: the lodger with influence and authority who will protect the family's living space. (890-892) Both old and new symbols are alike appropriated and exploited by these indomitable philistines: "Jesus tips his thorny crown and bows politely, and Marx, bitted and haltered in a pink frame" (an image first used in the poem "About Trash") "pulls his full weight in the middle-class ménage." (915-920)

But in this very apartment, out of the enemy's clutter and bric-a-brac, a fourth "double" of Mayakovsky suddenly materializes, and it becomes clear that the philistine poison is firmly lodged in the poet himself:

But the most awful thing was:
by his size, / his complexion
his clothes / —even by his walk
I recognized / one of them,
my very own / self / —me!
As like me as a twin. (893-903)

Among these acquaintances, his plea to save the man on the bridge is greeted with obtuse ridicule. The next section is entitled "No Way Out" (*Devatsya nekuda*), another phrase that occurs both in an earlier poem (the *Cloud*) and in his farewell letter, and that helps to tie into a single unity his personal and his literary biographies. There is no way out and nowhere for him to go, nowhere *else* to go, that is, but to *her*, and in a scene that even in its minutiae recalls Dostoevsky's *Crime and Punishment* he returns to the scene of his "crime"—*her* apartment. Like Raskolnikov, he climbs a dark and filthy staircase:

The pain in my heart, never silent,
forges link to link.
This is the way / Raskolnikov / who murdered
came back to ring the bell. (1133-1138)

Dostoevsky's scene is recalled in the poet's slinking behavior, his darting into corners to avoid being observed, his intense awareness of corridor and stairway noises, his eavesdropping at the door of "her" apartment. The scene recalls, moreover, not only *Crime and Punishment* but also *The Double*, especially the scene where Golyadkin Junior hides below the window of an apartment where there is a party in progress to which he has not been invited. The poet as he stands outside Lily's door overhears conversations each remark of which he, the rejected one, interprets paranoically as referring to himself.

This is not, of course, the first echo of Dostoevsky in the poem *About That*: we have already observed the correspondence of the young Communist's suicide note with Stavrogin's. Even the title of the poem *About That* is reminiscent of a number of passages in Dostoevsky's novels, as Lily Brik has pointed out.[31] Raskolnikov never names his crime as robbery or murder, but always refers only to "*that*," and compulsively dwells on his own thoughts "about *that*." In *The Possessed* the following exchange

[31] L. Brik, "Predlozhenie issledovaltelyam," pp. 203-208.

occurs between Stavrogin and his mad wife, Maria Timofeevna: "You must have had a bad dream. . . ." "But how did you know that I dreamed *about that*? . . ." In *The Brothers Karamazov* the pure young man Alyosha Karamazov stops his ears whenever anyone speaks "about that": "He couldn't listen to certain words, nor to a certain kind of conversation about women." We note that Mayakovsky's poem *About That* never mentions the word "love." An apparently minor but very interesting correspondence with *Crime and Punishment* is the situation of the man on the bridge, who, exactly like Raskolnikov, leans on the railing and thinks of throwing himself down.[32] Still another is the passage at the beginning of this section in which the word *obukh* (blunt end of an axe-head) occurs in a context strongly reminiscent of the distraught Raskolnikov's awakening from a troubled sleep at the sound of street noises outside his window, and his horrified realization that the time has come to take his axe and be off to perform his deed:

> Thus with an axe they break into sleep,
> and make a mark on sleepers' foreheads—
> then all at once / —everything is gone
> and all you see is the butt of the axe.
> And thus the drum of streets
> enters your sleep, / and all at once you remember
> that here's your grief
> and there's that corner
> and she's / around it—
> the culprit. (1093-1105)

These are some of the most striking echoes of Dostoevsky in the poem, but there are still others. The subtitle "No Way Out" recalls the drunkard Marmeladov in *Crime and Punishment*, who also had no way out and pointedly queried Raskolnikov as to whether the latter really understood the meaning of that phrase. We will presently address ourselves to the problem of the significance of the many reminiscences of Dostoevsky in *About That*.

But to return to the action of the poem. There is no hope in "her" house, either, for the man on the bridge. "She" and her friends are having a noisy party, dancing the one-step and the

[32] *Ibid.*, p. 205. On this subject see also I. Corten, "The Influence of Dostoevsky on Mayakovsky's Poem 'Pro eto,'" *Studies Presented to Roman Jakobson by His Students* (Cambridge, Massachusetts, 1968).

two-step. Through the walls of her apartment, as he stands in the corridor outside, his preternaturally sensitive ears pick up scraps of conversations that are made up of smart trivia without any real wit. The dreadful conclusion is forced upon him, and upon the reader, that even "she," like the girl in the *Cloud* who mentioned "money, passion, and Jack London," like the "red-head with a painted face" in *The Backbone Flute* who had "a husband, and music on her piano," and, if we may anticipate a little, like his last Parisian love, is a philistine and a member of the enemy camp—incapable of helping or even understanding the man on the bridge. But still he loves her. In verse he speaks more truthfully than other people (or even than himself), and it is in verse that he speaks of his love:

> Where, my dear one, / where, my sweet,
> have I ever wronged my love / in a song?
> In a song / every sound / is a confession / and a call.
> But in a song not a word can be changed.[33] (1240-1248)

And when he curses the established way of life (of which she is a part) he does not mean her, he avoids mentioning her!

Again there is a sharp shift in the images and a quick geographical progression through the towns on the road from Petrograd to Moscow, where he is confronted once more by the man on the bridge. Images of crucifixion now appear, and he represents himself as "nailed" to his sorrow, and presents to himself as the only possible solution a love that transcends the individual and embraces all human beings. To put it in other terms, Mayakovsky can be saved only if he transforms his *eros* into *agape*.[34] There is no real salvation for *oneself alone*, and his own suffering he now offers as a sacrifice:

> I'm waiting for love to come
> to all the unloved world at once,
> to the whole world-wide human mass.
> I've stood here seven years, I'll stand two hundred more,
> nailed here waiting for that.
> . . . .

[33] The last line is a phrase usually applied to the *byliny*.

[34] For an illuminating discussion of the relationship of *eros* and *agape* in Mayakovsky's poetry, see Stahlberger, *The Symbolic System of Mayakovsky*, pp. 91-93, 136-137.

And I must stand here. I stand here for everyone,
for each one I weep, for each I atone. (1328-1342)[35]

It has seemed to some readers that at this point there is a flaw in the structure of the poem since nothing in the progress of the work thus far has prepared the ground for this sudden moralistic departure. Soviet commentators of course emphasize the evidence of a healthy development in the poet's "world view" in the direction of a "collective" morality, and it would seem at first sight that something of the sort is intended. However, I shall soon advance the thesis that the abrupt reversal from total and uncompromising egotism to a universal love reflects not Marx nor the Soviet *ethos*, but rather, like so much of what is in the poem, a literary source, Dostoevsky.

Another cinematic scene-shift takes the poet to Paris and Montparnasse, where a brief adventure with the prostitutes convinces him that there is no help there either, since the Parisian whore insists on her own Parisian way of life. When he gets up on a table and cries out for help, "calling somewhere . . . to save someone," the *patron* explains the phenomenon with a single word: "a Russian."

The crucifixion images now become more insistent, when the poet alights upon the tower of Ivan the Great in Moscow and balances himself precariously, his arms outstretched cross-like. Suddenly the dream-like imagery transports him to the Caucasus, the place of his origin. Guilt and fear now dominate his emotions: "They see me. From here I'm all visible. Look—the Caucasus swarms with Pinkertons. They've noticed. They give the signal." Everyone attacks, insults, and *challenges* him. They spit on their palms till they are all wet, then

With their hands / with the wind
without mercy / uncounted times
they slap my face into ribbons. (1473-1477)

At this point, then, the old "Slap in the Face" that he and his comrades had administered to the public in 1912 is now returned to him with heavy measure. And they kill him, all of them together:

[35] The last line: "Za vsekh rasplachús / za vsekh raspláchus."

No / you are our inveterate enemy
Another like you once fell into our hands—a hussar![36]

. . . .

From all rifles / and batteries
from every Mauser and Browning
at a hundred paces / at ten / at two
point blank— / one cartridge after another.

. . . .

Get rid of him / lead into his heart!
So he can't even tremble!
But in the end / everything ends.
Trembling ends too. (1500-1527)

We note here the recurrence of the theme of the duel in which the poet is killed, an echo of both Pushkin and Lermontov, and the destruction of the poet as unnecessary and even dangerous reminds us once again of *Man*, a principal theme of which, we recall, was the rejection of the poet by the busy beings of the heavenly as well as the earthly realm. But in this poem there is a sudden emotional transition that prepares us, despite the poet's death, for the joyful utopian vision of the epilogue. Only a few shreds of him are left, but these fragments of the poet still fly—a red flag on the Kremlin tower. We recognize the repeated image from its first occurrence in the *Tragedy* (1913), where the shreds of the poet's soul are impaled on chimneys, and also from the *Cloud* (1915), where he stamped out his soul and offered it to the people, "a bloody banner." Here the poet's being is torn with suffering and broken into shreds, but in the process he nonetheless triumphs. His fate is still to save the people through his own suffering.

4) Epilogue: The Golden Age

From the ending of Part II it is clear that the poet has a choice: either he kills himself or the philistines kill him. As far as his own possessive and individual love is concerned, either he kills the object of that love or it kills him. Yet the ending of Part II, as we have seen, is a sudden, lyrical anticipation of happiness and light, and it recalls the bright optimism that closed the poem about the sun, and that suffuses the final part of the poem *Very*

[36] The reference is of course to the poet Lermontov.

Good; in this case the abrupt transition prepares the way for a dream of the golden age presented in the form of an official "application" (*proshenie*) addressed to an unnamed chemist of the thirtieth century, petitioning him most earnestly to use the chemical processes that by then have been developed, in order to resurrect the poet Mayakovsky so that he may "live out his life really" (*svoe dozhit*). This "application" to be resurrected calls up a vision of a future world in which there is no death and the already dead are easily resurrected. It contains a surging, exultant paean, issuing from the poem like a dazzling ray in the darkness of a tomb, to the earth and life on earth, and the joyous future when all men will have a single father, the world, and a single mother, the earth, in lines virtually impossible to translate because of the absence of gender in English nouns:

> So that our family / should be
> from now on
> our father— / at least the world,
> the earth at very least our mother. (1807-1812)

It is true that the thoughts of suicide and death in Parts I and II are not fully overcome, but the poet's resolute acceptance of life tends to dominate those thoughts, though at times it would seem that he protests too much:

> I'm not going to give anybody the satisfaction
> Of seeing me / stretched out with a bullet in me
> . . . .
> You can get me / from an ambush / with a knife,
> But I'm not offering my forehead to any D'Antheses.
> Four times I'll grow old—four times I'll be rejuvenated,
> Before I get to the grave.
> And whenever I die, / I'll die singing.
> And no matter what hole I lie in
> I know I deserve to lie
> with those who fell under the red flag. (1619-1634)

But immediately these lines are followed by dismal thoughts:

> But for whatever cause you finally stretch out
> death is still death.
> It's fearful, not to love, / it's awful, not to dare.
> There's a bullet / or a knife for everyone.
> But what about me—and where?

And the suicide clearly speaks again in these lines:

> Maybe, in my childhood, / deep down in it,
> I could find / ten bearable days. (1644-1647)

Yet these lines are in beautiful but precarious balance with statements such as this, which accept earthly life:

> What am I to do / if I / totally
> with every ounce of my heart,
> believed in this life / in this / world,
> and still / believe? (1661-1669)

Only on earth does Mayakovsky seek his paradise, and the utopia he foresees in the epilogue is one in which science has conquered the material problems of earthly existence, including death, and universal, all-pervasive love has conquered the social problems. When the human race as a whole learns the lesson learned and preached by the man on the bridge—that the only possible love is one which transcends individual demands and embraces all human beings—then men will no longer live as a sacrifice each to his own miserable little house and home, and love will leave the private bed and board and stride through the universe. (1790-1800)[37]

I have suggested above that the salvation offered the man on the bridge—unselfish love and the sacrifice of the self—probably has its origin in Dostoevsky. Moreover, there is a specific work of Dostoevsky in which the union of selfless and universal love is linked with the golden age of human happiness. The epilogue of the poem *About That* has so many correspondences with Dostoevsky's *Dream of a Ridiculous Man* (1877) that, considering the evidence already accumulated of a strong Dostoevskian element in the poem, there is little doubt that Mayakovsky drew important inspiration from that particular work.

Dostoevsky's *Dream of a Ridiculous Man*, and in particular its probable influence on Mayakovsky, may be better understood if we place that story and its principal character in a wider context. There are in Dostoevsky's works many characters who may be loosely described as "underground men" in the sense that they cultivate a protective isolation from contact with other human beings. These characters, in fact, do not fully recognize the real

[37] "Chtob vsei vselennoi shla lyubov."

existence of other human beings. The underground man in the story *Notes from Underground* spent forty years accumulating spite in isolation; the hero of *Mr. Prokharchin*, completely out of touch with reality, lives alone in his corner and accumulates money; the young recluse of *The Landlady* lives apart with his highly personal poetic visions; Raskolnikov hugs to himself his theory that he himself is a superman; Arkadii in *The Adolescent* has an idea that he will become wealthy and gain dominion over others, and he will not share his idea with anyone; Kirillov in *The Possessed* is effectively shut off from other human beings by his theory that in order to achieve complete freedom he must kill himself; Stavrogin in the same novel is different from the others in that he has no plan or idea or theory, but for him moral values do not exist, nor do people exist as beings that have any claim on his affections.

In the *Dream* this character-type has reached, so to speak, the outer limits of isolation. His shell is a metaphysical one: he becomes convinced that only he himself exists, and that therefore nothing in the world matters. He decides to kill himself, and thereby end at a stroke his own existence and that of everything else. The revolver is purchased and ready, and the idea of suicide actually comforts him. He found, however, that *something* did matter. A little girl in desperate need of help approached him on the street one dismal night, but he angrily brushed her away. Yet he felt a twinge of pity for the little girl and this opened a chink in his tough armadillo-cloak. He could not bring himself to end his life. In a dream he did shoot himself (in the heart) and seemed transported through space (as happens so frequently to Mayakovsky in his poetry) to a distant star. Its geographical outlines seen from a great height (a situation duplicated in *War and the Universe*, *The Fifth International*, and some other things) closely resembled our own earth, but on this star human beings still lived in a state of innocence and harmony, and the secret of their happiness is the unbounded love of each one for every other one:

> They knew love and they begat children, but I never noticed in them those outbursts of cruel sensuality which overtake almost everybody on our earth whether man or woman, and are the only source of almost every sin of our human race. . . . There were no quarrels or jealousy among them, and they did

not even know what the words meant. Their children were the children of them all, for they were all one family.[38]

Dostoevsky's distrust of the human reason and of modern science shows itself when the ridiculous man *corrupts* these innocents, like Satan in the garden of Eden, by introducing them to the fruits of knowledge; Mayakovsky rejected that viewpoint. In any case, the story ends when the ridiculous man awakens to a realization that universal love is both the meaning of life and the source of happiness; he says finally: "And I did find that little girl. . . . And I shall go on! I shall go on!"

The points of contact between this story and Mayakovsky's poem are too numerous, it would seem, to be accidental. Moreover, Mayakovsky's own life at the time he wrote the poem was not unlike that of the ridiculous man, especially his isolation from most of humanity and his recurrent thoughts of suicide: the revolver and the "healing death" it may bring are a real presence in *About That*, even in its final and more optimistic version. Curiously enough, Lily Brik, though she does not mention the *Dream of a Ridiculous Man*, records an incident in Mayakovsky's own life that vividly recalls the ridiculous man's encounter with the little girl who needed help. Lily wrote:

> I thought about Dostoevsky when, shortly after Mayakovsky's death, M. Yu. Levidov told me that in March 1930, he happened to meet Mayakovsky in Herzen House. They sat together at a table and Levidov asked him why he was so sad. The sense of Mayakovsky's answer was that he felt very sorry for people. They're all unhappy. And he then remembered a poor beggar to whom he had given nothing several years ago. And he couldn't forgive himself. And he kept saying that he never found her again, that beggar.[39]

Of course we must not lose sight of the distinction between life and literature, and what we are really concerned with here are parallels with Dostoevsky in a particular literary work. Yet there is never any sharp distinction between Mayakovsky and the central characters in his poems, and when we find biographical evidence that the poet himself responded to a character or situation in Dostoevsky, we may be fairly sure that such a re-

[38] F. M. Dostoevsky, *Sobranie sochinenii* (Moscow, 1956), x, 433-434.
[39] L. Brik, *Predlozhenie*, p. 207.

sponse will be mirrored in the imagined experiences of his characters.

We have traced in an earlier chapter a number of significant parallels with Dostoevsky in several of Mayakovsky's earlier works. The clearest and most specific parallels occur in *About That.* Lily Brik argues that Mayakovsky had a close emotional affinity with Dostoevsky himself, and that this explains the apparent anomaly of a revolutionary poet's echoing and even quoting the great conservative novelist. Mayakovsky's admiration of Dostoevsky as a novelist—though not of course as an ideologue—is well established by Lily's own testimony, and, given the sharp contrast between the two men in political outlook and allegiance, it is not surprising that Mayakovsky never emphasized this particular literary preference of his, and that, as a matter of fact, there are very few references to Dostoevsky in the thirteen volumes of his *Collected Works*, all of them routine and casual.

I would suggest that Mayakovsky was drawn to Dostoevsky because of that novelist's intense investigation of a number of characters who are in one way or another in rebellion, not only against society and social requirements, but against the rigid fact of existence itself. The number and variety of suicides that Dostoevsky examines in vivid psychological detail provided material that was congenial to Mayakovsky's own consciousness. Raskolnikov contemplates the deed, and his double, Svidrigailov, performs it; Kirillov plans his own suicide, and repeatedly explains the theory that drives him to it; Stavrogin is so empty of love that only suicide is left him ("Blame no one"); the ridiculous man plans suicide in his waking moments and carries it out in his dream. All these characters have reached an extreme of despair not unlike the condition of the central personage in the *Cloud, The Backbone Flute, Man*, and *About That*, and very like the psychological condition of Mayakovsky himself at certain points in his life.

There is another Russian source for many of the ideas and situations in *About That*, and, once again, that source is not directly related to Marx or Marxism: the Russian philosopher N. F. Fyodorov.[40] Viktor Shklovsky has suggested that Mayakovsky was

[40] It should be noted that Dostoevsky, too, was intrigued by the work of Fyodorov, and that he wrote of it enthusiastically to Fyodorov's disciple, N. P. Peterson, in March 1878: "We here, i.e. Solovyov and myself at least, believe in a real, literal, personal resurrection, and that it will take place on

acquainted with the work of Fyodorov. He may have derived from that philosopher the notions about the resurrection of the dead that appear in both *About That* and *The Bedbug*. It seems likely, then, that the utopian passages in the poem, not only where they tell of the future resurrection of the dead but also where they touch upon the necessity for universal love and brotherhood, derive in part from Fyodorov.

Fyodorov is a neglected Christian philosopher whose thought is original to the point of oddity. Though highly valued by both Dostoevsky and Tolstoy, he did not share their distrust of science; in fact he regarded science as a divinely provided means for realizing man's highest ends. For many years the librarian of the Rumyantsev Museum in Moscow, he lived simply, never sought publicity, and discussed his ideas only with a small circle of admirers that included the philosopher V. S. Solovyov, who called his teaching "the first forward movement of the human spirit along the path of Christ since the appearance of Christianity." Most of what he wrote he never published, and the few articles that did appear were usually unsigned. After his death his friends printed a collection of his writings under the title *The Philosophy of the Common Cause* (*Filosofiya obshchego dela*).[41] Only a few copies of this book were printed, and it has become a bibliographical rarity. It was reissued in 1928 in Harbin on the hundredth anniversary of Fyodorov's birth, and a photographic reprint of the original edition appeared in England in 1970.

The essays that express Fyodorov's ideas are numerous and tend to verbosity, and he never organized them into a systematic whole; nonetheless his thought may be summarized under two principal headings: 1) the need for brotherhood, or what he calls "kinship," among human beings; and 2) the need for the human community to bring the "blind forces" of nature under complete

---

this earth." See Konstantin Mochulsky, *Dostoevsky, His Life and Work*, trans. Michael A. Minihan (Princeton, 1967), p. 568.

[41] N. F. Fyodorov, *Filosofiya obshchego dela*, V. A. Kozhevnikov and N. P. Peterson, eds., I (Moscow, 1906), and II (1913). There is evidence in Maxim Gorky's published correspondence that he too had read Fyodorov with great interest. Moreover several of his correspondents—S. Grigoriev, Olga Forsh, Mikhail Prishvin—had also read Fyodorov and were curious about his ideas. See *Literaturnoe nasledstvo*, LXX, *M. Gorky i sovetskie pisateli; neizdannoe perepiska* (Moscow, 1963), pp. 134, 136, 335-336, 584-588, 591.

control in order to conquer not only all "natural" disasters but even death itself. The principal task of the "sons of man"—under God—is to achieve victory over the elemental forces, over hunger, disease, old age, and death. There would seem to be nothing particularly original in these thoughts, but the next step he takes is, to say the least, startling. He maintains that the task of all humans is to free from the "prison of death" those who gave them life, their fathers. The physical resurrection of those already dead, he believed, should be the sacred project, particularly of Christians, who believe in the physical resurrection of Christ.[42]

The first point on brotherhood or kinship also had some highly original implications. The reason for the failure to control nature is the fact that men are divided into classes and nations, and that the educated, those possessing knowledge, consider themselves a clan apart. The conquest of hierarchical and national divisions presupposes a philosophical reform in the course of which the division of the world into our "idea" or "representation," on the one hand, and some unknown reality on the other hand—the heritage from Kant—will break down, and men will recognize themselves not only as brothers each of every other but also as an integral part of everything that is. Positivism as an approach to human problems, he believed, also involved a division into theoretical and practical reason, and the modern infatuation with "progress" he deplored because it tended to cancel out the past and the labors of all our fathers.

It's not difficult to see some relationship to Marx in Fyodorov's thought, especially when he speaks of the "dis-relatedness" of human beings to labor in the modern world. As a librarian in the Rumyantsev Museum, he was curator of antiquities and a lover of the ornate printing of old books. Of the Gothic and so-called *ustavnyi* letters he says:

> . . . traced out with deep reverence, with love, even with delight, and executed like works of art . . . and produced with the same feelings with which churches were built and icons were painted in this epoch . . . then letters were something magnificent, like Gothic cathedrals, and did not, of course, have that womanish beauty which prevails now in the epoch of the cult of woman . . . they were produced neither hurriedly nor

[42] Fyodorov, I, 138-141.

impatiently, they were produced as a labor that was viewed as a blessing and not as a curse."[43]

The writing of Gothic, which gave pleasure in the present and the promise of greater pleasure in the future, is contrasted with the "rapid" modern satisfaction. "This rapidity deprives all work, not only mechanical but also intellectual work, of artistic attractiveness, turning it into a means of profit without any good whatever, if the sense of pleasure is to be considered a good."

In Mayakovsky's work there is more than a trace of Fyodorov. The idea that science will one day be able to resurrect the dead the poet took quite literally, at least for the purpose of his poem.[44] Fyodorov's own statements on the subject of resurrecting the "fathers" are direct and literal, though it may be that he also intends the "resurrection" of those who are dead as a metaphor of the attention and respect the present generation owes to the past. He lived and worked in a museum, he was in constant communication with the great minds of the past, and his concern that those minds and their priceless products not be lost to us perhaps took the figurative form of a moral imperative upon the present generation to "resurrect" past generations. The position Mayakovsky had reached in 1923 has implications inconsistent with his earlier views: instead of throwing the past "overboard from the steamship of modernity," he now looks forward to the possibility of resurrecting and preserving it.

5) The Poet and *Byt*

When the poem *About That* appeared in the first number of *Lef*, Mayakovsky's severest critic, N. Chuzhak, wrote a brief comment on it in which he said:

> Everything in this "Mystery" is *byt*. Everything is moved by *byt*. "My" house. "She," surrounded by friends and servants. . . . And "he" listens at the doors, rushes back and forth, genius that

[43] N. F. Fyodorov, "The Question of Brotherhood," as translated in James M. Edie, James P. Scanlon, and Mary-Barbara Zeldin, *Russian Philosophy*, III, 43.

[44] Roman Jakobson records a conversation with Mayakovsky that indicates that the poet did indeed believe literally in physical resurrection. See his "O pokolenii," p. 25.

> he is, from one set of philistines to another, talks with them about art, passionately mocks himself . . . and comes to the conclusion that "there's no way out" (*devatsya nekuda*).
>
> And really "there's no way out": the whole free world is enclosed by philistines and their way of life. In 1914 that poet was more perspicacious, and his hero did know a way out. . . .
>
> But still at the end of the poem, we see, "there is a way out." That way out is the faith that "in the future everything will be different, and there will be some kind of marvellous life. . . ."
>
> It seems to me that this is the faith of *despair. . . . This is not a way out, but a hopeless situation.*[45]

We can only say to this that even though he disapproved, Chuzhak has correctly understood the poem's deeper meaning; others on the editorial board of *Lef* shared Chuzhak's unhappiness. In the poem *Man* there is no hope in heaven or on earth for the poet, and earth's future offers no relief from the dominion of the philistines. In *About That* the outlook would seem to have altered for the better in that a happy future is allowed to mankind; yet for the poet in his own lifetime there is still no hope and no "way out," since the philistine dominates even "our red-flagged way of life." The old enemy has conquered again, and the world has grown gray with his breath.

Who exactly is the enemy? At first sight it seems a paradox that a towering ego such as Mayakovsky, an individualist whose sole topic was himself, should have lived constantly with the thought of suicide, with the compulsion, in other words, to destroy the self. In discussing the poem *Man*, Jakobson defines the poet's mortal contest with *byt* as an unresolvable opposition to everything that exists outside the self: "If we should attempt to translate Mayakovsky's mythology into the language of speculative philosophy, the exact equivalent of this enmity [for *byt*] would be the opposition of 'ego' and 'not ego.' It would be impossible to find a more adequate name for the enemy."[46]

Jakobson also points out that it is only in the poem *About That* that the struggle with *byt* is given directly: in his other works *byt* is usually personified—in *Man*, for instance, as the Ruler of All. No doubt the reason *byt* is attacked directly in *About That* (and also, we recall, in *The Fourth International*) is that at the

[45] *Lef*, No. 2, 1923, pp. 150-151. [46] Jakobson, "O pokolenii," p. 15.

time of writing it, his spirit was depressed by the immediate evidence that the revolutionary explosions of the century had changed nothing, that the old way of life had settled firmly into its old established ruts, that bureaucrats and policemen still held sway under the "new" regime, and that the immemorial enemy, just as he had once appropriated the symbols of Christ, now held sway under the aegis of Marx.

But the Soviet philistine is only one form the enemy took: we recall that in *Man* the angels busily concerned with ordering the heavenly realm are a kind of celestial variation of *byt*, they are bodiless philistines. The "ordinary young man" of the *Tragedy* is still another variation: like Fekla Davidovna's husband he wants to hear no dangerous revolutionary talk; he is attached to his sister Sonya and to material progress—his machine for cutting up chops automatically and his friend's invention, a trap for bedbugs. Moreover, he has a wife who will soon have a son or a daughter. The ordinary young man is in thrall to objective reality: in order to control it he has surrendered to it; he has accepted Marx's dictum that "freedom is knowledge of necessity."

Another shape of the enemy was "Wilson," the man whose city rests upon a screw and is completely "electro-dynamo-mechanized." Still others are Lloyd George, the "Negus," and those other "clean" characters in *Mystery-Bouffe* whom the flood washes away. The odious "fat ones" (*zhirnye*) that appear in the *Cloud* and in the short poem "That for You!" (*Nate!*) and elsewhere are another variation of the enemy. Obviously many of these "masks" fit the general concept of the bourgeois, a type to which Mayakovsky, both as a revolutionary and as a futurist poet, was organically hostile. But the angels in *Man* hardly fit into that category, and the Soviet philistines that are castigated in *The Fourth International* and in *About That* are certainly not bourgeois, whatever else they are. Heaven itself in *Man* has its own variety of *byt*—that is to say, a rigid organization with assigned songs to sing (an aria from Rigoletto, for instance), and assigned tasks for each bodiless being to perform. Like the angels, the whores of Montparnasse have their own habits and expectations. The source of all organization is of course God himself who, we recall, "made the stars light up their fires," who (as we have it in the *Cloud*) created man with imperative sexual needs but never "fixed it" so that those needs could be absolutely satisfied ("so that he could just kiss and kiss and kiss"). Repeatedly we find the poet rebelling against the fact that sexual love is part of a larger plan not devised by the poet himself, the terms of which he cannot accept. A family, stability, children, the home were never part of the bargain entered into by the frantic lover. Maria in the *Cloud* wants to get married, with all that implies as to regularity of life and provision for the consequences of sexual acts; Lily in *The Backbone Flute* is already married and has music on her piano (twice used as a symbol of *byt*); in *Man* the girl on Zhukovsky Street whose boudoir he invades has a husband categorized as to place and profession—he is an engineer—who claims his rights: "Why are you bothering my wife?"; Fekla Davidovna's husband boasts of his daughter, who is "the spit and image of him." And even "She" in that poem is caught in the tangles of convention and routine. The free, unfettered happiness of the poem "I Love You," in which the girl simply plays with his heart as with a child's ball, was an illusion. The exercise of sex brings about situations and consequences that do fetter the poet. Even the revolution, in the course of propagating and defending itself, has had to organize, define, and regulate life, and it had placed the poet in a confining niche.

We may now be in a better position to answer the question already posed: Why was the expansive Mayakovsky self so obsessed with the idea of destroying itself? Precisely because the poet's ego was so demanding, because he could not compromise his existential autonomy, because he could not accept the "plan" imposed upon him whether by God, by nature, or by the state, the act of suicide may have seemed an ultimate assertion of the self, and the only means to achieve perfect freedom. And there was literary precedent for such an action in the suicide of Kirillov in *The Possessed*, who had to kill himself in order to assert his independence.

But Mayakovsky recovered from the psychological crisis of 1923, and no doubt his work on the poem *About That* was a kind of occupational therapy inasmuch as the poem did objectify and externalize his problem. Soon after its completion he came out of isolation, began once again to see his friends, and plunged into a new kind of agitation and propaganda: commercial poetry. For a few more years the well-organized alter ego whom the poet recognized in Fekla Davidovna's apartment would dominate his life and save him from suicide. Once more the structural unity of his life and all his work strikes us with particular force: doomed to death as he was, he still continued for some years to shout his "commercials," like the man in the *Cloud* who recommends on the very gallows that we "drink Van Houten's cocoa."

Chapter Ten

A COMMERCIAL ARTIST DISCOVERS AMERICA

1) The Poet-Advertiser

Mayakovsky crossed the Mexican-American border at Laredo, Texas on July 27, 1925, having at long last received a visa after several unsuccessful attempts to visit the land where the "future," in terms at least of industrialization, was actually being realized.[1] Burliuk in New York had moved whatever could be moved in the State Department to procure the visa, and had arranged an invitation from the New York artist Willy Pogany, who wrote Mayakovsky offering him the good offices of the Pogany Studio at 152 West 46th Street in arranging exhibits of his own work and becoming acquainted with the work of American artists. Other procedures and pressures were undertaken, not all of which are clear at this distance in time, and the poet was indeed admitted for a five-month stay.

It's noteworthy that he was admitted as a commercial artist, which is broadly what he had become shortly after the completion of the poem *About That,* and before considering his travels we should look into that new development in his career. He had, in other words, capitulated to Soviet *byt* and found himself lucra-

[1] The most complete treatment of Mayakovsky's visit to America is S. Kemrad, *Mayakovsky v Amerike; stranitsy biografii* (Moscow, 1970). This book must be used with great care, however, since the author both consciously and unconsciously (which is worse) takes the viewpoint of a loyal Soviet citizen describing a confrontation with capitalism. A totally false impression is created, moreover, by the author's quotation of enthusiastic statements about Mayakovsky from such papers as the *Russian Voice* (*Russkii golos*) and *Freiheit,* when he fails to tell us that these were Communist papers.

The best treatment in English of Mayakovsky's travels is Charles Moser, "Mayakovsky's Unsentimental Journeys," *American Slavic and East European Review,* XIX (1960), 85-100. See also his "Mayakovsky and America," *Russian Review,* XXV (1966), 242-266.

Also useful is V. Katanyan, "Poezdki Mayakovskogo zagranitsu," in *Mayakovsky, PSS* (Moscow, 1939-1949), VII.

tive activity as a producer of illustrated advertising jingles from 1923 to 1925. This was his "*Mosselprom* period," so named for the many jingles written for the Moscow Food Stores (*Mosselprom*), which ended with the rhyming lines, "*nigde krome / kak v Mosselprome*": "Nowhere else but in the Moscow Food Stores." These scores of advertisements for *Mosselprom* and other Soviet retail trading organizations, jingles such as

> Where can you buy and eat for your money
> the best and the tastiest macaroni?
> Where? Nowhere else but in the Moscow Food Stores. . . .

were, said Mayakovsky, poetry of the highest caliber.[2] The phrase *nigde krome* became a kind of motto of *Mosselprom*, and was displayed in huge blue letters the whole height of its headquarters on the Arbat.

He wrote jingles for magazines: *Lef, Red Virgin Soil* (*Krasnaya nov*), *The Rattrap* (*Krysodav*), and others. The State Publishing House was one of his clients, as was the Rubber Trust: he wrote sales jingles for galoshes, tires, rubber balls, and, of all things, infant pacifiers: "The best pacifiers ever sold / He'll suck on them till he's very old."[3] He wrote for the Moscow clothing stores and for the tea administration. His numerous productions for the Moscow Food Stores include recommendations not only for macaroni and vermicelli but for cigarettes of various brands:

> *Joke* cigarettes are no joke
> Taste better than oranges
> Smell sweeter than the rose.[4]

Of course the verses alone on the printed page convey no adequate impression of the total "work of art," if that is what it is. Each verse was accompanied by drawings, and the words of the jingle are fitted into a composition in many interesting and amusing ways. The drawings were for the most part done by artists associated with him in the project, and many of these were the work of Rodchenko, his associate on *Lef*. His friend and advisor, Osip Brik, was engaged at the same period in producing advertising materials for *Mosselprom* and in writing theoretical rationalizations of such activity for *Lef*.

[2] *PSS*, I, 27.
[3] *PSS*, v, 278: "Luchshikh sosok nebylo i net / gotov sosat do starosti let."
[4] *PSS*, v, 285.

The jingles fit the typical Mayakovsky verse pattern in important ways. Each one turns on a humorous and offbeat rhyme (*eli-vermisheli*). The metrical beat is for the most part accentual, though the typical rhythm is simple, direct, and popular. The advertising jingles recall the "windows" and the propaganda pieces written in support of Russia during the First World War. Mayakovsky in these verses is using well-developed skills for new purposes, and it is difficult to agree with Tynyanov that the *Mosselprom* series was a retreat into "the everyday" (*byt*) for the purpose of "recruiting reinforcements," that is, for the purpose of renewing the poetic lexicon and the verse phrase. Tynyanov adds in parentheses, ". . . any regrets over the fact that the poet is 'wasting' his talent [in such work] are simply mistaken; where it seems to us that it is being wasted it is actually acquiring something new." Yet Tynyanov ends his comment with a question: "But will the cold-blooded *Mosselprom* profit Mayakovsky as once the ardent posters of ROSTA [the windows] profited him?"[5]

Tynyanov's thought seems a rather precious application of formalist dogma without regard to the real literary situation. There is nothing new about the *Mosselprom* series since it simply repeats for commercial purposes the formal tricks developed in earlier periods. The "renewal of the lexicon" consists simply in the appropriation for verse purposes of egregiously non-poetic vocabulary—"pacifiers," "galosh," "cigarette," "caramel," and so forth; this was no novelty for a poet trained in the futurist school. These verses are far inferior to the windows in versatility and variety. Perhaps because of the commercial subject matter, they offer nothing like the literary allusion and literary parody that we found in the windows.

The rationalization for this kind of work provided by Mayakovsky in his autobiography and by his colleagues in their articles on the social demand[6] is not convincing. The arguments that he was engaged in the "de-aestheticization" of the productive arts or that the function of the poet is simply to fulfill the "order" of his client, the proletarian state, are simply pretentious ways of saying that one must adjust to an environment unfriendly to poets; it does not follow at all that what he produced under these pressures was poetry, or is worth reading now except as evidence of the

[5] Yu. Tynyanov, "Promezhutok," in his *Arkhaisty i novatory* (Leningrad, 1929), pp. 556-557.

[6] See above, Chapter Eight.

times. Nevertheless his commercial *agitka* is usually clever, deftly pointed, and of course immeasurably superior to any commercial verse written since, in the east or in the west. Those verses display the inimitable Mayakovsky turn of phrase and his skill in the original use of non-poetic vocabulary. In this respect the advertising *agitki* were a perfect echo of Mayakovsky's first poetic "caper," so to speak: his original pose as a poet of anti-poetry, indeed as a brilliant non-poet. Perhaps that is why he engaged in this work with such obvious gusto. But of course the metaphor that is the heart of Mayakovsky's verse has gone; the lacerated ego is temporarily absent—except perhaps as an ironic background presence; and the rebellion against heaven and hell is in momentary abeyance.

2) The Restless Traveller

But let us return to Mayakovsky's travels as a "commercial artist." Most of his life he was a restless and compulsive traveller. The "tour" of provinces and far countries began in 1913, as we have seen, and did not end until the final months of his life. He visited Riga, Berlin, and Paris in 1922; Berlin once again in 1923; Riga, Berlin, and Paris in 1924; the western hemisphere in 1925, where he made his way during a six-month period to Mexico City, Laredo, New York, Rockaway Beach, Cleveland, Detroit, Chicago, Philadelphia, and Pittsburgh. The 1925 journey was planned as a trip around the world, but he reported that "after six months' travel I shot like a bullet back to the USSR. Didn't even go to San Francisco (they'd invited me for a lecture)."[7] As we shall presently see, his principal experience during these travels, as revealed in the direct, uninhibited documentation of his letters and telegrams to Lily Brik, was simple boredom (*skuka*), interrupted, it is true, by occasional onsets of poetic vision "clear to the point of hallucination," during one of which he produced the magnificent poem "Brooklyn Bridge." He travelled during 1926 and 1927 to twenty or thirty Soviet towns, and also managed to visit Prague, Berlin, Paris, and Warsaw. He visited Paris again in 1928 and early 1929, where another great love overwhelmed him. But that was a disappointment, perhaps a fatal one.

All his trips gave rise to literature, both poetry and prose, running the gamut of Mayakovsky's considerable range, that is to say,

[7] *PSS*, I, 27.

from trivial to magnificent. The poetry inspired by his journey to Paris in 1924 is interesting as a cycle which may be placed under the general heading of "metapoetry," since some of those poems betray a concern with the nature of the poet and his work. The cycle is interesting also in that through the scaffolding of political mythology that surrounds each one, we catch a glimpse of another apparatus, the lyrical one. In other words, the political and lyrical elements in the poet's work, as a rule temporally discrete, here coexist in many poems. We note the curious fact that in a letter written to Lily Brik from Paris at this time, he maintains that he is "drawn again to lyricism."[8] Incidentally, the letters betray an honest boredom with Paris and a perfectly genuine indifference to its sights and sounds (the latter were of course gibberish to Mayakovsky, who knew only Russian and Georgian).

The poem "On My Way" (*Edu*)[9] tells of the trip itself, giving immediate expression in rather feverish linguistic form to the sleepy sensations of a journey at night through northern France. The train ride through these foreign "place names" evokes nostalgic memories of Russia, a parody of Pushkin, and what is probably a Marinetti-like onomatopoeia, a verbal imitation of the click-clack noises made by a locomotive and its train of cars. The piece is fascinating for its treatment, not exactly of the delirious mental state that Mayakovsky sometimes favored, but of a kind of movement-and-distance-induced drowsiness on a train journey through far-off, exotic places. The poem "City" (*Gorod*) is a meditation on the *personal* plight occasioned by some Paris scenes, though the Paris setting is not really essential to the poem. It clearly fits into the category of "metapoetry." It conveys Mayakovsky's sense of loneliness even amid the crowd of admirers and supporters, his lack either of reliable friends or of "fellow-travellers." The latter term, often applied to him opprobriously by pure proletarians, he throws back at them ironically:

> Whose fellow-traveller am I?
> Nobody at all
> keeps step with me.[10]

He presents the image of himself as a lonely camel pulling the two-wheeled cart (*arb*) of his poetry: "I'm bored here way out / ahead of everybody."

[8] *Literaturnoe nasledstvo*, LXV, 140. [9] *PSS*, VI, 197-198.
[10] *PSS*, VI, 201.

In vivid contrast to his cart there is a paradoxical shift to the *Place de la Concorde* and a brilliant metaphorical study of Parisian light and rain: the lights burn in the rain, on the asphalt, over the earth, and are reflected a thousand times in a swirling mixture of rain and dust: "It's as though the lamps are memorizing the multiplication table." The poem ends with the often quoted lines, "If I were the Vendôme column, / I would marry the Place de la Concorde," in which the sexual symbolism is certainly deliberate.

"Verlaine and Cézanne"[11] is an imagined encounter with two great artists reduced to the proportions of a casual, but inwardly weighty, conversation over a table in the Rotonde. It reflects, once again, the boredom with Paris that we find expressed in his letters, and the imagined conversation with the great men is concerned exclusively with the current problems of poets in Moscow.

> I don't have enough room here / in the hotel Istria . . .
> I'm oppressed. / Parisian life is not ours—
> You just scatter your melancholy / over the boulevards.
> On the right of us— / the Boulevard Montparnasse,
> on the left— / the Boulevard Raspail. (5-14)

His only recourse is to "phantoms" groomed out in beards by the Paris fog: "good evening, M-r Turgenev / good evening, madame Viardot"—but we note that these are phantoms that speak Russian.

The encounter with Verlaine is another opportunity for the expression of irreverent attitudes—"I've hardly read you at all, Verlaine"—but it develops into a discussion of poetry as Mayakovsky unburdens himself to Verlaine on the subject of his difficulties with the Moscow establishment. He has some double-edged remarks to make, the most important of which is that a poet can live with *any* word. A poet is like a prostitute—he'll sleep with any word that will give him something, even such a word as "proletariat," which in fact provides a grandiose theme for some poets. (100-120) But when he tries to explain the situation of the poet in the Soviet Union, it turns out that there are drawbacks to practicing the trade there. Some of the lines appear to be a penetrating negative comment on the theory of the "social demand," which he himself helped to propagate. The attitude of official organization is that the poet is simply a crafts-

[11] *PSS*, vi, 204-210.

man—"poet—why that's just a craft"—give him an order (*zadanie*) and he carries it out: "Turn Toward the Village," for instance (*litsom k derevne*). He complains to Verlaine (and to his Moscow comrades) that he has his own individuality (*litso*) and that he is not a "weathercock" capable of turning as the winds of propaganda direct. Nor is he a thoughtless parrot:

> A poet / could never live / without ideas.
> What am I anyway— / a parrot? A gobbler?
> The worker / should be approached / more respectfully—
> we underestimate him.

This poem is clear evidence of Mayakovsky's unhappiness with the situation of the poet, and perhaps of art in general, in the Soviet Union, as well as his second thoughts concerning the theory of the "social demand," and it is interesting that such reflections appear in poems written from the far vantage point of Paris and the imagined company of "Verlaine and Cézanne."

"Notre-Dame"[12] is a genuine appreciation of Paris' Gothic wonder, but the poet's awe and admiration are partly concealed by the tone of friendly levity that characterizes all his poetic dealings with majesty, grandeur, and eminence. It is a not unfriendly, but distinctly irreverent, effort to lower the dignity and majesty of Notre-Dame, just as the Deity is brought down to an easy level in a number of poems, and Pushkin himself is reduced to a familiar drinking-companion in the matchless poem "Jubilee Year" (*Yubileinoe*, 1924). The touch of wonder in the poem about Notre Dame (as, indeed, in the poem about Pushkin) creates a teasing paradox of attitude and feeling. The magnificent edifice, a monument that is frozen in time and for all practical purposes indestructible, he describes as

> An exalted ship / of the past
> caught in time
> and held fast in the shallows. (6-9)

The poem "modernizes" that edifice in the sense that it becomes part of Mayakovsky's own world, a setting for amazing electronic advertisement, though of course it would not do for a worker's club ("a bit too dark inside"). The poem closes with an injunction to Parisian revolutionaries to take care:

[12] *PSS*, VI, 211.

Yes, / you have to be careful here
not to do any damage / with your shells.
Especially / if you're out
to smash
the Police Station
across the street. (102-112)

One critic contrasts this poem with Mandelshtam's "Notre Dame," and indeed the comparison is immensely illuminating.[13] Mandelshtam's poem is a direct contradiction of Mayakovsky in that he values particularly the accumulated evidence of culture preserved in architectural monuments; he feels reverence for the story of the human past that confronts and fascinates him in these magnificent relics. Mayakovsky the man may have felt some of this reverence, but reverence of any kind was incompatible with his nature as a poet, especially reverence for past glories.

"Versailles"[14] is an amusing poetic account of a visit to the palace and park, which are observed from the viewpoint of an "ordinary Russian chap," who happens also to be a revolutionary. It contains an example of what might be called "reverse hyperbole" in the lines:

The bastards had it really good.
The palaces
have a thousand bedrooms and halls—
And every room / has both a table / and a bed. (31-36)

The rococo magnificence of the palace and its rich supply of every conceivable furnishing is fully expressed in terms of the most minimal requirements of a room. We detect here a triple level of satire: directed at the palace itself with its superflux of rooms, ceilings, halls, alcoves, carved chairs, and gilded bedsteads; directed at the ordinary Moscow tourist (Mayakovsky), whose first response to it all is "The bastards had it really good"; and on a third level directed at the bare living conditions of the Moscow that is the tourist's normal habitat. The open-mouthed admiration he affects at a multiplicity of bedrooms, each with a bed and a table, reminds us of Zoshchenko's perfectly satisfac-

[13] Victor Terras, "Mayakovskij and Time," *Slavic and East European Journal*, XIII (1969), 152.
[14] *PSS*, VI, 215.

tory room that had absolutely everything: "a floor, a ceiling, a door—everything."[15]

The remaining poems in the 1925 Paris cycle have only minimal interest since they are direct propaganda motivated, no doubt, by conversation with Parisian radicals. "Jaures"[16] is a rhyming editorial giving the Communist Party view of the transference to the French Pantheon of the bones of the martyred socialist Jean Jaures, a ceremony which Mayakovsky apparently witnessed. "Farewell (the Café)" (*Proshchanie* [*Kafe*])[17] deals with the Russian émigrés in Paris and their supposedly uninformed "gossip" about the poet and all things Soviet. But in a final note to Paris, the poem "Farewell!" (*Proshchanie*)[18] he drops completely the role of a simple Moscow chap not taken in by foreign tricks and expresses uninhibited, direct admiration:

> Paris / runs along / seeing me off
> in all / her incredible beauty.
> Let the bilge of parting tears
> rise / in my eyes,
> may my heart / melt / with sentimentality!
> I would like / to live / and die in Paris
> If there were not / such a place / as Moscow. (4-20)

Mayakovsky's nature as traveller and tourist is more clearly revealed in the sketches of Paris and Berlin written in 1922 and 1923 on the occasion of earlier visits to Western Europe.[19] His comments on Parisian life make no pretense to objectivity, and his persistent reminders that life in Russia is purer and more promising recall the disillusionment with the west and nostalgic admiration for the homeland experienced by Russian travellers of the nineteenth century, especially Herzen and Dostoevsky. In fact, he closely follows certain of their comments on western life in comparison with Russian life and especially Russian prospects, although his confidence is based not on a future transformation of Russian life, but on the revolution that has already occurred. In the essay entitled "The Plan of Paris" (*Skhema Parizha*) there is a distinct note of moral outrage at the Parisian pursuit of money and purchasable pleasures; in these passages Mayakovsky is

[15] In the story "Pushkin."
[16] *PSS*, VI, 219.
[17] *PSS*, VI, 223.
[18] *PSS*, VI, 227.
[19] *PSS*, IV, 205-261.

simply one of those Russian writers who made pilgrimages to the west in search of a higher civilization, only to find materialism, egotism, and moral decay. He fits the stereotype remarkably well. There is a passage in the sketch entitled "Paris" that closely reproduces Dostoevsky's own ideas on the disappointments of Russians who depend too much on lessons learned from the west and also reminds us of Herzen's remark on the Germanizing philosophers of the eighteen-forties.

> Before the war pilgrims from the whole world came together to kiss the relics of Parisian art.
>
> They knew Paris by heart.
>
> You didn't have to be interested in anything that happened on Tverskaya-Yamskaya St., but you couldn't get along without knowing about the latest daubings of the hundred studios on the rue Jacques Caillot.
>
> Now there are more people acquainted with the poles than with Paris.
>
> The pole has no Poincarés. It's more congenial.[20]

But Mayakovsky is, as usual, ambivalent. Though he professes to find Paris, and especially Parisian art, in a state if not of decay then of stagnation, yet he grants the authority of the French in matters of form and technique. The "social system" in the west, he maintains, retards the development of art, and Russia has the priceless advantage of having cast off the impediment of the old system and thereby acquired unlimited freedom to develop new ideas and new forms. Picasso, for instance, strives through mastery of form to find an application for everything he knows, but is unable to function fully in the "stuffy atmosphere of French life," and Mayakovsky contrasts Picasso's position with that of Tatlin and the Russian "constructivists."[21] Of course he believed all this at the time, and no doubt the French painters with whom he conversed, and whose eager inquiries about developments in the Soviet Union he reports, believed it also.[22]

There is no doubt also that the people in France under whose auspices he travelled provided him with a carefully conditioned view of French life, the capitalist system, the decaying bourgeois society, and so forth. His visits were extremely brief, and, bereft as he was of the French language, he could have no basis for the

[20] *PSS*, IV, 205. [21] *PSS*, IV, 246. [22] *PSS*, IV, 212.

observations he made, other than the opinions he heard expressed (and himself held even before his visit) in the milieu where he was welcomed. His remarks on Parisian art he prepared for publication separately under the title "A Seven-Day Inspection of French Painting,"[23] and the title seems intended to underline the necessarily superficial nature of his observations. In the foreword to that essay he gives special credit to Sergei Pavlovich Diaghilev, "who aided my inspection through his knowledge of Parisian painting and because of his exceptionally loyal attitude toward the RSFSR, and who helped me to obtain materials for this book."[24] It is worth noting at this point that Mayakovsky dispatched a letter from Paris to A. V. Lunacharsky, the Commissar for Education, urging that he expedite a visit by Diaghilev to Russia:

Paris 20.XI.24

Honored Anatolii Vasilevich:

This "introductory" letter is rather unnecessary: you know Sergei Pavlovich Diaghilev as well as I do and S. P. is in no need of an introduction. Nevertheless I'm writing you this letter in the hope that S. P. may the more quickly break through the red tape of the secretariat, which might be disposed to be excessively defensive. . . . Of course those former Russians who have become habitués of Paris have S. P. thoroughly terrified of Moscow. But his own desire to see us has overcome that, as also my assurances that in delicacy and grace we outdo the French, and in "efficiency" the Americans. I hope that with your help S. P. will become convinced of this by his own experience. Especially since his principal purpose is to look us over.

It wouldn't hurt to speak of our pavilion at the Paris Exhibit. S. P. knows all about the taste of the French and he knows their art. That art, to my regret, still plays a considerable role in Paris.

I press your hand.
With comradely greetings,
Vl. Mayakovsky

On the same day Mayakovsky wrote to Osip Brik urging his good offices in the project of making an impression on Diaghilev:

[23] It was not published during his lifetime.
[24] *PSS*, IV, 233.

Dear Osip,

Be a guiding light to Sergei Pavlovich—show him everything in Moscow that ought to be seen—and when you get tired of showing him yourself, write it all down.

If S. P. doesn't like Rodchenko, Lavinsky, Eisenstein and the rest, soften him up with caviar. . . . If he doesn't like that there's nothing to be done.

I kiss you.
All yours,
Vol

We should never forget, in this connection, that Mayakovsky on his frequent trips abroad was a conscious representative of Soviet interests; this probably explains the ease with which he could obtain permission to travel as well as the large advances he occasionally received from publishers.[25] His position as "plenipotentiary of Soviet poetry" (*Polpred sovetskoi poezii*) seems to have been formalized in 1926 when he became an active member of a body founded within VOKS (All-Union Organization for Cultural Connections with Foreign Countries), the purpose of which was to serve the cause of "literary liaison" with foreign lands. A Soviet historian has pointed out that his trips abroad from 1927 to 1929 were undertaken as a mission (*zadanie*) assigned him by VOKS, and letters from the VOKS archives indicate that Mayakovsky's travels were officially regarded as important propaganda undertakings.[26]

3) America at Last

The visit to America in the summer of 1925 was, as we have seen, the realization of a plan entertained at least since 1923. The journey provided a rich yield of both poetry and journalistic prose, and, as is usually the case with Mayakovsky, it is more

[25] See, for instance his letter concerning the theft of his money in Paris, and his request for additional funds from the State Publishing House (*GIZ*), in *Literaturnoe nasledstvo*, LXV, 145.

[26] E. Dinershtein, ed., "Polpred sovetskoi poezii," *Voprosy literatury*, No. 8, 1968, pp. 250-251.

His visits to Berlin yielded comparatively little poetry and only a few sketches, though he lectured many times, gave out generously with Soviet propaganda, and seems to have sympathized with the problem of Germany in the era of reparations and Poincaré. See Moser, p. 88.

interesting and immeasurably more illuminating to give attention first to the poetry. In fact, Mayakovsky always treated the "Poems About America" as a special cycle of his work, and he published them separately as such. They provide a far more reliable diary of his visit than do the sketches he subsequently published under the title *My Discovery of America.*

The cycle is framed, so to speak, by the two poems about ocean voyages with which it begins and ends, "The Atlantic Ocean" and "Homeward!" (*Domoi!* 1925), not a surprising circumstance in view of the fact that the journey itself began and ended with transatlantic crossings.[27] Yet the two poems, and a third that we shall examine, do remind us of the frequent occurrence of water in Mayakovsky's poetry and the symbolic meanings that may be attached to it.

The poems inspired by the visit are more interesting than the prose chiefly because Mayakovsky's ambivalence appears in many of them, though never in the prose. For instance, "I Bear Witness" (*Svidetelstvuyu*) complains of simplistic propaganda of the kind that he himself must occasionally be charged with, and "Camp Nitgedaige"[28] is an abortive effort at escape into purely lyrical motifs. As in the poems of the Parisian cycle, Mayakovsky's range is incredibly wide, from the ill-natured and humorless triviality of "Six Nuns" (*Shest Monakhin*) to the ecstatic wonder of "Brooklyn Bridge."

"The Atlantic Ocean" we have already commented upon and analyzed[29] as a meditation on deep matters composed on shipboard. Also in a meditative mood he produced a short piece called "Shallow Philosophy in Deep Places" (*Melkaya filosofiya na glubokikh mestakh*),[30] which seems out of character for Mayakovsky since it treats time not as a creator but as a destroyer: the poet, as he experiences the deliberate movement of the ship over the boundless ocean and observes the accumulating evidence of its passage through space, reflects on the equally imperceptible movement of the years and the disappearance with them of—everything. The idea of constant flow, change, and passage is deeply embedded in the poem and is set forth in a number of images:

[27] Papernyi in his *Poeticheskii obraz* offers some interesting commentary on the oceans that "embrace the soul of the poet," as well as the "American cycle" of poems.

[28] *PSS*, VII, 58, 88.

[29] See above, Chapter Eight.

[30] *PSS*, VII, 17.

Yesterday / the ocean was mean / as a devil.
Today / it's as quiet / as a nesting dove.
What a difference!
Everything flows,
everything changes.
The water / has its own times
its hours of flood, / its hours of ebbing. (8-20)

And again:

Toward us / slower than a seal's bulk,
A ship from Mexico— / and we're / headed there.
How could it be otherwise. / It's the division
of labor. (35-42)

And on the disappearance of gulls:

The years are seagulls. / They fly off one after another,
then into the water— / to stuff their stomachs with fish.
The gulls have gone. / As a matter of fact,
Where are the birds? (50-56)[31]

And on himself:

I was born / grew / fed on a nipple—
lived / worked / got a bit old . . .
So life will have passed, / just as the Azores / passed us by.
(57-65)

Those final lines of the poem offer a rare instance in Mayakovsky's poetry of relative stillness and reflection; the effect of time's certain passage, in fact the near identity of past and future, is achieved by the abrupt insertion of a single future perfective tense (life will have passed, *zhizn proidyot*) in a long series of past-tense verbs, with the result that the mind apperceives that future as something already accomplished and gone. Indeed, the sense of the lines is that life too has passed. Nor is the sense of time's loss mitigated here by the usual "futurist" faith in the ultimate efficacy of time's work.

[31] Lily Brik remembers that this phrase was a domestic favorite of Mayakovsky in the sense of an "amusingly profound" query. According to her reminiscence the question was first asked by her own father when he noted the disappearance of the caged birds that Mayakovsky himself first collected, then got bored with and let go. See L. Brik, "Iz vospominanii o stikhakh Mayakovskogo," *Znamya*, No. 4, 1941, p. 233.

As we continue to consider the poems in the American cycle in the approximate order in which Mayakovsky arranged them for publication,[32] it will be necessary to perform an evaluation: some of them are poor poems and interesting only because Mayakovsky wrote them, others are interesting also because of the political message they contain, and a few belong with the best of Mayakovsky's work. In the first group, "Black and White" reveals the American phenomenon of a bitter class struggle complicated by racial hatreds, and is apparently based on some observations made during a brief stay in Havana. The highly political audiences that gathered to hear him read it in New York and other places may well have "raised the roof," as the *Chicago Daily Worker* reported,[33] at Mayakovsky's advice to black Willy, the oppressed worker:

> How was he to know
> that his question
> should be directed
> to the Comintern
> in Moscow?[34]

[32] There is difficulty in dating some of the poems. Katanyan is able to give precise dates for only a few. "Baryshnya i Vulvort," "Vyzov," "Amerikanskie russkie," "Bruklinsky most," "100%" were written during his stay in America, that is, between August 1 and October 28. "Domoi!" was apparently begun on shipboard on the way home. The rest ("Sifilis," "Tropiki," "Meksika-Nyu York," "Svidetelstvuyu") were written during the first half of the following year. See Katanyan, *Khronika*, p. 254.

[33] *PSS*, vii, 467.

[34] A note appended to this poem in *PSS*, vii, 474 (and repeated in Kemrad's book) offers the curious information that "in 1947 in Berlin a collection of Mayakovsky's works in German appeared which included the poem 'Black and White.' The son of the 'cigar king,' General Lucius Clay, who was then the chief commissar of the USA in Germany, issued an order that all copies of this collection in the American zone be destroyed."

This is an example of Soviet journalistic inventiveness at its worst, and it may even be pointless to dignify such matter by answering it. Whatever else might be said of General Clay, his father was not named Henry, as the poem says, and had nothing to do with Cuban tobacco. Moreover, Mayakovsky has clearly misunderstood something when he speaks of the tobacco firm as "Henry Clay and Bok Limited." No American firm could have such a name and there is no indication that we have to do here with British or Canadians. The name "Henry Clay"—an echo of the "great compromiser"—is itself suspicious. Perhaps additional research would clear up the point, but would it be worthwhile?

"Syphilis" is a lame effort to blame the exploiters for the spread of disease among the colonial peoples. "Christopher Columbus" employs once again the irreverent approach to greatness of "The Sun," "Jubilee Year," and "Notre-Dame," but the effect is lost when the poem (also a ringing success with his highly selected American audiences) lowers itself to simple propaganda:

> You're stupid, Columbus— / I tell you straight.
> As for me / why I / personally—
> would have closed America / cleaned it up a little
> and then / I would have opened it again / a second time.
> (253-261)

But then the propaganda note disappears without a trace in the poem "The Tropics," conceived on the railway journey from Vera Cruz to Mexico City, which is a purely lyrical impression of the onset of a tropical night, full of botanical wonders, strange colors and fragrances, and "packed" with stars so numerous that even the best accountant could not total them up. "Mexico" is probably the most successful piece of pure agitation in the American cycle, and the reason for its success is that it engages both the poet himself and the reader in the cause of liberating the colonial people: the poet's own memories of the Indian games he played during his childhood when, like so many Russian children, he drank deeply from the works of Fenimore Cooper and Mayne Reid, serve as introduction to the actual Indians of Vera Cruz who lift his suitcases, and no longer have any of the pride and beauty of Montihomo Hawk's-Claw: "The pile of suitcases / takes the place / of arrows / that couldn't miss—" (70-73) The poem contains also a beautiful evocation of past glory and ancient wars, and moments of historical meditation (rare in Mayakovsky): "That / was / so long ago / it almost never was." (87-90) The poem is so rich with actual images of Indians, with memories of the past in ironic contrast with the present: "Heroism / is not for now. / Montezuma is only a brand name of beer . . ." (169-171) and with unfeigned sorrow (the word is not too strong) at the humiliation and poverty of the aborigines, that Mayakovsky's closing agitational shout seems natural, and artistically acceptable in the context of the poem: "Soon / crimson flag, / fly over the Mexican melon!" (287-289)

The poem "Mexico" succeeds as propaganda because its message grows naturally out of a personal disenchantment. Others of the same cycle seem to be based on anecdotes or newspaper stories that Mayakovsky could have known only at second hand —for instance, the poem "Prayers" (*Bogomolnoe*). "Mexico-New York," suggested by the long train trip across the country from Laredo, Texas, is both slight and jaundiced.

"Broadway" was composed in a mood of linguistic gaiety, and combines English and Russian words in regular rhyming patterns that have a quality of antic humor. English words and phrases regularly used by New York Russians are set in rhyming juxtaposition with Russian words and phrases, and the rhymes are often of the broken variety. Let us see some examples:

> Asphalt like glass. / I walk and I clink (*idu i zvenyu*).
> Trees and grass / shaved off clean (*sbrity*).
> North / and south / the avenues go (*idut avenyu*),
> east / and west / the streets (*striti*).
>
> . . . .
>
> The mechanical city grinds its teeth, / everywhere /
>   noise and confusion (*zvon i gam*),
> but the people / are mute mid the noise (*v zvone*)
> and they stop / chewing gum (*chuingam*)
> only to toss off the greeting / "Make money?" (*Mek monei*).[35]
> When Mommie / her breast / to the baby gave (*dalá*)
> the kid, / drops falling from his nose, (*íz nosu*),
> sucks it / just like he'd suck / on a dollar (*dollár*)—
> He's occupied / with serious / business (*bíznesom*). (1-45)

The poem is remarkable not only for the freshness and surprise of its foreign vocabulary but also for the unconventional imagery provoked in the poet by the fantastic metropolis. The verbal play and ready metaphors remind us forcefully that even in his American cycle we still have to do with Mayakovsky, whose wonder and admiration break through all the restraints imposed by his "mission" as a representative of the proletarian state. The structures of the city are almost beyond measure, and certainly beyond comprehension:

[35] Mayakovsky in his own note to this line explains that in the United States the phrase "Make money?!" is used as a greeting. Obviously he misunderstood something reported to him by his Russian-American friends, possibly a comment on the widespread use of the appellation "Mac" as a generalized form of address.

Houses / of an impossible height.
Some houses / are as high as the stars
others / as high as the moon. (12-17)

And the coming and going of the human throng seems so well regulated: "At seven / a human floodtide. / At five / an ebbing of the tide." (23-26) And when the day's work is done: "You want to go underground / take the subway. / You want to go skyward / take the elevated."[36] (50-53) And the subway trains: "Stretch out their tails / onto Brooklyn Bridge / Then slither into / holes / 'neath the Hudson."[37] (60-64)

And the lights of Broadway, which have impressed so many travellers, also worked their magic on Mayakovsky, whose reaction is a frank and disarticulated cry of wonder:

And the lights / when they start / to dig into the night,
well I'll tell you / it's a hell of a brightness
You look to the right of you, / Jesus Christ!
(*mamochka mat!*)
You look to the left of you, / Christ, Jesus!
(*mat moya mamochka!*) (76-84)

Yet the travelling commercial artist and proletarian revolutionary quite rightly keeps in mind that this New York, which "delights him," is still a product of the bourgeoisie, and in need of revolution:

But / I'm not tipping / my cap.
We Soviets / have our own pride:
we look with disdain / on the bourgeois. (93-99)

"The Young Lady and Woolworth's" (*Baryshnya i Vulvort*) is amusing as a genre picture of American urban promotion methods of the twenties, as an image of the complete failure of communication between extremes of language and attitude, and as pure verbal play. Mayakovsky deftly sketches a familiar street situation of the time: a pretty girl sits in a Woolworth window demonstrating the use of a new "stropper" for Gillette razor blades:

[36] Mayakovsky here uses the word *eleveitor*, "elevator," which he apparently misunderstood to mean "elevated."

[37] It is clear that Mayakovsky does not properly distinguish the Hudson from the East River.

Although / it's out of the question
that she should have a moustache
She runs the blade / along her upper lip
pretending to take it off—
As though to say— / very simple,
just sharpen then shave. (30-38)

She then performs a manual gesture (no doubt well rehearsed) indicating that the potential customers should by all means come into the store and buy the gadget. The poet, repelled by this crude example of capitalist huckstering (and wholly forgetful of his own contributions to store-window promotion) speaks to her through the window in Russian, being careful to move his lips as though he were speaking in English. His remarks concerning her and her job are most uncomplimentary, but she translates everything into romantic compliments:

". . . You're the worst fool." (*dura iz dur*)
But the girl only hears:
"*Open*
open di dor"

. . . .

Look
they've set you here
like a blockhead (*kak duru elóvuyu*)
But the girl's imagination
swells out at full sail
And she only hears / "*Ai lóv yu.*" (70-82)

The message from Moscow is lost on a young lady who is only capable of imagining that the handsome youngish man is a rich Wall Street operator who would like to marry her.

The word play is interesting as a preview of the language used in the play *The Bathhouse* by the Englishman Pont Kich, whose foreign gibberish consists entirely of actual Russian words in combinations that mean nothing but sound like English. Also, it is characteristic of Mayakovsky's verse procedures, and perhaps lends evidence to the contention that his verse should be thought of as "rhyming" rather than "tonic," that the message, misunderstood though it is, is conveyed entirely by alternating end rhymes. Here we have an example, clear to the point of caricature, of the extent to which rhyme bears the emphasis, rhythm, and movement in a poem of Mayakovsky.

Most other poems of the cycle have less content or verbal interest than this one, though all carry ("Brooklyn Bridge" is an interesting exception) the clear stamp of the revolutionary poet speaking about bourgeois America to other revolutionaries who readily take his meaning. Perhaps the poem "A Skyscraper in Cross-Section" (*Neboskryob v razreze*) may be studied as typical of the genre, since it offers an example of a familiar situation: the tourist who is conditioned to see only what he already knew before he came. The poet (is it Mayakovsky or just one of his episodic masks?) is at first astonished by the power and beauty of a thing like New York, but he has learned about the decay of capitalism, and so in his poetry, he "sees through" the industrial miracle of the age—a skyscraper—to the rotting human corpses it encases. We shall see that the circumstances of his visit—his lectures, interviews, and meetings were, with few exceptions, sponsored and arranged for him by Russian or Jewish Communist groups, and he had almost no free contact with American life—helped him, indeed required him, to maintain at all times a dogmatic Marxist stance. One must remember also that in the twenties a large segment of American intellectual society, whether Marxist or not, held a negative view of the American money-culture, its Babbitts, Daddy Brownings, and Pinkertons, its "American tragedies," its hypocrisy built into law, as well as of the mute nonentity who presided over the official show. A surprisingly large number of Americans were ready to accept as sober history the "myth" of the world revolution that Mayakovsky propagated, and to turn hopefully, as he bade them do, to the Comintern. Many of the poems that now carry little conviction even to American radicals were probably not uncongenial to the taste of radical intellectuals in the twenties, and indeed some of them were translated and published in *The Nation*.[38] The hindsight we now have on the Russian revolution, the Comintern, and the Russian Party dictatorship should not blind us to the fact that Mayakovsky's propaganda, dated and forced though it seems to us now, was not out of tune with the intellectual attitudes of his time. But that does not mean at all that it is poetry or should be studied as such.

[38] Katanyan, *Khronika*, p. 469.

We now turn to a truly magnificent thing before which criticism either stands mute or lapses into superlatives and even the most eloquent efforts at interpretation seem tongue-tied.

"Brooklyn Bridge" was written in New York City in the late fall of 1925, recited to audiences there, and published in Moscow in the magazine *Projector* in December of that year. The poem as originally conceived is the purest lyricism, a hymn of praise by a modern artist of futurist antecedents and constructivist convictions to those unnamed artists who "made" their own great poem, the bridge. The poem is an abstraction from immediate reality. The poet confronts the bridge in a kind of solitude: the noises of New York are barely audible to him, the lights are distant and ghostly, the ships in the river below are foreshortened to an infinite smallness, and time is displaced to make way for a "geologist" of the far-distant future who examines the fragmental remains of New York and the bridge.

The poem is itself interesting as a structure. It consists of an elated "exordium" addressed to President Coolidge, a set of similes that establish the poet's variegated emotions as he views the bridge, a description of the setting and background from the high vantage point of the bridge, a personal statement of Mayakovsky's affinity with the builders ("I'm proud . . ."), a difficult reconstruction of the bridge and of the history of the times by that "geologist," and a conclusion that expresses the very personal and deep admiration of a maker of poems, Mayakovsky, for another kind of artistic structure.

There are a few lines that seem out of tune with the work as a whole, and the story of how those lines found their way into the poem, duly reported by our Soviet authorities,[39] is instructive as to the nature of the pressures that were constantly at work on Mayakovsky throughout the twenties, making difficult if not impossible the cultivation of his lyric gift. The lines in question read:

> Here / life / for some / was carefree
> for others / it was a long / and hungry howl.
> From this place / men without work
> threw themselves down / into the Hudson. (141-151)

Those lines appear in the handwritten copy of the poem as a later addition, and would seem to be an afterthought forced

[39] *PSS*, VII, 487.

upon the poet by the hostile reaction of one of his American audiences, as reported in the New York Communist paper *Russian Voice*: "When Mayakovsky had recited his new poem 'Brooklyn Bridge' before a large working-class audience in New York, a poem in which he expressed his rapture at technology and the greatness of human genius, someone in the balcony shouted: 'Don't forget, Comrade Mayakovsky, that unemployed men often jump off of that bridge into the water. . . .' "[40]

The pure flight of the poet's imagination, unencumbered by a social theme, was not what his audience wanted, and he readily adjusted himself to their spontaneous "censorship." We shall see another instance of his adjustment to quite unofficial censorship in the case of the poem "Homeward!" and these examples help us to understand the extremely complex nature of the psychological as well as social pressures under which he labored.

But let us return to the poem itself. What I have called the exordium bids Coolidge (that block of Vermont granite) "give a shout of joy" over Brooklyn Bridge. And "I too will not spare words when it comes to a really good thing," adds the poet. The country may not have been converted to communism by his anti-capitalist propaganda lectures, but "At my praise / you'll blush all red / like our flag, / however / United-States-of-America / you may be." (5-11)

There follows a set of three parallel similes that establish the poet's humility, his elation and pride, and the open-mouthed awe that one artist experiences before the work of another.

> As a crazed believer / enters / a church,
> . . . .
> so I / in evening's / gray haze
> humbly / set foot on Brooklyn Bridge.
> As a conqueror / marches / into a smashed city
> . . . .
> so, drunk with glory / ready for life,
> I climb / full of pride / onto Brooklyn Bridge.
> As a stupefied painter / fixes his eye
> lovesick and shrewd / on a museum madonna,
> so I / from the star-scattered height
> look / at New York / through Brooklyn Bridge. (12-42)

[40] *Ibid.*

New York City and the river on which it stands are then moved into place as a distancing backdrop for the poet's solitary experience of the bridge:

> New York, / in the daytime / so painful and stifling
> Now forgets / that it's excruciating / and high
> . . . .
> Here / the drone of the elevated / barely drones
> . . . .
> The masts passing under the bridge / Seem of a size /
> no larger than pins. (43-72)

Mayakovsky, alone with this monster work of art, identifies himself with it completely, associates the work of the builders with his own futurist artistic creed, and insists that he too is above all a careful craftsman:

> I am proud / of just this / mile of steel.
> My own visions have come to life / and stand erect.
> My struggle / for structures / instead of style,
> the stern / calculus / of bolts and steel. (73-83)

These lines are the best, quite possibly the only, poetic realization of the theories about art and literature developed in the *Lef* milieu. "We know," wrote Brik, "that so-called pure art is a craft like any other. We do not understand why a man who makes pictures is spiritually superior to the man who manufactures fabrics."[41] The bridge seemed to Mayakovsky a supreme example of what he would call "production-art," an art involved with everyday life and the needs of people, an art both developing out of and molding industrial processes; such an art must be explicitly rational, its effects fully explicable in mathematical terms (the "stern calculus"). Yet the poem is miraculously free of the sectarian dogmatism that usually characterized *Lef* theorizing. We sense no rejection of the "stupefied" (*glupyi*) artist adoring an ancient madonna in a museum, nor indeed any rejection of the past or of museums. Mayakovsky seems rather to associate his experience of reverence for creative power with the experience of all artists at all times.

[41] Osip Brik, *Iskusstvo v proizvodstve* (Moscow, 1921), p. 7.

The poet then invites us to imagine the end of the world and the planet smashed to pieces, with the only thing remaining this bridge "rearing above the dust of destruction" (93):

> Then, / as ancient lizards / standing in museums
> are filled out / from a few bones / tinier than needles,
> just so / the geologist of the centuries
> will succeed / in recreating
> the present day / from this bridge.
> He will say / "That steel paw
> once joined / the seas and the prairies,
> from this spot / Europe / tore westward,
> scattering / Indian feathers / on the wind.
> This rib here / suggests / a machine—
> just imagine, / would there be enough hands
> when you've planted / one steel foot / on Manhattan
> to drag Brooklyn / to yourself / by the lip?
> From the wires / and electrical strands
> I recognize / the era / right after steam.
> Here / people / already / ranted on radio,
> here / already / they'd flown / in airplanes." (94-140)

At this point the lines quoted above on the unemployed workers who threw themselves from the bridge intrude upon the movement of the poem. We may recognize the fact that much human misery went hand in hand with the development of capitalism in America, and that the bridge was indeed the scene of frequent suicides, but still insist that those lines are in disaccord with the rest of the poem, and do not at all fit the remarks of the "geologist," whose sole effort has been to reconstruct the *technology* of a former era from the evidence of the bridge; that evidence would tell him nothing about the class structure of the society that built it. After this interruption the "geologist" completes his remarks:

> And the rest / of my picture / is now very clear.
> Along cable-strings / it reaches to the stars.
> And I see / that here / Mayakovsky
> stood / and composed / verses, syllable by syllable. (153-162)

The last lines have also seemed to some critics an intrusion on the movement of the poem, but we are accustomed to the fact that, whatever the theme or setting of his lyric poetry, the center of apperception and feeling must always be the poet himself. The "chemist" of the distant future is called upon to "resurrect" Mayakovsky; why shouldn't the "geologist" also find a trace of Mayakovsky in the ruins of the bridge?

At this point the poet himself speaks again in his own person, to give a final statement of his total fascination:

> I stare / as an Eskimo stares at a train,
> I fasten on it / as a tick fastens on an ear.
> Brooklyn Bridge—
> Yes—
> It is really a creation! (*veshch*) (162-168)

The final word, *veshch,* suggests a self-quotation. The word *veshch* has two meanings here: 1) a thing, an object; and 2) a long poem, a major artistic undertaking; and it is the word he used as a subtitle of the poem *Man.* The pun upon the two meanings in the reference to the bridge—it is both an object, a structure, and a great work of art—reminds us once more of the futurist orientation in the mid-twenties toward art as the production of objects both useful and beautiful. The word serves as an accolade that accepts the bridge and its American builders into the company of modern artists to which Mayakovsky belonged.

4) Activities in America

The poems we have analyzed are the most immediate and the most characteristic record of Mayakovsky's experience of America.

Three other records of that visit exist, and we shall consider them briefly: 1) the telegrams from America to Lily Brik, 2) newspaper reports of his activities, and 3) the sketches he published in Moscow after his return under the title *My Discovery of America.* The wires to Lily are a revelation that he suffered from loneliness and boredom almost from the day he arrived in Mexico City. He sent telegrams from New York on July 31, August 2, and August 6, the last of which carried the message: "Trying very hard to get you visa. If impossible, coming right home. Terribly lonely. I kiss you. I love you." The next telegram did not come until a month later and it informed her that the death of the Amtorg representative I. Ya. Khurgin had upset the visa plans. A telegram from Chicago on October 3 reads: "I kiss you from Chicago. Lonely. I love you. I'll try to make it Italy." Three days later from New York: "My own sunlight! Telegraph when you leave. Give me address Italy. Lonely and bored. I love you kiss you." Two weeks later from New York: "Very bored. In two or three weeks find out visa date. Most likely I'll go home. It's awful here. I kiss you. I love you." Two more wires from New York (there were eleven in all from America) develop the same themes of his boredom, loneliness, and eagerness to get back to Lily.

It would seem from these telegrams—there are no known letters at all describing his stay in America—that in spite of his frequent meetings, lectures, and interviews in America, in spite of the new and amazing experiences he records in his poems, Mayakovsky was desperately unhappy during his visit. Patricia Blake maintains that he was "personally miserable during his three-month stay in America. He felt desperately homesick as he travelled alone, in the infernal summer heat, to Chicago, Detroit, Pittsburgh, and other unlovely monuments to industrialization. . . ."[42] It should be pointed out, however, that those telegrams from the U.S.A. are not very different in content from letters and wires dispatched to Lily from many other points he visited during his travels, both in Europe and in the Soviet Union. A sampling of excerpts from these will make the point. From Kharkov, January 1924: "I'm very terribly lonely for you . . . I may return even sooner than I thought." From Paris, November 1924:

> . . . How I get along during this period—I don't know myself. My basic feeling is one of anxiety [*trevoga*], anxiety to the point of tears and a complete lack of interest in this place.
>
> I *terribly want* to go back to Moscow. If I weren't ashamed of what you and the editors would think, I'd leave today. . . .
>
> Kiss Levka, Kolka, Ksanochka, Malochka and Levin for me. Any one of them is a hundred times smarter than all the Picassos.

From Paris, December 1924:

> I'm terribly sad without you. . . .
>
> . . . I miss you and the others *terribly*.
>
> I'm bored here. Can't stand it without something to do. . . .

[42] Introduction to *The Bedbug and Selected Poetry*, p. 35.

> I don't go to the theater any more, and I don't go to the bars either. I'm fed up; I stay home and gnaw chicken legs and goose livers with salad. My landlady Madame Sonet serves me. Astonishingly aesthetic city.

From Paris, June 1925:

> . . . That so-called "Paris in the spring" isn't worth anything, since nothing blossoms, and all they do is repair the streets. The first day we rode about, but now I don't go out at all, sleep twice a day, breakfast twice, and wash myself, that's all.
>
> Tomorrow I begin writing for *Lef.* I haven't met any old friends and the best of my new friends is a certain Buza, a dog belonging to some friends of Elsa. . . .

From Paris, June 1925: ". . . I'm more bored here even than usual. . . ."[43]

Clearly, the telegrams from America contain no special animus against the country or its industrial cities. They can be explained in part as a series of formulaic statements from a lover to his absent mistress: "I'm lonely without you. I'm bored. I'm coming home." Yet the long circumstantial expressions of boredom and disgust with Paris suggest that Mayakovsky in his role of world traveller was genuinely unhappy no matter where he went, and probably would always be. Something drove him to be constantly on the move, as a glance at Katanyan's schedule of his "itineraries" shows,[44] but in each new place his personal problem would once more assert itself. The monstrous ego whose imperative and unlimited need is registered in each of the major poems was apparently incapable of rest.

There are some special puzzles, however, concerning his American trip, and though Katanyan notes these, neither he nor others who have researched his stay in America offer any plausible explanations. In the first place, the eleven brief wires to Lily Brik are, in comparison with his usual behavior, an extremely lean harvest for a three-month period spent in an "awful" place. Lily, sensing at one point that something was amiss, sent *him* a wire that read simply: "What's happened to you?" (*Kuda ty propal?*).[45] There are, as a matter of fact, quite long periods of his

[43] The letters appeared in *Literaturnoe nasledstvo*, LXV, 135-140.

[44] Katanyan, *Khronika*, pp. 532-533.

[45] Katanyan, "Poezdki," p. 318.

stay in America not fully accounted for by letters, wires, records of lectures or poetry readings, or by the reminiscences of those who claimed to have met him.

It may be interesting to review briefly at this point his activities as reported in the press. He arrived in New York on July 30. On August 2, *The Russian Voice* (*Russkii golos*), organ of the American Workers (Communist) Party, published an interview with him by David Burliuk, who had of course hurried over to meet him at the quarters of the Amtorg representative at 3 Fifth Avenue, where he stayed while in New York. A few days later, at Burliuk's apartment, he met with a group of young proletarian poets who belonged to an organization called "The Hammer and Sickle." One of them made him a present of a book of his own poems, and was immensely gratified on a later visit when he surprised Mayakovsky reciting those poems to himself.[46] The poets, most of whom spoke Russian, were obviously enchanted and deeply impressed by Mayakovsky. During his first few days in New York he had an interview with Michael Gold, editor of *New Masses*, which was published in the *New York World.* The interview was a lengthy statement, elicited by Gold's leading questions, which ranged freely over a number of American topics: industrialization, the "chaos" of New York City, the anarchic nature of American life and its sharp contrast to Soviet Russia, where production is planned and there is a steady improvement in the cultural level of the masses. It was perfect material for the *New Masses* readers of the day. A somewhat similar interview with Shakhno Epstein was published on August 14 in the Communist Yiddish-language newspaper *Freiheit* under the title "With Mayakovsky on Fifth Avenue." These "interviews" were printed, not in the form of answers to questions but as extended remarks, oral essays on the theme of the decline of capitalism and the bright future of communism. The essays sound more like Epstein or Gold than like Mayakovsky, and it would be a mistake to incriminate him with that mixture of doctrinaire dogmatism, naive sentimentality, and hatred of one's nearest neighbors which characterized the writing of Gold and Epstein and many other American radicals of that time. Let us sample their style. Mayakovsky supposedly said:

[46] This is based on remarks made to me by the man in question.

"Here I am walking with you down one of the richest streets in the world. It has skyscrapers, palaces, hotels, stores, and crowds of people, but I feel as though I'm walking among ruins, and melancholy feelings oppress me. Why is it I don't feel this in Moscow, where the pavement is broken, many houses are in ruins, and the streetcars are crowded and terribly overused. The answer is very simple: because in Moscow life is seething and the energies of the whole liberated people—the collective—have been released. Every new brick, every new board on a construction project is the result of collective initiative. But here? There's no energy, only the muddled activity of a formless and senseless mob of stupefied people, a people whom someone drives like a herd, into the subway, out of the subway, onto the El, off the El . . ."

We were so fascinated by the conversation that we didn't notice we'd already walked as far as Central Park.[47]

That none of this represents Mayakovsky's authentic response to America is evident if one remembers the content and spirit of the poems "Broadway" and "Brooklyn Bridge." Of course it is impossible to tell how much Epstein suggested, or even supplied, but it is worth remarking that these points about New York had already been made many years earlier by Gorky, and in strikingly similar language. Mayakovsky, or certainly Epstein, had been studying *The City of the Yellow Devil.*

But to return to the events of Mayakovsky's stay. On August 14 his first lecture and recitation took place at what was then the Central Opera House, on East 67th Street near Third Avenue. *The Russian Voice* reported: "Radvansky, Chairman of the Russian Section of the Workers' Party and editor of *New World*, opened the meeting. . . . Finally Mayakovsky himself appeared on the platform, tall, strong, and healthy. It is hard to describe what happened to the audience. Unceasing applause filled the hall. Mayakovsky tried to speak. But the applause did not stop. Everybody stood up. Feet stamped on the floor. . . ."[48]

Soon after that date Mayakovsky visited the summer home of the artist Manievich at Rockaway Beach. Sometime during the second half of August he met with the editors of the *New Masses* in a far-ranging discussion. At the end of August he visited for

[47] Katanyan, *Khronika*, p. 241. [48] *Ibid.*, p. 243.

a few days at Camp Nitgedaiget, a summer camp run by *Freiheit.* But it was not until September 10, almost a month after his first appearance, that his second recital in New York took place. That period, except for the visits noted, is comparatively bare of recorded activities; interestingly enough, there are no wires to Lily during almost exactly the same interval. She may have had reason to worry.

We may conjecture that during this period Mayakovsky was engaged in activities that he and his friends preferred not to make public, and certainly he had a right to privacy in some part of his life. Perhaps we should observe the injunction in his suicide note not to "gossip" about the deceased, but rumors about certain adventures during his stay in America are so widespread and so widely believed in Moscow (and elsewhere) that we must deal with them briefly. The story, corroborated by Lily Brik, who claimed to have seen epistolary evidence supporting it, is that Mayakovsky became sexually involved with a young woman in New York who eventually bore him a daughter. No printed source on Mayakovsky published in the Soviet Union has ever emitted a single breath concerning this affair,[49] but the specialists on Mayakovsky have all heard of it and seem to believe it implicitly. What is more, they profess to know the name of the woman involved, and many express eager interest in the whereabouts of both mother and daughter. But perhaps both women deserve to have their privacy respected, and even to be proud, in private, one that she mothered Mayakovsky's child, and the other that she is that child—if the story is true.

I report this story with misgiving, and even with apologies, since it has only peripheral interest in a study of the poet Mayakovsky. It is neither sensational nor surprising news that one of Mayakovsky's sexual escapades had an issue, and for all we know there may be other daughters, or sons, of Mayakovsky in other places. The story is interesting not for any light it throws on Mayakovsky's poetry or even on his biography, but for the curious fact that Russians interested in Mayakovsky attach so much importance to it. Their pride, apparently, is titillated by the thought that the poet conquered America in more than one department, and that somewhere his seed exists in the new world.

[49] A possible exception is Kemrad, who does mention the woman's name with a kind of cryptic emphasis, and in several contexts.

The third variety of evidence concerning the journey, the collection of essays, was the occasion of a stormy controversy in the Soviet literary world. Talnikov, one of the contributors to *Red Virgin Soil*, published there some remarks on Russian travellers in America[50] that contained a devastating and basically sound review of Mayakovsky's *My Discovery of America*. On certain points he has Mayakovsky dead to rights: the superficiality of his observations in his essays, the mechanical repetition of second-hand or casual impressions of many countries, and the circumstance that the traveller himself is the center of every stage he describes. "Mayakovsky," says Talnikov, "is himself more important than any country, or for that matter any universe he has ever discovered." Not knowing any of the details, Mayakovsky still can hold forth with confidence on the "general picture." On his "galloping itinerary" he saw many places in a short time, but could he possibly have learned much about any of them? And Talnikov complains that those essays are written in the tone of vulgar familiarity that characterizes the cheap journalist. Talnikov's own tone is contemptuously polemical: he calls Mayakovsky "the boy without trousers," and compares him to the empty-headed braggart Khlestakov in Gogol's *The Inspector General*. Much of what Mayakovsky wrote during and after the trip he describes as "pot-boiling" (*khaltura*), and this is a just though not very brilliant or original judgment. Talnikov is quite unperceptive in dealing with the poems connected with America, the real virtues of which he simply does not see, but there is no denying that *My Discovery of America* is *khaltura*, written in haste, readied for publication less than two months after Mayakovsky's return, and published with the simple object of getting money.[51] He had little to learn in this respect from American "money-grubbers."

The bloody aftermath of this article is not without interest, since it reveals the tangled involvement of Mayakovsky and his *Lef* group in the polemics and the politics of the day, the quality of which was both sordid and dangerous. A section of the "proletarian" press, especially *Young Guard* (*Molodaya Gvardiya*) un-

[50] D. Talnikov, "Literaturnye zametki," *Krasnaya nov*, No. 8, 1928, pp. 259-281.

[51] See Kemrad for an account of his financial straits during and immediately after the trip, especially p. 85 and pp. 262-263. On the publication of the essays see *PSS*, VII, 515, 516.

der the editorship of Kostrov, who frequently published Mayakovsky and whose name we shall hear again, released a barrage of pointless vituperation in the general direction of Talnikov and *Red Virgin Soil.* Its editor, Aleksandr Voronsky, held, as we know, a low opinion of Mayakovsky and despised the ideas of *Lef* concerning the "social demand" and art as craft. The attack in *Young Guard* had little to do with the points actually raised in Talnikov's article, but was directed at him personally as a dangerous element simply because he "didn't like Mayakovsky." Talnikov's own description of the dispute reveals the disastrous level of information, taste, and morality that sometimes set the tone for literary discussion, and he warns, all too prophetically, of what would certainly happen if slander in the guise of debate should go unchecked.[52] In fact, it would appear that this dispute over Mayakovsky was one of the important incidents in the successful campaign to bring about fundamental changes in the journal founded by Voronsky. Mayakovsky himself contributed to the dispute with a poem in his own defense, "Running Roughshod over the Writers" (*"Galopshchik po pisatelyam"*),[53] which further lowered the level of discussion by completely distorting Talnikov's position.

Talnikov was certainly right that Mayakovsky's information about America was hastily assembled from biased sources, and that his essays are quite useless as a guide to American life in the twenties. Many of his facts and statistics betray their origin in the Russian-American Communist press, the only one he could read. The material on the eating habits of New Yorkers (pp. 310-311) is really very poor, and must have come to him second-hand either from the Communist papers or from conversations with his hosts. Or let us look at the Daddy Browning story, which occupies a page or more in Mayakovsky's "discovery" of America. Old "Daddy Browning," with his pretty young adopted daughters, was an inflated sensation of the day on the front pages of the Hearst chain and other venal newspapers, and the episode was used by the radical press as an indictment of capitalist mores. Mayakovsky uses it for the same purpose.[54] A strange story about Miss Vanderbilt's "palace" on Fifth Avenue and 53rd Street and how she sold it for six million dollars "because there's a Child's restaurant across the street, and on one side a bakery and on the

[52] "Zametki pisatelya," *Krasnaya nov*, No. 11, 1928, pp. 241-244.

[53] *PSS*, IX, 29.

[54] *PSS*, VII, 316-317.

other a barber,"[55] makes some kind of sense when we learn that the Vanderbilt *Hotel* at that location was actually sold during his stay, and the sale reported in the press.[56] We can only conjecture as to how the misconception arose.

Some comments on the mores of New York bandits, their bondsmen, and the police are probably based on misunderstanding or else on the exaggerations of his informant.[57] "Lynch law" was bad enough at the time of his visit, but Mayakovsky makes it worse: "a Negro who approaches a white woman is judged by lynch law; that is, they tear off his arms and legs and roast him alive over a fire."[58] He has some stirring words to say about the anarchist labor leaders who were hanged in Chicago after the Haymarket riot of 1886, but either he or his informants suppressed the information that a bomb thrown at the police was important in starting the "riot." His story is not quite accurate, but it loses nothing in propaganda appeal because of that.[59] We may be inclined to question both the statistic that "Detroit has the highest incidence of divorces," and his explanation that "the Ford system of production makes the workers impotent." He leaves us in no doubt, however, as to the source of that information: a group of workers in the Ford plant who were also "correspondents" of the *Daily Worker*.[60] These examples—and many others might be adduced—demonstrate that Mayakovsky's essays about America are a shabby piece of work, considered as a guide to America. A certain type of Soviet reader finds them an edifying experience, however, since in them Mayakovsky "exposes American capitalism in all its nakedness."[61] But this he could have done without ever leaving the Soviet Union.

There is another way of considering those essays, or at least certain passages in them. Mayakovsky was an artist in spite of himself, and the essays contain many passages in which he describes his own experiences directly, uncomplicated by ideology or the supposed "social demand" of his Soviet readers. Those passages are among the finest examples of his prose style. He recounts with the fervor of a raconteur the stories told him in

[55] *PSS*, VII, 311.

[56] See Moser, "Mayakovsky's Unsentimental Journeys," p. 94.

[57] *PSS*, VII, 306.

[58] *PSS*, VII, 328.

[59] *PSS*, VII, 335.

[60] *PSS*, VII, 341.

[61] B. P. Goncharov, "Mayakovsky v krivom zerkale 'sovetologii,'" *Voprosy literatury*, No. 3, 1970, pp. 100ff.

Laredo, Texas by his Russian-Jewish interpreter, who was the owner of a small business, about the misadventures of his brother during travels in many countries in search of beautiful women, money, sensations—in a word, life.[62] The account of his entertainment by this interpreter is warm and perceptive, and brings more than one character to life.

Another brief passage where the artist is in complete control is his description of a trip on the New York Central Railroad from Albany to New York City, as well as the description of Grand Central Station and the tracks and tunnels that lead out of New York from that terminal.[63] Those passages are an impressionistic picture of the railway ambience written by an alert, observant, and innocent traveller, and the important thing in it is the traveller's awed reaction to that brilliant industrial pandemonium. The following passage about Broadway, full of genuine admiration for a city laid out on rational lines, shows Mayakovsky in the role of a traveller eager to learn the most necessary things, but still, like Broadway itself, intent on going his own way.

> Beginning at six or seven Broadway lights up—and it's my favorite street, since among all those streets and avenues as regular and even as the bars of a jail cell Broadway alone boldly and capriciously goes at an oblique slant. It's harder to get lost in New York than in Tula. The avenues go north and south, the streets go east and west. Fifth Avenue divides the city into two parts, West and East. That's all you need to know. I'm on Eighth St., at the corner of Fifth Avenue, and I have to get to 53rd St. at the corner of Second; all I have to do is walk 45 blocks, turn right and walk to Second Avenue.[64]

He notes with interest the enforcement of male hat-styles in New York through the practice of smashing any straw hat seen after September 15, and the spectacle provokes some sharp comment on a new face of his old enemy, *byt*:

> What I've been saying about New York's mores (*byt*) is of course not a full face, but just separate features—eyebrows, a freckle, a nostril.
>
> But these freckles and nostrils are very characteristic of the whole petty-bourgeois mass, a mass that includes all the

[62] *PSS*, VII, 294-295.
[63] *PSS*, VII, 298-299.
[64] *PSS*, VII, 304.

bourgeoisie; a mass that's leavened by intermediate layers of the population; a mass that's tied into itself even the well-to-do among the working class, those who have bought a house on time payments—and are afraid above all of being unemployed.[65]

Sometimes he is capable of a shrewd insight, without any help from his Russian immigrant guides:

> In spite of the grandeur of American structures, in spite of the unattainable, for Europe, tempos of construction that have been achieved and the height of American skyscrapers, with their conveniences and capaciousness—still American houses, in general, produce an uncanny impression of temporariness.
>
> Or maybe it only seems so. . . .
>
> Even the huge, most modern and most convenient buildings seem temporary, because America, and New York in particular, is constantly in process of construction. Ten-story houses are torn down to make way for twenty-story houses; twenty-story houses to make way for thirty- or forty-story ones, and so on.[66]

Such passages are a meager harvest from the eighty or so printed pages of Mayakovsky's "discovery" of America. We must note, in passing, that he displays no curiosity about American art or music; that Burliuk, who continued to paint in America and to experiment with new styles, is not even mentioned; and that apart from the incidental reference to Sandburg in connection with the industrial marvels of Chicago there is no discussion at all of American literature. During his visit Mayakovsky apparently kept his horizons narrow, and the impulse to create poetry or write impressionistic prose was effectively checked, as a rule, by ideology, or by his image of himself as a representative of the revolution ("agent of the Soviet government" is what the Russian anti-Soviet press called him, and the term is accurate enough), or by the insistent pressures of the American Communist milieu that welcomed and entertained him.[67]

65 *PSS*, VII, 319.

66 *PSS*, VII, 324.

67 Joseph Freeman in his *An American Testament: a Narrative of Rebels and Romantics* (New York, 1936) gives a vivid account of a rather wild party for Mayakovsky organized by the staff of the Communist journal *New Masses*, an account that throws some light on Mayakovsky but much more on the American radicals of the time. Freeman's story of this affair is used by Soviet writers, but only in a form that carefully expurgates all references to drunkenness, unconventional behavior, or maudlin radical sentiment. Freeman writes:

Some months after his return from America, Mayakovsky wrote an unpretentious and amusing essay that illuminates his difficulty in communicating with "workers," and quite incidentally throws light on the circumstances of his visit to America. The essay "How I Made Her Laugh" (*Kak ya eyo rassmeshil*, 1926) describes a number of occasions on which his brightly humorous remarks had found no response, and tells also of a party in New York at which the failure of communication was absolute:

> Possibly foreigners admire me, but it's possible also that they consider me an idiot. I say nothing for the moment of Russians. But just consider my situation in America. A poet's been invited. They've been told he's a genius. A genius—that's even better than being well-known. I arrive and right off I say:
>
> "Gif me pliz sam tee."
>
> OK. They serve me. I wait a bit, and then:
>
> "Gif me pliz . . ."
>
> They serve me again.
>
> And I keep it up, varying the intonation and the phrasing:
>
> "Gif me de sam tee; sam tee de gif me." I say my say. And the evening proceeds.

. . . the group which was organizing the New Masses gave Mayakovsky a party at a private house. It was typical of the gay twenties—jazz records, bathtub gin, dancing in shirtsleeves. Mayakovsky danced with the strength and awkwardness of a bear, and liked it. So did the girls. Then the poet was urged to read his verses. He took a little notebook out of his pocket and read his latest. We all drank too much. Mayakovsky, twice my size, lifted me to the ceiling to show his strength. I made fun of his booming voice by reciting the first two lines of his poem in mangled form without knowing their meaning.

"Take the potatoes out of your mouth," he said.

"The Revolution doesn't need a megaphone voice," I said. "Look at Lenin."

"Lenin's voice did not matter. He talked with cannon. I have no cannon, but I have my voice."

Mike Gold recited *A Strange Funeral at Braddock*, broke into tears, and made an eloquent speech about the proletarian revolution. The gin was bad; my head ached; my conscience bothered me; revolutionary writers shouldn't drink.

"Don't get foolish," Mike Gold said. "Mayakovsky drinks three times as much as we do."

Mayakovsky admitted it.

"Yes, I am a bohemian," he added. "That is my great problem: to burn out all my bohemian past, to rise to the heights of the Revolution" (pp. 367-368).

Respectful old fellows listen reverently and think: "There's a Russian for you. Doesn't waste words. He's a thinker . . . Tolstoy . . . The North."

But the ladies move away from me when they hear for the hundredth time that same request for tea, enunciated it's true in a pleasant bass voice, and the gentlemen distribute themselves in the corners of the room laughing reverentially at my expense.

So I shouted to Burliuk: "You translate this for them. Tell them that if they knew Russian I could, without even dirtying my shirtfront, nail them with my tongue to the cross of their own suspenders, that I could roast this whole collection of insects on the sharp turnspit of my tongue."

And the honest Burliuk translated:

"My eminent friend Vladimir Vladimirovich wants another cup of tea."

5) Homeward

Mayakovsky set out for home aboard the French steamer *Rochambeau* on October 28, having remained in the country only three of his alloted six months. He refused an eager invitation from comrades in San Francisco to come there for a lecture with all expenses paid, and he had long since given up his plans for a trip around the world. Part of the reason for his depressed mood, and certainly the chief reason he aborted his trip around the world, may have been the rather desperate condition of his finances. All the money he took with him for the trip to America had been stolen in Paris before his departure by a "highly talented thief." As a result he had to borrow money insistently and constantly from friends both old and new in Paris, in Mexico, and in New York, and the debts he incurred were not fully repaid for some time. An advance from the State Publishing House against future royalties also helped to make the trip possible in spite of the theft.[68] The reduced condition of his finances explains those other-

[68] The details are covered very well in Kemrad, pp. 22-27.

Bertram Wolfe, who met Mayakovsky at the Soviet Embassy in Mexico City, is authority for the story that Mayakovsky borrowed $500 from Mrs. Wolfe's mother in New York, which he repaid many months later, but in rubles worth only a fraction of the original amount. Even that repayment he made only after Wolfe complained of the matter to Pyatnitsky, an official of the Comintern.

wise inexplicable lines in the poem "Homeward!" that describe his cabin on the *Rochambeau* as "the worst of all possible cabins." His accommodations on the outward voyage had been first class, but the home trip had to be made in a third-class cabin below decks, where the popular music and dancing feet of the first-class salon were painfully audible. He did not have enough money even to buy a decent overcoat or hat and he got himself instead that cheap mackintosh and peaked cap we see in the well-known photograph taken when he arrived in Paris, the curious ensemble completed by an incongruous pair of spats. His "lecture tour" of the United States netted him nothing except debts. It goes without saying that as a rule no admission fees were charged at his public appearances, though collections were regularly taken up to support the *New Masses*, the *Daily Worker*, *Russian Voice*, and other Communist publishing enterprises. His Communist hosts exploited him, in other words, not only politically but financially.

The poem "Homeward!" which he wrote on board the *Rochambeau*,[69] is a reflection on the kind of poetic career that he had chosen in the homeland; to all appearances he has no regret over his choice. The poem expresses in the plainest possible terms Mayakovsky's acceptance of social purpose, but it does much more than that. "Homeward!" compresses into a few lines the principal structural components of his poetry as a whole. As in all his major poetry, the real experience of the poet in a concrete situation is the subject of the work, in this case the thoughts of home that run randomly through his head as he lies, supine and lethargic ("I can hardly move / the parts of my machine"), in his narrow bunk. It reminds us of *A Cloud in Pants* in that it is an inner monologue whose movement is seemingly prompted by random associations. The first lines, "Leave me, thoughts, go your way. / Embrace / depths of the soul and sea," clear the way for the subliminal self to seek expression. The next lines mark the mood as morose, "Anyone / who's always cheerful / is in my opinion / simply stupid." The noise of vulgar music and dancing feet that bruise the floor on the first-class deck above him deepens his melancholy mood. And here we see reproduced almost exactly the scene from *About That* in which the rejected Mayakovsky stands listening outside Lily's door to music and dancing ("one-step, two-step") in which he has no part. The slow, strong accents of

[69] *PSS*, VII, 92.

his own verse line are broken in upon by the insipid rhythm of a popular song:

> Marquíta, / Marquíta,
> Marquíta my lóve,
> O whý, / O Marquíta
> Can't yoú love me trúe . . . (17-22)

His impoverished condition supplies the answer: "Why / should Marquita love me? / I don't own / a single franc." (23-26) Money is indispensable for bourgeois love, and he has little of it, though he reflects that "Marquita" could be had easily and for a small sum. The thought has a certain appeal ("not much money— / have a little fun—"). That thought is rejected by an ironic reflection on the intellectual's traditional answer to the problem of the prostitute, an answer which is accommodated metaphorically to Mayakovsky's own profession. The radical intellectual of the nineteenth century—we think of Belinsky and of Chernyskevsky's *What Is To Be Done*—saved prostitutes from their fate by finding them useful employment, often as "seamstresses":

> But no / you intellectual / ruffling up your filthy hair,
> You'll push / a sewing machine at her
> one that stitches / and scribbles / the silks of your verse.
> (33-40)

This image suggests, by an association not too distant to follow, the general lot of the dispossessed and their easy road to communism. They come to it "by the low road / of mines / sickles / and pitchforks." (43-46)

But Mayakovsky's trip to communism is both an act of will and an act of love, since he normally occupies the "heavenly heights" of poetry. The reason he must "dive into communism" is that "without it / there is no love / for me." (50-52) Here once again the need for love is as imperious and as desperate as it was in the *Cloud*, *The Flute*, *Man*, and *About That*, but now the satisfaction of that need, as in the epilogue to *About That*, is linked with the love of mankind generally, and with a social organization that will join all men in a close community. This dream might well be betrayed by reality, but it clearly has an important function in the poet's life. The fact that it is still love he is looking for is borne out by a later passage in which he speaks of his demands upon the state: "I want / the heart / to receive its wage of love / At the premium rate paid to specialists." (85-88)

The abrupt associative movement of the poem turns to thoughts of his recent "exile" in America, and the effect upon his metallic "muse" of separation from the native land:

It doesn't matter / whether I exile myself /
  or I'm sent to the devil—
The steel of my words rusts /
  and the brass of my bass gets discolored.
Why / should I get soaked / and rot / and rust
under foreign rains?
I lie here / far away across the waters;
listless, / can hardly move /
  the parts of my machine. (52-66)

The metaphor of the poet's work is taken from the industrial world, which leads into an ultimate image of Mayakovsky himself as a poet-factory, an image familiar from earlier poems: "I feel / that I / am a Soviet factory / manufacturing happiness." (68-71)

He then reverts to that paradoxical image of himself as an anti-poet, a poet in rebellion against all poetry, which runs as a persistent leitmotif through all his work. In "Order No. 2 to the Army of Art" (1921), he addressed himself to all poets, "futurists, imaginists, acmeists, entangled in the cobweb of rhymes," with an urgent command that "before getting chased off with rifle butts," they "Give it up! / forget it, / spit / on rhymes / and on arias / and on the rosebush." We recall in the *Cloud* his scornful rejection of Igor Severyanin and all lyrics addressed to some Tiana or other, and we shall see that his conflict with Sergei Yesenin was simply an episode in his struggle against lyric poetry; it goes without saying that his most persistent enemy in the struggle was himself. After announcing in "Homeward!" that he does *not* want, as a poet, to be "plucked like a flower from the fields after the day's work is done," he lists six demands upon the state, each introduced anaphorically by a firm "I want . . ." ("*Ya khochu*"). With the exception of the demand for an extra ration of love, these absolute requirements are a sure prescription for the extinction of all poetry, including his own. But Mayakovsky in this poem is not afraid of state control; on the contrary he *demands* that the State Planning Agency earnestly debate an annual order to him for poetry, that the commissar of the day hover over his thought with a command, that when his day's work is done the factory committee shut his lips and lock them, that the pen be equated with the bayonet, and, finally, as a culminating monstrosity, that

> Along with his reports on pigiron / and steel
> Stalin / should read a report / on verse production
> On behalf of the Politburo. (97-102)

We may react to these lines with revulsion at the ideas in them, with amusement at the ironies they contain, with admiration for the verbal artistry they display, or, finally, with appreciation of Mayakovsky's most completely realized image: the irreverent anti-poet of the futurist days whose literary pose it was to pillory symbolists, acmeists, and all their breed, now proposes quite literally to destroy them as poets. His poetic metaphors of state direction and control for poetry, unless they are taken as ironic hyperbole, go far beyond anything that had yet been proposed by the Soviet government itself, or by any of its official bodies.

The lines about Stalin were written long before Stalin had reached his exclusive eminence and may have had something to do with forming his opinion of Mayakovsky as "the greatest poet of our socialist epoch," but those lines probably do not contain the flattery he might have seen in them. The name Stalin (man of steel) was chosen, not from political but from poetic considerations: it furnishes both a pun and a rhyme for the word *stali* (steel). At the same time the choice of the person heightens the irony of the line and the humor of the pun, since the prosaic Stalin, who never had anything to say about literature, was the least suitable member of the Politburo to read a report on poetry.

The version of "Homeward!" first published in the Soviet press ended with the following lines:

> I want my country to understand me.
> But if I'm not understood / what of it.
> I shall pass through my native land / to one side
> as a slanting rain passes by.

Those lines were later eliminated from the poem, and Mayakovsky on two occasions explained why. In a letter to an ambitious beginning poet who had submitted some verses to *Lef* with a request for criticism, Mayakovsky argued against the note of whining and complaint in the young poet's treatment of the themes of hunger, unemployment and the like. And he said:

> . . . What you need is more tendentiousness. Plaintive words in your work too are stronger than the descriptive and joyful ones. It's easy to strike a plaintive note—such stuff tweaks the heart not because of the verbal quality but by way of some sad though extraneous parallel reminiscences associated in some way with the lines. One of my own lumbering behemoth-poems I once decked out with this paradisiacal tail—[he quotes the lines given above].
>
> In spite of all their romance-like sensibility (people reached for their handkerchiefs when they heard them), I plucked out those beautiful feathers, all wet with the rain.[70]

On another occasion he informed Roman Jakobson that Osip Brik had found fault with the final lines as being out of harmony with the poem as a whole, and had advised eliminating them. "So I took them out."[71]

There is no reason to doubt that Brik advised "plucking out" those final lines, since Brik was the principal theorist of the "social demand" and those lines, a cryptic comment on the poet's individual fate, call in question the strong social message in the main body of the poem. But Brik when he advised removing those lines and Mayakovsky when he agreed to this self-censorship—and it is important to emphasize that there was no question here of official censorship, since the lines had already been accepted and published—really emasculated the poem. We recall Mayakovsky's poetic program as announced in the *Cloud*: "If you like I'll rage and roar on raw meat; or . . . I'll be unimpeachably tender . . ." A poem by Mayakovsky accommodates by its nature opposite extremes of feeling, and to argue that the closing minor note is out of place in "Homeward!" is to do violence to the poet's special gift. That Mayakovsky himself acquiesced in the mutilation of his poems, that he "plucked out their tail feathers" or himself "stepped on the throat of his own song" is the tragedy of his final years.

[70] "Pismo Ravicha i Ravichu," *PSS*, XII, 182.

[71] Jakobson, "O pokolenii," pp. 35-36.

Chapter Eleven

CONTEMPORARIES

1) "I Became a Newspaper Poet"

Under the heading "1926" in his autobiography, Mayakovsky wrote: "In my work I consciously transform myself into a newspaper man. Feuilletons, slogans. Poets halloo and shout at me, only they can't do newspaper work but mostly publish irresponsible supplements. To me their lyrical junk is funny to look at. It's so easy to do that kind of thing, and nobody cares about it but your wife."[1]

Faithful to the literary tenets held at the time by the *Lef* group, Mayakovsky during the last years of his life devoted a major part of his activity to the production of poetry on topical matters for the Soviet press. This was hardly a "transformation," as he suggests, but rather a strengthening of old and well-established habits of work. His journalistic activity during those years was not essentially different from the production of "windows" or the more recent commercial agitation, though the techniques employed were different, and he had far greater thematic scope. Poetry on topical themes is by definition ephemeral and of little interest beyond the day of its appearance, yet those years did yield a small harvest of memorable verses, including the long poem written on the occasion of the tenth anniversary of the revolution, *Very Good!*

He consciously and more or less consistently subordinated his poetic gift to social purposes, or, to put it more simply, he placed his unusual talents at the disposal of the Soviet state. Literary history offers few comparable examples of such absolute abnegation on the part of a major lyric poet. It might be argued that the production of literature is always conditioned to some extent by extra-literary factors and even that writers are usually a part of social processes. But Mayakovsky's position was unique in the sense that the theory of the "social demand," which originated in the *Lef* milieu, required the writer to submit consciously

[1] *PSS*, I, 28.

and deliberately to the "orders" of his client, the proletarian state. The State Planning Commission may not actually have given direct annual orders for poetry (though some extremists urged that it do just that, indeed that it "sweat over them"), but Mayakovsky was usually at the service of those organizations that asserted the social demand in practice: the editorial boards of journals and newspapers. Needless to say, he did them an enormous service, and they paid him well.[2] The mass of poetry he produced is surely one of the finest examples of didactic verse in the world's literature, considered as an exhibition of verbal versatility. It is true that there were purely lyrical interludes, especially in 1928 and 1929, but they were simply an interruption of his main work.

There were important antecedents in Russian nineteenth-century thought and criticism for the nihilistic rejection of art as a specific and autonomous sphere. The critic Chernyshevsky was held in high esteem by Mayakovsky, by the Briks and by the *Lef* group as a whole. Chernyshevsky's fictional account of a sensible and practical *ménage à trois* in the novel *What Is to Be Done?* served as the principal model for the domestic arrangements worked out by Mayakovsky and the Briks, though there were indeed other nineteenth-century models.[3] In his critical writings Chernyshevsky maintained that reality was superior to art and that the latter possessed value and beauty only to the extent that it reflected and dealt with "life," that, in fact, poets should produce "textbooks of life." That doctrine is not fundamentally different from the *Lef* preachments concerning "factography," the superiority of the "sketch" genre, etc., though of course Chernyshevsky could not have foreseen that a particular state apparatus would control the content and the "lessons" of literature. And the critic Dmitrii Pisarev had far antedated the futurists in the business of throwing Pushkin overboard, in favor of practical needs, like chemists and boots. Turgenev's fictional character Bazarov in *Fathers and Sons*, to whom Mayakovsky bore a conscious resemblance,[4] rejected poetry and all imaginative literature as a frivolous luxury for which Russia had no need. And need we mention Leo Tolstoy in his late period, who regarded all the art that served the tastes of the upper classes, including his own

[2] Note the reference to royalties in the letter to Ravich, *PSS*, XII, 182.

[3] This is based on Lily Brik's oral account of these matters.

[4] A fact hardly in need of documentation.

great novels, as an abomination. Indeed, Mayakovsky and the Briks were simply elaborating in theory and carrying out in practice a tendency to the denigration of art that lay deeply embedded in the Russian tradition.

What Mayakovsky himself attempted, very simply, was to eliminate—perhaps "liquidate" is a better word—the element of the irrational which was always present in his own best work, and which would seem to be a necessary ingredient of all art. We shall return later to the problem of the relationship of the *Lef* group to other literary movements and organizations and to the Soviet government itself, but I should point out once more that the *Lef* theories were vigorously attacked by the liberal critic Voronsky, who could not accept the liquidation of imaginative literature, as well as by the leaders of the proletarian literary organization, RAPP, who believed in the revival of the nineteenth-century realistic novel. The *Lef*-futurists Mayakovsky and Brik were far ahead of any other organization in their demand for a purposeful and didactic literature closely tied to the Party.[5] Osip Brik, who was Mayakovsky's chief theoretician in these matters, would seem to have been more closely attuned to the actual spirit of the time and to the realities of the Soviet Union than most other literary figures.[6]

A survey of his journalistic poetry during the period in question would reveal to us that Mayakovsky, with only occasional lapses, played the part of a highly skilled craftsman producing verbal artifacts in answer to the demands of his employer. The poems he produced successfully versify editorial policies and political campaigns of the day. He entered into each poetic enterprise with so much creative gusto that we can only conclude that the work was done with a degree of conviction. And the work he did was highly skilled. Though necessarily ephemeral considered as poetry, it has genuine historical interest in that it reflects with extraordinary faithfulness the principal concerns of party organs during the late twenties. And it is quite clear that Mayakovsky himself shared many of these concerns.

There are poems that respond to the events of the day on the

[5] An exception to this statement was the *Litfront*, a minority opposition group within RAPP. See E. J. Brown, *The Proletarian Episode in Russian Literature* (New York, 1953), pp. 150-171.

[6] Nadezhda Mandelshtam's comments on the character and purposes of Osip Brik are very penetrating. See *Hope Against Hope*, pp. 172-173.

international scene. "To the English Workers" (1926) is a reaction to the British general strike; "Moscow-China" (1926) to the revolutionary developments in China. A number of poems are hymns to industrial construction and material progress throughout the Soviet Union: "Two Moscows" (1926), "The Crimea" (1926), "Ekaterinburg—Sverdlovsk" (1928), "The Story of the Smelter Ivan Kozyrev about How He Moved into a New Apartment" (1928), and many others. An intense and mordant poem entitled "Kike" (1928), written as Mayakovsky's contribution to a newspaper campaign against anti-Semitism, reveals incidentally how deep and widespread was the feeling against Jews in the Soviet Union. (Yevtushenko's *Babii Yar*, written more than a generation later, reminds us of Mayakovsky's poem in its ugly picture of racial prejudice among Russians.) Many poems are directed against survivals of old habits among bureaucrats, for instance "Pompadour" (1928), and "Bribe-Takers" (1926), the latter an attack on corruption and nepotism in the "new" Soviet apparatus of government.

There is a fairly large cycle of poems that deal with the revival of petty-bourgeois and philistine attitudes among working-class youth; some of these, as we shall see, foreshadow both the characters and the problems of the play *The Bedbug*. A social phenomenon known during the twenties as "decadence" (*upadochnichestvo*) was widely discussed, explained, and condemned in the Soviet press of the day, and Mayakovsky contributed some excellent poems to the campaign against it, the most famous of which is his "To Sergei Yesenin" (1926). The urban hooligan was a constant source of terror, and Mayakovsky wrote a powerful indictment both of the type and of the authorities who handled them leniently. The most impressive of these is a piece entitled "A Character" (1926), which graphically contrasts the teachers and theorists who dispense copy-book lessons in Marxism, with ugly reality in the form of a young brute totally devoid of intelligence and morality, impervious to human ambition or human feeling: "He's a bomb / made of oaths and flourishes / of beer / and stupidities / . . ." It is a frightening picture and no doubt it tells us something about the reasons for the ultimate deformation of Marx's ideas in Russia. Several poems are a stirring expression of purely Soviet patriotism, and these naturally have found their way into schoolbook anthologies. "We" (1929) fully exploits Mayakovsky's verbal powers in the assertion of Soviet ascendancy over the ordinary Edisons and Marconis of Europe. The best in this genre is undoubtedly "Verses about the Soviet Passport" (1929), which expresses genuine pride in that symbol of his Soviet citizenship, and reveals quite incidentally and unconsciously, albeit humorously, feelings of contempt for the holders of other passports, such for example as "Danes, and various other Swedes."

Interspersed among poems of this sort are a number of pieces that express only Mayakovsky himself, and were not written to the specification of any "social demand": "Conversation with a Tax Collector about Poetry" (1926), "A Conversation in the Odessa Roadstead between the Ships 'Soviet Dagestan' and 'Red Abkhaziya'" (1926), "A Letter to Comrade Kostrov from Paris on the Nature of Love" (1928), and the "Letter to Tatyana Yakovleva" (1928). Some of these we will deal with in other contexts.

2) Mayakovsky and His Contemporaries

Mayakovsky was at odds during the last years of his life with a number of his most famous contemporaries, including Gorky, Pasternak, the proletarian poets and theorists whose work he constantly satirized as dull and technically old-fashioned, Mandelshtam, the critics Polonsky and Voronsky, and of course Yesenin.

The origin of the long quarrel with Gorky is obscure, and Soviet sources have so far thrown little light on it. I would suggest that the quarrel began not long after the revolution when Gorky found occasion to express his distaste for the program and tactics adopted by the futurists in the journal they controlled, *Art of the Commune*. One incident in particular led to bitterness and recrimination. In December 1918 the futurists organized discussions of "The Old and the New" in art, and at one such meeting Gorky had been invited to function as chairman. The main speakers announced for the affair included Benois, Chaliapin, Dobuzhinsky, Mayakovsky, and Brik. But Gorky refused to appear, as did other representatives of what the futurists considered "old" art, and the noisy audience agitated for a return of their entrance money. Mayakovsky took the floor and insisted that the absence of representatives of the "old art" should not serve as a pretext for refusing to discuss art at all. He himself was then elected chairman of the meeting in Gorky's place, and after restoring order, apparently with some difficulty, he proceeded with the discussion.[7] This is the clearest instance of a direct "slap in the face" of the futurists from the potent hand of Gorky, and apparently Mayakovsky never forgot it. I have already referred to the scornful treatment of Gorky in Mayakovsky's autobiography, where he is described as a sentimental old buffoon, prone to slobber his tears over any "poetic vest."[8]

We would expect disagreement between the two men on literary matters, since Gorky was a representative of a kind of verbose didactic realism basically in the nineteenth-century tradition, and Mayakovsky was a futurist innovator, and as a matter of fact it is known that they differed sharply on the merits of a number of literary figures. But these literary disagreements do not explain the note of personal animosity in Mayakovsky's "Letter from the Writer Vladimir Mayakovsky to the Writer Maxim Gorky" (1926) addressed to Gorky at his residence in Capri and published in the first issue of *New Lef.* Many appeals that he return to the Soviet Union had been addressed to Gorky during the twenties, when the possibility still existed that he might decide to stay in the west, but Mayakovsky's "letter" is not so much an appeal to return as a reproach for his absence. It contains no trace of the flattery normally expressed in such appeals to the "great proletarian writer," but rather castigates him for his unhealthy influence, even at a distance, on literary life in the Soviet Union. The poem is made up of disparaging phrases and pointed innuendoes, some of which seem quite unfair from any viewpoint. "I'm very sorry," it says, "that you are not to be found at the building of our new life." "Do you think / that from your little hill / on Capri / You can see us better?" (26-29)

The fact that Gorky has given encouragement to such writers as Gladkov is a heavy score against him:

> *Cement* is sold at all the stores.
> But you, / what about it? / Do you value such a book?
> There's no cement anywhere in it. / Gladkov
> wrote / a thanksgiving service / on the subject of cement.
> (43-50)

Gladkov was a writer of no merit whatever who constantly curried favor with Gorky, sometimes to good advantage: the coryphaeus

[7] *Iskusstvo kommuny,* January 5, 1919.
[8] See above, Chapter Five.

had opined, for instance, that *Cement* was "a very good and significant book."[9]

Mayakovsky suggests that Gorky had something to do with the publication of a cheap bit of pornography, Kallinikov's novel *Relics.* Gorky is somehow to blame also for the bad situation on the poetry sector, where beginning proletarian poets are taught to use old-fashioned anapests. The new school of realists with which Gorky is associated, moreover, have *nothing* to offer, according to Mayakovsky, who maintains that the history of literature is being moved forward only by "us and our friends of *Lef.*" There are references to "Gorky the émigré," and a query as to whether he prefers to live like Chaliapin, who was then regarded as a traitor. The tuberculosis which required Gorky's travel to the kinder climate of Italy Mayakovsky dismisses as a pretext, pointing to the example of Dzherzhinsky, who gave everything to the revolution in spite of a fatally bad heart. In short, says Mayakovsky, come back from your comfortable Capri and join us in the hard work of building the future. The poem addressed to Gorky is sharp, polemical, and more than faintly contemptuous.

Not long after the publication of the "letter" Mayakovsky had occasion once more to take sharp issue with Gorky in the matter of the Molchanov controversy, a major episode of the twenties that has now retreated to the dimensions of the trivial and absurd. In this case Mayakovsky's disagreement with Gorky was neither direct nor personal, but he was to be found nonetheless on the side of Averbakh, Bezymensky, and other proletarian litterateurs in a curious polemic with Gorky. A young proletarian poet (and apparently in this case the poet did indeed have proper working-class credentials) named Ivan Molchanov had published in *Young Communist Truth*[10] a rather long poem expressing his honest weariness with the constant struggle and his need for peace, recreation and above all *love.* The poem, entitled "Rendezvous," is a series of sentimental iambic tetrameters with alternating masculine and feminine rhymes (Pushkin is implicitly invoked as model and aegis) in which the poet bids a sad farewell to his working-class girl friend, whose buxom plainness (we judge) was cloaked

[9] M. Gorky, *Sobranie sochinenii,* xxix, 438. It should be pointed out that Gorky was merciless in his criticism of Gladkov's novel *Energy,* which was dedicated to him. See *Literaturnoe nasledstvo,* lxx, *M. Gorky i sovetskie pisateli* (Moscow, 1963).

[10] *Komsomolskaya pravda,* September 25, 1927.

in the usual blue blouse, and announces that he has found another, more delicate, more sensitive, and (of all things) rich:

> My sweet, I love another—
> She's fairer and shapelier
> And a finely tailored jacket
> Supports her tight, neat bosom . . .
> And to her, so rich and fair,
> I've given my old flame.

Leopold Averbakh, the leading figure in the Association of Proletarian Writers, responded immediately with a severe lecture on the need to struggle against all evidences of proletarian "degeneration," and the revival of bourgeois tastes and bourgeois vulgarity in love and elsewhere.[11] Mayakovsky responded with a poem entitled "A Letter to Molchanov's Love, Whom He Abandoned,"[12] which offers among other things a delightful parody of the original poem and advises the forsaken girl to send her Molchanov packing. (We shall see presently that this incident found its way into the play *The Bedbug*, and that Mayakovsky, in belaboring Molchanov, is also belaboring himself.) Gorky entered the dispute over Molchanov's loves with an article published in no less an organ than *Izvestiya*[13] in which he defended the poet's right to change loves under "purely biological motivation," pointed out that Molchanov was a "true proletarian" while his detractors were either middle class intellectuals or merchant types (a telling point), and faulted Averbakh particularly for the offensive tone of his comments on Molchanov (of course Mayakovsky's were no less offensive). Averbakh, not at all impressed by Gorky's intervention, wrote a sharp and politically pointed answer which he published in his proletarian journal.[14] This incident reveals much about the vicious but fictive "class struggles" of the twenties in the Soviet Union, but it is particularly interesting here as evidence that during that decade Mayakovsky was consistently in opposition to Gorky and deplored his influence on literature.

A serious rift between Mayakovsky and Pasternak developed in the middle twenties, though the two poets had at first been

[11] *Ibid.*, October 2, 1927. [12] *PSS*, VIII, 196.
[13] May 1, 1928.
[14] *Na literaturnom postu*, No. 10, 1928, pp. 6-14.

very close and always held each other in high esteem. As a matter of fact Pasternak's sophisticated appreciation in his autobiography *Safe Conduct* is one of the best brief criticisms of Mayakovsky ever written.[15] Pasternak was a member of the *Lef* group in the early twenties and some of his poetry was published in the journal, but his liaison with the *Lef*-futurists, maintained only because of his friendship with Mayakovsky and their common interest in poetic innovation, was both brief and unstable. The *Lef* program, with its emphasis on agitational art and poetry as a "useful craft," was alien to Pasternak, and he tells of a bitter epistolary exchange with Mayakovsky, after which he publicly severed his connection with the group.[16] Only the early, lyrical Mayakovsky had any meaning for Pasternak; he was totally deaf to Mayakovsky's agitational verse. In his own words:

> . . . I shall never understand what benefit he derived from the demagnetising of the magnet, when, retaining its whole appearance, the horseshoe which before had reared up every idea and attracted every weight with its twin poles, could no longer move a single grain. There will hardly be found another example in history when a man who was so far advanced in a new proficiency would renounce it so fully, in the hour foretold by himself when that proficiency even at the price of inconveniences would have fulfilled such a vital need.

Many other eminent contemporaries were for one reason or another alienated from Mayakovsky. Mandelshtam apparently regarded the poet-agitator with ironic amusement, and according to one reliable source Mayakovsky was actually ill at ease in Mandelshtam's presence—an unusual condition for him.[17] The record is clear that Mayakovsky was no less fervent than the RAPP-ites in the journalistic persecution of Pilnyak, Zamyatin, and Bulgakov.[18] Nor was he friendly to "proletarian" poets: Utkin, Zharov, Bezymensky, and others of that literary camp are the frequent targets of his biting satire. The literary politics of the day apparently necessitated a tight group loyalty, and Mayakovsky was always ready to defend and praise his colleagues of

[15] In *Safe Conduct*, pp. 88-94.
[16] *I Remember* (New York, 1959), p. 100.
[17] See V. Kataev, "Trava zabveniya," *Novyi mir*, No. 3, 1967, p. 93.
[18] See *PSS*, XII, 331; IX, 148.

Lef even when he disagreed with them, but ultimately, as we shall see, he became alienated even from them.

But Mayakovsky's principal rival during the twenties, the poet who had taken the place of Igor Severyanin as a threat to be fought with every weapon, was Sergei Yesenin. Severyanin, who sang songs about the modern city's amenities and comforts, was of course very different from the Ryazan peasant Yesenin, whose specialty was village scenes and village memories, yet the two had this in common: they were both highly successful and immensely popular platform artists whose style was the antithesis of Mayakovsky's. Yesenin's poems are melodious and eminently singable; in fact many of them have been set to music, and many others consciously invite such treatment. His style has none of the harsh urban accent that marks Mayakovsky. The city in Yesenin's personal mythology is a labyrinth where men lose their souls, and he shrinks from the iron march of industry. The principal content of his work is nostalgia for the old Russian village that is already disappearing. It may not be an exaggeration to say that Yesenin fashioned a body of poetry out of the childhood memories that he brought with him from his native Ryazan, whose birches and cottages become brilliantly visible again in his lines. Of course all this was alien to Mayakovsky, who repeatedly and from every possible tribunal and even after Yesenin's suicide pronounced his dread anathema upon the backward and decadent tendency represented by Yesenin and "Yeseninism" (*Yeseninshchina*).

At a meeting in 1920 chaired by the poet Valerii Bryusov, Mayakovsky met head on with Yesenin and the group of "imaginists" gathered around him. Mayakovsky, so one of the memoirists tells us, stood in the middle of the auditorium and proclaimed the following: "Attention, listen! Sensational news! An extraordinary court case has just been tried. . . . I've just come from the people's court. An unusual case. Some children killed their mother. They justified themselves by saying that their mother was no good—she was dissolute and a whore. But the fact of the matter is that the mother had been poetry herself, and the children were the imaginists." There took place a noisy verbal duel between Mayakovsky and the assembled imaginists, in the course of which Yesenin leaped up on the chairman's table: "Like an angry child he tore off his tie, ruffled his golden wavy hair and shouted in his sonorous, fine, and strong . . . voice: 'We are not the murderers of poetry! You are! You don't write poems, but propaganda.' "[19]

According to the memoirist Mayakovsky on that occasion easily conquered Yesenin because of the "verbal expressiveness and political saturation" of his verses, but there is no doubt that readers and hearers of poetry in the Soviet Union usually responded to Yesenin with immediate and spontaneous sympathy, while Mayakovsky was often enough not understood or was regarded as no more than a talented buffoon.

Yesenin, moreover, fashioned for himself a biography intended to be read along with his poems as commentary and supplement. Lost in "Tavern Moscow," he instigated wild and impossible scenes, drank and fought in grand excess, and was a frequent visitor at various police stations. Isadora Duncan fell in love with him and married him, and he travelled with her to Europe and America, where he not infrequently acted out the violent component of his "Ryazan soul." He was deeply unhappy. He left Isadora (or she left him) and returned to Russia suffering from alcoholism and hypochondria. On December 27, 1925 he hanged himself in the Angleterre Hotel in Leningrad. He was thirty years old.

Yesenin left behind a farewell poem of two stanzas, written in his own blood, which ended with the lines: "Dying is nothing new in this life / But then, living is nothing new either." Mayakovsky, who would end his own life just a few years later, undertook as his own special mission a literary polemic against the pessimism those last lines express, and specifically with Yesenin's last act, his suicide. The major item in that polemic was the remarkable poem "To Sergei Yesenin," but there were some important contributions in prose also. One of these was a speech on Yesenin and "decadent moods among the youth" delivered at two successive discussions of that topic organized by the Communist Academy in Moscow in February and March 1927.[20] That speech is a kind of inadvertent confessional in which Mayakovsky fully exposes his intense rivalry with Yesenin, his envy of Yesenin's popularity, and his unwillingness to give the dead man his due. He expresses shock at the fact that a large percentage even of proletarian poets

[19] Lidiya Seifullina, *Vospominaniya* (Moscow, 1941), as quoted in Katanyan, *Khronika*, p. 134.

[20] *PSS*, XII, 312-320.

write under Yesenin's influence, and some of them are printed in millions of copies. He blames the editors of literary publications for not giving Yesenin better advice, and implies that they were responsible for putting him "on the path of vodka." He questions Yesenin's value as a poet: "Did he know how to write poetry? That's absolute trash. Trivial stuff. Nowadays everybody writes and not badly. But tell me if you can make of your verses or if you've made of them a weapon of the working class, of the revolution?" He is indignant that in spite of the fact that party leaders have spoken out against Yesenin—he mentions Bukharin—the magazines are still printing his verses, even featuring them. The speech was a poor performance, confused, rambling, ill-natured, and highly emotional. One passage was so distressing and at the same time so revealing that he left it out of the printed version, though it was later published among the variants.

> In the Publishing House (*Dom pechati*) he [Yesenin] used to force himself on everybody, grab them by the throat and demand that his primacy be acknowledged, not only on the territory of the USSR but in the whole world, and not only in poetry, but in his knowledge of the English language. (A voice from the hall: "Speak decently of the dead!") No I won't. I don't acknowledge this practice of not speaking ill of the dead. I abused Yesenin when he was alive and I'll abuse him now and with the greatest pleasure. And one final remark, if somebody hadn't at one time grabbed Sergei Yesenin and held him by the paws, I might be lying in that same coffin, and my books would enjoy such wide circulation as the books of Sergei Yesenin. I had to knock down the dagger that he was brandishing. . . .[21]

That passage expresses in stark form the fierce rivalry between the two poets, and it hints at a physical encounter that would not have been at all out of character for the drink-sodden Yesenin. But we must note once more the baldly expressed envy of those editions of Yesenin's poetry that were published in so many thousands of copies at a time when Mayakovsky's own popularity was often in doubt.

The fact that so many public meetings were organized after his suicide to combat Yesenin, Yeseninism, and the "decadent" feelings he seems to have encouraged is itself evidence that not only Yesenin's poetry, but also his tragic death, must have struck chords

[21] *PSS*, XII, 533.

of sympathy in the reading public. As I have said, it was Mayakovsky's self-appointed mission to "combat" that death. The essay *How to Make Verses*, written in May 1926, which has many interesting observations about Mayakovsky's own verse-making habits, offers as its most important concrete example an account of how the poem "To Sergei Yesenin" was made. The purpose of that poem as a social fact as well as its function in Mayakovsky's own psychology becomes terribly clear in the following passage:

> . . . Yesenin's death grieved me, grieved me in the ordinary sense, as a human being. But at first that death seemed quite natural and logical. I learned about it at night, and my grief no doubt would have remained just grief, and would have abated a little by morning, but that morning the newspapers carried those farewell lines:
>
> Dying is nothing new in this life,
> But then living is nothing new either.
>
> With those lines Yesenin's death became a literary fact.
>
> *It was clear at once how many people who were still hesitating would be brought to the rope or the revolver by those powerful lines—just by the lines themselves.* [My italics.]
>
> No newspaper articles or journalistic analyses could wipe out and annul that poem.
>
> Only with another poem could you fight that one, and you must.
>
> So the poets of the USSR were assigned the social task [*zakaz*] of writing verses about Yesenin. That task was exceptionally important and urgent since Yesenin's verses took effect swiftly and surely. Many poets accepted the assignment. But what should one write? And how? . . .[22]
>
> Considering his death from every angle and getting rid of all extraneous material, I finally formulated and set myself a definite task.
>
> My purpose: *deliberately to paralyze the action of Yesenin's final verses, to make Yesenin's death uninteresting*, and to set up in place of the easy beauty of death, another kind of beauty, since laboring humanity needs all its strength for the revolution it has begun . . . and demands that we celebrate the joy of life, the bright gaiety of the hard march to communism. [My italics.]

[22] *PSS*, XII, 95-97.

That passage is an indispensable background for a correct interpretation of the poem on Sergei Yesenin, which shocks us at first with its harshness and its cold denial of sympathy or understanding. It would have been easy to write a lament over the sad life that had brought the suicide to his fatal impasse, with perhaps some moral reflections on the need for courage and confidence; indeed the elegiac note would normally be difficult to avoid in a poem about anybody's suicide. But Mayakovsky tried to write a poem about Yesenin's death that would make it not only uninteresting, but ridiculous. The apparent lack of sympathy in the poem is easier to understand if we remember that the words are addressed, not only to Yesenin, but also (and even more) to another suicide-prone poet, Mayakovsky.

The opening lines parody the religious associations of the dead one's departure:

> You've left us / as they say / for another world
> Nothingness. / There you hover / mingling with the stars.
> No more advances / no more bars.
> Sobriety. (1-9)

And as he contemplates the suicide hanging there, his veins cut open:

> Stop it! / Cut it out! / Are you out of your mind?
> Letting / your cheeks / get smeared over / with death's chalk?!
> You! / Who could do things with words / that nobody else on earth / can do.
> Why? / What for? / The mind boggles. (21-36)

(Note that the third line above is addressed to himself rather than to Yesenin.) He suggests ways the commentators might explain the death: 1) "lack of contact with the working class," but the working class is pretty good at drinking too; 2) "should have assigned to him a proletarian critic or poet from the 'On Guard' group who would have guided him," but it is better to die from vodka than from boredom. (We shall see that certain "On Guard" critics were actually assigned to Mayakovsky shortly before his death to help him with his political development.)

And on the subject of that suicide poem written in the poet's own blood:

Maybe / if there'd been ink / in that room in the "Angleterre,"
You wouldn't have had to / cut open / your veins.
Your imitators / are delighted: / "Encore!" they shout.
A whole platoon / have already settled all scores with
themselves.
Why increase / the number / of suicides?
Better / to increase / the output of ink! (82-98)

A number of lines speak disdainfully of the writers of funeral elegies and singers of sad songs who held forth immediately after the poet's death:

Get up / and be a roaring scandalmonger:
"I won't let you / mangle verse / and mess it up!"
I'd drown them out / with a three-fingered whistle. (147-152)

These days are difficult ones for those who want to write, but:

Where, / when, / has anybody great / ever
picked out a path / that was travelled / and easy? (181-187)

Our planet / is poorly equipped / for delight.
You've got to / tear joy / from the days to come. (199-204)

And the poem ends with an ironic paraphrase of the last two lines of Yesenin's farewell poem:

Dying / in this life / is not hard.
Making life / is much harder. (206-210)

The poem is a stern lecture, not only to Yesenin and his sympathizers, but, as I have said, to Mayakovsky. Considered as the fulfillment of a healthful social assignment to combat the rising suicide rate, the poem is ambivalent, to say the least. A man ready to "settle all scores with himself" would derive cold comfort from the thought expressed in the last two lines that dying is easier than living. The poem as a whole is one of Mayakovsky's most moving accomplishments, even though it was undertaken as a social assignment. The poet's own frustration, his fear, and above all his identification with the suicide, emerge from it in spite of all his protests—and he does protest too much.

Chapter Twelve

THE CINEMA AND THE STAGE

1) Thirteen Scenarios

Mayakovsky's scenarios and last plays are connected by an intricate allusive pattern to his poetry as a whole. Though he gave much attention and energy to the art of the film, it can hardly be said that he achieved success in it. He is known to have written thirteen scenarios, but only five were produced and shown. He also wrote a number of articles on the problems and prospects of the film.

There were three periods when he showed a special interest in the cinema, the first during the earliest days of the futurist movement, in 1913 and 1914. At that time the film was held in low esteem by the established art world, and it was perhaps to be expected that the futurists, who rejected everything respectable and established, should become interested in the cinema as an art form. The Russian formalists at the same time were paying attention to cinematic form, and Brik's, Tynyanov's, and Shklovsky's interest in the subject is well known.[1] During those years Mayakovsky wrote at least three articles for *Kine-zhurnal*, a periodical whose purpose was both to discuss and to promote the new medium.[2] The three articles whose authorship is definitely established present a pungent defense of futurist ideas about art, expressing also the belief that the film offers the best hope of realizing them. Those articles contain, moreover, both a justification and an explanation of cubism in painting, and the last of the three attempts a careful definition of the relationship of the camera itself to the various arts on which it depends. Two young Mayakovsky scholars in the Soviet Union, R. Duganov and V. Radzishevsky, say that they have discovered twenty-four additional articles in *Kine-zhurnal* that, though signed by various pseudonyms, must be the work of Mayakovsky. Their arguments

[1] These matters are covered in an unpublished Harvard dissertation: William Rudy, "Mayakovsky and Film Art" (1955).

[2] *PSS*, I, 275-286.

are interesting and throw light on many things, but they are not fully convincing. The chief reason for doubting Mayakovsky's authorship of those twenty-four articles is that their style and intellectual quality represent a sharp downward gradient by comparison with the three articles we know he wrote.[3]

The importance of the film for Mayakovsky is best illustrated in his earliest poems. We have remarked in passing that parts of the *Cloud* are structured like the scenario of an old film. The hotel scene is a case in point: the girl comes in, fusses with her gloves; then comes her remark: "Look—I'm getting married." Then there is a quick shift to the telephone conversation. The scene fades to the burning building, then to the Lusitania, then to the harbor fire. All this bears the mark of film technique.

I may add that Mayakovsky's early poems as a whole display an absolute freedom of viewpoint that may also be the result of the influence on him of film technique. The swift movement from one scene to another in the *Cloud*, the soaring, "demon's-eye" view of the earth in *Man*, the abrupt shift from one exotic locale to another in *The Backbone Flute*, the free-ranging "camera-eye" of *War and the Universe* that takes in the whole war on all its fronts much like an old newsreel—such things could probably not have been written before the movie camera converted the old theater auditorium into an "eye" on all the world. The same techniques are suggested in some of the shorter poems, for instance in *Morning*, where the city is asleep and *suddenly* a burning ray of sunlight turns everything into brightness, and in "From Street to Street" where the rails seem to be "drawn out" of the *moving* streetcar (a scene repeated, by the way, in his later scenario *How Are You?*). Mayakovsky's poetry has the whole world as its locale,

[3] R. Duganov and V. Radzishevsky, "Neizvestnye stati Vladimira Mayakovskogo," *Voprosy literatury*, No. 8, 1970, pp. 157-203. This is not the place to enter into a polemic with the Soviet scholars who have labored so long over this problem. However, I cannot accept the newly ascribed articles as Mayakovsky's, chiefly because their style and sentence structure is utterly unlike any prose of Mayakovsky that we know, and also because they are largely devoid of the verbal figures he always used; they lack the analogies, the comparisons, the apt phrases, and above all the emotionalism and excitement that we find in his articles of 1913 and 1914. The arguments that he *probably* contributed drawings to the *Kine-zhurnal* ("certain drawings are 'clearly' [?] in the style of Mayakovsky") and that the articles in question refer to persons, books, ideas, and other things discussed in Mayakovsky's own articles of the time are extremely shaky. But at the present writing the two scholars have not yet published their full argumentation.

in certain cases even the universe, and this has seemed quite natural in a poet of "world" revolution, and "world" war. No doubt that universal setting of his poems is the result also of the mind's liberation from the local and particular, partly through the agency of the moving-picture reel.

Mayakovsky made three films in 1918, for each of which he authored the scenario and played the principal part. The first, entitled *Not Born for Money* (*No dlya deneg rodivshiisya*), was based on Jack London's novel *Martin Eden*, with some characteristic modification by Mayakovsky. The hero Ivan Nov (Mayakovsky) is a worker who has fallen in love with a "girl from another world," and because of his love for her undertakes to educate himself. Fame and fortune come to him when he joins the futurists and recites his poems in one of their cafes. There is a scene in which the poet bursts into a solemn literary meeting and overturns a bust of Pushkin. When he has become rich, Ivan Nov dresses like a dandy in frock coat, spats, and top hat. The girl (to shorten a long story) acknowledges her love for him, but Ivan Nov knows that she is drawn to him only by his wealth, so he rejects her. He suffers, broods, contemplates suicide but in the end only simulates the deed, then returns to his old identity as a worker.[4] Interestingly enough, Mayakovsky at this point changed the plot of *Martin Eden*, which does end in suicide.

The Young Lady and the Hooligan (*Baryshnya i khuligan*) is a story of hopeless love. The hooligan (played by Mayakovsky) falls in love with a nice young girl who has been sent into the slums to teach adult classes. She is on his mind constantly, he "sees" her wherever he goes. He contrives to meet her in a park, where he tells her of his love. She is frightened and runs away. Meanwhile he has changed his ways and is no longer a hooligan, but his former friends make fun of him for loving the girl and giving up the old life. There is a fight and he suffers a fatal knife wound. Before dying he begs his mother to have the teacher come to him. She comes, she kisses him on the lips, and he dies.[5]

Held Fast in Film (*Zakovannaya filmoi*) is a more complex and intricately symbolic piece of work, in which Mayakovsky attempted to exploit the possibilities of the new medium in order to escape from realism. An artist (Mayakovsky) is the main character. He is bored and depressed. He paces the boulevards

[4] *PSS*, XI, 481. [5] *PSS*, XI, 482.

looking for something, he does not know what. He approaches a woman and strikes up a conversation, but suddenly she becomes transparent and he can see that instead of a heart she has a hat, a necklace, and some hatpins. At home he sees through his wife: instead of a heart she has frying pans. He meets a friend: instead of a heart he has a bottle and a deck of cards. He meets a gypsy: instead of a heart she has a string of coins. Nothing comforts him. He leaves home. A gentleman not unlike Mephistopheles has produced a film that has had a great success, entitled "Heart of the Screen." A ballerina (Lily Brik) is that heart, but the whole world of the cinema surrounds her with all its brilliant personalities, cowboys, detectives, etc. After seeing the picture, the artist stays in the auditorium and continues to applaud. The ballerina reappears on the screen, then comes down from it and joins the artist. He takes her with him, but it is cold and dark outside. She escapes from him and re-enters the theater through the closed doors. The artist despairingly pounds on the door. (Once again I shorten what was a long story.) The artist falls sick. Some medicine is brought to him wrapped in an advertisement of the film—a picture of the ballerina. The ballerina comes to life and is suddenly sitting on a little table. She approaches the artist and he is immediately well again. At that very moment the ballerina disappears completely, from the advertisement, from the film—totally. The artist has appropriated her and takes her away with him, but she yearns for the screen and is drawn to everything white and bright that looks like the screen. After more adventures she finds her way back to the studio and "melts" into film, where she really wanted to be. The film ends with a shot of the desolate artist at the window of a train on a journey to the "country of the cinema."[6]

Even an unaided eye could see the correspondences between these three scenarios and Mayakovsky's prerevolutionary poetry. Each scenario deals with a hopeless love; in each the loved object is inaccessible ("Let me in, Maria! I can't stay out here!" he said in the *Cloud*); always the frustration of love is connected with death, or thoughts of death, or mortal sickness, or the idea of escape from an arid, unutterably boring existence. And all three present variations on the theme of *unrequited* love.

Mayakovsky once again had a sudden access of interest in the cinema shortly after his return from America. He produced six

[6] *PSS*, XI, 483.

scenarios in 1926, three in 1927, and one in 1928 which is known only from a *précis* of its content in French. Of these scenarios three have special interest for their relationship to his poetic work at various periods, as well as to his work in the drama: *How Are You?* (*Kak pozhivaete?* 1926), *Forget about the Hearth* (*Pozabud pro kamin*, 1927), and the last-mentioned, *The Ideal and the Disguise* (*Ideal i odeyalo*, 1928).[7] None of the three was ever produced and presented.

How Are You? is quite frankly a recapitulation of Mayakovsky's own career, and many of the motifs of his early poetry reappear in it.[8] The image of Mayakovsky and his double appears in the first scene, where two Mayakovskys join to introduce the movie, and continues throughout, the attention shifting from Mayakovsky himself to "a man" who is his alter ego. The gestural signature of the actual Mayakovsky—an elaborate waving of the arms—is imitated by both of the cinema Mayakovskys. The transformation of his bedroom into an ocean in *About That* takes place once again in the film. The city, the street, the pounding feet of pedestrians disturb him in his sleep, and city sounds awaken him. All this is imported directly from the poems of 1912 and 1913, including the street in perspective and streetcar tracks moving directly at the camera.[9] He is drinking tea and reading the paper. In the paper he reads of a young girl who attempted suicide. She materializes out of the paper. Mayakovsky jumps through the paper like a dog through a hoop and tries to take the revolver away from her, but it's too late.[10] The "man" shrinks from the scene. His face expresses horror. But "Mayakovsky crushes the paper, pushes the tea away with distaste and leaps back in his chair." The "man's" face gradually becomes calm. He again fastens his eyes on the paper. He finds an advertisement in Mayakovsky's *Mosselprom* style: "Buy your clothes and make your dress only at 'The Moscow seamstress.'" Then the various

[7] The other scenarios are discussed in the dissertation by William Rudy mentioned above, n. 1.

[8] This has been pointed out by Roman Jakobson in "Novye stroki Mayakovskogo," p. 183.

[9] *PSS*, XI, 134.

[10] Here Mayakovsky, we have been told, reproduces an item from a dream told to him by Roman Jakobson: Mayakovsky leaping into a room through a round mirror. The scene of the suicide also, we have been told, alludes to the suicide of a young girl who loved Mayakovsky but whose love was not returned.

types of clothing walk along the street without people in them, displaying prices instead of heads, a reminiscence of the animation of "Things" in the *Tragedy.* A series of scenes involving money and books then follows, and the first part ends when two pens form an equal sign between books and money. "One must work" is the title.

The second part concerns Mayakovsky's problems in producing poetry for the masses. The young Communists want verses. But Papa doesn't need them. He turns into an orangutan and says "I don't need your verses." Drawing on two early poems, Mayakovsky describes himself as "A factory without smoke or smokestack." A number of frames are required to show how he rejects such lyrical lines as "How fine, how fresh were the roses" in favor of "Left! Left! Left!" Several more present a fantastic sequence of pictures involving changes in size and shifts of focus, which demonstrate Mayakovsky's troubles with hidebound editors. Young people are on the side of Mayakovsky; a set of orangutans on the side of the editors.

Part three called for a reversed time sequence. Mayakovsky has thrown away a crust of bread. The crust is taken back through all the processes of its production to show "How much work it takes just to make a piece of bread"—apparently a lesson in the value of things.

Part four shows two houses, one set afire through carelessness, the other containing a wedding. Mayakovsky is in a crowd watching the fire; a young girl is in a crowd watching the wedding. Both are bored. The two crowds move toward one another. The girl looks at Mayakovsky. Mayakovsky looks at the girl. She becomes the girl from the newspaper who had tried to kill herself. He overtakes her. There follows a deftly understated seduction scene.

"I'm not going to talk to you." Moves away and shakes her head.

"I'm not going to walk with you—well, only a short way." Walks with him, then takes his arm and they go off together. They reach his house.

"You're not going to come in to my place—well, only for a minute." It is winter, but suddenly it is bright summer just in front of his house. They are "on the wings of love." They sprout airplane wings and dance up the stairs. It is a filthy room but everything in it suddenly blossoms. He pours a drink.

"We're not even going to drink—just one glass."
"What powerful water you serve."
He takes the glass away and sidles up to her.
"We aren't even going to kiss." They kiss.

The room returns to its normal filthy state. No more flowers. It is winter. They come out. They slip and slide. They yawn. He points to his watch. Time to go. They part. No more "wings of love"; it is all over. Love is both satisfied and disappointed.

Part five shows Mayakovsky's entertainment of a dull philistine family at tea. They invite themselves to his house on the occasion of "Robespierre's birthday eve." A policeman's uniform hangs in the kitchen while the policeman entertains himself with the cook. A worker calls Mayakovsky. He is wanted at a meeting. "I'll come if I can get rid of them." The family comes in, Papa, Mama, their daughter, their little boy Toto, and his dog. The father: "The price of pig kidneys is unsteady again." The daughter: "Tell me, have you ever known an ideal love?" The son (lisping): "My dog has discipline. He never pees when he wants, but only when I want." The mother: "Isn't my Toto wonderful. He's smart beyond his years." Mayakovsky answers each one politely, but turns away from them with a distressed look on his face. He must get rid of them, but they plan to stay. He puts on the policeman's uniform and a moustache and presents an order to the effect that "in view of the danger of a repetition of the Tokyo earthquake in Moscow, everybody must spend the night on the street." They rush out in blind obedience to the order and spend the night under an umbrella. Mayakovsky removes his disguise and roars with laughter. Relieved of the family, he goes to his meeting, where he recites, lectures, and answers questions. They applaud. Tired, he reaches home. A daydream of a future when he won't have to attend in person but can dictate his speech into a microphone and answer the questions by radio. Mayakovsky goes to sleep. The sun rises over the sea.

Mayakovsky reports that a famous director (Kuleshov) and two members of the literary staff of Sovkino (Shklovsky and Solsky) were delighted with the scenario and wanted to produce it, but that the administrative heads of the Soviet film organization turned it down out of hand (as indeed they did almost all his scenarios)[11] as "ideologically weak," as "not reflecting life,"

[11] "Karaul!" *PSS*, XII, 130-132.

and as "utter nonsense." This is one more evidence of the growing weakness of Mayakovsky's position in the Soviet Union, though it is possible to sympathize with the administrators' viewpoint. We can only agree with Kuleshov, Shklovsky, and Solsky that *How Are You?* is original and powerful, but the trouble with it from a producer's viewpoint is that it is purely lyrical. Its only unifying theme is the poet himself: his early poems about the city, his unhappy and frustrated love affairs, his conversion from a lyric poet to a producer of political and commercial agitation, his constant struggle with editors for the acceptance of his style, his distaste for the narrow philistinism of family life, his weariness with platform work. It is really not surprising that the film was never made.

The scenario *Forget about the Hearth* (*Pozabud pro kamin*) is an early variant of *The Bedbug*, and it contains much of what later went into the play: the proletarian-turned-philistine who abandons his working-class girl friend for a beauty-shop operator, the vulgar "red" wedding ceremony ending in a fire, the resurrection of the dead proletarian twenty-five years later when communism has been already achieved, the bedbug resurrected with him, his guitar and his sentimental songs. All the ingredients of the scenario were used in *The Bedbug*, and yet in its final effect the play is a radically new thing.

2) Two Plays

The plays written by Mayakovsky in 1928 and 1929 constitute a two-part dramatic satire directed against old enemies whom we have already met under the generic name *byt* and who appear now in the form of *bourgeoisis vulgaris*, a species closely allied with *bedbugus normalis*, and "the Soviet bureaucrat." Both plays are satiric utopias in the sense that they present a vision of a future in which the world will be purified of such specimens. *The Bedbug* is a two-part drama in which the action of the first part takes place in the year 1928 and of the second part fifty years later in a well-ordered communist state. The principal character is one Prisypkin, a successful Soviet "promoted worker," for whom proletarian blood, callused palms, and the trade-union card have become symbols of privilege and power. As the play opens, he has jilted his working-class girl friend for a beauty-shop operator and manicurist, Elzevir Renaissance, and is shopping in a huge department store in preparation for the wedding. Various street salesmen are promoting their wares—buttons, dolls, whetstones, lampshades, glue, perfumes, fur-lined brassieres, and the like—in jingles that parody Mayakovsky's own commercial poetry. Prisypkin, as acquisitive as any bourgeois, purchases a variety of such wares, announcing that his house must be filled with such things "like a horn of plenty." Prisypkin is accompanied by a poet named Oleg Bayan, whose function is to educate this working-class person in an appreciation of the "finer" things, such as poetry, the fox-trot, and the tango. Oleg Bayan is a barely disguised portrait of an actual poet, Vladimir Ivanovich Sidorov, who had adopted a pseudonym redolent of Russia and poetry, "Vadim Bayan." He had taken part with Mayakovsky in the futurist tour of the provinces in 1914, presenting his verses in competition with Burliuk, Severyanin, and Mayakovsky himself. After the revolution Sidorov had indeed occupied himself with the literary education of young workers and he had composed communist wedding songs, as well as politically oriented games (*igry*) and dances to be performed by peasants. This activity Mayakovsky satirizes directly and without mercy, and when Sidorov-Bayan complained of it in an open letter published in the *Literary Gazette*, Mayakovsky answered briefly and scornfully, suggesting that if he objected to the character in the play he should change his own name.[12]

Prisypkin's rejection of his working-class girl friend, Zoya Berezkina, who tries to commit suicide, revives in dramatic form two recent polemical episodes, his answer to Molchanov,[13] and his poem "Marusya Has Poisoned Herself" (*Marusya otravilas*),[14] concerning a girl who committed suicide in desperation over her abandonment by such a one as Molchanov. Both these poems, as well as the main plot of the scenario *Forget about the Hearth*, are closely connected with Mayakovsky's work on the newspaper *Young Communist Truth*, and with the campaign against decadence and backsliding sponsored during those years by its editor, Taras Kostrov, who was deeply troubled about the tendency of young people, often under the influence of foreign movies, to adopt bourgeois dress and manners. The basic idea of *The Bedbug* and much of the material in the play, it would seem, grew out of Mayakovsky's work as a newspaper propagandist. Yet the

[12] *PSS*, I, 368; XII, 588.
[13] See above, Chapter Eleven.
[14] *PSS*, VIII, 188.

play itself deviated strangely from its announced and initial direction, as we shall presently see.

Prisypkin's wedding ceremony takes place in the "Renaissance" beauty-shop amid the odor of hair-tonic, curling tongs, and perfumes. The beauty shop serves as a mighty symbol of resurgent philistinism and is actually prophetic of the revival under Stalin of make-up, manicures, and brilliantine. Oleg Bayan's production of this "red wedding," moreover, suggests the flowery sentimental ceremonies, with bride and groom bedecked and attended, that developed much later as an appendix to simple registration of the marriage as a vital statistic at a government office. Prisypkin, whose speech is cluttered with clichés mechanically transferred from Party and trade-union life to other spheres, declares the wedding "open." The guests, soon drunk in the traditional fashion, repeatedly shout the traditional Russian wedding toast "Bitter!" (*Gorko!*) whereupon the bride and bridegroom must kiss (Prisypkin kissing "with a sense of his worth as a member of the proletariat") and the guests again drain their glasses. Oleg Bayan (Sidorov, we remember) recites speeches and poetry on the subject of the good life and the elegant luxuries (vodka and herring, for example) now at the disposal of the working class, lines certainly intended as a parody of the ego-futurist Severyanin.[15] A drunken "best man" serves as a kind of self-appointed policeman enforcing order and propriety, and when Bayan intones "Beauty is the mother . . ." the "best man" thinks he's heard a "mother-oath": "Who said 'mother' . . . ? Don't talk like that in front of the newlyweds." (161)

The directions for stage business call for an ignorant mixture of attempted elegance and vulgarity. Someone calls for "Beethoven and the Kamarinsky," the latter a peasant dance. The "best man" understands Elzevira's French affectations in his own way:

> ELZEVIRA: Ah, that's so *charmant*, oh, it's simply a *petite histoire*. . . .
>
> BEST MAN: Who said *pissoir*!? Please! In front of the newlyweds. . . . (172-173)

The "red" wedding of the petty bourgeois Elzevira and the proletarian Prisypkin (who has changed his name to Pierre Skripkin)

[15] This was first suggested, as far as I know, by A. M. Ripellino in his *Majakovskij e il teatro russo d'avanguardia* (Milan, 1959), p. 185. I am indebted to this excellent study for many of its insights.

symbolizes the continuing debasement of revolutionary ideas in the Soviet Union. The color red, which belonged properly to the Soviet flag and the blood of the working class, is now bestowed on ham, wine-bottles and painted lips.

At last the drunken guests set fire to the house, which burns to the ground destroying the inmates and all their neo-bourgeois trappings. In Scene IV the firemen report to one another on the burnt-out remains, and incidentally offer a Mayakovskyan rhymed homily on the dangers of vodka when mixed with fireplaces and primus stoves.

Each of Mayakovsky's plays, beginning with the *Tragedy*, divides more or less evenly into two parts, one concerned with the present, the other with the future. *The Bedbug* is closely reminiscent of the *Tragedy* in its structure in that the second part shows us a future world that has come about as the result of a revolution and a reordering of life. Fifty years after the fire the bridegroom Prisypkin, together with his close companion, a bedbug, is found, by workmen excavating for a new structure, perfectly preserved in a block of ice, and both are brought to life by scientists of the "Bureau for the Resurrection of the Dead." Prisypkin's "unfreezing," though a scientific success, is not an unmixed blessing to the inhabitants of the future, for he is found to contain a petty-bourgeois infection called "love," along with a fondness for strong drink and sentimental songs. Moreover, the citizens of the socialist future are not immune to these infections, which they pick up much too easily, and it is necessary to isolate Prisypkin and encompass him with disinfectants. Otherwise he will spread by contagion that ancient disease called love, "a state in which a person's sexual energy, instead of being rationally distributed over the whole of his life, was compressed into a single week and concentrated in one hectic process. This made him commit the most absurd and impossible acts."

The authorities of the State of the future place Prisypkin in a cage in the municipal zoo, where he is displayed in all his natural filth for the education and edification of the citizens. These people of utopia have, supposedly, forgotten a way of life that called for the use of poison (vodka), the disorderly and unhealthful consumption of tobacco, the use of foul language, the strumming of guitars, and idle talk about one's "heartstrings." And when the director of the zoo lets Prisypkin out of his cage to see the spectators and to address a few words to them in order to prove that he has mastered human speech, Prisypkin, suddenly looking out at the theater audience, is overjoyed at seeing so many people like himself: "Citizens! Brothers! My own people! Darlings! How did you get here? So many of you! When were you unfrozen? Why am I alone in the cage? Darlings, friends, come and join me! Why should I alone suffer? Citizens!"

This pathetic appeal of the caged Prisypkin has been interpreted in recent times as a veiled attack on the police state, but of course it is nothing of the sort. Prisypkin's apostrophe to the Soviet audience of 1928 is reminiscent of a very similar scene in Gogol's *Inspector General*, when the dishonest and foolish mayor turns to the audience to ask them whether they are not laughing at themselves rather than at him. You all have a bit of Prisypkin in you, Mayakovsky is saying in this scene, you are all attached to vulgar bourgeois values. Like Prisypkin you smoke, drink, and use intemperate language. Like him you want your houses to be "horns of plenty," crammed with buttons, brassieres, and bathos, and like him you have debased the humanitarian ideals of the revolution to the pursuit of comfort and power. Worst of all, you still preserve the infections of individualism and sexual love.

This is Mayakovsky's ostensible and consciously devised message in the play, yet something went wrong with the images in which he presents it. In the first place, there crept into the figure of Prisypkin a measure of identification with the poet himself, and this resulted in sudden, unexpected, and discordant notes of pathos throughout the second part, and especially at the end of the play.

Mayakovsky's satire in *The Bedbug* is clearly directed at himself as well as at his contemporaries. We have already noted that the ditties recited by the peddlers in the first scene are a parody of his own verse written for the Moscow Food Stores. Mayakovsky's most accomplished work is a poetic expression of that "disease of the brain" known as sexual love. It has been pointed out that Mayakovsky, in satirizing Prisypkin's yearning for "roses" and "visions," may be lecturing himself: "Only books on horticulture have anything about roses, and visions are mentioned only in the medical books, in the section on dreaming."[16] And the ugly caricature of a "bourgeoisified" proletarian Prisypkin in search of conventional marital bliss may be that alter ego of the poet with whom he disputed in the poem *About That*:

[16] *PSS*, xi, 263.

Have you greased your way
  into that caste of theirs?
Will you kiss?
  Feed yourself?
    Grow fat?
Do you intend
  yourself
to dig yourself into their way of life
and practice that family happiness of theirs?

The identification of Prisypkin-Skripkin with the poet himself is borne out in a curious reminiscence of the actor who played the part, Igor Ilinsky, in which he tells us, almost inadvertently, of this identification:

> In his author's interpretation Mayakovsky did not endow Prisypkin with any characteristic traits or moral attributes. He read the part in his usual manner of monumental authoritativeness and with a solemn, even noble . . . pathos, peculiar to himself.
>
> . . . I built Prisypkin's part as a "monumental" flunkey and boor. . . . Though it may seem paradoxical, I adopted for Prisypkin, even externally . . . Mayakovsky's manner.[17]

Other evidence tends to support Ilinsky's interpretation of the part. Prisypkin is brought back from death by a chemist of the future (possibly "broad-domed") very like the one to whom Mayakovsky himself applied for resurrection in the poem *About That*; but Prisypkin's experience in the brave new world represents later and gloomier thoughts on the rationalized future society: "Comrades, I protest. I didn't get unfrozen just so you could dry me out!" (368)

The zoo itself and Prisypkin's cage in it suggest Mayakovsky's own identification with animals, and the sympathy both he and Khlebnikov felt for the beast, who offers the poet both moral analogies and metaphors. Mayakovsky's menagerie of animal-selves would serve as a very respectable small public zoo: it included, as we have seen, dog, elephant, giraffe, bear, and ostrich; he signed most of his letters to Lily Brik "Puppy" (*Shchen*), and in some of them the pathetic puppy is shown behind bars; in *About That* he says the zoo is where he would prefer to work in

[17] *V. Mayakovsky v vospominaniyakh sovremennikov*, p. 300.

the future world, and "she herself" would come there, because "she loved animals, too." "She herself" wrote a delightful character sketch of Mayakovsky, entitled "Puppy" (*Shchen*),[18] in the disguise of a delicate vignette about a stray dog adopted by the Briks and Mayakovsky. Her sketch is not only a humorous and sensitive treatment of a dog by a woman who knows and understands the character, quality, and life style of dogs, but it is also an extended metonymy for the proper name Mayakovsky: "They were very like one another. They were both huge and had huge heads. They both carried their tails high. They both whined pathetically when they wanted something and wouldn't give up until they got it. Sometimes they barked for no good reason at anybody who came along, just to have something to say."

The caged clown and cretin Prisypkin suddenly turns pathetic when we realize that this is Mayakovsky himself caught in the cage of the futurist world that he and his comrades were so busily building. The petty-bourgeois ambience in the first part of the play smells of hair-tonic, as Ripellino has pointed out, but the principal odor of Mayakovsky's world of the future is that of disinfectant. It is a painfully disinfected world, clean not only of emotion, but of germs. We recall in this connection Mayakovsky's own neurotic fear of germs, his compulsive hand-washing, and his habit of drinking coffee through a straw to avoid contact with dubious cups.[19] The second part of *The Bedbug* is a nightmarish realization of his deep fear of contagion. *The Bedbug* is, therefore, an extremely complex satiric system, so complex that at times it does not hold together. Voices from the crowd in the last scene break in upon the action and the mood with a sudden plea that mercy be shown the caged beast, Prisypkin-Skripkin:

"Don't, don't! Don't torment the poor animal. . . ."

"Oh how awful!"
"Professor, stop!"
"Oh, please don't shoot!"

Prisypkin himself in his apostrophe to the audience asks pathetically, "Why am I suffering?" The philistine symbolized by Prisypkin-Skripkin is the normal Soviet man of the late twenties who has deserted the "trenches" of revolution for the sake of

18 Lily Brik, *Shchen* (Molotovgiz, 1942).
19 Elsa Triolet, *Maiakovski, poète russe*, p. 126.

middle-class happiness. He is also Mayakovsky himself, the unreconstructed poet of his own all-important self, who no matter how hard he tried never quite succeeded in choking off the love lyric. With his barbarous ways, Prisypkin seems no better than an animal to the citizens of the rationalized world of the future. That world itself is presented in satiric images by the Mayakovsky who is himself part Prisypkin: the world-wide mechanical voting-apparatus; the organized mass dances which are the only kind that survived; the comical search among old books for something on "love"; and the steel, concrete, and glass backdrop against which the man of the future lives—a construction worthy of Tatlin—are hardly offered as a happy prospect.

Mayakovsky in this play is caught in a dilemma that is both historical and personal: he abhors the philistine individualism of Prisypkin and the tawdry values that survive in him, but he does not really believe either in the hardening scientific utopia that threatens to crush Prisypkin—and Mayakovsky. The future world he shows is something like the Single State of Zamyatin's *We*, where human beings are simply numbers, each one specialized for a certain job, and where love "has long since been forgotten." In that state there could be no surprises and no unforeseen events; similarly in Mayakovsky's future: "External events are rare . . . ," though "Our years are full of deep experiences and disturbances of an internal nature" (394). That statement might have been made of Zamyatin's D-503, who, though he lives in a perfectly organized state, suddenly experiences inward conflicts due to the re-assertion of his individual self. Indeed it is most likely that Mayakovsky when he wrote the second part of *The Bedbug* was responding in his own way to *We* (1921), and even engaging Zamyatin in dispute over the importance of values that, both thought, would probably disappear in a fully rational world. Ostensibly, Mayakovsky despised Prisypkin's "heart strings," his individualism, and his dirty indulgence in cigarettes and vodka. For Zamyatin in *We* those very things are symbols of rebellion against social regimentation. But Mayakovsky throws a perverse doubt on his own argument by making his prehistoric bourgeois animal into a pathetic creature imprisoned in a world he never made and can't understand. Into a play that was planned as a simple propaganda exercise Mayakovsky, characteristically, injected a moment of his own pain, and a muffled cry for help.

Flawed though it is as a play and uncertain in its final effect, *The Bedbug* is nevertheless a valid record of human experience. *The Bathhouse*, on the other hand, is derivative in its plot, deficient in action, devoid of dramatic suspense or interest, and, what is worst of all, Mayakovsky himself is not present in it. The play is stiff and schematic, without feeling or conviction, and even as spectacle it is uninteresting. *The Bathhouse*, like *The Bedbug*, was cut to a propaganda pattern. It is simply and pointedly directed against the Stalinist bureaucracy that was taking form at the time—in this it has much in common with Bezymensky's play *Vystrel* (1930)—and it echoes the continuing campaign of Kostrov's *Young Communist Truth* against the abuse of power at high levels.

The character Pobedonosikov, whose name recalls the nineteenth-century reactionary minister Pobedonostsev, dominates a paper apparatus that is indifferent to human beings and incapable of action. The generation of bureaucrats he represents is narrow and conformist; they are sycophants, opportunists and time-servers, people of vulgar ambition, vulgar tastes, and no education, interested only in power and the exercise of power. The inventor Chudakov (whose name means approximately "The Eccentric") has devised a time machine not very different from the one invented by H. G. Wells, but with some refinements derived from second-hand accounts of Einstein's theories. His assistant Velosipedkin ("the bicycle man") is a busy and importunate pleader of Chudakov's need for funds to develop this invention. Foreign interests are conspiring to steal the idea, or buy it from him. Mr. Pont-Kich (whose name mixes a suggestion of Pierpont Morgan with the German word *Kitsch*, "cheap display")[20] is a "British Anglo-Saxon" very much interested in appropriating the discoveries of Soviet science.

This enterprising Englishman and "spy" is the most delightful character in the play, even though he speaks in a kind of "transsense" idiom, made up of actual Russian phrases that resemble English utterances but are difficult to apprehend fully in either language.[21] For instance, Mr. Pont-Kich says, if we translate his

[20] See Hugh McLean, "How the Beasts Roared . . ." in *For Roman Jakobson* (The Hague, 1957).

[21] Mayakovsky's invention of this language is described in Rita Rait, "Tolko vospominaniya," in *V. Mayakovsky v vospominaniyakh sovremennikov*, pp. 236-279.

Russian into English, "Hey! Ivan roared at the door, but the beasts were dining. Hey! A mannequin was on its way to paradise, and a raccoon to Indostan, Akh! too much pepper! Akh! Very inventiveness." The Russian sounds like this: *Ai Ivan v dver revel, a zveri obedali. Ai shol v rai maneken, a enot v Indostan, pereperchil oi zveri izobreteishen,* which we understand with some difficulty as meaning, approximately, in English, "I want that very well and very badly. I shall buy many kinds, and you don't understand that Churchill is very British." Mr. Pont-Kich's remarks are nonsense that conceals meaning, and the play is occasionally amusing when he is on the stage. Chudakov is unable to get money to support his project from Pobedonosikov, who is so tangled in paper, routine, and official clichés that he cannot deal sensibly with any problem. Nevertheless the machine is properly plugged in and a "phosphorescent woman" from the future arrives to make a number of set speeches on the glorious struggles of the present that will lead—from her point of view already have led—to the communist future. She is moralistic, puritanical, didactic, and, like the people of the future in *The Bedbug*, she diffuses the aroma of disinfectant. When she is about to take the time machine into the future she says that the future (i.e., the machine) "will accept all those who have any features that show their kinship with the commune," and of course the machine when it takes off rejects and leaves behind Pobedonosikov, his secretary Optimistenko, the painter Belvedonsky, who does portraits of notables, Pont-Kich, and various official and unofficial sycophants. The last remark of the play would seem to be a superfluous hammer blow on a didactic nail already driven home:

> POBEDONOSIKOV: "She, and you, and the author—what do you mean by all this, that I and my like are not needed for communism?"

The play was a failure, and knowledgeable people (with the exception of the director, Meyerhold, who compared it to Molière and others) were understandably disappointed. Zoshchenko, who was present at a reading of the play, reported: ". . . I did not like the play. I thought it was theatrically clumsy. On that occasion I was, for the first time in my life, insincere, thinking that perhaps I did not understand something in it. When Mayakovsky asked me whether the play was good, I said it was."

Igor Ilinsky, who had created the part of Prisypkin, also reacted negatively to Mayakovsky's new play.[22] When it was produced in Leningrad in January 1930, Zoshchenko reported, "The audience received the play with murderous coldness. I do not recall a single burst of laughter. After the first two acts there was not the slightest applause. I have never seen a more terrible flop." Mayakovsky's good intention—to castigate the Soviet bureaucracy—was poorly implemented in a bad play.

Perhaps part of the reason for Mayakovsky's failure as a dramatist—and there is now no question that he did fail—was that the lyricist Mayakovsky could not refrain from injecting himself and his own personal concerns into the plays, thereby abandoning disciplined development of character and conflict. The central, even at times the sole, character in those plays, is Mayakovsky himself and the cast of characters is at least partly illusory. We recall that his earliest play, *Vladimir Mayakovsky, A Tragedy*, features the poet himself as author, director, and hero, and the other characters, the mutilated men, the women with tears, and so forth, are fragments of Mayakovsky himself. The characters in *Mystery-Bouffe* are conventional puppets whom Mayakovsky manipulates, and though it may have been successful as spectacle, it had little dramatic quality. *The Bedbug* ends on a note of emotional confusion when Prisypkin, suddenly and without any preparation, speaks for Mayakovsky. *The Bathhouse* was a puppet-show rather than a play, and its doll-like characters, with their conventional names (Mr. Eccentric, Mr. Bicycle-Man, Mr. Momentarily, Mr. Optimist, and so forth), are manipulated by Mayakovsky himself in the character of the "phosphorescent woman," who brings us his "message" from the future. In spite of the occasional flashes of Mayakovsky's genius that are in it, *The Bathhouse* is now quite dead, and probably could not be revived.

[22] V. *Mayakovsky v vospominaniyakh sovremennikov*, p. 303.

Chapter Thirteen

A GIRL FROM A DIFFERENT WORLD

We have had occasion to trace the strands that connect Mayakovsky's poetry with his life. It should be clear now that the poetry is to a large extent his own created autobiography: it is particularly interesting to note that in certain important details the structure of his work in terms of imagery, ideas, and emotional content closely parallels the pattern of his own life, so much so that at times the critic may shift unwittingly from literary to biographical commentary. Love he lavishes, both in his poetry and in his life, on female objects who are unattainable and who do not return his love: recall the Maria of *The Cloud*, the redhead with a painted face and a husband in *The Flute*, the woman in *Man* who sold herself to the enemy, and the girl in *About That* whose apartment is bedecked with geraniums and canaries, and who has sent him away. The early cycle of love poems are all inspired by Lily Brik, and indeed dedicated to her: a new cycle begun in 1928 but rapidly aborted was inspired by Tatiana Alekseevna Yakovleva, a young emigrée Russian whom he met in Paris in 1928 and with whom he fell once again totally and abjectly in love.

The character and personality of Tatiana neatly fits both his life pattern and the structure of his love poetry as a whole. Beautiful, tall, and stately, she was a desirable object in the Parisian milieu of prestigious males. She made a place for herself in that world, though she may have loved, after her fashion, the extravagant Soviet poet who offered her his heavy heart. There are conflicting accounts concerning how she met Mayakovsky, her relations with him in Paris, and the circumstances of their aborted romance. Jakobson reports that they met in October 1928 in the house of a Parisian doctor. "The fashion of the day—beads and furs—" he adds, "was very becoming to her." This account, written years after the event, gives no credit to any particular persons for bringing them together. Elsa Triolet, a witness hostile to Tatiana, had another version, that she herself had introduced them at the apartment of a friend, who may indeed have been the doctor Jakobson mentions. She adds, with her claws bared, that Tatiana was very anti-Soviet, but suggests that Mayakovsky's passionate suit may not have been totally rejected: "There was only one thing she would not do for him, go with him to Russia as he wanted her to do."[1]

Jakobson's account makes no mention of any radical, pro-Soviet Russians such as Ehrenburg or Triolet as agents of their meeting, but the letters Tatiana wrote at the time to her mother in Russia seem to reveal that the meeting was not accidental but was arranged for her by Left Bank acquaintances. Those letters were published in 1968 in the Soviet mass journal *Ogonyok* in a series of articles whose method and intent are questionable, although there is no reason to doubt the authenticity of the letters:

> Here's how we met. Here on Montparnasse (where I spend a lot of time) Ehrenburg and some of my friends kept telling him about me all the time, and I'd gotten greetings from him before he'd even seen me. Then I was invited to a certain house especially to meet him. That was on the 25th of October. And until the second of November (the day he left) I saw him every day and became very friendly with him. If I've ever really liked one of my admirers then it's him, mostly because of his talent, but even more because of the surprising and even touching way he treats me. In his attentiveness and care for me (and you know I'm spoiled as it is) he's really astonishing. I still miss him very much. The main thing is that the people I know are mostly "high society" and they don't have any desire to stir their minds or else they have certain conventional thoughts and feelings. But Mayakovsky stimulated me, and forced me (because I'm awfully afraid of seeming stupid when I'm with him) to extend myself mentally, but most of all to remember Russia with a kind of pang [*ostro*]. . . .

The same letter gives evidence that under Mayakovsky's influence she did at least consider the idea of returning to Russia: "He awakened in me such lonesomeness for Russia that I almost returned." Yet she assures her mother that she is not likely to do anything foolish: "You know here I never felt lonesome for the

[1] Jakobson, "Novye stroki," p. 183. Elsa Triolet's statement is quoted from Woroczylski, *Życie Majakowskiego*, p. 681.

'Volodyas,' but for this third Volodya I do feel lonesome. But don't get upset! This is certainly no hopeless love. Quite the contrary. His own feelings are so powerful that you can't help returning them, even if only a little bit."

Another letter written in August 1929 reveals that her mother was disturbed at the Mayakovsky affair and by no means approved of the prospect of her daughter's marriage to a "dissolute" poet and her return to Russia. The letter suggests also that the family may have had some hope of securing, through Mayakovsky's influence, an exit visa for Tatiana's sister:

> I'm very sad that you, with all your troubles, should worry about me. Let me answer the main thing. I've certainly not decided to go for, or, as you put it, throw myself into marriage with M, and he's not after me but comes to see me and for a short time. Of course in any case he won't fail to look out for Lilyusha. There's not even any thought of that and so she should study her lessons and come in the spring. Her lack of faith in us makes me terribly sad. We're always thinking about her, but for the present there's no way of dragging her out. But you can see from grandma's letter that *everything is decided.* To get a visa right away (M. leaves on the thirteenth) is impossible but with his departure *nothing* in her life will be changed.

She reassures her worried mother about the poet's character by pointing out that the "verses" Mama is concerned about were written when Mayakovsky was only twenty; reminds her that her "little girl" is now old enough to take care of herself; and announces that in any case she does not really want to get married, adding in parentheses that she has the reputation of a *femme fatale.* She goes on, "There are an awful lot of dramas in my life. Even if I wanted to be with M. then what would happen to Ilya, and besides him there's still another. It's a charmed circle."[2]

Tatiana Yakovleva was obviously very young, unformed, and fond of herself (but also fond of Mayakovsky). She enjoys her reputation of a *femme fatale,* and worries sweetly about what will happen to all her other admirers should she choose her poet. She appreciates Mayakovsky's mind, his wit, his glittering reputation,

[2] Tatiana's letters to her mother were first published in V. Vorontsov and A. Koloskov, "Lyubov poeta," *Ogonyok,* April 14, 1968.

and she is impressed by the attention and time he lavishes upon her and upon her family in Russia, whom he apparently helped in many ways.[3] But the letters reveal not a trace of passionate self-surrender, nor any evidence that she was ready to follow her lover back to the Soviet Union. The affair came to an abrupt end, though certain details are still obscure.

Mayakovsky spent the summer and early fall of 1929 in Moscow in a kind of fever of work on *The Bathhouse*. He was driven by deadlines and harassed by difficulties with the Repertory Committee and other bodies, and the pressure upon him at the time shows plainly in the shortcomings of the play. He bombarded Tatiana with letters and wires—there were, according to Jakobson, seven letters and twenty-five telegrams dispatched to her between December 27, 1928, and October 5, 1929, the date of his last letter.[4] Excerpts from the messages published by Jakobson reveal the state of his mind and of his nerves:

> ". . . I'll be writing *The Bathhouse*. Please don't find fault with me and don't reproach me. I've had so many troubles, both large and small, that you must not be angry with me . . ." (May 15, 1929).
>
> "I'm trying to get to you as soon as possible. . . . I've begun to write *The Bathhouse* (with a hellish delay!). . . . I have not written a single line of verse. After your verses all others seem insipid. . . .[5] It's impossible that we should not be together for all time . . ." (June 8, 1929).
>
> "I'm lonesome for you. I'll try to see you as soon as possible. . . . I can't imagine life without you after October (the date we've fixed). . . . I'm so huge, bear-pawed, and disgusting. And today I'm also very morose. . . . I write very little. My head isn't working right. I need a rest. . . ."

And the telegrams: "Lonesome will try to see you soon. . . . Very lonesome (*toskuyu*). . . . You wouldn't believe how lonesome. . . . Infinitely melancholy . . . absolutely lonesome. . . . I miss you regularly, and lately even more often." He invites Tatiana to come and work as an engineer somewhere in the Altai range of mountains: "Come on! What about it?"

[3] See his letter to Lily Brik on this subject in *Literaturnoe nasledstvo*, LXV, 170.

[4] Jakobson, "Novye stroki," p. 185.

[5] He means the poems he had written to her, or about his love for her.

In these repeated notes of lonesomeness, disgust for any place where the beloved is not present, lack of interest in activities that don't include her, we find repeated the major motifs of the love letters to Lily Brik. The style of the letters and telegrams to Tatiana demonstrates that Mayakovsky had really transferred his affections to her, along with his insistent, restless, all-consuming demand for attentive love.

Mayakovsky was straining for Paris during the early fall of 1929, but he never made the trip—in fact, he never again left Russia. There are conflicting accounts as to why he remained in Russia, but the weight of evidence supports the accepted belief that he was refused an exit visa by the Soviet government. That account is supported by Vorontsov and Koloskov in their article "A Poet's Love,"[6] and we must assume that those Soviet authors had some access to Soviet records of the event. Elsa Triolet disputes their statement, insisting that he did not get a visa because he did not apply for one, and that he did not apply for one because Tatiana had married someone else.[7] It is a fact that she married, but Tatiana maintains that the marriage took place, not in October but in December, and only after she had learned that Mayakovsky would not be joining her. She had waited two months, then married Vicomte du Plessix, a member of the French diplomatic corps, and accompanied him to his post in Warsaw.

Mayakovsky learned of this event from a letter that Elsa Triolet wrote to her sister Lily Brik and that Lily read aloud to him. There are two distinct versions of his immediate reaction to the news, one that he greeted it with ironic resignation, the other that it was a tragic moment for him. Elsa says that he responded by recalling the well-known joke about the inexpert horseman who slid backward toward his horse's tail and when he reached it said, "This horse is finished, get me another one." Jakobson's version includes the remark "This horse is finished," but refers the word "horse" not to Tatiana but to Mayakovsky himself, and connects the remark with his famous poem "Be Better to Horses." Elsa Triolet's version, which comes directly from Lily Brik, has the effect of minimizing the strength of Mayakovsky's attachment to Tatiana and the effect upon him of her sudden marriage. All the

[6] See above, n. 2.

[7] See her "N'accusez personne de ma morte," in *Les lettres françaises*, No. 1239, July 3-9, 1968. This is one of two articles she wrote in answer to the articles in *Ogonyok*.

other evidence—his letters and telegrams to her, the depressed state of his spirit during the following months, his sudden and hopeless infatuation with Veronika Polonskaya (the other "horse"?), an actress who reminded him of Tatiana[8]—tends to support Jakobson when he maintains that the end of the affair with Tatiana was a mortal frustration.

The force of the blow was surely multiplied many times by the poet's consciousness that the brief affair with Tatiana was only a dull re-enactment of the persistent theme that ran through all his lyric poetry. "Look! I'm getting married"; "God brought that woman up out of hell and gave her a husband and music to put on her piano"; "His 'little flute,' his 'little cloud' "; "I'm Nikolaev, an engineer, don't bother my wife." "Live alone and comfort yourself somehow. I'm in love to the top of my masts with a three-stacked cruiser." And now, instead of joining him in Moscow to live in a state of pure love, or going off to the Altai mountains for adventure and service, his latest love says, in effect: "Look! I'm marrying a fine gentleman." No doubt if she had told him in person she would have "fussed nervously with her suède gloves," as Maria did in the *Cloud.* The repetitions seemed endless, the pattern fixed and inescapable.

The lost love affair with Tatiana gave rise to two beautiful lyrics, some unfinished poems, and, as he himself put it in a letter to her, much material for further lyrical treatment: ". . . if I were to make a record of all my conversations with myself about you, unwritten letters, unspoken words of love, my collected works would swell to twice their size, and all pure lyricism" (January 3, 1929).[9] The two completed poems, "A Letter to Tatiana Yakovleva" (*Pismo Tatyane Yakovlevoi* 1928) and "A Letter to Comrade Kostrov from Paris on the True Nature of Love" (*Pismo tovarishchu Kostrovu iz Parizha o sushchnosti lyubvi*, 1928), remind us that the affair with Tatiana was in many of its features a re-enactment, supported by poems written in Mayakovsky's own idiom, of Ivan Molchanov's adventure in love, when he exchanged his proletarian inamorata for a love object "fairer and more stately."[10] It is true that Molchanov was explicit in his rejection of the struggle and of girls who were immersed in it, and that there is nothing

[8] On the last days with Polonskaya, see Pertsov, *Mayakovsky, zhizn i tvorchestvo* [III], *V poslednie gody* (Moscow, 1965), 371ff.

[9] Jakobson, "Novye stroki," p. 187.

[10] See above, Chapter Eleven.

like that in Mayakovsky's two poems; yet this sudden eruption of love poems addressed to a "girl from another world" suggests that Mayakovsky was suffering from the same kind of "weakness" that he castigated so severely in Ivan Molchanov. In fact Molchanov seems in retrospect an incarnation of that double of his—"as like me as a twin"—that he discovered among the philistines in *About That.* And I might mention in passing that Tatiana did not command all his affection during his visits to Paris, but was obliged to share him with an object of bourgeois comfort which he described in loving terms in his letters to Lily: a four-cylinder, six-horsepower Renault. "A gray-colored beauty," he called it, and "very appealing."[11] Somewhat uneasy about the purchase of this Parisian beauty for his own personal use in hungry and miserable Russia, he wrote an "Answer to Future Gossip" (*Otvet na budushchie spletni*, 1928)[12] in which he acknowledged the purchase, praised his auto in loving terms, and suggested that, though his "thousands of sleepless lines" gave him a right to it, he would gladly surrender it to the commune if need be. But meanwhile that machine is his thing of pride and glory: "The whole street / falls on its face / When my six beauties / neigh." (47-51)

The "Letter" to Comrade Kostrov, the editor of *Young Guard* and *Young Communist Truth* with whom Mayakovsky worked closely during the last years of his life, marks a new access of poetic energy as well as a return to the old theme of love. But the accent of the poem, rhythmic as well as emotional, is strikingly different from that of his characteristic love lyrics: in its strength and assurance that poem recalls the earlier "I Love You," which expressed a happy moment in the affair with Lily. The regular beat of a predominantly iambic-anapest meter, the unfailing succession of masculine and feminine and dactylic rhymes, the neat epigrammatic quality of almost every stanza—all these formal features give sure support to a series of happy definitions of the state into which the poet has fallen. He begins with an ironic apology to Comrade Kostrov, who had commissioned a certain number of lines on Paris, for the fact that he now "squanders" some of these lines on a lyrical theme. He tells of his meeting with a type clearly Parisian and obviously bourgeois: "Just think: / a real beauty / walks into the hall, / All decked / in furs / and beads." (11-16)

[11] See his letter to Lily Brik in *Literaturnoe nasledstvo*, LXV, 169.
[12] *PSS*, IX, 390.

The rest of the poem takes the form of a series of remarks about love that he addressed to the woman: "I took / that beauty / and I said to her / (Was I right or wrong?) . . ." (16-20)

He introduces himself as a poet "to whom girls are partial"; he is "bright and loudmouthed"; he will "charm you to death" if you will just listen. But he knows all about love: "I'm wounded / for life / by love / I can hardly / drag myself about." (40-43) Then comes the series of metaphoric definitions of the state he is in: love means to chop wood in the yard until the dead of night, "the axe glistening, playing with your strength." It means to get up out of your sleepless bed and "envy Copernicus, considering him your rival, not Maria Ivanovna's husband." Love is a claxon announcing that the heart's "stalled motor" has again set to work. "She" can hardly understand his state of mind:

> You've broken / your tie / to Moscow
> Years have passed— / it's a great distance.
> How could I / explain / the situation?
> On the earth / there are fires—as high as heaven
> In the dark blue sky / there's the devil of a lot /
> of stars. (98-111)

Once again the stars enter Mayakovsky's poetry in a lyrical context. Earth's fires are linked by contiguity to the starry heavens, and love means that one takes in, contemplates (in the last poem he wrote "holds converse with"), the universe itself: "If I were not / a poet / I would become / a stargazer (*zvezdochot*)." (112-116) In his transported state the poet is a hazard to Parisian traffic, but the autos do not run him down for they, too, are sympathetic to his condition: "Good fellows / they understand / The man / is simply ecstatic." (126-129)

He is full of visions and ideas to the very top of his head and when all that comes to a boil in some cheap restaurant, "From my gullet / to the stars / My word shoots up, / a comet born of gold." (142-145) And the effect of viewing such a comet is salubrious for all lovers, and indeed for others too: "To lift up / and lead / and draw on / Those whose eyes have grown tired." (155-158)

The final lines of the poem seem addressed rather to Comrade Kostrov than to Tatiana and have the effect of chiding him (and Mayakovsky himself) for his efforts to domesticate the emotions of one Ivan Molchanov (and of one Vladimir Mayakovsky):

Storm / fire / water
Rush forward rumbling.
Who knows / how / to control them?
You do? / Just try it. . . . (172-180)

The second letter that tells of this love affair was addressed to Tatiana herself, and though it contains the usual sparks of jealousy and frustration, those emotions do not dominate the poem, which is in effect a proposal of marriage, ending on the confident note that some day "I'll take you back with me / alone, or together with Paris."

The poem contains also a statement of his identification with the Soviet Union and its purposes, and an expression of "Soviet patriotism" that would have warmed the red cockles of Comrade Kostrov, and it is certain that Mayakovsky planned to publish the work in Moscow. Tatiana, however, for reasons of her own persuaded him to withhold it, and it remained unpublished and virtually unknown until 1955 when the complete text was published in facsimile by Roman Jakobson, from a copy Tatiana preserved in a notebook Mayakovsky had given her.[13]

His love poem stipulates that the crimson color of his republics must blaze forth in kisses on hand or lip, and even in the body's trembling. It stipulates also that he has no use for Parisian love:

You dress up / some female / in silks—
I nod / and yawn / and say *"tout beau"*
to the hounds / of passion. (11-19)

He then establishes the setting of a quiet *tête-à-tête*:

You're the only one / as tall as I am,
so then stand beside me / brow to brow,
and let's / speak in human fashion
about this / important night. (20-28)

His old jealousy raises its head in the following lines, which allude to a plan of hers to travel to Barcelona, where the singer Chaliapin, whom he suspected of designs on Tatiana, was appearing:

[13] See *Harvard Library Bulletin*, Vol. IX, No. 2, 1955, pp. 285-287. A part of the poem was published, in a version given by Tatiana from memory, in *Novosele*, No. 2, 1942, pp. 57-62. See also Jakobson, "Novye stroki," pp. 173-180.

. . . the peopled city / has died out,
all you can hear / is the whistled argument
of trains to Barcelona. (34-38)

His jealousy of her other affairs appears again in the lines that tell her that her fine legs, which have walked through Russia's snow and typhus, should never be fondled at dinners by oil magnates. But he promises to master his jealousy and love her with a simple love:

The rash of my passion / will disappear in harmless scabs,
but of my joy / inexhaustible / I shall speak
simply and at length / in my verses. (57-63)

The whole gamut of love's pain and anguish he puts behind him: "Jealousy / wives / tears . . . / the hell with it— . . . / It's not me, / I'm jealous / for Soviet Russia." (64-73)

Images of Russia's poverty, disease, and misery are then opposed to the elegance of Parisian females in their "beads, furs, and silks," and there is a reference to Tatiana's own bout with tuberculosis, which had left scars ("patches") on her body: "I've seen / the patches on your shoulders, / The breath / of consumption on them." (74-77) The millions who suffer are his concern, and his suit to Tatiana is only strengthened by the thought that she too could help: "And we need you too / in Moscow, / we don't have enough / long-legged girls." (88-91)

For a moment the curious, puzzled face of Tatiana, doubtful about her lover's invitation to come home to Russia, appears in the poem:

Don't just think about it / screwing up your eyes
under the straightened bows of your eyebrows.
Come here, / come to the crossroads
of my huge / awkward arms. (102-108)

He knows that she is not ready for such a move now, yet he refuses to give up hope:

You don't want to? / Then stay and spend the winter,
and this wound / I'll add to the general account.
But anyway / some day I'll take you back with me
alone / or together with Paris. (111-118)

Of course the day never comes, and in fact, not long after those lines were written, the love he planned to speak about "simply and at length" was irretrievably lost when Tatiana turned her back on both the Soviet Union and Mayakovsky.

The question of Mayakovsky's romance with Tatiana Yakovleva was revived almost forty years later in the Soviet Union with the appearance of the two articles to which I have already referred: "A Poet's Love," and "A Poet's Tragedy," the first written by V. Vorontsov and A. Koloskov, and the second by Koloskov alone.[14] They are evidence that long after his death the patterns of his poetry continue to be repeated in his "red republic," and that Soviet *byt* and the Soviet philistine at last envelop and enshroud the poet. The primary purpose of the two articles was to destroy Lily Brik as the great love of Mayakovsky's life in order to install in her place a "true Russian" girl (not a Jew, of course), Tatiana Yakovleva. Had things worked out right, they say, the great Soviet poet would have repatriated his Russian beauty, married her, and lived with her happily ever after, building "socialism." They quote the artist Lavinskaya on Mayakovsky's need for the tender hand of a "wife and good comrade" who would free him just a little from himself, and they add, "He had hoped to find such a comrade in Tatiana Yakovleva. But someone interfered!"

Who was that someone? Who was the jealous, evil enchantress that spoiled Mayakovsky's chance for family happiness? Who else but Lily Brik? The authors point significantly to the fact that there are no extant letters from Tatiana that would prove her attachment to Mayakovsky, and conjecture: "Some evil hand destroyed those letters."[15] The reference is of course to Lily, with whom he was living at the time of his death, whom he named as a member of his immediate family, who did dispose of his papers and manuscripts and now stands accused of having destroyed Tatiana's letters to him. What machinations did she employ to prevent the wedding in the first place? They hint that she frustrated the plans for a reunion with his beloved in Paris! How? They do not know how, but let them speak for themselves: "Who could have prevented a trip to Paris that was so important for the poet? And isn't it strange that just five months after Mayakovsky was refused a

[14] *Ogonyok*, April 14, 1968; June 1 and June 22, 1968.

[15] *Ibid.*, April 14, p. 12. Tatiana herself supports this version, maintaining that she wrote Mayakovsky regularly during the period in question.

visa the Brik pair set out on a long journey abroad [to England]?"[16]

That, of course, proves nothing (except that the Briks maintained some kind of connection with foreign places—actually, they visited Lily's mother, who lived in England), but it sets up a suspicion in the reader's mind, and in the Soviet environment that is often enough for conviction. Mayakovsky's prediction of the future in the poem *Man* is here realized, not in the details but in the spirit: a dishonest and foolish legend masks the harsh inescapable reality of his life. His love was never satisfied, but a tale is told in its honor that features the cheap claptrap of melodrama: a beautiful and purely Russian girl who had to be rescued from the meshes of the emigration; a true Russian poet who loved her, was loved by her, and wanted to fly to Paris, marry her, and restore her to her native land; a wicked beauty (not really a Russian) with her claws in the poet, who employed her wiles to prevent that trip and that happy ending.

In the second of the two articles, which purports to investigate the poet's death, Lily Brik still figures as the false friend who contrived so much unhappiness for Mayakovsky, but the range of Koloskov's attack has widened to include Osip Brik and many others.

The Briks—Koloskov thinks he has discovered—were the center of a wide-ranging conspiracy against Mayakovsky. He has mined the critical literature of the teens and twenties and found (*horribile dictu!*) that unfriendly reviews, severe criticism, and even outright hostility often greeted Mayakovsky's work. This sort of thing dated back to 1913, he found, but became particularly offensive during the twenties. The inattentive reader—and no doubt many of the readers of *Ogonyok*, which has a circulation of over two million, are uninformed and inattentive—would certainly be left with the impression that the literary world at that time was full of traitors and Trotskyites, all dedicated to destroying a great Soviet poet. "His contemporaries knew," says Kolo-

[16] *Ibid.*, p. 13. The belief is firmly held in some quarters that Brik, through his connections in the GPU, maneuvered the refusal of Mayakovsky's visa, since he had reason to believe that Mayakovsky's marriage would be a distinct loss to both of the Briks. This story has the virtue of plausibility, but it cannot be verified. A version repeated and widely believed in the Soviet Union is that Lily, through her own connections with a GPU official, Yakov Saulovich Agranov, herself brought about the refusal of Mayakovsky's visa. Until documentary evidence is produced we can only withhold judgment.

skov, "that the prototype of Pobedonosikov [in *The Bathhouse*] was L. Trotsky," and of course that is why Trotskyite critics attacked the play. No contemporary or competent person has ever suggested that the erudite, intellectual Trotsky had anything in common with the ignoramus Pobedonosikov, but Koloskov has nonetheless made another telling point. The Briks, the Trotskyites—who else?

Koloskov's article gives a surprisingly complete inventory of negative statements about Mayakovsky's work, though usually without bibliographical references, since his *Ogonyok* readers would not require them. Some of the names are familiar from the critical discussions of the period, others are strange and fortuitous. Lvov-Rogachevsky wrote a criticism of the "Me" cycle in 1914; Yartsev was displeased with the play *Vladimir Mayakovsky*, and wrote about it in the Kadet paper *Speech* (*Rech*) that it was "senseless and vulgar"; one Chunosov wrote of the *Cloud* that it "inspired horror and deep pity"; Ivanov-Razumnik wrote a satiric review of *Mystery-Bouffe*; Zamyatin in his "malicious article" ("I'm Afraid") complained that Mayakovsky was engaged in working out "official topics in official rhythms." Sergei Spassky, Osip Mandelshtam, Kornei Chukovsky, Ilya Ehrenburg, the Marxist critic P. S. Kogan, A. Lezhnyov, who wrote about Mayakovsky and the revived *Lef* under the title "Matter of a Corpse" (Mayakovsky answered, "That's funny. I'm a corpse but he stinks"), Boris Bukhshtab, and many others contributed not criticism of Mayakovsky or a polemic with him but "abuse, lies, and slander." They were "enemies" who never wished him well. Koloskov weightily recalls those lines in *About That* where the poet describes himself as fired upon from every kind of weapon, but now it turns out that these attacks were not from philistines but from critics and Marxist theoreticians of the twenties.

The articles we have examined are intended to leave with the readers of *Ogonyok* the impression that two circumstances adequately account for Mayakovsky's suicide, and that Lily Brik's talk of his "obsession with suicide and fear of old age" must be dismissed. The twin causes of his death were 1) Lily's own frustration of his marriage plans; and 2) the constant attacks upon him in the literary world by "intellectuals" nearly all of whom are now forgotten, suspect, or alien in their mental attitude and writing style, often enough in their strange names. The list of "accessories" to the suicide ranges from Trotsky through the Briks and Lvov-Rogachevsky to Lezhnyov, Shengeli, Averbakh, and Bukhshtab. Koloskov quotes Aseev's query to the poet, "Who did this to you?" and, taking it literally, proposes to find out the criminals. Those primarily responsible, he thinks, were the members of the poet's own circle, the avant-garde critics, poets, and artists with whom Mayakovsky was most closely associated; but apart from them the whole literary and intellectual world of the twenties bears a heavy share of blame.

Who were his true friends? Who else but the ones he once turned to in his extremity, "Mama, Lyuda and Olya?" There were also the friends of his childhood and youth; the friends he acquired doing Party work; and his friends among Georgian writers and artists. These "friends" figure very little in Mayakovsky's literary biography, and Koloskov admits that they were "not favored" in the poet's immediate entourage, where "the chief places were occupied by L. and O. Brik."[17] The articles in *Ogonyok* are late evidence of a competition over the "inheritance" of Mayakovsky between his immediate family and their supporters on the one hand and Lily Brik on the other. His suicide note named the members of his family as "Lily Brik, Mama, my sisters, and Veronika Vitoldovna Polonskaya," and Lily had immediate access to his manuscripts and papers as well as to the literary milieu of which Mayakovsky was a part. His "real" family never forgave her for that, nor ever accepted her as one of themselves. Indeed the alienation of Mayakovsky's mother and sisters from the bohemian intellectuals for whom he left them dates far back, and glints of animosity occasionally appear in the "reminiscences" his relatives wrote.[18] Mayakovsky was sensitive to the strains created by his

[17] *Ogonyok*, June 22, 1968, p. 19.

[18] See, for instance, L. Mayakovskaya, "Vospominaniya," in *Molodaya gvardiya*, December 1963, and February 1937, where resentment of Shklovsky and Livshits appears very clearly.

The contest between Lyudmila Mayakovsky and Lily Brik over the "legacy" of Mayakovsky has to all appearances been settled in the Soviet Union in favor of Lyudmila, who died in 1972. The Mayakovsky Museum and Library that had for many years been located in the apartment near Taganka Place in Moscow once occupied by Mayakovsky and the Briks was closed in 1972, and all its appurtenances, including the excellent library and collection of manuscript materials, were removed to a new "Mayakovsky State Museum" set up in the building on Lyubyansky Place (now Proezd Serova) where the poet maintained an office and where he shot himself. Four floors in that building have been converted into an elaborate and impressive display devoted to every period of the poet's life; the library is located in the same

abandonment of home and "Mama," and the emotional problem the break created was, as we have seen, the theme of "A Few Words About My Mama," which he wrote in 1913. Vorontsov and Koloskov, working closely with Lyudmila Mayakovsky, have made a belated effort to heal an old and inevitable breach, to bring Mayakovsky home from the Brik *ménage à trois* and restore him to his true family and his "real" friends, to rescue him from that degenerate bohemian world "ruled" by Lily Brik and her husband.

The articles in question would waste our time if we used them simply as evidence of the low intellectual and moral state of Soviet mass journalism; as such they are surely redundant. Vorontsov and Koloskov, though never prominent among the Soviet specialists on Mayakovsky (indeed they are "not favored" in that milieu), have worked long and diligently in their efforts to turn up evidence, and their articles do reveal a number of things. Tatiana's letters to her mother (published, of course, without her consent) tell us all we need to know not only about the state of her mind at the time, but also about the real nature of her feeling for Mayakovsky. Moreover, those articles confirm the evidence that the poet was actually refused an exit visa in 1929. And the long recital of negative statements covering Mayakovsky's work drives home the fact that Mayakovsky's agitational verse of the twenties was actually in wide disfavor in the literary world, and that his abandonment of his own metier in favor of steady employment as a purveyor of agitation and propaganda for mass circulation organs such as *Izvestiya* and *Young Communist Truth* had alienated him from a large and probably decisive segment of contemporary Russian literature. His discord with the outstanding poets of his time I have already documented: Pasternak, Mandelshtam, and Akhmatova regarded with shame and distaste his daily labor at the production of *agitki* on any topic assigned to him. They

---

building. The poet's life and work have thus been physically detached from the bohemian ambience of the Briks and all its memories. The director of the new museum, Vladimir Makarov, has worked indefatigably and successfully to discover new materials. He is the author of a recent study of the "real-life" Maria of the poem *A Cloud in Pants*, already mentioned in Chapter Five.

From the point of view of the proletarian revolutionaries Mayakovsky's most dubious characteristic was his "bohemianism," and he himself set himself the task of "burning out his bohemian past." The curators of his image in the Soviet Union have succeeded, many years after his death (which they never refer to as "suicide"), in overcoming that "bohemianism."

walked a thorny path in the Soviet Union, but Mayakovsky prospered and even rode about in a chauffeured Renault. Mayakovsky himself attacked Bulgakov, Zamyatin, and Pilnyak, as we have seen, without mercy, pitching his remarks to the tone of the journalistic campaigns against those writers.[19] He was at odds with Gorky. The leading critics of the day—Voronsky, Lezhnyov, and Polonsky, to name a few—wrote with disdain of his work and of the *Lef* theory that served as its rationalization. The critics of RAPP rejected him as a bohemian intellectual. The "proletarian" poets—Bezymensky, Zharov, Utkin, and others—did not share his ideas about poetry, and his arguments with them over content and method continued until the end of his life. His reliable supporters were the members or close relatives of his own literary group, the *Lef*-ists, Nikolai Aseev, Sergei Tretyakov, Rodchenko, Shklovsky, the Briks, Boris Kushner, S. Kirsanov, V. Pertsov, his old friend Kamensky, and a few others. Yet he succeeded in alienating himself from them, too, as Koloskov has demonstrated, during the last months of his life, when, without consultation or discussion, he abandoned them to join—as an individual—the semi-official Russian Association of Proletarian Writers.

[19] See *PSS*, IX, 48, 148; XII, 43, 301, 304, 331. Pasternak's disagreements with Mayakovsky are referred to in the former's autobiography *I Remember* (New York, 1959), pp. 99-101, and in his letter announcing his final break with *Lef*, which appeared in *Novyi mir*, No. 10, 1964, pp. 195-196.

Chapter Fourteen

THE HEART YEARNS FOR A BULLET

1) The "Note" and the Last Lyrics

On April 14, 1930 in the office he maintained in Lyubyansky Street, Mayakovsky shot himself through the heart. There was only one bullet in the revolver he used, and some of his friends maintained that he played Russian roulette and lost, and that it was not the first time he had played the game. Ilya Ehrenburg in his memoirs accepts this story, reminding us of the poet's passion for gambling, his compulsion to place a bet on any event involving chance—the turn of a card, heads or tails, odd or even.[1] In Russian roulette the significance of the wager is both heightened and confused by the fact that the stake is life itself and that the gambler stands to lose everything or win nothing. And the odds in favor of losing increase drastically each time the gambler plays. The player of Russian roulette, therefore, is actually a suicide who seeks higher sanction for his deed from the turn of chance. The game was congenial to Mayakovsky's psychological makeup, but since he fired the shot in private, there could be no evidence that he actually played it. The fact that there was only one bullet in the revolver proves nothing: only one was needed. And the suicide note, written two days earlier, is clear proof of his intention, this time, to end it all. Here is the note:

To All of You:

Don't blame anyone for my death, and please don't gossip about it. The deceased hated gossip.

Mama, sisters, comrades, forgive me. This is not a good method (I don't recommend it to others), but for me there's no other way out.

Lily, love me.

Comrade Government, my family consists of Lily Brik, Mama, my sisters, and Veronika Vitoldovna Polonskaya.

If you can provide a decent life for them, thank you.

[1] Ilya Ehrenburg, *Lyudi, gody, zhizn* (Moscow, 1961), p. 399.

The verses I have begun give to the Briks. They'll figure them out.

As they say, "The incident is closed."

Love boat
  smashed on convention.
I don't owe life a thing
  and there's no point
in counting over
  mutual hurts,
    harms,
      and slights.

Best of luck to all of you!

Vladimir Mayakovsky
4/12/30

Comrades of the Proletarian Literary Organization, don't think me a coward.

Really, it couldn't be helped.

Greetings!

Tell Yermilov it's too bad he removed the slogan; we should have fought it out.

V. M.

In the desk drawer I have 2,000 rubles. Use them to pay my taxes. The rest can be gotten from the State Publishing House.[2]

The suicide note invites commentary as a literary document that can hardly be understood apart from Mayakovsky's life as a poet; indeed literature and biography are indissolubly linked in this his last production. As a suicide note it is a model of the genre. There is not a scintilla of self-accusation or self-pity in it; neither is there any suggestion that others—the world, society, the government, his friends or enemies—bear any share of blame. Nor is "life" to blame, since the suicide, having paid his own debts (including some taxes due the state!) refuses to count over any that may be owed to him. The quiet tone and gentle ironies of this last "poem" are, paradoxically, in happy contrast to the manic-depressive poetry of his earliest period, the great revolutionary songs of the twenties, *Lenin* and *Very Good!*, or the hopeless invocation of the future that we find in *About That*, or *At the Top*

[2] The full text of the note, together with a photographic reproduction, is given in *Literaturnoe nasledstvo*, LXV, 199.

of My Voice. The poet has at last reached a place of rest; he is calm and self-possessed; and though almost all his other poems express a towering and intransigent egotism, in this one he attends entirely to "others": Lily Brik, Mama, his sisters, Polonskaya, his new "comrades" of RAPP, even the doctrinaire ignoramus who had caused him grief in connection with his play *The Bathhouse*, the critic Yermilov. And he even shows concern that his survivors have at hand the money to pay his income tax, a considerable sum, incidentally.[3]

The note is a kind of recapitulation of his life and work, composed during a period of deep peace induced by the decision to "put a period to his line with a bullet." It powerfully recalls the lover of the *Cloud* who turned in his extremity to his mother and sisters with the message that he had no way out (*emu nekuda detsya*), as well as the young man in *About That* who, with a love song on his lips, shot himself and left a note: "Please don't blame anyone." The last, simple plea, "Lily, love me" reminds us of his major lyric poems, all of which were dedicated to Lily Brik, a woman who did not love him. The friendly and familiar address to his "Comrade Government" reminds that body of the enormous poetic service he had performed, and he seems quietly confident that the debt will be repaid and that Lily and his family, as well as Polonskaya, will not want. There is no suggestion in the note that he is at odds with the Soviet government, however impatient he may have been for the future it promised. In writing his note, he first used the formal pronoun in addressing that august body, but then crossed it out and wrote the familiar *ty*;[4] thus the Soviet government, like the sun, and Pushkin, and other remarkable things he dealt with in his poetry, is made to stand on easy terms with the poet, Mayakovsky.

Like the lad in *About That*, he died with a kind of love song on his lips. The four lines of poetry included in the note are part of a lyric poem he had been working on during the last weeks of his life, supposedly a second, lyrical introduction to a poem about the First Five-Year Plan. The verses we have already met in chapter one under the title *At the Top of My Voice* are an introduction to that poem; and they are not even the whole introduc-

[3] One of the stories that circulated in Moscow after the suicide was that the "man on the street" couldn't understand such a thing. "What? two thousand rubles in his drawer and he kills himself?"

[4] *Literaturnoe nasledstvo, loc. cit.*

tion but only the first part of it. *At the Top of My Voice* is a "civic" poem, boldly declaring Communist beliefs and presenting the poet as an agitator and a rabble rouser. Apparently there was to have been a second introduction, and the few fragments found in the poet's papers after his death reveal that the Mayakovsky of the second introduction was to have been a lyric instead of a civic poet, as soft and tender, indeed, as a cloud in pants. Those fragments deal chiefly with love, and fall into three parts:[5] eleven lines on the theme "She loves me, she loves me not," the twelve-line poem "It's After One," together with some lines either discarded or reworked, and eleven lines that begin "I know the power of words." The first two parts are of special interest because of their connection with the suicide note itself.

> She loves me, she loves me not? I wring my hands.
> My fingers I tear apart having wrung them.
> Thus people pluck off petals of daisies,
> trying to find out, and then drop them onto the winds
> of May.
> Let the scissors and the razor expose my gray hairs.
> Let the silver of my years ring out in their throng;
> I hope I trust that never ever
> will your shameful common sense ever come to me.

The fragment is especially interesting as a bold vindication of the poet's anti-rational, emotional self. It revives a recurrent image, first used in the *Me* cycle of 1913, the hands wrung in agony, and appropriates from that same poem the daisy whose petals, when plucked, tell of the lover's fate. It confirms other evidence that the poet was acutely conscious—at thirty-seven—of his advancing age, and tells of his determination never to succumb to the concomitant of old age, reasonableness.

The second fragment contains in one of its variants the two lines:

> The sea draws back
> The sea goes off to sleep

and those lines remind us one final time of the overwhelming presence in Mayakovsky's poetry of water imagery and its connection with the theme of death and disappointed love. The lines suggest, moreover, the ebbing of all the forces of life that once

[5] *PSS*, x, 286-287.

surged in the poet, and they are a clear warning that death may not be far off.

That second fragment of twelve lines is in its final form one of Mayakovsky's most tender and moving lyric poems:

It's after one.
  You must have gone to bed.
The Milky Way runs like a silvery river through the night.
I'm in no hurry
  and with lightning telegrams
there's no need to wake and worry you.
As they say
  the incident is closed
The love boat
  has smashed against convention
Now you and I are through
  No need then
To count over mutual hurts, harms, and slights.
Just see how quiet the world is!
Night has laid a heavy tax of stars upon the sky.
In hours like these you get up and you speak
To the ages, to history, and to the universe.

As we have seen, he included four lines from this poem in the suicide note, with the change of "you" to "life." The "love boat smashed against convention" is in its form and rhythm a mock-sentimental phrase, but in its content deeply personal and very serious. The "love boat" is more than a metaphor of love's fragile passage over rough seas and among threatening obstacles; it is also a reference to Mayakovsky's office on the Lyubyanka, which he always referred to as a boat; "love boat" (*lyubovnaya lodka*) surely suggests his "Lyubyanka-boat." The "convention" against which it has broken is Mayakovsky's old enemy, *byt*, in this case the ingrained habits and encrusted prejudice that, as he believed, had doomed his romance with Tatiana Yakovleva. But that incident is now "closed"—and here the poet develops a neat pun, using the word *izperchen* (over-peppered), instead of *izcherpan* (closed), thus attaining the superior stance of humorous detachment toward his latest misadventure. Mutual pain there had been, but the poet is both beyond and above blaming anyone for that. Indeed the magnificent simile that contemplates the Milky Way as the heavenly reflection of a Central Russian river (the Oka) whose broad, slow stream flows through the night, raises the level of the lyric to the contemplation of the mysterious reality of the universe itself. The stars are as essential to his poem now as they were when he wrote "Listen!" in 1914, and the tone of this last lyric repeats the stillness in the last lines of the *Cloud*:

> The universe is asleep
> its huge ear,
> star-infested,
> rests on a paw.

The wild torment of his life is now almost over, and after the end of love's manic exercise with its lightning-like wires and its implacable and unsatisfied demand ("Why didn't you fix it / so that one could, without torment / just kiss and kiss and kiss?!") the poet is ready for quiet converse with "the ages, history, and the universe."

2) The Final Depression

The note refers to certain events of the last few months in his life that, along with the disappointment of his love for Tatiana, helped to deepen his mood of despair. We have not commented on the presence of Veronika Polonskaya among the members of his "family." She was an actress whom he met not long after the end of the affair with Tatiana Yakovleva and who attracted him because she reminded him of Tatiana. The attraction developed into an emotional involvement—on his part—of serious proportions, and Valentin Kataev, who entertained both of them at a supper the night before the suicide, describes Mayakovsky's behavior then as that of a man "in love, passionately, openly, honestly," though he adds the cautionary statement that "perhaps he was only sick, and couldn't control his feelings." Indeed he was ill during that spring, and constantly complained of "the grippe." Kataev describes Polonskaya, known to her familiars as "Nora":

> . . . she was quite young, charming, blonde, with dimples on pink cheeks, wearing a tight knitted blouse with short sleeves, also pale pink—a kind of jersey that lent her the aspect of a young sportswoman, a ping-pong champion among beginners, rather than an actress of the second rank in the Moscow Art Theater.

The scene that developed on that occasion between them Kataev characterizes as a kind of "love duel" (we recall the duel in *About That*), carried on in a silent exchange of notes: "With a somewhat frightened smile she wrote, on little pieces of cardboard broken off a candy box, answers to Mayakovsky's notes, which he tossed across the table to her with the gesture of a roulette player." They went off into a separate room together, and continued the mute exchange of written messages: "He made demands. She refused. She made demands. He wouldn't agree. It was the eternal love duel." The floor afterward was littered with little scraps of paper.[6]

Veronika Polonskaya was the last person, as far as we know, to see the poet alive, and she has left a kind of diary concerning his final days that has not yet been published, though some of her comments appear in the third volume of Pertsov's work.[7] According to her account, they had agreed to meet in his office on Lyubyansky Street on the morning of April 14. It is obvious from the distracted and sometimes unintelligible jottings he had prepared for a meeting two days earlier that their affair was not progressing smoothly, that he was irritated, angry, and demanding, and although he underlined in that note the statement that his grief was not caused by jealousy, yet he obviously felt that her behavior had placed him in a ridiculous situation.[8] She recalled that he was in a very bad frame of mind; he was sick, and he demanded that she stay with him and not even leave the room. But she was on her way to a rehearsal at the Art Theater, and would not think of being late for it. Nor would she consider giving up her work in the theater. Here is what she supposedly said in her memoirs:

> That would have caused difficulty for him first of all. Once you've known work as interesting as being an actress in the Art Theater, it would be impossible just to be your husband's wife, even the wife of such a great man as Mayakovsky. . . .
>
> . . . I left, and walked a few steps toward the front door. There was a shot. I almost fell in a faint. I screamed and rushed along the corridor. I couldn't bring myself to open the door. . . .[9]

So much for the last of Mayakovsky's luckless affairs.

[6] V. Kataev, "Trava zabveniya," *Novyi mir*, No. 3, 1967, p. 111.

[7] Pertsov, *Mayakovsky, zhizn i tvorchestvo* [III], *V poslednie gody*, 372-373.

[8] *Ibid.*

[9] *Ibid.*, p. 374.

The suicide note at first closed with the lyrical lines that we have already examined. Then he wrote the farewell greeting, both old-fashioned and ironical, which I have translated "Best of luck to all of you," a greeting used by a traveller departing on a long journey that means literally "May those who remain behind be happy." Then he had an afterthought that is very significant since it reveals one of the worries that plagued him during the last month of his life. He sent greetings to RAPP (Russian Association of Proletarian Writers), and specifically to his enemy Yermilov. The reference recalls his entrance into RAPP and all the unhappy circumstances attending it, just two months before his suicide. Mayakovsky had for many years carried on a violent polemic with the leaders of RAPP, whose literary doctrines favored the revival of Tolstoyan realism and psychological probing of what they called "the living man," and even his last play, *The Bathhouse*, contains satiric references to the theories dominant in that organization. The "slogan" referred to in the letter was one of many agitational verses with which the auditorium was decorated during the performance of that play, and was a personal attack on one of the leaders of RAPP:

> It isn't easy to clean out
>   the bureaucratic swarm.
> There aren't enough baths
>   nor is there soap enough
> And these bureaucrats
>   are given aid and comfort by critics
>   like Yermilov.[10]

At the insistence of the proletarian literary leadership, the slogan was removed from the hall. It was actually an answer to an article Yermilov had published in *Pravda*, after having read only part of the play, attacking it as an expression of a false and petty-bourgeois "leftishness" characteristic of "intellectuals" who had lately joined the proletariat.[11] We need not be concerned with the dismal polemic that raged briefly around Yermilov's doctrinaire pronouncements.[12]

Mayakovsky's entrance into RAPP involved the abandonment of his former comrades of *Lef*, as well as of their doctrines; it

[10] *PSS*, xi, 350.
[11] *Pravda*, March 9, 1930.
[12] *Vechernyaya Moskva*, March 13, 1930, and March 17, 1930.

aroused the anger of some and alienated almost all of them. His motivation for the action he took is not difficult to establish, and there is evidence, moreover, that he was disenchanted with the group that surrounded him even before he finally left them.

Valentin Kataev's reminiscences throw unexpected light on the state of affairs within the *Lef* milieu at this time, and on Mayakovsky's relationships with his former comrades. Kataev reports that when he was arranging to invite certain people to spend the evening with Mayakovsky and himself, Mayakovsky expressed strong distaste for most of his consorts of *Lef*, suggesting that they not be invited:

> It was hard to see what guided him in his selection [of *invitées*]. I was surprised that he rejected some of his generally acknowledged friends and comrades of *Lef*, and did so with an expression, I would say, of violent disgust: "O to hell with him!"
>
> Such was also the fate of a poet of another camp, who called me on the phone. "Don't invite him," Mayakovsky growled, and turned his back to the phone.[13]

At this point Kataev gives voice to his own distaste for the *Lef*-ists, which he ascribes, perhaps with some justice, to Mayakovsky also. He describes them, not quite fairly, as a coterie of mediocre hangers-on who clung to Mayakovsky like barnacles to a ship and through him found an undeserved place for themselves in literature: "He was in despair. He didn't know how to get rid of them, of all those homebred '*Lef*-ists,' those illiterate and self-assured theoreticians, who sucked their theory of literature out of high-school textbooks.[14]

It is impossible to say with certainty to whom Kataev may be referring, but certain specific comments seem directed at Shklovsky and Brik. We know, of course, that Brik was Mayakovsky's principal theoretical guide and literary mentor, and we know also that it was at Brik's suggestion that he sometimes modified his verses. Brik is the one who urged him to exclude from the poem "Homeward!" its wonderful concluding lines because they were "out of phase" with the poem as a whole.[15] Kataev refers to that episode, and probably to Brik, though he does not mention him by name. Mayakovsky, says Kataev, had at last asserted his inde-

[13] Kataev, p. 103.
[14] *Ibid.*, p. 104.
[15] See above, Chapter Ten.

pendence of all the pseudo-learned guidance to which he had so long been enslaved:

> A time of great changes had begun for him with the return of his inner freedom and of spiritual confidence. He no longer had to "step on the throat of his own song" to satisfy somebody's invented theory of literature, and strike out of his verses such powerful fragments as:
>
> I want my country to understand me,
> but if it doesn't—what of it?
> I will pass by my native land to the side
> as a slanting rain passes.[16]

Osip Brik's role in the final episodes of Mayakovsky's life is clouded, but some things are fairly certain. When, in the latter part of 1928, disagreement developed between the editors of *New Lef* and Mayakovsky, he withdrew from the magazine and in a speech entitled "More Left than *Lef*" he publicly dissociated himself from the critical theories espoused by Brik and his followers. He rehabilitated traditional art in the phrase "I've granted Rembrandt an amnesty." The *Lef* theories on "fixation of fact," the "social demand," and so on he rejected with the announcement that "we need poetry and song too, and not just the newspaper," and that "not every boy who can work a camera and take a picture of something is a *Lef*-ist."[17] The amnesty granted Rembrandt (a painter of the realist school, incidentally) had less immediate consequence than the meed of praise awarded somewhat later to Fadeev, one of the leaders of RAPP and a theoretician of the "back to Tolstoy" movement in the literature of the time. Osip Brik, as we have seen, had published in an early issue of *New Lef* a contemptuous critique of Fadeev's novel *The Rout* under the title "Fadeev's Rout," in which he rejected that work as an arid imitation of dead literary styles. But now Mayakovsky avers that " 'Fadeev's *Rout*' is more important for us than the notes of that factographer Isadora Duncan," thus associating Brik with the famous dancer whose book of reminiscences *My Life* had just appeared in a Russian translation.

[16] Kataev, p. 104.
[17] Pertsov, [III], 353; *PSS*, XII, 503-507.

The evidence is scant at this point, but it would seem that Brik adjusted to the new situation with his usual agility. Shklovsky is reported to have said that if they ever cut off Brik's legs he would simply say that he found it more convenient that way.[18] When Mayakovsky showed dangerous symptoms of breaking free of the theories Brik had developed and propounded, Brik proceeded to modify those theories, and since *Lef* was clearly doomed by Mayakovsky's defection, to work out the framework of a new organization. According to Pertsov's testimony (admittedly not always a sure guide), Brik was the one who broached to Pertsov the idea that a simple change of the letter L to R (for revolutionary) would preserve the essentials of the group while adjusting to new demands. "With a mysterious look he told me that he proposed to change the letter 'L' to 'R.' He proceeded to explain to me the necessity of transforming *Lef* into *Ref* (Revolutionary Front of Art), and he explained the difference quite subtly . . . pointing out that the designation 'Left,' [in the name *Lef*] had to do mainly with questions of form."[19]

The new organization was duly formed, and was accepted into the Federation of Soviet Writers[20] during the summer of 1929. Not all the former members of *Lef* joined Mayakovsky and Brik in *Ref*; Shklovsky, Chuzhak, Tretyakov, and some others who had been prominent in *Lef* do not appear as members of the new organization. In his public statements on the role of *Ref*, Mayakovsky tried to salvage as much as possible of the literary experience of innovation that the futurists had accumulated over the years, but he clearly capitulated to the contemporary demand for an art intelligible to the masses, and free of strangeness and "difficulty." He proposed, in fact, to combat those "apolitical and aesthetic tendencies" that had been present in *Lef* and to place political action and social purpose in the forefront of the artists' attention. "We insist," he said, "on the primacy of purpose over both form and content."[21]

Mayakovsky's last days are marked by frequent statements on the need for contact with the masses and work in the mass organizations of literature. There is no doubt that he felt his own increasing isolation and sensed the cloud of disapproval that in

18 Pertsov [III], 352. See Shklovsky, *Tretya fabrika* (Moscow, 1926), p. 62.
19 *Ibid.*
20 On the "Federation" see Brown, *The Proletarian Episode*, pp. 48ff.
21 *PSS*, XII, 510-511.

fact hung over him. Yet each effort of his to break out of his little group and enter the main stream of Soviet literature led, paradoxically, to an even greater isolation. He lost friends and supporters when he abandoned *Lef* and formed his new and more "revolutionary" *Ref*. He alienated those who had loyally followed him into the new organization when he organized an exhibit devoted to himself alone and called "Twenty Years of Work." This seems in retrospect to have been a pathetic exercise in ego-exaltation, a mistaken effort to demonstrate something already well enough known, namely that Mayakovsky had performed yeoman service for the Soviet state. The exhibit was organized in the name of *Ref*, but almost all its members boycotted Mayakovsky's elaborate self-display, as did other writers of the day, and representatives of publishing houses and writers' organizations. Aseev and Kirsanov both objected that if an exhibit were to be organized, it should include the work of the Left Front of Art as a whole, not of just one poet, and Mayakovsky's insistence on exhibiting only his own work led to an angry and fatal split with some of his oldest and closest friends. While the exhibit was in progress Mayakovsky applied for admission to RAPP and was accepted. He brought some of his new comrades of RAPP with him to the exhibit, and they were photographed with him there: Fadeev, Stavsky, and Surkov.[22] With his entry into RAPP the last tie binding him to former associates was broken. And only dismal reproval and "re-education" awaited him in RAPP itself.

Aseev wrote a moving and sympathetic account of the quarrel that developed between Mayakovsky and his friends as a result of his entering RAPP:

> I saw him alive for the last time on Friday, April 11. I must say that shortly before that we had our first and only quarrel[23] —because he left *Ref* to join RAPP without any preliminary agreement with the other members of our association. This seemed to us arbitrary and undemocratic; to tell the truth we felt ourselves abandoned in a kind of thicket of contradictions.

[22] On the exhibit see S. Kovalenko, "20 let raboty Mayakovskogo," *Voprosy literatury*, No. 4, 1963, pp. 95-102; Pertsov [III], 356-357; A. G. Bromberg, "Vystavka 'dvadtsat let raboty'" in *V. Mayakovsky v vospominaniyakh sovremennikov*, pp. 549-577.

[23] This is not quite accurate. Mayakovsky and his friends had quarreled over the exhibit of his works.

Where should we go? What should we do next? And Mayakovsky's responsibility for not having worked out these problems irritated and annoyed us. . . .

And so all his former associates of *Lef*, whom he had later taken into *Ref*, rebelled against his individualistic moves, and we decided to make Mayakovsky understand that we didn't approve of his dissolving *Ref* and entering RAPP without his comrades. . . .[24]

Mayakovsky's comrades were rightly indignant at his action. It seemed to them a betrayal. The official literary "line" of RAPP—the revival of classical realism and the creation of a "new Leo Tolstoy"—had long been the target of their scornful polemical articles, and RAPP's doctrinaire insistence on "proletarian" background and orthodox views tended to set Mayakovsky and his comrades beyond the pale of the Communist literary world. For many years *Lef* had been carrying on a brave struggle against the sloganized literary dictates of RAPP in favor of formal innovation and experiment. Suddenly their eminent leader, without consulting any of them, had capitulated. Why?

The answer to that question requires some reference to the literary situation of the day. The year 1930 was crucial and tragic in the history of Soviet literature. The relative freedom and variety of the twenties had been eroded, and the political climate had become cold to difference and dispute. "Consolidation of literary forces" for the attainment of political and economic ends had become the official policy toward the end of 1929, and consolidation meant organizational unity as well as ideological conformity. The final organizational "reform" that was to bring all writers into one big union was still two years ahead, but 1930 saw the absorption by RAPP of many formerly independent groups and individuals.[25] In December 1929 an editorial in *Pravda* asserted that RAPP was carrying on a line in literature "closest" to the line of the Party, and from this drew the conclusion that all "proletarian" literary forces should close ranks around RAPP. The article expressed suspicion of the fact that Marxists

[24] V. *Mayakovsky v vospominaniyakh sovremennikov*, pp. 395-396.

[25] On this process see Brown, *The Proletarian Episode*, pp. 96-105; and E. J. Brown "The Year of Acquiescence," in *Literature and Revolution in Soviet Russia, 1917-1962* (London, 1963), pp. 44-61.

were broken up into "competing groups" and that these groups not only disagreed but fought one another violently. The immediate result of the article was the dampening down of controversy in the literary field. The "consolidation of forces" meant in practice that many writers and critics from groups previously hostile to RAPP now joined it, ostensibly of their own accord. Mayakovsky was one of them.

Brik may have had a hand in that decision, too. Writing of this period ten years later, he opined that "*Ref* had become an anachronism" after the publication of the "consolidation of forces" policy, and that Mayakovsky had simply drawn the inescapable conclusion.[26]

Mayakovsky's action was certainly in part a response to the new policy announced in the *Pravda* editorial, but it was also the result of a complex set of pressures. His official entry into RAPP took place on February 6 at a meeting of the Moscow branch of the Association held in the building on Vorovsky Street that housed his one-man exhibition. But the announcement of adherence to RAPP read at that meeting had been written earlier and is actually dated January 3, 1930. It has been suggested that this was a mistake and that he meant to write February 3, but that is unlikely and in any case there is other evidence that he reached his decision soon after the publication of the editorial in *Pravda* referred to above. Libedinsky, one of the leaders of RAPP, claimed in his volume of reminiscences *Contemporaries* (*Sovremenniki*) that Mayakovsky had decided to enter RAPP late in 1929. Sutyrin, a secretary of RAPP, said that Mayakovsky had first announced his intention of joining early in January, but that nothing could be done about it then because a number of key officials of RAPP were absent from Moscow.[27] The announcement of his intention to join RAPP reveals in its language that this action was an answer to the call for a "consolidation of forces":

> In order to realize in practice the slogan for the consolidation of all the forces of proletarian literature, I request that I be accepted as a member of RAPP.

[26] Osip Brik, "Mayakovsky redaktor i organizator," *Literaturnyi kritik*, No. 4, 1936, p. 145.

[27] *PSS*, XIII, 350.

(1) I have not, and have never had, any disagreements as to the literary-political line of the Party, which is being carried out by RAPP.

(2) Stylistic and methodological differences can be resolved with benefit for proletarian literature within the Association.

I believe that all active members of *Ref* should draw the same conclusion that I have drawn, a conclusion dictated by all our previous history.

V. Mayakovsky[28]

The date of this document, January 3, 1930, presents an interesting problem. Why was there a delay of more than a month in accepting Mayakovsky into RAPP? Why should there have been any delay in acknowledging the capitulation of a powerful adversary? Sutyrin's explanation does not fully cover the case. There is evidence, moreover, that the bureaucrats in control of RAPP were afraid of the poet and did not very much want him in their organization, since his entrance, along with many others, might have threatened to upset the balance of power within the Association.[29] There is also evidence that Mayakovsky himself forced their hand. The evidence in question is Libedinsky's account of how Mayakovsky became a member of RAPP on February 6, 1930:

In February 1930 I arrived at a conference of RAPP, and at the door Sutyrin, a member of the secretariat, met me. . . . He looked a little bit upset. "I have to consult you on one question," he said. "You know, Mayakovsky is here and he says he's going to speak now and announce he's joining RAPP. I said I'd have to consult with some of my colleagues, with Fadeev or Libedinsky. . . ."

"What is there to consult about?" I asked, though I was myself somewhat upset. I rejoiced at the entrance of Mayakovsky into RAPP, but for me, too, it was somewhat unexpected. . . .

The leaders of RAPP looked upon Mayakovsky's adherence with a kind of worry. It was as though we were concerned lest our weak vessel be hurt by the weight of such an elephant. . . .[30]

[28] *PSS*, XIII, 134.

[29] On the struggle in progress at that time for control of RAPP see Brown, *The Proletarian Episode*, pp. 150-172.

[30] Yurii Libedinsky, *Sovremenniki* (Moscow, 1958), p. 173.

Libedinsky admits that Mayakovsky was not warmly welcomed into RAPP, and that in this mass organization he felt isolated and alone. His comrades of *Ref* did not join him and he had no new friends in RAPP. "I know," said Libedinsky, "that from February until April 1930 the secretariat of RAPP constantly hauled Mayakovsky over the coals—and in a trivial and didactic fashion. . . ."

The account in the *Literary Gazette* of February 10, 1930, of the meeting at which Mayakovsky joined RAPP bears out Libedinsky's memory of the cold reception accorded the poet. From the moment of his entry until his suicide, the "secretariat" of that organization occupied itself with "re-educating" him in the spirit of proletarian ideology and literature, a truly depressing experience. Some people recalled that on the eve of his suicide, already cut off from friends and collaborators of long standing, he was in a state of defenseless misery as a result of his sessions with the talentless dogmatists and petty literary tyrants whose organization he had joined.[31] Shklovsky's memory of the last days is especially poignant:

> I saw him for the last time in the House of Writers on Vorovsky Street. . . .
>
> I was sitting there talking to Lev Nikulin about Paris.
>
> One RAPP-ist passed us, then another. They had briefcases. They'd come to discuss their RAPP-ist business. They'd come to re-educate Mayakovsky. Vladimir came over and stopped for a moment. He began to talk. He had words of praise for the communal life, in which at first he didn't believe. It seems they'd convinced him.
>
> He told us wearily about the little box where the money is put and everyone takes as much as he needs. Nikulin answered with a joke. Mayakovsky didn't argue. He just smiled and followed the RAPP-ists into another room.[32]

His capitulation to RAPP was probably the one event that made his suicide inevitable. His motive was to establish himself firmly in a mass organization, break out of the isolation of *Lef* and *Ref*, acquire new and powerful allies, and thus combat the hostility that he felt around him and that was so clearly demonstrated at

[31] Pertsov [III], 350.

[32] As quoted in Katanyan, *Khronika*, p. 419.

his last recital. Some advantages did accrue to him. The leaders of RAPP paid a visit to his exhibit. A portion of his last poem *At the Top of My Voice* was published in the RAPP journal *On Literary Guard* (*Na literaturnom postu*), though the editors made a curious slip in mis-titling it *At Full Gallop* (*Vo ves galop*, instead of *Vo ves golos*). The manuscript of his play *The Bathhouse* had been held up for two months by *Glavrepertkom*, the chief committee on the repertory of Soviet theaters, because of its sharply satirical attacks on contemporary personalities and tendencies and on the bureaucratic nature as exhibited in recognizable commissar types. Some of these barbs were softened at the behest of *Glavrepertkom*, and permission to produce the play was finally granted on February 9, just three days after Mayakovsky joined RAPP. There may have been a connection between the two events.

But the cost to Mayakovsky was far too great. By April 1930 he was a psychological bankrupt, and the suicidal tendencies that had always been present in him met no resistance. There was no way out. "Really, comrades."

The cloud that had been settling over Mayakovsky's reputation during the last years of his life was not dispelled by his senseless death. During the early thirties his work was neglected and his example as a poet-agitator not always held in high esteem. An examination of the library holdings of the Mayakovsky Museum in Moscow reveals that in the first four years after his suicide articles and books about him were rather sparse. The *Collected Works* begun before his death appeared slowly and desultorily, and was completed, with no particular fanfare, only in 1933. The poet's friends and literary colleagues had reason to believe that, in spite of his immense service to the Soviet state, he might sink into something like official oblivion.

All that ended in 1935. We recall that in the poem "Homeward!" Mayakovsky expressed the ultimate hope of an anti-poet, that Stalin should read reports on verse-making along with his reports on the production of pig-iron and steel. It was therefore an appropriate irony that the coarse dictator and enemy of poets himself rescued Mayakovsky's reputation, made sure that he would not be forgotten, and in fact initiated the cult of collective worship that raised Mayakovsky onto the pedestal he occupies. That curious development involved not only Stalin, but Osip and Lily Brik, the bolshevik political leader Bukharin, and, as a peripheral and passive but important figure, the poet Boris Pasternak.

Bukharin read a report on Soviet poetry at the First Congress of Soviet Writers in 1934 that though not directly downgrading Mayakovsky, tended to deplore the influence on certain other poets of his agitational style. At the same time Bukharin paid tribute to Pasternak as a superlative poetic craftsman; in fact a tendency developed, as Pasternak himself later put it, to "inflate" his importance.[1] Osip and Lily Brik could only view such a turn of affairs with alarm: the elevation of Pasternak lent prestige to an uninvolved poet who had expressed scorn for *Lef* and its ideas; moreover, this was a clear threat to the value of the legacy Lily had inherited from her lover (remember his farewell letter). But the Briks were resourceful, and they had excellent connections in

[1] Pasternak, *I Remember*, p. 101.

the Party. They had no intention of seeing the enemies of Mayakovsky win the day.

According to Hugo Huppert, a German radical who knew all the major figures well (and his version is amply supported by other authorities), Brik himself composed for Stalin's perusal a complaint over the neglect of Mayakovsky that contained the phrase "Mayakovsky was and remains the best and most talented poet of our Soviet epoch."[2] Osip and Lily managed to deliver this statement to Stalin personally, and they found in him a sympathetic listener to their grievance over the neglect of Mayakovsky. In fact, he accepted Brik's formulation of the matter, adding to it his own ominous phrase, "Indifference to his memory and his works is a crime." Thus that famous Stalinist evaluation of Mayakovsky, which until Stalin's own disgrace in the mid-fifties was repeated *ad nauseam* in books and articles about the poet, was actually the joint product of Stalin and Osip Brik. But it was Stalin alone who introduced the idea that the neglect of Mayakovsky was a *crime*. And that statement was given prominent space in the newspaper *Pravda*.

After that there was no lack of attention to Mayakovsky's work. The Soviet presses began turning out a plethora of books and articles about the poet, as well as new and large editions of his works. Readers were reminded constantly that he was a "patriot," a "citizen," a "poet of the revolution." There were hundreds of articles whose titles are a litany-like repetition of all his civic attributes. A thousand times Brik's words, "was and remains," "the best and most talented," were hammered into the consciousness of the Soviet reader. Squares and streets were named in Mayakovsky's honor. Statues of him proliferated in parks and public buildings. Subway stations were called "Mayakovsky," as were trawlers, tractors, mine-sweepers, and tanks. In Pasternak's scornful phrase, he was "propagated compulsorily, like potatoes in the reign of Catherine the Great." His lifelong mortal enemy, *byt*, had enshrined him.

[2] Hugo Huppert, *Erinnerungen an Majakowskij* (Frankfurt am Main, 1966), p. 141.

Bibliographical Essay

The material on the subject of this work is so abundant that a simple listing, even a highly selective one, would scarcely help the reader find his way in the maze of pre-Soviet, Soviet, and western literature. Therefore it has seemed preferable to present here a critical guide, under a number of headings, to the most important items. Except for the various editions of the poet's collected works, which are given in chronological order, the items discussed under each heading are given in what seems to the author their order of importance.

1) Collected Works

The first nearly complete collection of Mayakovsky's works, *Sobranie sochinenii*, in ten volumes, was begun in 1927 and completed in 1933. It omitted many things, but has special interest as an edition the poet himself had a hand in preparing. In many ways the most valuable edition is the *Polnoe sobranie sochinenii Mayakovskogo* (Moscow, 1934-1938) in twelve volumes, edited by Lily Brik. This contains especially interesting annotation and some excellent essays on certain aspects of Mayakovsky's work—for instance one by Nikolai Aseev on the composition of the poem *Pro eto*. A second *Polnoe sobranie sochinenii* (Moscow, 1939-1949), also in twelve volumes, contains some material not in the first and some useful information. The most complete available edition is *Polnoe sobranie sochinenii* (Moscow, 1955-1961), in thirteen volumes, which has good annotation, excellent coverage of variants, and much material from Mayakovsky's pen that is not to be found in earlier editions.

2) Bibliographies

A very useful bibliography of works about Mayakovsky is Gerald Darring, "Mayakovsky: A Bibliography of Criticism (1912-1930)," in *Russian Literature Triquarterly*, No. 2, Winter 1972, p. 510. This work includes no critical material published since Mayakovsky's death, but it is very complete (605 items) for the period covered. It also provides a listing of some basic bibliographical sources.

V. Sillov and P. Neznamov, "Materialy k bibliografii Mayakovskogo" appeared in *V. V. Mayakovsky; sobranie sochinenii*, Volume I (Moscow, 1928), pp. 337-356. It has many defects, but is invaluable for the record of early criticism, and for the account of Mayakovsky's publications in various collections (*sborniki*) and in periodical publications.

A chronological account of critical literature with brief annotation is L. M. Polyak and N. V. Reformatskaya, "Iz bibliografii kriticheskoi literatury o Mayakovskom (1918-1936)," *Literaturnyi kritik*, No. 4, 1936, pp. 244-262.

A bibliography of Mayakovsky's works in all genres is included in *Polnoe sobranie sochinenii v 12-ti tomakh*, Volume XII (Moscow, 1949), pp. 123-198. This bibliography was compiled by Polyak and Reformatskaya, with assistance from N. Khardzhiev.

We are still not served well with bibliographies of critical materials published in the Soviet Union since 1936, or of works on the poet published outside the Soviet Union in various languages. Many of the books we will mention here contain useful bibliographies of such materials; for example, Vladimir Markov, *Russian Futurism; a History* (Berkeley, 1968) contains the most complete bibliography of the futurist movement, and an excellent selection of articles and books on Mayakovsky. Needless to say, footnotes to the various chapters of the present book contain references to materials in several languages and from all periods.

3) Biographies

The most complete record of Mayakovsky's life is V. Katanyan, *Mayakovsky, literaturnaya khronika*, 4th ed. (Moscow, 1961). Mayakovsky's activities are listed here day by day in chronological sequence, with generous selections from journalistic accounts and from criticism. The book must be used with great caution, however, since the materials are selected and edited with a view to presenting Mayakovsky in a consistently favorable light. Negative statements concerning his work are as a rule not allowed to appear.

V. O. Pertsov's three-volume treatment of the poet, which appeared between 1951 and 1969, is an ambitious effort conceived and executed in a hagiographical spirit. It deals with all the important acts and words of Mayakovsky. In the discussion of the poem *Man* in Chapter Five, I have dealt at length with Pertsov's critical method. The three volumes are:

Mayakovsky, zhizn i tvorchestvo do velikoi oktyabrskoi sotsialisticheskoi revolyutsii (Moscow, 1951; 2nd ed., 1969).
Mayakovsky, zhizn i tvorchestvo, Volume II (Moscow, 1958).
Mayakovsky, zhizn i tvorchestvo v poslednie gody (1925-1930) (Moscow, 1965).

Much information on the life of Mayakovsky is contained in *Literaturnoe nasledstvo,* Volume LXV (Moscow, 1958), to which I have referred many times. Mayakovsky's letters to Lily Brik, an intimate personal revelation, were published in that volume, as well as V. Zemskov's account of Mayakovsky's revolutionary activities, "Uchastie Mayakovskogo v revolyutsionnom dvizhenii," pp. 433-540; and E. A. Dinershtein's "Mayakovsky v fevrale-oktyabre 1917 g.," pp. 541-570.

Some important primary materials on Mayakovsky's life were published by his close associate in the futurist movement, Vasilii Kamensky. His *Zhizn s Mayakovskim* (Moscow, 1940) is a close friend's report on the varied prerevolutionary activities of the poet and his group. The work draws on the author's own memories, which are curiously detailed and vivid, as well as on published evidence.

Viktor Shklovsky's *O Mayakovskom* (Moscow, 1940) is a laconic, cryptic, and clever memoir with many excellent insights. It is subjective in its method and sometimes mistaken in its facts. Tr. L. Feiler, *Mayakovsky and His Circle* (New York, 1972).

Elsa Triolet's *Maiakovski, poète russe* (Paris, 1945) is a sympathetic account of Mayakovsky's life by the sister of Lily Brik and wife of Louis Aragon. It reveals many things about Mayakovsky's personality that Soviet sources tend to obscure.

The Polish poet and critic Wiktor Woroszylski is the author of *Życie Majakowskiego* (Warsaw, 1965), which has appeared in English as *The Life of Mayakovsky,* translated from the Polish by Boleslaw Taborski (New York, 1971). This work is a useful collection of excerpts from published materials touching on the poet's life, interspersed with translations from some of his major works. Woroszylski covers the primary sources with admirable thoroughness.

4) Contemporary Literary Movements

The most valuable book on the Russian futurist movement is Vladimir Markov, *Russian Futurism; a History* (Berkeley, 1968). All the major groups and figures in the movement and their principal publications are dealt with exhaustively and wisely in this work. Subsequent works on any aspect of Mayakovsky or futurism owe an enormous debt to Professor Markov's research.

Benedikt Livshits, *Polutoraglazyi strelets* (Moscow, 1932) is a fascinating account of the Russian literary and artistic worlds in the early years of the century.

V. Mayakovsky v vospominaniyakh sovremennikov, Z. S. Papernyi, ed. (Moscow, 1963) is a collection of memoirs concerning the poet by an impressive array of people who knew him at every stage of his career. Like almost all Soviet materials it has been sanitized, and much is concealed. But it is still an indispensable source for materials on Mayakovsky and literary groups with which he was associated.

5) Criticism

Probably no one would question the statement that the most interesting critical studies of Mayakovsky are those of Roman Jakobson:

Noveishaya russkaya poeziya (Prague, 1921), is a penetrating study of Khlebnikov, which offers incidentally many insights on Mayakovsky.

O cheshskom stikhe, preimushchestvenno v sopostavlenii s russkim (Berlin, 1923; repr. Providence, 1969) contained the first authoritative analysis, from a formalist point of view, of Mayakovsky's verse system.

"O pokolenii, rastrativshem svoikh poetov," in *Smert Vladimira Mayakovskogo* (Berlin, 1930), offers insights on the structure and imagery of Mayakovsky's work as a whole.

"Novye stroki Mayakovskogo," in *Russkii literaturnyi arkhiv* (New York, 1956) presents manuscript materials that were new at the time and offers pointed critical comments, both general and particular.

The work of N. Khardzhiev and V. Trenin ranks very high as critical analysis. The major critical articles on which they collaborated (together with one by Khardzhiev alone) have been reissued in the Soviet Union: *Poeticheskaya kultura Mayakovskogo* (Moscow, 1970).

V. Trenin, *V masterskoi stikha Mayakovskogo* (Moscow, 1937) is an invaluable study of poetic language, meter and rhythm, rhyme and imagery.

Z. S. Papernyi, *Poeticheskii obraz u Mayakovskogo* (Moscow, 1961) is specifically a study of the "lyrical hero" and images of the revolution, but it actually encompasses the whole work of Mayakovsky and offers valid insights into the process of his image-making.

Lawrence L. Stahlberger, *The Symbolic System of Mayakovsky* (The Hague, 1964) is an excellent systematic treatment of archetypal symbols that appear primarily in the early works.

G. S. Cheremin, *Rannii Mayakovsky* (Moscow, 1962) is an interesting and original treatment of the poet's futurist period, which emphasizes and documents the important debt Mayakovsky owed to the futurist movement.

Zdenek Mathauser, *Umeni poezie; Vladimir Majakovskij a jeho doba* (Prague, 1964) is in the main a study of Mayakovsky's relationship to contemporary movements in literature and the other arts.

Karel Teige, *Vladimir Majakovskij (k historii ruského futurismu)* (Prague, 1935) is an interesting treatment of Mayakovsky in the context of Russian avant-garde art movements.

6) Additional Works of Special Interest

Aseev, N. *Mayakovsky nachinaetsya*. Moscow, 1940.

Blake, Patricia. "The Two Deaths of Vladimir Mayakovsky," introduction to *The Bedbug and Selected Poetry*. New York, 1960.

Brik, Lily. "Mayakovsky i chuzhie stikhi," *Znamya*, No. 3, 1940.

———. "Predlozhenie issledovatelyam," *Voprosy literatury*, No. 4, 1966.

Brik, Osip. "Mayakovsky redaktor i organizator," *Literaturnyi kritik*, No. 4, 1936.

Bryusov, V. "Zdravogo smysla tartarary," *Russkaya mysl*, No. 3, 1914.

———. "Novye techeniya v russkoi poezii: futurizm," *Russkaya mysl*, No. 3, 1913.

Burliuk, David. *Color and Rhyme*, No. 26, 1952; No. 31, 1957; No. 41, 1959.
Chukovsky, K. "Akhmatova i Mayakovsky," *Dom Iskusstv*, No. 1, 1920.
———. *Futuristy*. Petrograd, 1922.
Ehrlich, Victor. "The Dead Hand of the Future," in *The Double Image*. Baltimore, 1964.
Evstigneeva, L. A. (and others) eds. *Poet i sotsializm. K estetike Mayakovskogo*. Moscow, 1971.
Goncharov, B. P. "Ob izuchenii stikha Mayakovskogo," in *Poet i sotsializm. K estetike Mayakovskogo*. Moscow, 1971.
———. "Intonatsionnaya organizatsiya stikha Mayakovskogo," *Russkaya literatura*, No. 2, 1972.
Humesky, Asya. *Mayakovsky and His Neologisms*. New York, 1964.
Ivanov-Razumnik, R. *Vladimir Mayakovsky* (*Misteriya ili Buff*). Berlin, 1922.
Kassil, Lev. *Mayakovsky—sam; ocherk zhizni i raboty poeta*. Moscow, 1940.
Khodasevich, V. "O Mayakovskom," in his *Literaturnye stati i vospominaniya*. New York, 1954.
Kolmogorov, A. "K izuchenii ritmiki Mayakovskogo," *Voprosy yazykoznaniya*, No. 4, 1963.
Kondratov, A. "Evolyutsiya ritmiki Mayakovskogo," *Voprosy yazykoznaniya*, No. 4, 1962.
Kondratov, A. and Kolmogorov, A. "Ritmika poem Mayakovskogo," *Voprosy yazykoznaniya*, No. 3, 1962.
Kosman, S. *Mayakovsky, mif i deistvitelnost*. Paris, 1968.
Kruchonykh, A. *Stikhi Vladimira Mayakovskogo*. Petrograd, 1914.
———. *Zhivoi Mayakovsky*. Moscow, 1930.
Marshall, Herbert, trans. and ed. *Mayakovsky*. London, 1965.
Mayakovskomu: sbornik vospominanii i statei. Leningrad, 1940.
Mayakovsky: materialy i issledovaniya. Moscow, 1940.
Mayakovsky, 1930-1940: stati i materialy. Leningrad, 1940.
Moser, Charles. "Mayakovsky's Unsentimental Journeys," *American Slavic and East European Review*, XIX (1960), 85-100.
Muchnic, Helen. *From Gorky to Pasternak*. New York, 1962.
Nag, Martin. "Fantastical Realism: the Problem of Realism in Mayakovsky's *Pro eto*," *Scando-Slavica*, IV (1959), 3-22.
Naumov, E. V. *Mayakovsky; seminarii*. 3d ed., Leningrad, 1955.

Pomorska, Krystina. *Russian Formalist Theory and Its Poetic Ambience*. The Hague, 1968.
Ripellino, E. M. *Majakovskij e il teatro russo d'avanguardia*. Torino, 1959.
Rostotsky, V. *Mayakovsky i teatr*. Moscow, 1952.
Shengeli, G. *Mayakovsky vo ves rost*. Moscow, 1927.
Taranovsky, Kirill. "Vzaimootnoshenie stikhotvornogo ritma i tematiki," in *American Contributions to the Fifth International Congress of Slavicists*. The Hague, 1963.
Terras, V. "Majakovskij and Time," *Slavic and East European Journal*, XIII, No. 2 (1969), 151-161.
Thomson, R. D. B. "Mayakovsky and His Time Imagery," *Slavonic and East European Review*, XLVIII (1970), 181-200.
Timofeeva, V. V. *Yazyk poeta i vremya; poeticheskii yazyk Mayakovskogo*. Moscow, 1962.
Trotsky, L. *Literatura i revolyutsiya*. Moscow, 1925.
Tvorchestvo Mayakovskogo; sbornik statei. Moscow, 1952.
Tynyanov, Y. "Promezhutok," in *Arkhaisty i novatory*. Leningrad, 1929.
Vinokur, V. *Mayakovsky novator yazyka*. Moscow, 1943.
Voronsky, A. "Vladimir Mayakovsky," *Krasnaya nov*, No. 4, 1925.
Zhirmunsky, V. "Stikhoslozhenie Mayakovskogo," *Russkaya literatura*, No. 4, 1964. Tr.: "The Versification of Mayakovsky," in *Poetics. Poetyka. Poetika II*. Warsaw, 1966.

Index of Names

Index of Titles of Mayakovsky's Works

Index of Titles